ŚRĪ CAITANYA-CARITĀMṚTA

BOOKS by
His Divine Grace A.C. Bhaktivedanta Swami Prabhupāda

Bhagavad-gītā As It Is
Śrīmad-Bhāgavatam, Cantos 1-5 (15 Vols.)
Śrī Caitanya-caritāmṛta (17 Vols.)
Teachings of Lord Caitanya
The Nectar of Devotion
Śrī Īśopaniṣad
Easy Journey to Other Planets
Kṛṣṇa Consciousness: The Topmost Yoga System
Kṛṣṇa, The Supreme Personality of Godhead (3 Vols.)
Transcendental Teachings of Prahlād Mahārāja
Kṛṣṇa, the Reservoir of Pleasure
The Perfection of Yoga
Beyond Birth and Death
On the Way to Kṛṣṇa
Rāja-vidyā: The King of Knowledge
Elevation to Kṛṣṇa Consciousness
Kṛṣṇa Consciousness: The Matchless Gift
Back to Godhead Magazine (Founder)

A complete catalogue is available upon request

International Society for Krishna Consciousness
3764 Watseka Avenue
Los Angeles, California 90034

All Glory to Śrī Guru and Gaurāṅga

ŚRĪ CAITANYA-CARITĀMṚTA

of Kṛṣṇadāsa Kavirāja Gosvāmī

Madhya-līlā
Volume Six

"Śrī Caitanya Mahāprabhu Leaves for Vṛndāvana"

with the original Bengali text, Roman transliterations, synonyms, translation and elaborate purports

by

HIS DIVINE GRACE

A.C. Bhaktivedanta Swami Prabhupāda

Founder-Ācārya of the International Society for Krishna Consciousness

THE BHAKTIVEDANTA BOOK TRUST
New York · Los Angeles · London · Bombay

Readers interested in the subject matter of this book
are invited by the International Society for Krishna Consciousness
to correspond with its Secretary.

International Society for Krishna Consciousness
3764 Watseka Avenue
Los Angeles, California 90034

Library of Congress Catalogue Card Number: 73-93206
International Standard Book Number: 0-912776-68-4

First printing, 1975: 20,000 copies

Printed in the United States of America

Contents

Introduction

Śrī Caitanya-caritāmṛta is the principal work on the life and teachings of Śrī Kṛṣṇa Caitanya. Śrī Caitanya is the pioneer of a great social and religious movement which began in India a little less than five hundred years ago and which has directly and indirectly influenced the subsequent course of religious and philosophical thinking not only in India but in the recent West as well.

Caitanya Mahāprabhu is regarded as a figure of great historical significance. However, our conventional method of historical analysis—that of seeing a man as a product of his times—fails here. Śrī Caitanya is a personality who transcends the limited scope of historical settings.

At a time when, in the West, man was directing his explorative spirit toward studying the structure of the physical universe and circumnavigating the world in search of new oceans and continents, Śrī Kṛṣṇa Caitanya, in the East, was inaugurating and masterminding a revolution directed inward, toward a scientific understanding of the highest knowledge of man's spiritual nature.

The chief historical sources for the life of Śrī Kṛṣṇa Caitanya are the *kaḍacās* (diaries) kept by Murāri Gupta and Svarūpa Dāmodara Gosvāmī. Murāri Gupta, a physician and close associate of Śrī Caitanya's, recorded extensive notes on the first twenty-four years of Śrī Caitanya's life, culminating in his initiation into the renounced order, *sannyāsa*. The events of the rest of Caitanya Mahāprabhu's forty-eight years are recorded in the diary of Svarūpa Dāmodora Gosvāmī, another of Caitanya Mahāprabhu's intimate associates.

Śrī Caitanya-caritāmṛta is divided into three sections called *līlās*, which literally means "pastimes"—*Ādi-līlā* (the early period), *Madhya-līlā* (the middle period) and *Antya-līlā* (the final period). The notes of Murāri Gupta form the basis of the *Ādi-līlā*, and Svarūpa Dāmodara's diary provides the details for the *Madhya-* and *Antya-līlās*.

The first twelve of the seventeen chapters of *Ādi-līlā* constitute the preface for the entire work. By referring to Vedic scriptural evidence, this preface establishes Śrī Caitanya as the *avatāra* (incarnation) of Kṛṣṇa (God) for the age of Kali—the current epoch, beginning five thousand years ago and characterized by materialism, hypocrisy and dissension. In these descriptions, Caitanya Mahāprabhu, who is identical with Lord Kṛṣṇa, descends to liberally grant pure love of God to the fallen souls of this degraded age by propagating *saṅkīrtana*—literally, "congregational glorification of God"—especially by organizing massive public chanting of the *mahā-mantra* (Great Chant for Deliverance). The esoteric purpose of Lord Caitanya's appearance in the world is revealed, his co-*avatāras* and principal devotees are described and his teachings are summarized. The remaining portion of *Ādi-līlā*, chapters thirteen through seventeen, briefly recounts his divine birth and his life until he accepted the renounced order. This includes his childhood miracles, schooling, marriage and early philosophical confrontations, as well as his organization of a widespread *saṅkīrtana* movement and his civil disobedience against the repression of the Mohammedan government.

The subject of *Madhya-līlā,* the longest of the three divisions, is a detailed narration of Lord Caitanya's extensive and eventful travels throughout India as a renounced mendicant, teacher, philosopher, spiritual preceptor and mystic. During this period of six years, Śrī Caitanya transmits his teachings to his principal disciples. He debates and converts many of the most renowned philosophers and theologians of his time, including Śaṅkarites, Buddhists and Muslims, and incorporates their many thousands of followers and disciples into his own burgeoning numbers. A dramatic account of Caitanya Mahāprabhu's miraculous activities at the giant Jagannātha Cart Festival in Orissa is also included in this section.

Antya-līlā concerns the last eighteen years of Śrī Caitanya's manifest presence, spent in semiseclusion near the famous Jagannātha temple at Jagannātha Purī in Orissa. During these final years, Śrī Caitanya drifted deeper and deeper into trances of spiritual ecstasy unparalleled in all of religious and literary history, Eastern or Western. Śrī Caitanya's perpetual and ever-increasing religious beatitude, graphically described in the eyewitness accounts of Svarūpa Dāmodara Gosvāmī, his constant companion during this period, clearly defy the investigative and descriptive abilities of modern psychologists and phenomenologists of religious experience.

The author of this great classic, Kṛṣṇadāsa Kavirāja Gosvāmī, born in the year 1507, was a disciple of Raghunātha dāsa Gosvāmī, a confidential follower of Caitanya Mahāprabhu. Raghunātha dāsa, a renowned ascetic saint, heard and memorized all the activities of Caitanya Mahāprabhu told to him by Svarūpa Dāmodara. After the passing away of Śrī Caitanya and Svarūpa Dāmodara, Raghunātha dāsa, unable to bear the pain of separation from these objects of his complete devotion, traveled to Vṛndāvana, intending to commit suicide by jumping from Govardhana Hill. In Vṛndāvana, however, he encountered Rūpa Gosvāmī and Sanātana Gosvāmī, the most confidential disciples of Caitanya Mahāprabhu. They convinced him to give up his plan of suicide and impelled him to reveal to them the spiritually inspiring events of Lord Caitanya's later life. Kṛṣṇadāsa Kavirāja Gosvāmī was also residing in Vṛndāvana at this time, and Raghunātha dāsa Gosvāmī endowed him with a full comprehension of the transcendental life of Śrī Caitanya.

By this time, several biographical works had already been written on the life of Śrī Caitanya by contemporary and near-contemporary scholars and devotees. These included *Śrī Caitanya-carita* by Murāri Gupta, *Caitanya-maṅgala* by Locana dāsa Ṭhākura and *Caitanya-bhāgavata.* This latter text, a work by Vṛndāvana dāsa Ṭhākura, who was then considered the principal authority on Śrī Caitanya's life, was highly revered. While composing his important work, Vṛndāvana dāsa, fearing that it would become too voluminous, avoided elaborately describing many of the events of Śrī Caitanya's life, particulary the later ones. Anxious to hear of these later pastimes, the devotees of Vṛndāvana requested Kṛṣṇadāsa Kavirāja Gosvāmī, whom they respected as a great saint, to compose a book to narrate these episodes in detail. Upon this request, and with the permission and blessings of the Madana-mohana Deity of Vṛndāvana, he began compiling *Śrī Caitanya-caritāmṛta,* which, due to its biographical excellence and thorough exposition of Lord Caitanya's profound philosophy and teachings, is regarded as the most significant of biographical works on Śrī Caitanya.

He commenced work on the text while in his late nineties and in failing health, as he vividly describes in the text itself: "I have now become too old and disturbed in invalidity. While writing, my hands tremble. I cannot remember anything, nor can I see or hear properly. Still I write, and this is a great wonder." That he nevertheless completed, under such debilitating conditions, the greatest literary gem of medieval India is surely one of the wonders of literary history.

This English translation and commentary is the work of His Divine Grace A. C. Bhaktivedanta Swami Prabhupāda, the world's most distinguished teacher of Indian religious and philosophical thought. His commentary is based upon two Bengali commentaries, one by his teacher Śrīla Bhaktisiddhānta Sarasvatī Gosvāmī, the eminent Vedic scholar who predicted, "The time will come when the people of the world will learn Bengali to read *Śrī Caitanya-caritāmṛta,"* and the other by Śrīla Bhaktisiddhānta's father, Bhaktivinoda Ṭhākura.

His Divine Grace A. C. Bhaktivedanta Swami Prabhupāda is himself a disciplic descendant of Śrī Caitanya Mahāprabhu, and he is the first scholar to execute systematic English translations of the major works of Śrī Caitanya's followers. His consummate Bengali and Sanskrit scholarship and intimate familiarity with the precepts of Śrī Kṛṣṇa Caitanya are a fitting combination that eminently qualifies him to present this important classic to the English-speaking world. The ease and clarity with which he expounds upon difficult philosophical concepts lures even a reader totally unfamiliar with Indian religious tradition into a genuine understanding and appreciation of this profound and monumental work.

The entire text, with commentary, presented in seventeen lavishly illustrated volumes by the Bhaktivedanta Book Trust, represents a contribution of major importance to the intellectual, cultural and spiritual life of contemporary man.

—The Publishers

His Divine Grace
A. C. Bhaktivedanta Swami Prabhupāda
Founder-Ācārya of the International Society for Krishna Consciousness

The place known as Yājapura on the bank of the Vaitaraṇī River, where great sages formerly performed sacrifices. Śrī Caitanya Mahāprabhu visited this *tīrtha* on His way to Vṛndāvana. (*p.231*)

The house of Śrī Rāghava Paṇḍita, Lord Caitanya Mahāprabhu's original follower, located in Pāṇihāṭi, West Bengal. (*p.259*)

A reconstruction of the house in Hālisahara where Śrīvāsa Ṭhākura lived feeling separation from Śrī Caitanya Mahāprabhu after the Lord accepted *sannyāsa*. (*p.259*)

In Śāntipura, a reconstruction of the house of Śrī Advaita Ācārya (left) and a temple commemorating the site where He resided (right). Lord Caitanya Mahāprabhu visited Advaita Ācārya there before returning to Jagannātha Purī. (*p.265*)

The Śrī Śrī Kṛṣṇa-Balarāma Mandira and International Guest House in Vṛndāvana, established by His Divine Grace A. C. Bhaktivedanta Swami Prabhupāda to broadcast to the world that worship of Gaura-Nitāi is the same as worship of Kṛṣṇa-Balarāma. (*p.299*)

The Deities of Śrī Śrī Kṛṣṇa-Balarāma, installed in Vṛndāvana on April 20, 1975, by His Divine Grace A. C. Bhaktivedanta Swami Prabhupāda, founder-*ācārya* of the International Society for Krishna Consciousness. (*p.299*)

PLATE ONE

"The devotees celebrated the festival of Janmāṣṭamī, Kṛṣṇa's birthday, which is also called Nanda-mahotsava, the festival of Nanda Mahārāja. At that time Śrī Caitanya Mahāprabhu and His devotees dressed themselves as cowherd boys. It was at this time that Śrīla Advaita Ācārya said, 'Please do not be angry. I speak the truth. I shall know whether You are a cowherd boy only if You can wheel this rod about.' Accepting Advaita Ācārya's challenge, Śrī Caitanya Mahāprabhu took a big rod and began to wheel it around and around. Again and again He threw the rod into the sky and caught it when it fell. Śrī Caitanya Mahāprabhu wheeled and threw the rod, sometimes over His head, sometimes behind His back, sometimes in front of Him, sometimes to His side and sometimes between His legs. Indeed, all the people laughed to see this." (*pp.9-12*)

PLATE TWO

"On the victory day celebrating the conquest of Laṅkā—a day known as Vijaya-daśamī—Śrī Caitanya Mahāprabhu dressed up all His devotees like monkey soldiers. Displaying the emotions of Hanumān, Śrī Caitanya Mahāprabhu took up a large tree branch, and, mounting the walls of Laṅkā fort, began to dismantle it. In the ecstasy of Hanumān, Śrī Caitanya Mahāprabhu angrily said, 'Where is the rascal Rāvaṇa? He has kidnapped the universal mother, Sītā. Now I shall kill him and all his family.' Everyone became very astonished to see the emotional ecstasy of Śrī Caitanya Mahāprabhu, and everyone began to chant, 'All glories! All glories!' again and again." (*pp.16-17*)

PLATE THREE

"Kṛṣṇa is the Supreme Personality of Godhead, the origin of all incarnations and the source of everything. He is pure transcendental love itself, and He is the reservoir of all pleasure. Kṛṣṇa is the reservoir of all transcendental qualities. He is like a mine of gems. He is expert at everything, very intelligent and sober, and He is the summit of all humors. His character is very sweet, and His pastimes are melodious. He is expert in intelligence, and thus He enjoys all His pastimes and mellows." (*pp. 73-74*)

PLATE FOUR

"Sārvabhauma Bhaṭṭācārya had a son-in-law named Amogha, who was the husband of his daughter named Sathi. Although born in an aristocratic *brāhmaṇa* family, this Amogha was a great faultfinder and blasphemer. Amogha wanted to see Śrī Caitanya Mahāprabhu eat, but he was not allowed to enter. Indeed, Bhaṭṭācārya guarded the threshold of his house with a stick in his hand. However, as soon as Bhaṭṭācārya began distributing *prasāda* and was a little inattentive, Amogha came in. Seeing the quantity of food, he began to blaspheme. 'This much food is sufficient to satisfy ten or twelve men, but this *sannyāsī* alone is eating so much!' As soon as Amogha said this, Sārvabhauma Bhaṭṭācārya turned his eyes upon him. Seeing Bhaṭṭācārya's attitude, Amogha immediately left. Bhaṭṭācārya ran after him to strike him with a stick, but Amogha fled so fast that Bhaṭṭācārya could not catch him. Bhaṭṭācārya then began to curse and call his son-in-law ill names. When Bhaṭṭācārya returned, he saw that Śrī Caitanya Mahāprabhu was laughing to hear him criticize Amogha. When Ṣāṭhī's mother, Bhaṭṭācārya's wife, heard of this incident, she immediately began to strike her head and chest, saying again, 'Let Ṣāṭhī become a widow!' Seeing the lamentation of both husband and wife, Śrī Caitanya Mahāprabhu tried to pacify them. According to their desire, He ate the *prasāda* and was very satisfied." (*pp.125-129*)

PLATE FIVE

"Gopīnātha Ācārya went to see Śrī Caitanya Mahāprabhu, and the Lord asked him about the events taking place in Sārvabhauma Bhaṭṭācārya's house. Gopīnātha Ācārya informed the Lord that both the husband and wife were fasting and that their son-in-law Amogha was dying of cholera. As soon as Caitanya Mahāprabhu heard that Amogha was going to die, He immediately ran to him in great haste. Placing His hand on Amogha's chest, He spoke to him as follows. 'The heart of a *brāhmaṇa* is by nature very clean; therefore it is a proper place for Kṛṣṇa to sit. Why have you allowed jealousy to sit there also? Because of this, you have become like a *caṇḍāla,* the lowest of men, and you have also contaminated a most purified place—your heart.' However, due to the association of Sārvabhauma Bhaṭṭācārya, all your contamination is now vanquished. When a person's heart is cleansed of all contamination, he is able to chant the *mahā-mantra,* Hare Kṛṣṇa. Therefore, Amogha, get up and chant the Hare Kṛṣṇa *mahā-mantra!* If you do so, Kṛṣṇa will unfailingly bestow mercy upon you.' After hearing Śrī Caitanya Mahāprabhu and being touched by Him, Amogha, who was on his deathbed, immediately stood up and began to chant the holy name of Kṛṣṇa. Thus he became mad with ecstatic love." (*pp.141-146*)

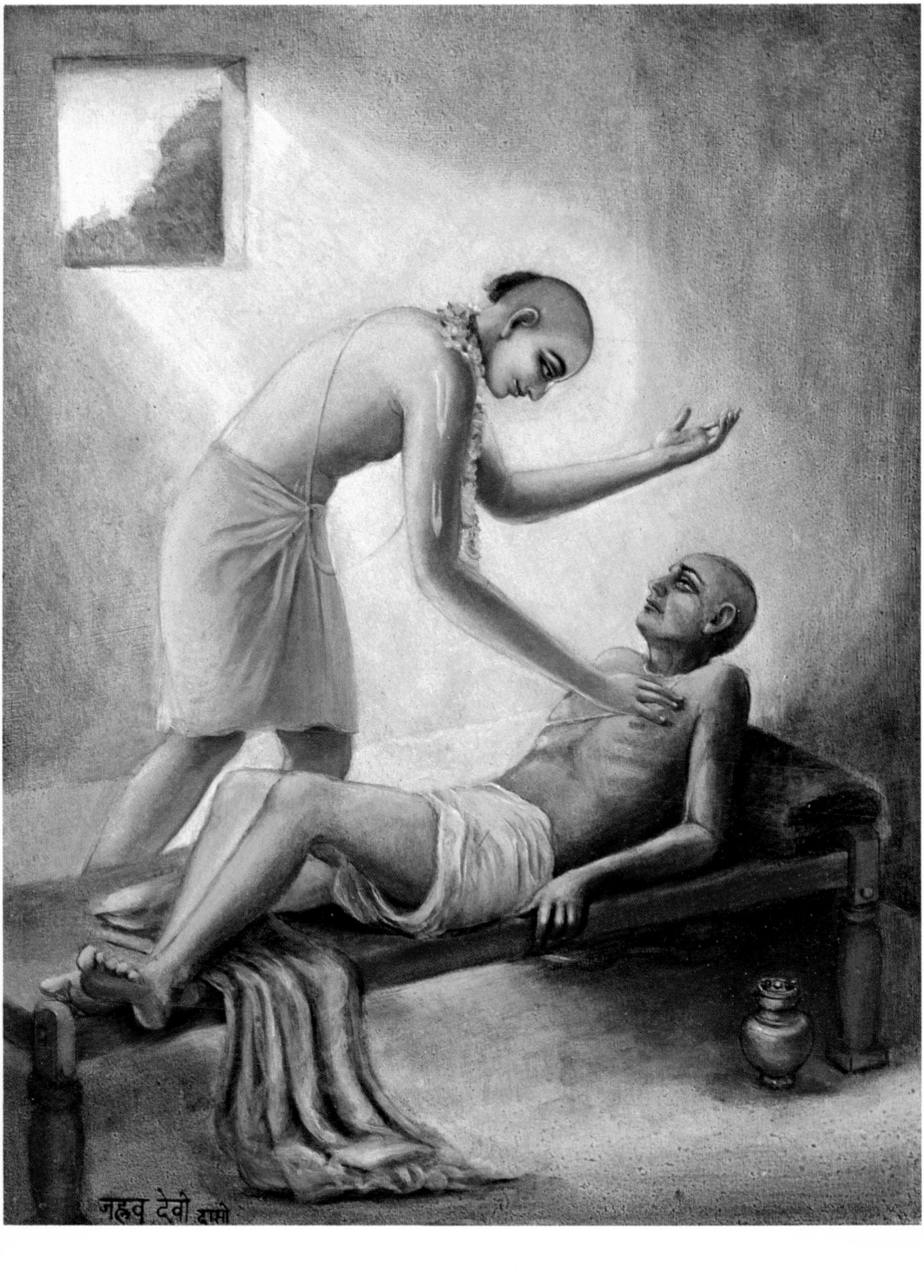
जह्नव देवी दासी

PLATE SIX

"Puṇḍarīka Vidyānidhi initiated Gadādhara Paṇḍita for the second time, and on the day of Odana-ṣaṣṭhī he saw the festival. When Puṇḍarīka Vidyānidhi saw that Lord Jagannātha was given a starched garment, he became a little hateful. In this way his mind was polluted. That night the brothers Lord Jagannātha and Balarāma came to Puṇḍarīka Vidyānidhi and, smiling, began to slap him. Although his cheeks were swollen from the slapping, Puṇḍarīka Vidyānidhi was very happy within." (*pp.200-201*)

PLATE SEVEN

"When the king heard that the Lord was leaving that evening, he immediately made arrangements for some elephants with small tents on their backs to be brought there. Then all the ladies of the palace got on the elephants. All these ladies went to the road the Lord was taking and remained there in a line. That evening, the Lord departed with His devotees. When Śrī Caitanya Mahāprabhu went to the bank of the river Citrotpalā to take His bath, all the queens and ladies of the palace offered their obeisances to Him. Upon seeing the Lord, they all felt themselves overwhelmed with love of Godhead, and, tears pouring from their eyes, they began to chant the holy name, 'Kṛṣṇa! Kṛṣṇa!'" (*pp.216-217*)

PLATE EIGHT

"Gadādhara Paṇḍita Gosvāmī traveled alone, but when they all arrived at Kaṭaka, Śrī Caitanya Mahāprabhu called him, and he went in the Lord's company. No one can understand the loving intimacy between Gadādhara Paṇḍita and Śrī Caitanya Mahāprabhu. Gadādhara Paṇḍita gave up his vow and service to Gopīnātha just as one gives up a piece of straw. Gadādhara Paṇḍita's behavior was very pleasing to Śrī Caitanya Mahāprabhu's heart. Nevertheless, the Lord took his hand and spoke to him, displaying the anger of love. 'You have abandoned Gopīnātha's service and broken your vow to live in Purī. All that is now complete because you have come so far. Your wanting to go with me is simply a desire for sense gratification. In this way, you are breaking two religious principles, and because of this I am very unhappy. If you want My happiness, please return to Nīlācala. You will simply condemn Me if you say any more about this matter.' Saying this, Śrī Caitanya Mahāprabhu got into a boat, and Gadādhara Paṇḍita immediately fell down in an unconscious state." (*pp.224-227*)

CHAPTER 15

The Lord Accepts Prasāda at the House of Sārvabhauma Bhaṭṭācārya

The following summary of this chapter is given by Śrīla Bhaktivinoda Ṭhākura in his *Amṛta-pravāha-bhāṣya.* After the Ratha-yātrā festival, Śrī Advaita Ācārya Prabhu worshiped Śrī Caitanya Mahāprabhu with flowers and *tulasī.* Śrī Caitanya Mahāprabhu, in return, worshiped Advaita Ācārya with the flowers and *tulasī* that remained on the offered plate and said a *mantra, yo 'si so 'si* ("What You are, You are"). Then Advaita Ācārya Prabhu invited Śrī Caitanya Mahāprabhu for *prasāda.* When Lord Śrī Caitanya Mahāprabhu and His devotees performed the Nandotsava ceremony, the Lord personally dressed Himself as a cowherd boy. Thus the ceremony was very jubilant. Then the Lord and His devotees observed Vijayā-daśamī, the day of victory when Lord Rāmacandra conquered Laṅkā. The devotees all became soldiers of Lord Rāmacandra, and Śrī Caitanya Mahāprabhu, in the ecstasy of Hanumān, manifested various transcendentally blissful activities. Thereafter, the Lord and His devotees observed various other ceremonies.

Śrī Caitanya Mahāprabhu then asked all the devotees to return to Bengal. Lord Śrī Caitanya Mahāprabhu sent Nityānanda Prabhu to Bengal for preaching and also sent Rāmadāsa, Gadādhara dāsa and several other devotees with Him. Then Śrī Caitanya Mahāprabhu, with great humility, sent some Jagannātha *prasāda* and a cloth from Lord Jagannātha to His mother through Śrīvāsa Ṭhākura. When the Lord bade farewell to Rāghava Paṇḍita, Vāsudeva Datta, the residents of Kulīna-grāma and other devotees, He praised them for their transcendental qualities. Rāmānanda Vasu and Satyarāja Khān asked some questions, and Lord Śrī Caitanya Mahāprabhu instructed them that all householder devotees must engage themselves in the service of Vaiṣṇavas exclusively devoted to chanting the holy name of the Lord. He also directed the Vaiṣṇavas from Khaṇḍa, instructed Sārvabhauma Bhaṭṭācārya and Vidyā-vācaspati, and praised Murāri Gupta for his firm faith in the lotus feet of Lord Rāmacandra. Considering the humble prayer of Vāsudeva Datta, He established that Lord Śrī Kṛṣṇa is qualified to deliver all the conditioned souls.

Thereafter, when Śrī Caitanya Mahāprabhu was accepting *prasāda* at the house of Sārvabhauma Bhaṭṭācārya, Sārvabhauma's son-in-law, Amogha, created trouble in the family with his criticisms. The following morning, he was attacked by the disease of *visūcikā* (cholera). Lord Śrī Caitanya Mahāprabhu very kindly saved him from death and enlivened him in chanting the holy name of Lord Kṛṣṇa.

TEXT 1

সার্বভৌমগৃহে ভুঞ্জন্ স্বনিন্দকমমোঘকম্ ।
অঙ্গীকুর্বন্ স্ফুটাং চক্রে গৌরঃ স্বাং ভক্তবশ্যতাম্ ॥ ১ ॥

sārvabhauma-gṛhe bhuñjan
sva-nindakam amoghakam
aṅgīkurvan sphuṭāṁ cakre
gauraḥ svāṁ bhakta-vaśyatām

SYNONYMS

sārvabhauma-gṛhe—at the house of Sārvabhauma Bhaṭṭācārya; *bhuñjan*—while eating; *sva-nindakam*—a person who was criticizing Him; *amoghakam*—named Amogha; *aṅgīkurvan*—accepting; *sphuṭām*—manifested; *cakre*—made; *gauraḥ*—Lord Śrī Caitanya Mahāprabhu; *svām*—His; *bhakta-vaśyatām*—obligation to His devotees.

TRANSLATION

While Śrī Caitanya Mahāprabhu was accepting prasāda at the house of Sārvabhauma Bhaṭṭācārya, Amogha criticized Him. At that time the Lord also showed how much He was obliged to His devotees.

TEXT 2

জয় জয় শ্রীচৈতন্য জয় নিত্যানন্দ ।
জয়াদ্বৈতচন্দ্র জয় গৌরভক্তবৃন্দ ॥ ২ ॥

jaya jaya śrī-caitanya jaya nityānanda
jayādvaita-candra jaya gaura-bhakta-vṛnda

SYNONYMS

jaya jaya—all glories; *śrī-caitanya*—to Lord Caitanya Mahāprabhu; *jaya*—all glories; *nityānanda*—unto Nityānanda Prabhu; *jaya advaita-candra*—all glories to Advaita Prabhu; *jaya*—all glories; *gaura-bhakta-vṛnda*—to the devotees of Lord Śrī Caitanya Mahāprabhu.

TRANSLATION

All glories to Śrī Caitanya Mahāprabhu! All glories to Lord Nityānanda Prabhu! All glories to Advaitacandra! And all glories to all the devotees of Lord Caitanya!

TEXT 3

জয় শ্রীচৈতন্যচরিতামৃত-শ্রোতাগণ ।
চৈতন্যচরিতামৃত - যাঁর প্রাণধন ॥ ৩ ॥

jaya śrī-caitanya-caritāmṛta-śrotā-gaṇa
caitanya-caritāmṛta——yāṅra prāṇa-dhana

SYNONYMS

jaya—all glories; *śrī-caitanya-caritāmṛta-śrotā-gaṇa*—to the listeners of *Śrī Caitanya-caritāmṛta; caitanya-caritāmṛta*—*Caitanya-caritāmṛta; yāṅra*—of whom; *prāṇa-dhana*—the life and soul.

TRANSLATION

All glories to the listeners of Śrī Caitanya-caritāmṛta who have accepted it as their life and soul.

TEXT 4

এইমত মহাপ্রভু ভক্তগণ-সঙ্গে ।
নীলাচলে রহি' করে নৃত্যগীত-রঙ্গে ॥ ৪ ॥

ei-mata mahāprabhu bhakta-gaṇa-saṅge
nīlācale rahi' kare nṛtya-gīta-raṅge

SYNONYMS

ei-mata—in this way; *mahāprabhu*—Śrī Caitanya Mahāprabhu; *bhakta-gaṇa-saṅge*—with His devotees; *nīlācale rahi'*—staying at Nīlācala, Jagannātha Purī; *kare*—performs; *nṛtya-gīta-raṅge*—chanting and dancing with great pleasure.

TRANSLATION

While Śrī Caitanya Mahāprabhu stayed at Jagannātha Purī, He constantly enjoyed chanting and dancing with His devotees.

TEXT 5

প্রথমাবসরে জগন্নাথ-দরশন ।
নৃত্যগীত করে দণ্ডপরণাম, স্তবন ॥ ৫ ॥

prathamāvasare jagannātha-daraśana
nṛtya-gīta kare daṇḍa-paraṇāma, stavana

SYNONYMS

prathama-avasare—in the beginning; *jagannātha-daraśana*—seeing the Deity of Lord Jagannātha; *nṛtya-gīta kare*—performs chanting and dancing; *daṇḍa-paraṇāma*—offering obeisances; *stavana*—offering prayers.

TRANSLATION

In the beginning, Śrī Caitanya Mahāprabhu saw the Deity of Lord Jagannātha in the temple. He offered Him obeisances and prayers and danced and sang before Him.

TEXT 6

'উপলভোগ' লাগিলে করে বাহিরে বিজয়।
হরিদাস মিলি' আইসে আপন নিলয় ॥ ৬ ॥

'upala-bhoga' lāgile kare bāhire viyaja
haridāsa mili' āise āpana nilaya

SYNONYMS

upala-bhoga lāgile—when there is an offering of food known as *upala-bhoga; kare bāhire vijaya*—He remains outside; *haridāsa mili'*—meeting Haridāsa Ṭhākura; *āise*—comes back; *āpana nilaya*—to His residence.

TRANSLATION

After visiting the temple, Śrī Caitanya Mahāprabhu would remain outside during the upala-bhoga offering. He would then go meet Haridāsa Ṭhākura and return to His residence.

PURPORT

At noon, when there was an *upala-bhoga* offering in a place called *bhoga-vardhana-khaṇḍa,* Śrī Caitanya Mahāprabhu would go outside the temple. Before going outside, He used to stand near the Garuḍa-stambha column and offer His obeisances and prayers. Afterwards, the Lord would visit Siddha-bakula, where Haridāsa Ṭhākura lived. After visiting with Haridāsa Ṭhākura, the Lord would return to His own place at the abode of Kāśī Miśra.

TEXT 7

ঘরে বসি' করে প্রভু নাম সঙ্কীর্তন।
অদ্বৈত আসিয়া করে প্রভুর পূজন ॥ ৭ ॥

ghare vasi' kare prabhu nāma saṅkīrtana
advaita āsiyā kare prabhura pūjana

SYNONYMS

ghare vasi'—sitting in His room; *kare*—performs; *prabhu*—Lord Śrī Caitanya Mahāprabhu; *nāma saṅkīrtana*—chanting on beads; *advaita*—Advaita Ācārya; *āsiyā*—coming; *kare*—performs; *prabhura pūjana*—worship of the Lord.

TRANSLATION

Sitting in His room, Śrī Caitanya Mahāprabhu would chant on His beads, and Advaita Prabhu would come there to worship the Lord.

TEXT 8

সুগন্ধি-সলিলে দেন পাদ্য, আচমন।
সর্বাঙ্গে লেপয়ে প্রভুর সুগন্ধি চন্দন ॥ ৮ ॥

sugandhi-salile dena pādya, ācamana
sarvāṅge lepaye prabhura sugandhi candana

SYNONYMS

su-gandhi-salile—with scented water; *dena*—offers; *pādya*—water for washing the feet; *ācamana*—washing the mouth; *sarva-aṅge*—all over the body; *lepaye*—smears; *prabhura*—of the Lord; *su-gandhi candana*—fragrant sandalwood pulp.

TRANSLATION

While worshiping Śrī Caitanya Mahāprabhu, Advaita Ācārya would offer Him scented water to wash His mouth and feet. Then Advaita Ācārya would smear very fragrant sandalwood pulp all over His body.

TEXT 9

গলে মালা দেন, মাথায় তুলসী-মঞ্জরী।
যোড়-হাতে স্তুতি করে পদে নমস্করি' ॥ ৯ ॥

gale mālā dena, māthāya tulasī-mañjarī
yoḍa-hāte stuti kare pade namaskari'

SYNONYMS

gale—on the neck; *mālā*—garland; *dena*—offers; *māthāya*—on the head; *tulasī-mañjarī*—flowers of *tulasī; yoḍa-hāte*—with folded hands; *stuti kare*—offers prayers; *pade*—unto the lotus feet; *namaskari'*—offering obeisances.

TRANSLATION

Śrī Advaita Prabhu would also place a flower garland around the Lord's neck and tulasī flowers [mañjarīs] on His head. Then, with folded hands, Advaita Ācārya would offer obeisances and prayers unto the Lord.

TEXT 10

পূজা-পাত্রে পুষ্প-তুলসী শেষ যে আছিল।
সেই সব লঞা প্রভু আচার্যে পূজিল ॥ ১০ ॥

pūjā-pātre puṣpa-tulasī śeṣa ye āchila
sei saba lañā prabhu ācārye pūjila

SYNONYMS

pūjā-pātre—on the dish that holds flowers and *tulasī; puṣpa-tulasī*—flowers and *tulasī; śeṣa*—remaining; *ye āchila*—whatever there were; *sei saba*—all of them; *lañā*—taking; *prabhu*—Śrī Caitanya Mahāprabhu; *ācārye pūjila*—worshiped Advaita Ācārya.

TRANSLATION

After being worshiped by Advaita Ācārya, Śrī Caitanya Mahāprabhu would take the dish containing flowers and tulasī and, with whatever paraphernalia remained, would also worship Advaita Ācārya.

TEXT 11

"যোঽসি সোঽসি নমোঽস্তু তে" এই মন্ত্র পড়ে।
মুখবাদ্য করি' প্রভু হাসায় আচার্যেরে ॥ ১১ ॥

"yo 'si so 'si namo 'stu te" ei mantra paḍe
mukha-vādya kari' prabhu hāsāya ācāryere

SYNONYMS

yaḥ asi—whatever You are; *saḥ asi*—so You are; *namaḥ astu te*—I offer My respects unto You; *ei mantra paḍe*—chants this *mantra; mukha-vādya kari'*—making a sound within the mouth; *prabhu*—Lord Śrī Caitanya Mahāprabhu; *hāsāya*—causes to laugh; *ācāryere*—Advaita Ācārya.

TRANSLATION

Śrī Caitanya Mahāprabhu would worship Advaita Ācārya by chanting the mantra, "Whatever You are, You are—but I offer My respects unto You." In addition, the Lord would make some sounds within His mouth that would make Advaita Ācārya laugh.

TEXT 12

এইমত অন্যোন্যে করেন নমস্কার ।
প্রভুরে নিমন্ত্রণ করে আচার্য বার বার ॥ ১২ ॥

ei-mata anyonye karena namaskāra
prabhure nimantraṇa kare ācārya bāra bāra

SYNONYMS

ei-mata—in this way; *anyonye*—to one another; *karena*—offer; *namaskāra*—obeisances; *prabhure*—unto Lord Caitanya Mahāprabhu; *nimantraṇa*—invitation; *kare*—does; *ācārya*—Advaita Ācārya; *bāra bāra*—again and again.

TRANSLATION

In this way both Advaita Ācārya and Śrī Caitanya Mahāprabhu would offer Their respectful obeisances unto one another. Then Advaita Ācārya would extend invitations to Śrī Caitanya Mahāprabhu again and again.

TEXT 13

আচার্যের নিমন্ত্রণ—আশ্চর্য-কথন ।
বিস্তারি' বর্ণিয়াছেন দাস-বৃন্দাবন ॥ ১৩ ॥

ācāryera nimantraṇa——āścarya-kathana
vistāri' varṇiyāchena dāsa-vṛndāvana

SYNONYMS

ācāryera nimantraṇa—the invitation of Advaita Ācārya; *āścarya-kathana*—wonderful story; *vistāri'*—very vividly; *varṇiyāchena*—described; *dāsa-vṛndāvana*—Vṛndāvana dāsa Ṭhākura.

TRANSLATION

Indeed, Śrī Advaita Ācārya's invitation is another wonderful story. It has been very vividly described by Vṛndāvana dāsa Ṭhākura.

TEXT 14

পুনরুক্তি হয়, তাহা না কৈলুঁ বর্ণন ।
আর ভক্তগণ করে প্রভুরে নিমন্ত্রণ ॥ ১৪ ॥

punarukti haya, tāhā nā kailuṅ varṇana
āra bhakta-gaṇa kare prabhure nimantraṇa

SYNONYMS

punaḥ-ukti—reputation; *haya*—there is; *tāhā*—that; *nā*—not; *kailuṅ*—I have done; *varṇana*—description; *āra bhakta-gaṇa*—other devotees; *kare*—do; *prabhure*—unto Lord Caitanya Mahāprabhu; *nimantraṇa*—invitation.

TRANSLATION

Since Advaita Ācārya's invitation has been described by Vṛndāvana dāsa Ṭhākura, I shall not repeat the story. However, I shall say that other devotees also extended invitations to Śrī Caitanya Mahāprabhu.

TEXT 15

এক এক দিন এক এক ভক্তগৃহে মহোৎসব ।
প্রভু-সঙ্গে তাহাঁ ভোজন করে ভক্ত সব ॥ ১৫ ॥

eka eka dina eka eka bhakta-gṛhe mahotsava
prabhu-saṅge tāhāṅ bhojana kare bhakta saba

SYNONYMS

eka eka dina—each and every day; *eka eka bhakta-gṛhe*—in the house of one devotee after another; *mahotsava*—festival; *prabhu-saṅge*—with Lord Śrī Caitanya Mahāprabhu; *tāhāṅ*—there; *bhojana*—lunch; *kare*—accept; *bhakta*—devotees; *saba*—all.

TRANSLATION

Every day one devotee after another would invite Śrī Caitanya Mahāprabhu and the other devotees to lunch and would also hold a festival.

TEXT 16

চারিমাস রহিলা সবে মহাপ্রভু-সঙ্গে ।
জগন্নাথের নানা যাত্রা দেখে মহারঙ্গে ॥ ১৬ ॥

cāri-māsa rahilā sabe mahāprabhu-saṅge
jagannāthera nānā yātrā dekhe mahā-raṅge

SYNONYMS

cāri-māsa—four months; *rahilā*—remain; *sabe*—all the devotees; *mahāprabhu-saṅge*—with Lord Caitanya Mahāprabhu, *jagannāthera*—of Lord Jagannātha; *nānā yātrā*—many festivals; *dekhe*—they see; *mahā-raṅge*—with great pleasure.

TRANSLATION

All the devotees remained at Jagannātha Purī for four continuous months, and they observed all Lord Jagannātha's festivals with great pleasure.

TEXT 17

কৃষ্ণজন্মযাত্রা-দিনে নন্দ-মহোৎসব ।
গোপবেশ হৈলা প্রভু লঞা ভক্ত সব ॥ ১৭ ॥

kṛṣṇa-janma-yātrā-dine nanda-mahotsava
gopa-veśa hailā prabhu lañā bhakta saba

SYNONYMS

kṛṣṇa-janma-yātrā—observance of the birth of Lord Kṛṣṇa; *dine*—on the day of; *nanda-mahotsava*—the festival observed by Nanda Mahārāja, the father of Kṛṣṇa; *gopa-veśa hailā*—dressed Himself as a cowherd boy; *prabhu*—Śrī Caitanya Mahāprabhu; *lañā*—taking; *bhakta saba*—all the devotees.

TRANSLATION

The devotees also celebrated the festival of Janmāṣṭamī, Kṛṣṇa's birthday, which is also called Nanda-mahotsava, the festival of Nanda Mahārāja. At that time Śrī Caitanya Mahāprabhu and His devotees dressed themselves as cowherd boys.

TEXT 18

দধিদুগ্ধ-ভার সবে নিজ-স্কন্ধে করি' ।
মহোৎসব-স্থানে আইলা বলি 'হরি' 'হরি' ॥ ১৮ ॥

dadhi-dugdha-bhāra sabe nija-skandhe kari'
mahotsava-sthāne āilā bali 'hari' 'hari'

SYNONYMS

dadhi-dugdha—of milk and yogurt; *bhāra*—carriers; *sabe*—all of them; *nija-skandhe*—on their shoulders; *kari'*—keeping; *mahotsava-sthāne*—to the place of the festival; *āilā*—came; *bali hari hari*—chanting Hari, Hari.

TRANSLATION

Having dressed up like cowherd boys, all the devotees carried pots of milk and yogurt balanced on rods over their shoulders. Thus they all arrived at the festival grounds chanting the holy name of Hari.

TEXT 19

কানাঞি-খুটিয়া আছেন 'নন্দ'-বেশ ধরি' ।
জগন্নাথ-মাহাতি হঞাছেন 'ব্রজেশ্বরী' ॥ ১৯ ॥

kānāñi-khuṭiyā āchena 'nanda'-veśa dhari'
jagannātha-māhāti hañāchena 'vrajeśvarī'

SYNONYMS

kānāñi-khuṭiyā—Kānāñi Khuṭiyā; *āchena*—is; *nanda-veśa dhari'*—in the dress of Nanda Mahārāja; *jagannātha-māhāti*—Jagannātha Māhāti; *hañāchena*—was; *vrajeśvarī*—mother Yaśodā.

TRANSLATION

Kānāñi Khuṭiyā dressed himself like Nanda Mahārāja, and Jagannātha Māhāti dressed himself as mother Yaśodā.

TEXT 20

আপনে প্রতাপরুদ্র, আর মিশ্র-কাশী ।
সার্বভৌম, আর পড়িছা-পাত্র তুলসী ॥ ২০ ॥

āpane pratāparudra, āra miśra-kāśī
sārvabhauma, āra paḍichā-pātra tulasī

SYNONYMS

āpane pratāparudra—personally King Pratāparudra; *āra*—and; *miśra-kāśī*—Kāśī Miśra; *sārvabhauma*—Sārvabhauma Bhaṭṭācārya; *āra*—and; *paḍichā-pātra tulasī*—Paḍichāpātra Tulasī, the temple superintendent.

TRANSLATION

At that time, King Pratāparudra was also personally present with Kāśī Miśra, Sārvabhauma Bhaṭṭācārya and Tulasī Paḍichāpātra.

TEXT 21

ইঁহা-সবা লঞা প্রভু করে নৃত্য-রঙ্গ ।
দধি-দুগ্ধ হরিদ্রা-জলে ভরে সবার অঙ্গ ॥ ২১ ॥

iṅhā-sabā lañā prabhu kare nṛtya-raṅga
dadhi-dugdha haridrā-jale bhare sabāra aṅga

SYNONYMS

iṅhā-sabā lañā—taking all of them; *prabhu*—Lord Caitanya Mahāprabhu; *kare nṛtya-raṅga*—performed dancing in jubilation; *dadhi*—yogurt; *dugdha*—milk; *haridrā*—turmeric; *jale*—with water; *bhare*—covered; *sabāra*—of all of them; *aṅga*—bodies.

TRANSLATION

As usual, Śrī Caitanya Mahāprabhu danced jubilantly. Everyone was covered with milk, yogurt and yellow turmeric water.

TEXT 22

অদ্বৈত কহে,—সত্য কহি, না করিহ কোপ ।
লগুড় ফিরাইতে পার, তবে জানি গোপ ॥ ২২ ॥

advaita kahe,——satya kahi, nā kariha kopa
laguḍa phirāite pāra, tabe jāni gopa

SYNONYMS

advaita kahe—Advaita Ācārya says; *satya kahi*—I speak the truth; *nā kariha kopa*—please do not be angry; *laguḍa*—stick, staff; *phirāite pāra*—if You can wheel around; *tabe jāni*—then I shall understand; *gopa*—cowherd boy.

TRANSLATION

It was at this time that Śrīla Advaita Ācārya said, "Please do not be angry. I speak the truth. I shall know whether You are a cowherd boy only if You can wheel this rod about."

TEXT 23

তবে লগুড় লঞা প্রভু ফিরাইতে লাগিলা ।
বার বার আকাশে ফেলি' লুফিয়া ধরিলা ॥ ২৩ ॥

tabe laguḍa lañā prabhu phirāite lāgilā
bāra bāra ākāśe pheli' luphiyā dharilā

SYNONYMS

tabe—then; *laguḍa*—rod; *lañā*—taking; *prabhu*—Śrī Caitanya Mahāprabhu; *phirāite lāgilā*—began to wheel it around; *bāra bāra*—again and again; *ākāśe*—in the sky; *pheli'*—throwing; *luphiyā*—tossing; *dharilā*—He captured.

TRANSLATION

Accepting Advaita Ācārya's challenge, Śrī Caitanya Mahāprabhu took a big rod and began to wheel it around and around. Again and again He threw the rod into the sky and caught it when it fell.

TEXT 24

শিরের উপরে, পৃষ্ঠে, সম্মুখে, দুই-পাশে ।
পাদমধ্যে ফিরায় লগুড়,—দেখি' লোক হাসে ॥ ২৪ ॥

śirera upare, pṛṣṭhe, sammukhe, dui-pāśe
pāda-madhye phirāya laguḍa,——dekhi' loka hāse

SYNONYMS

śirera upare—over the head; *pṛṣṭhe*—behind the back; *sammukhe*—in front; *dui-pāśe*—on the two sides; *pāda-madhye*—between the two legs; *phirāya*—wheels around; *laguḍa*—the rod; *dekhi'*—seeing; *loka hāse*—all the people began to laugh.

TRANSLATION

Śrī Caitanya Mahāprabhu wheeled and threw the rod, sometimes over His head, sometimes behind His back, sometimes in front of Him, sometimes to His side and sometimes between His legs. Indeed, all the people laughed to see this.

TEXT 25

অলাত-চক্রের প্রায় লগুড় ফিরায় ।
দেখি' সর্বলোক-চিত্তে চমৎকার পায় ॥ ২৫ ॥

alāta-cakrera prāya laguḍa phirāya
dekhi' sarva-loka-citte camatkāra pāya

SYNONYMS

alāta-cakrera—the circle of a firebrand; *prāya*—like; *laguḍa phirāya*—wheels the rod; *dekhi'*—seeing; *sarva-loka*—all the people; *citte*—within the heart; *camatkāra pāya*—became very astonished.

TRANSLATION

When Śrī Caitanya Mahāprabhu whirled the rod in a circle like a firebrand, the heart of everyone who saw it was astonished.

TEXT 26

এইমত নিত্যানন্দ ফিরায় লগুড় ।
কে বুঝিবে তাঁহা দুঁহার গোপভাব গূঢ় ॥ ২৬ ॥

ei-mata nityānanda phirāya laguḍa
ke bujhibe tāṅhā duṅhāra gopa-bhāva gūḍha

SYNONYMS

ei-mata—in this way; *nityānanda*—Lord Nityānanda Prabhu; *phirāya laguḍa*—wheels a rod; *ke*—who; *bujhibe*—will understand; *tāṅhā*—there; *duṅhāra*—of both of Them; *gopa-bhāva*—the ecstasy of the cowherd boys; *gūḍha*—very deep.

TRANSLATION

Nityānanda Prabhu also played at whirling the rod. Who can understand how They were ecstatically immersed in the deep emotions of the cowherd boys?

TEXT 27

প্রতাপরুদ্রের আজ্ঞায় পড়িছা-তুলসী ।
জগন্নাথের প্রসাদ-বস্ত্র এক লঞা আসি ॥ ২৭ ॥

pratāparudrera ājñāya paḍichā-tulasī
jagannāthera prasāda-vastra eka lañā āsi

SYNONYMS

pratāparudrera—of King Pratāparudra; *ājñāya*—on the order; *paḍichā-tulasī*—the temple superintendent named Tulasī; *jagannāthera*—of Lord Jagannātha; *prasāda-vastra*—used cloth; *eka*—one; *lañā*—taking; *āsi*—came.

TRANSLATION

Following the orders of Mahārāja Pratāparudra, the temple superintendent named Tulasī brought one of Lord Jagannātha's used cloths.

TEXT 28

**বহুমূল্য বস্ত্র প্রভুমস্তকে বান্ধিল ।
আচার্যাদি প্রভুর গণেরে পরাইল ॥ ২৮ ॥**

bahu-mūlya vastra prabhu-mastake bāndhila
ācāryādi prabhura gaṇere parāila

SYNONYMS

bahu-mūlya—very valuable; *vastra*—cloth; *prabhu-mastake*—on the head of Śrī Caitanya Mahāprabhu; *bāndhila*—wrapped; *ācārya-ādi*—headed by Advaita Ācārya; *prabhura*—of Śrī Caitanya Mahāprabhu; *gaṇere*—on the associates; *parāila*—put.

TRANSLATION

This valuable cloth was wrapped around the head of Śrī Caitanya Mahāprabhu. The other devotees, headed by Advaita Ācārya, also had cloths wrapped about their heads.

TEXT 29

**কানাঞি-খুটিয়া, জগন্নাথ,—দুইজন ।
আবেশে বিলাইল ঘরে ছিল যত ধন ॥ ২৯ ॥**

kānāñi-khuṭiyā, jagannātha,——dui-jana
āveśe bilāila ghare chila yata dhana

SYNONYMS

kānāñi-khuṭiyā—Kānāñi Khuṭiyā; *jagannātha*—Jagannātha Māhāti; *dui-jana*—two persons; *āveśe*—in ecstatic love; *bilāila*—distributed; *ghare*—at home; *chila*—was; *yata*—all; *dhana*—riches.

TRANSLATION

In ecstasy, Kānāñi Khuṭiyā, who was dressed as Nanda Mahārāja, and Jagannātha Māhāti, who was dressed as mother Yaśodā, distributed all the riches they had stocked at home.

TEXT 30

দেখি' মহাপ্রভু বড় সন্তোষ পাইলা ।
মাতাপিতা-জ্ঞানে দুঁহে নমস্কার কৈলা ॥ ৩০ ॥

dekhi' mahāprabhu baḍa santoṣa pāilā
mātā-pitā-jñāne duṅhe namaskāra kailā

SYNONYMS

dekhi'—seeing; *mahāprabhu*—Śrī Caitanya Mahāprabhu; *baḍa*—very much; *santoṣa*—satisfaction; *pāilā*—felt; *mātā-pitā-jñāne*—accepting as father and mother; *duṅhe*—unto both of them; *namaskāra kailā*—offered obeisances.

TRANSLATION

Śrī Caitanya Mahāprabhu was greatly satisfied to see this. Accepting them both as His father and mother, He offered them obeisances.

TEXT 31

পরম-আবেশে প্রভু আইলা নিজ-ঘর ।
এইমত লীলা করে গৌরাঙ্গসুন্দর ॥ ৩১ ॥

parama-āveśe prabhu āilā nija-ghara
ei-mata līlā kare gaurāṅga-sundara

SYNONYMS

parama-āveśe—in great ecstasy; *prabhu*—Śrī Caitanya Mahāprabhu; *āilā*—returned; *nija-ghara*—to His own residence; *ei-mata*—in this way; *līlā*—pastimes; *kare*—performed; *gaurāṅga-sundara*—Śrī Caitanya Mahāprabhu.

TRANSLATION

In great ecstasy, Śrī Caitanya Mahāprabhu returned to His residence. In this way, Śrī Caitanya Mahāprabhu, known as Gaurāṅga-sundara, performed various pastimes.

TEXT 32

বিজয়া-দশমী—লঙ্কা-বিজয়ের দিনে ।
বানর-সৈন্য কৈলা প্রভু লঞা ভক্তগণে ॥ ৩২ ॥

vijayā-daśamī——laṅkā-vijayera dine
vānara-sainya kailā prabhu lañā bhakta-gaṇe

SYNONYMS

vijayā—victory; *daśamī*—tenth day; *laṅkā-vijayera dine*—on the day celebrating the conquering of Laṅkā; *vānara-sainya*—monkey soldiers; *kailā*—arranged; *prabhu*—Śrī Caitanya Mahāprabhu; *lañā bhakta-gaṇe*—taking all the devotees.

TRANSLATION

On the victory day celebrating the conquest of Laṅkā—a day known as Vijayā-daśamī—Śrī Caitanya Mahāprabhu dressed up all His devotees like monkey soldiers.

TEXT 33

হনুমান্-আবেশে প্রভু বৃক্ষশাখা লঞা ।
লঙ্কা-গড়ে চড়ি' ফেলে গড় ভাঙ্গিয়া ॥ ৩৩ ॥

hanumān-āveśe prabhu vṛkṣa-śākhā lañā
laṅkā-gaḍe caḍi' phele gaḍa bhāṅgiyā

SYNONYMS

hanumān-āveśe—in the emotion of being Hanumān; *prabhu*—Śrī Caitanya Mahāprabhu; *vṛkṣa-śākhā lañā*—taking a large branch of a tree; *laṅkā-gaḍe*—on the Laṅkā fort; *caḍi'*—ascending; *phele*—breaks down; *gaḍa*—the fort; *bhāṅgiyā*—dismantling.

TRANSLATION

Displaying the emotions of Hanumān, Śrī Caitanya Mahāprabhu took up a large tree branch, and, mounting the walls of the Laṅkā fort, began to dismantle it.

TEXT 34

'কাহাঁরে রাব্ণা' প্রভু কহে ক্রোধাবেশে ।
'জগন্মাতা হরে পাপী, মারিমু সবংশে ॥' ৩৪ ॥

'kāhāṅre rāvṇā' prabhu kahe krodhāveśe
'jagan-mātā hare pāpī, mārimu savaṁśe'

SYNONYMS

kāhāṅre rāvṇā—where is the rascal Rāvaṇa; *prabhu*—Śrī Caitanya Mahāprabhu; *kahe*—says; *krodha-āveśe*—in great anger; *jagat-mātā*—the mother of the universe; *hare*—kidnaps; *pāpī*—sinful; *mārimu*—I shall kill; *sa-vaṁśe*—with all his family.

TRANSLATION

In the ecstasy of Hanumān, Śrī Caitanya Mahāprabhu angrily said, "Where is the rascal Rāvaṇa? He has kidnapped the universal mother, Sītā. Now I shall kill him and all his family."

TEXT 35

গোসাঞির আবেশ দেখি' লোকে চমৎকার ।
সর্বলোক 'জয়' 'জয়' বলে বার বার ॥ ৩৫ ॥

gosāñira āveśa dekhi' loke camatkāra
sarva-loka 'jaya' 'jaya' bale bāra bāra

SYNONYMS

gosāñira—of Śrī Caitanya Mahāprabhu; *āveśa*—ecstasy; *dekhi'*—by seeing; *loke*—all people; *camatkāra*—astonished; *sarva-loka*—all people; *jaya jaya*—all glories; *bale*—speak; *bāra bāra*—again and again.

TRANSLATION

Everyone became very astonished to see the emotional ecstasy of Śrī Caitanya Mahāprabhu, and everyone began to chant, "All glories! All glories!" again and again.

TEXT 36

এইমত রাসযাত্রা, আর দীপাবলী ।
উত্থান-দ্বাদশীযাত্রা দেখিলা সকলি ॥ ৩৬ ॥

ei-mata rāsa-yātrā, āra dīpāvalī
utthāna-dvādaśī-yātrā dekhilā sakali

SYNONYMS

ei-mata—in this way; *rāsa-yātrā*—*rāsa* dancing of Lord Kṛṣṇa; *āra*—and; *dīpa-āvalī*—a row of lights, the day of Dīpāvalī; *utthāna-dvādaśī-yātrā*—the festival of Utthāna-dvādaśī; *dekhilā sakali*—participated in all of them.

TRANSLATION

Śrī Caitanya Mahāprabhu and His devotees participated in all the festivals known as Rāsa-yātrā, Dīpāvalī and Utthāna-dvādaśī.

PURPORT

The Dīpāvalī festival takes place on the dark-moon night in the month of Kārttika (October-November). The Rāsa-yātrā, or *rāsa* dancing of Kṛṣṇa, takes place on the full-moon night of the same month. Utthāna-dvādaśī takes place the day after Ekādaśī in the waxing fortnight of the moon in the same month. All the devotees of Śrī Caitanya Mahāprabhu participated in all these festivals.

TEXT 37

একদিন মহাপ্রভু নিত্যানন্দে লঞা ।
দুই ভাই যুক্তি কৈল নিভৃতে বসিয়া ॥ ৩৭ ॥

eka-dina mahāprabhu nityānande lañā
dui bhāi yukti kaila nibhṛte vasiyā

SYNONYMS

eka-dina—one day; *mahāprabhu*—Śrī Caitanya Mahāprabhu; *nityānande lañā*—taking Lord Nityānanda Prabhu; *dui bhāi*—two brothers; *yukti kaila*—consulted; *nibhṛte vasiyā*—sitting in a solitary place.

TRANSLATION

One day the two brothers, Śrī Caitanya Mahāprabhu and Nityānanda Prabhu, consulted one another, sitting together in a solitary place.

TEXT 38

কিবা যুক্তি কৈল দুঁহে, কেহ নাহি জানে ।
ফলে অনুমান পাছে কৈল ভক্তগণে ॥ ৩৮ ॥

kibā yukti kaila duṅhe, keha nāhi jāne
phale anumāna pāche kaila bhakta-gaṇe

SYNONYMS

kibā yukti kaila—what consultation They had; *duṅhe*—both of Them; *keha nāhi jāne*—no one knows; *phale*—by the result; *anumāna*—guess; *pāche*—later; *kaila*—did; *bhakta-gaṇe*—all the devotees.

TRANSLATION

No one could understand what the brothers discussed between Themselves, but later all the devotees could guess what the subject matter was.

TEXT 39

তবে মহাপ্রভু সব ভক্তে বোলাইল ।
গৌড়দেশে যাহ সবে বিদায় করিল ॥ ৩৯ ॥

tabe mahāprabhu saba bhakte bolāila
gauḍa-deśe yāha sabe vidāya karila

SYNONYMS

tabe mahāprabhu—thereafter Śrī Caitanya Mahāprabhu; *saba*—all; *bhakte*—the devotees; *bolāila*—called; *gauḍa-deśe*—to Bengal; *yāha*—return; *sabe*—all of you; *vidāya karila*—bade farewell.

TRANSLATION

Thereafter, Śrī Caitanya Mahāprabhu called for all the devotees and asked them to return to Bengal. In this way, He bade farewell to them.

TEXT 40

সবারে কহিল প্রভু—প্রত্যব্দ আসিয়া ।
গুণ্ডিচা দেখিয়া যাবে আমারে মিলিয়া ॥ ৪০ ॥

sabāre kahila prabhu——pratyabda āsiyā
guṇḍicā dekhiyā yābe āmāre miliyā

SYNONYMS

sabāre—to all of them; *kahila*—said; *prabhu*—Śrī Caitanya Mahāprabhu; *prati-abda*—every year; *āsiyā*—coming; *guṇḍicā*—the function at the Guṇḍicā temple; *dekhiyā*—seeing; *yābe*—you should go; *āmāre miliyā*—after meeting Me.

TRANSLATION

Bidding farewell to all the devotees, Śrī Caitanya Mahāprabhu requested them to return to Jagannātha Purī every year to see Him and then see the cleansing of the Guṇḍicā temple.

TEXT 41

আচার্যেরে আজ্ঞা দিল করিয়া সম্মান ।
'আ-চণ্ডাল আদি কৃষ্ণভক্তি দিও দান' ॥ ৪১ ॥

ācāryere ājñā dila kariyā sammāna
'ā-caṇḍāla ādi kṛṣṇa-bhakti dio dāna'

SYNONYMS

ācāryere—unto Advaita Ācārya; *ājñā dila*—ordered; *kariyā sammāna*—with great respect; *ā-caṇḍāla*—even to the lowest of men, known as the *caṇḍāla; ādi*—beginning with; *kṛṣṇa-bhakti*—Kṛṣṇa consciousness, or devotional service to Lord Kṛṣṇa; *dio*—deliver; *dāna*—in charity.

TRANSLATION

With great respect, Śrī Caitanya Mahāprabhu requested Advaita Ācārya, "Give Kṛṣṇa consciousness, devotion to Kṛṣṇa, even to the lowest of men [caṇḍālas]."

PURPORT

This is Śrī Caitanya Mahāprabhu's order to all His devotees. *Kṛṣṇa-bhakti,* devotion to Kṛṣṇa, is open to everyone, even low-class men like *caṇḍālas.* One should follow this order in the disciplic succession stemming from Śrī Advaita and Nityānanda Prabhu and distribute Kṛṣṇa consciousness without discrimination throughout the world.

There are different kinds of men, beginning with the *brāhmaṇa* and going down to the lowest platform known as *caṇḍāla.* Whatever one's position, everyone in this age of Kali needs to be enlightened in Kṛṣṇa consciousness. That is the greatest need of the day. Everyone is acutely feeling the pangs of material existence. Even in the ranks and files of the American Senate, the pinpricks of material existence are felt, so much so that April 30, 1974, was actually set aside as Prayer Day. Thus everyone is feeling the resultant pinpricks of Kali-yuga brought about by human society's indulging in illicit sex, meat-eating, gambling and intoxication. Now is the time for the members of the International Society for Krishna Consciousness to distribute *kṛṣṇa-bhakti* all over the world and thus follow the orders of Śrī Caitanya Mahāprabhu. The Lord has ordered everyone to become a *guru* (Cc. *Madhya* 7.128): *āmāra ājñāya guru hañā tāra' ei deśa.* Everyone in every town and village should be enlightened by the instructions of Śrī Caitanya Mahāprabhu. Kṛṣṇa consciousness should be distributed to everyone indiscriminately. In this way, the entire world will be peaceful and happy, and everyone will glorify Śrī Caitanya Mahāprabhu, as He desires.

The word *caṇḍāla* actually refers to a dog-eater, who is considered the lowest of men. Even *caṇḍālas* can be enlightened in Kṛṣṇa consciousness due to Śrī Caitanya Mahāprabhu's benedictions. *Kṛṣṇa-bhakti* is not the monopoly of a certain caste. Everyone is eligible to receive this great benediction given by Śrī Caitanya Mahāprabhu. Everyone should be given a chance to receive it and be happy.

The word *dāna,* meaning "charity," is also significant in this verse. Whoever engages in the distribution of Kṛṣṇa consciousness is a charitable person. Professional men recite *Śrīmad-Bhāgavatam* and discuss *kṛṣṇa-bhakti* for an exchange of money. They cannot distribute such exalted transcendental property to everyone and anyone. Only pure devotees who have no motive other than serving Kṛṣṇa can give such transcendentally valuable benedictions out of charity.

TEXT 42

নিত্যানন্দে আজ্ঞা দিল,—'যাহ গৌড়দেশে ।
অনর্গল প্রেমভক্তি করিহ প্রকাশে ॥ ৪২ ॥

nityānande ājñā dila,——'yāha gauḍa-deśe
anargala prema-bhakti kariha prakāśe

SYNONYMS

nityānande—unto Nityānanda Prabhu; *ājñā dila*—Lord Śrī Caitanya Mahāprabhu ordered; *yāha gauḍa-deśe*—go to Gauḍa-deśa (Bengal); *anargala*—without restriction; *prema-bhakti*—devotional service in love of Godhead; *kariha prakāśe*—manifest.

TRANSLATION

Śrī Caitanya Mahāprabhu ordered Nityānanda Prabhu, "Go to Bengal and, without restriction, manifest devotional service to the Lord, Kṛṣṇa consciousness."

PURPORT

Śrī Caitanya Mahāprabhu thus ordered Nityānanda Prabhu to deliver all the Bengalis to devotional service. In *Bhagavad-gītā* (9.32) it is said:

māṁ hi pārtha vyapāśritya
ye 'pi syuḥ pāpa-yonayaḥ
striyo vaiśyās tathā śūdrās
te 'pi yānti parāṁ gatim

"O son of Pṛthā, those who take shelter in Me, though they be of lower birth—women, *vaiśyas* [merchants], as well as *śūdras* [workers]—can approach the supreme destination." Whoever takes to Kṛṣṇa consciousness and follows the regulative principles can return home, back to Godhead.

In his *Anubhāṣya,* Śrīla Bhaktisiddhānta Sarasvatī Ṭhākura writes: "There is a class of so-called devotees called *prākṛta-sahajiyās* who think that Nityānanda Prabhu is an ordinary human being. They have spread the news that Śrī Caitanya Mahāprabhu ordered Nityānanda Prabhu to return to Bengal from Orissa just to marry and beget children. This is certainly a great offense against Nityānanda Prabhu."

Such an offense is called *pāṣaṇḍa-buddhi,* or an atheistic remark. Offenders consider Nityānanda Prabhu to be like one of them, an ordinary human being. They do not know of Nityānanda Prabhu's identity with the *viṣṇu-tattva.* Thinking Nityānanda Prabhu to be an ordinary human being is the business of mental speculators known as *kuṇapātma-vādīs.* These people accept the material body, which is a bag of three material elements (*kuṇape tridhātuke*), as themselves. They think that Nityānanda Prabhu's body was similarly material and that it was meant for sense gratification. Whoever thinks in this way is a candidate for the darkest regions of hell. Those who hanker after women and money, who are self-interested and have the mentality of merchants, can certainly discover many things with their fertile brains and speak against the authorized revealed scriptures. They also engage in some moneymaking businesses to cheat innocent people, and they try to support their business programs by making such offensive statements. Actually Nityānanda Prabhu, being the expansion of Śrī Caitanya Mahāprabhu, is the most munificent incarnation. No one should consider Him an ordinary human being or an entity like the *prajāpatis,* who were ordered by Brahmā to increase generation. Nityānanda Prabhu should not be considered instrumental for sense gratification. Although professional so-called preachers support this, such statements are not found in any authorized revealed scriptures. Actually there is no support for these statements made by *sahajiyās* or other professional distributors of *kṛṣṇa-bhakti.*

TEXT 43

রামদাস, গদাধর আদি কত জনে।
তোমার সহায় লাগি' দিলু তোমার সনে ॥ ৪৩ ॥

rāma-dāsa, gadādhara ādi kata jane
tomāra sahāya lāgi' dilu tomāra sane

SYNONYMS

rāma-dāsa—Rāmadāsa; *gadādhara*—Gadādhara dāsa; *ādi*—and others; *kata jane*—some people; *tomāra*—Your; *sahāya*—assistants; *lāgi'*—as; *dilu*—I give; *tomāra sane*—with You.

TRANSLATION

Nityānanda Prabhu was given assistants like Rāmadāsa, Gadādhara dāsa and several others. Śrī Caitanya Mahāprabhu said, "I give them to You to assist You.

TEXT 44

মধ্যে মধ্যে আমি তোমার নিকট যাইব ।
অলক্ষিতে রহি' তোমার নৃত্য দেখিব' ॥ ৪৪ ॥

madhye madhye āmi tomāra nikaṭa yāiba
alakṣite rahi' tomāra nṛtya dekhiba'

SYNONYMS

madhye madhye—at intervals; *āmi*—I; *tomāra nikaṭa*—near You; *yāiba*—shall go; *alakṣite rahi'*—keeping invisible; *tomāra nṛtya*—Your dancing; *dekhiba*—I shall see.

TRANSLATION

"I shall also go to see You at intervals. Keeping Myself invisible, I shall watch You dance."

TEXT 45

শ্রীবাস-পণ্ডিতে প্রভু করি' আলিঙ্গন ।
কণ্ঠে ধরি' কহে তাঁরে মধুর বচন ॥ ৪৫ ॥

śrīvāsa-paṇḍite prabhu kari' āliṅgana
kaṇṭhe dhari' kahe tāṅre madhura vacana

SYNONYMS

śrīvāsa-paṇḍite—unto Śrīvāsa Paṇḍita; *prabhu*—Lord Śrī Caitanya Mahāprabhu; *kari'*—doing; *āliṅgana*—embracing; *kaṇṭhe dhari'*—catching his neck; *kahe*—says; *tāṅre*—unto him; *madhura vacana*—sweet words.

TRANSLATION

Śrī Caitanya Mahāprabhu then embraced Śrīvāsa Paṇḍita and, with His arm about his neck, began to speak to him in sweet words.

TEXT 46

তোমার ঘরে কীর্তনে আমি নিত্য নাচিব ।
তুমি দেখা পাবে, আর কেহ না দেখিব ॥ ৪৬ ॥

tomāra ghare kīrtane āmi nitya nāciba
tumi dekhā pābe, āra keha nā dekhiba

SYNONYMS

tomāra ghare—in your house; *kīrtane*—in the performance of congregational chanting; *āmi*—I; *nitya*—daily; *nāciba*—shall dance; *tumi*—you; *dekhā pābe*—will be able to see; *āra*—else; *keha*—anyone; *nā dekhiba*—will not see.

TRANSLATION

Śrī Caitanya Mahāprabhu requested Śrīvāsa Ṭhākura, "Perform congregational chanting daily, and be assured that I shall also dance in your presence. You will be able to see this dancing, but not others.

TEXT 47

এই বস্ত্র মাতাকে দিহ', এই সব প্রসাদ ।
দণ্ডবৎ করি' আমার ক্ষমাইহ অপরাধ ॥ ৪৭ ॥

ei vastra mātāke diha', ei saba prasāda
daṇḍavat kari' āmāra kṣamāiha aparādha

SYNONYMS

ei vastra—this cloth; *mātāke diha'*—deliver to My mother, Śacīdevī; *ei saba prasāda*—all these remnants of the food of Jagannātha; *daṇḍavat kari'*—offering obeisances; *āmāra*—My; *kṣamāiha*—cause to be excused; *aparādha*—offenses.

TRANSLATION

"Take this prasāda of Lord Jagannātha's and this cloth and deliver them to My mother, Śacīdevī. After offering her obeisances, please request her to excuse My offenses.

TEXT 48

তাঁর সেবা ছাড়ি' আমি করিয়াছি সন্ন্যাস ।
ধর্ম নহে, করি আমি নিজ ধর্ম-নাশ ॥ ৪৮ ॥

tāṅra sevā chāḍi' āmi kariyāchi sannyāsa
dharma nahe, kari āmi nija dharma-nāśa

SYNONYMS

tāṅra sevā chāḍi'—giving up her service; *āmi*—I; *kariyāchi*—accepted; *sannyāsa*—the renounced order of life; *dharma nahe*—it is not My religion; *kari*—perform; *āmi*—I; *nija dharma-nāśa*—destruction of My religious principles.

TRANSLATION

"I have given up the service of My mother and have accepted the sannyāsa order. Actually I should not have done this, for by so doing, I have destroyed My religious principles.

TEXT 49

তাঁর প্রেমবশ আমি, তাঁর সেবা– ধর্ম ।
তাহা ছাড়ি' করিয়াছি বাতুলের কর্ম ॥ ৪৯ ॥

tāṅra prema-vaśa āmi, tāṅra sevā——dharma
tāhā chāḍi' kariyāchi vātulera karma

SYNONYMS

tāṅra prema-vaśa—subordinate to her love; *āmi*—I; *tāṅra sevā*—her service; *dharma*—My religion; *tāhā chāḍi'*—giving up that; *kariyāchi*—I performed; *vātulera karma*—the acts of a madman.

TRANSLATION

"I am subordinate to the love of My mother, and it is My duty to serve her in return. Instead of doing so, I have accepted this renounced order. Certainly this is the act of a madman.

TEXT 50

বাতুল বালকের মাতা নাহি লয় দোষ ।
এই জানি' মাতা মোরে না করয় রোষ ॥ ৫০ ॥

vātula bālakera mātā nāhi laya doṣa
ei jāni' mātā more nā karaya roṣa

SYNONYMS

vātula bālakera—of a mad son; *mātā*—mother; *nāhi*—does not; *laya*—accept; *doṣa*—fault; *ei jāni'*—knowing this; *mātā*—mother; *more*—unto Me; *nā karaya roṣa*—is not at all angry.

TRANSLATION

"A mother is not offended by her mad son, and, knowing this, My mother is not offended by Me.

TEXT 51

কি কায সন্ন্যাসে মোর, প্রেম নিজ-ধন ।
যে-কালে সন্ন্যাস কৈলুঁ, ছন্ন হৈল মন ॥ ৫১ ॥

ki kāya sannyāse mora, prema nija-dhana
ye-kāle sannyāsa kailuṅ, channa haila mana

SYNONYMS

ki kāya—what business; *sannyāse*—in the renounced order; *mora*—of Me; *prema*—love; *nija-dhana*—My real wealth; *ye-kāle*—at which time; *sannyāsa kailuṅ*—I accepted the renounced order; *channa*—deranged; *haila*—was; *mana*—mind.

TRANSLATION

"I had no business in accepting this renounced order and sacrificing My love for My mother, which is My real property. Actually I was in a crazy state of mind when I accepted sannyāsa.

TEXT 52

নীলাচলে আছোঁ মুঞি তাঁহার আজ্ঞাতে ।
মধ্যে মধ্যে আসিমু তাঁর চরণ দেখিতে ॥ ৫২ ॥

nīlācale āchoṅ muñi tāṅhāra ājñāte
madhye madhye āsimu tāṅra caraṇa dekhite

SYNONYMS

nīlācale āchoṅ—stay at Jagannātha Purī, Nīlācala; *muñi*—I; *tāṅhāra ājñāte*—under her order; *madhye madhye*—at intervals; *āsimu*—I shall go; *tāṅra*—her; *caraṇa dekhite*—to see the lotus feet.

TRANSLATION

"I am staying here at Jagannātha Purī, Nīlācala, to comply with her orders. However, at intervals I shall go see her lotus feet.

TEXT 53

নিত্য যাই' দেখি মুঞি তাঁহার চরণে ।
স্ফূর্তি-জ্ঞানে তেঁহো তাহা সত্য নাহি মানে ॥ ৫৩ ॥

nitya yāi' dekhi muñi tāṅhāra caraṇe
sphūrti-jñāne teṅho tāhā satya nāhi māne

SYNONYMS

nitya yāi'—going daily; *dekhi*—see; *muñi*—I; *tāṅhāra caraṇe*—her lotus feet; *sphūrti-jñāne*—feeling My appearance; *teṅho*—she; *tāhā*—that; *satya nāhi māne*—does not accept as true.

TRANSLATION

"Indeed, I go there daily to see her lotus feet. She is able to feel My presence, although she does not believe it to be true.

TEXTS 54-55

একদিন শাল্যন্ন, ব্যঞ্জন পাঁচ-সাত ।
শাক, মোচা-ঘণ্ট, ভৃষ্ট-পটোল-নিম্বপাত ॥ ৫৪ ॥
লেম্বু-আদাখণ্ড, দধি, দুগ্ধ, খণ্ড-সার ।
শালগ্রামে সমর্পিলেন বহু উপহার ॥ ৫৫ ॥

eka-dina śālyanna, vyañjana pāṅca-sāta
śāka, mocā-ghaṇṭa, bhṛṣṭa-paṭola-nimba-pāta

lembu-ādā-khaṇḍa, dadhi, dugdha, khaṇḍa-sāra
śālagrāme samarpilena bahu upahāra

SYNONYMS

eka-dina—one day; *śāli-anna*—cooked rice made of *śāli* paddy; *vyañjana*—vegetables; *pāṅca-sāta*—five to seven different kinds; *śāka*—spinach; *mocā-ghaṇṭa*—curry made from banana flowers; *bhṛṣṭa*—fried; *paṭola*—*paṭola* vegetables; *nimba-pāta*—with leaves of the *nimba* tree; *lembu*—lemon; *ādā-khaṇḍa*—pieces of ginger; *dadhi*—yogurt; *dugdha*—milk; *khaṇḍa-sāra*—sugar candy; *śālagrāme*—unto Lord Viṣṇu in the form of the *śālagrāma; samarpilena*—offered; *bahu upahāra*—many other varieties of food.

TRANSLATION

"One day My mother, Śacī, offered food to Śālagrāma Viṣṇu. She offered rice cooked from śāli paddies, various kinds of vegetables, spinach, curry made of banana flowers, fried paṭola with nimba leaves, pieces of ginger with lemon, and also yogurt, milk, sugar candy and many other foods.

TEXT 56

প্রসাদ লঞা কোলে করেন ক্রন্দন ।
নিমাইর প্রিয় মোর—এসব ব্যঞ্জন ॥ ৫৬ ॥

prasāda lañā kole karena krandana
nimāira priya mora——e-saba vyañjana

SYNONYMS

prasāda lañā—taking the remnants of food; *kole*—on her lap; *karena krandana*—was crying; *nimāira*—of Nimāi; *priya*—favorite; *mora*—My; *e-saba vyañjana*—all these varieties of cooked food.

TRANSLATION

"Taking the food upon her lap, Mother was crying to think that all that food was very dear to her Nimāi.

TEXT 57

নিমাঞি নাহিক এথা, কে করে ভোজন ।
মোর ধ্যানে অশ্রুজলে ভরিল নয়ন ॥ ৫৭ ॥

nimāñi nāhika ethā, ke kare bhojana
mora dhyāne aśru-jale bharila nayana

SYNONYMS

nimāñi—Nimāi; *nāhika ethā*—is not present here; *ke kare bhojana*—who will eat them; *mora dhyāne*—on meditation upon Me; *aśru-jale*—with tears; *bharila nayana*—eyes become filled.

TRANSLATION

"My mother was thinking, 'Nimāi is not here. Who will accept all this food?' As she meditated upon Me in this way, her eyes filled with tears.

TEXT 58

শীঘ্র যাই' মুঞি সব করিনু ভক্ষণ ।
শূন্যপাত্র দেখি' অশ্রু করিয়া মার্জন ॥ ৫৮ ॥

śīghra yāi' muñi saba karinu bhakṣaṇa
śūnya-pātra dekhi' aśru kariyā mārjana

SYNONYMS

śīghra—very soon; *yāi'*—going; *muñi*—I; *saba*—all; *karinu bhakṣaṇa*—ate; *śūnya-pātra dekhi'*—seeing the dish empty; *aśru*—tears; *kariyā mārjana*—smearing with her hands.

TRANSLATION

"While she was thus thinking and crying, I immediately went there with great haste and ate everything. Seeing the dish empty, she wiped her tears away.

TEXT 59

'কে অন্ন-ব্যঞ্জন খাইল, শূন্য কেনে পাত ?
বালগোপাল কিবা খাইল সব ভাত ? ৫৯ ॥

'ke anna-vyañjana khāila, śūnya kene pāta?
bālagopāla kibā khāila saba bhāta?

SYNONYMS

ke—who; *anna-vyañjana khāila*—has eaten all this food; *śūnya kene pāta*—why is the dish empty; *bāla-gopāla*—the Deity Bāla-gopāla; *kibā khāila*—did He eat; *saba bhāta*—all the rice.

TRANSLATION

"She then began to wonder who had eaten all that food. 'Why is the plate empty?' she wondered, doubting that Bāla-gopāla had eaten it all.

TEXT 60

কিবা মোর কথায় মনে ভ্রম হঞা গেল !
কিবা কোন জন্তু আসি' সকল খাইল ? ৬০ ॥

kibā mora kathāya mane bhrama hañā gela!
kibā kona jantu āsi' sakala khāila?

SYNONYMS

kibā—or; *mora kathāya*—when I was thinking like that; *mane*—in the mind; *bhrama hañā gela*—I was mistaken; *kibā*—or; *kona jantu*—some animal; *āsi'*—coming; *sakala khāila*—ate everything.

TRANSLATION

"She began to wonder whether there was actually anything on the plate in the first place. Then again she thought that some animal might have come and eaten everything.

TEXT 61

কিবা আমি অন্নপাত্রে ভ্রমে না বাড়িল !'
এত চিন্তি' পাক-পাত্র যাঞা দেখিল ॥ ৬১ ॥

kibā āmi anna-pātre bhrame nā bāḍila!'
eta cinti' pāka-pātra yāñā dekhila

SYNONYMS

kibā—or; *āmi*—I; *anna-pātre*—on the plate for food; *bhrame*—by mistake; *nā bāḍila*—did not put anything; *eta cinti'*—thinking this; *pāka-pātra*—the kitchen pots; *yāñā dekhila*—went and saw.

TRANSLATION

"She thought, 'Perhaps by mistake I did not put any food on the plate.' So thinking, she went into the kitchen and saw the pots.

TEXT 62

অন্নব্যঞ্জনপূর্ণ দেখি' সকল ভাজনে ।
দেখিয়া সংশয় হৈল কিছু চমৎকার মনে ॥ ৬২

anna-vyañjana-pūrṇa dekhi' sakala bhājane
dekhiyā saṁśaya haila kichu camatkāra mane

SYNONYMS

anna-vyañjana-pūrṇa—filled with rice and vegetables; *dekhi'*—seeing; *sakala bhājane*—all the cooking pots; *dekhiyā*—seeing; *saṁśaya haila*—there was doubt; *kichu*—some; *camatkāra*—wonder; *mane*—in the mind.

TRANSLATION

"When she saw that all the pots were still filled with rice and vegetables, there was some doubt in her mind, and she was astonished.

TEXT 63

ঈশানে বোলাঞা পুনঃ স্থান লেপাইল ।
পুনরপি গোপালকে অন্ন সমর্পিল ॥ ৬৩ ॥

īśāne bolāñā punaḥ sthāna lepāila
punarapi gopālake anna samarpila

SYNONYMS

īśāne—to Īśāna, the servant; *bolāñā*—calling; *punaḥ*—again; *sthāna*—the place; *lepāila*—cleaned; *punarapi*—again; *gopālake*—unto Gopāla; *anna*—cooked rice and vegetables; *samarpila*—offered.

TRANSLATION

"Thus wondering, she called Īśāna, the servant, and had the place cleaned again. She then offered another plate to Gopāla.

TEXT 64

এইমত যবে করেন উত্তম রন্ধন।
মোরে খাওয়াইতে করে উৎকণ্ঠায় রোদন ॥ ৩৪ ॥

ei-mata yabe karena uttama randhana
more khāoyāite kare utkaṇṭhāya rodana

SYNONYMS

ei-mata—in this way; *yabe*—when; *karena*—does; *uttama randhana*—first-class cooking; *more*—Me; *khāoyāite*—to feed; *kare*—does; *utkaṇṭhāya*—with great anxiety; *rodana*—crying.

TRANSLATION

"Now whenever she prepares some good cooked food and wants to feed it to Me, she cries in great anxiety.

TEXT 65

তাঁর প্রেমে আনি' আমায় করায় ভোজনে।
অন্তরে মানয়ে সুখ, বাহ্যে নাহি মানে ॥ ৬৫ ॥

tāṅra preme āni' āmāya karāya bhojane
antare mānaye sukha, bāhye nāhi māne

SYNONYMS

tāṅra preme—by her love; *āni'*—bringing; *āmāya*—Me; *karāya bhojane*—causes to eat; *antare*—within herself; *mānaye*—she feels; *sukha*—happiness; *bāhye*—externally; *nāhi māne*—does not accept.

TRANSLATION

"Being obliged by her love, I am brought there to eat. Mother knows all these things internally and feels happiness, but externally she does not accept them.

TEXT 66

এই বিজয়া-দশমীতে হৈল এই রীতি ।
তাঁহাকে পুছিয়া তাঁর করাইহ প্রতীতি ॥ ৬৬ ॥

ei vijayā-daśamīte haila ei rīti
tāṅhāke puchiyā tāṅra karāiha pratīti

SYNONYMS

ei vijayā-daśamīte—on the previous Vijayā-daśamī day; *haila*—there was; *ei rīti*—such an incident; *tāṅhāke*—unto her; *puchiyā*—asking; *tāṅra*—her; *karāiha*—make; *pratīti*—belief.

TRANSLATION

"Such an incident took place on the last Vijayā-daśamī day. You can ask her about this incident and thus make her believe that I actually go there."

TEXT 67

এতেক কহিতে প্রভু বিহ্বল হইলা ।
লোক বিদায় করিতে প্রভু ধৈর্য ধরিলা ॥ ৬৭ ॥

eteka kahite prabhu vihvala ha-ilā
loka vidāya karite prabhu dhairya dharilā

SYNONYMS

eteka kahite—saying this; *prabhu*—Lord Śrī Caitanya Mahāprabhu; *vihvala ha-ilā*—became overwhelmed; *loka vidāya karite*—to bid farewell to the devotees; *prabhu*—Lord Śrī Caitanya Mahāprabhu; *dhairya dharilā*—maintained patience.

TRANSLATION

While describing all this, Śrī Caitanya Mahāprabhu was a little overwhelmed, but just to finish bidding farewell to the devotees, He remained patient.

TEXT 68

রাঘব পণ্ডিতে কহেন বচন সরস ।
'তোমার শুদ্ধ প্রেমে আমি হই' তোমার বশ' ॥৬৮॥

rāghava paṇḍite kahena vacana sarasa
'tomāra śuddha preme āmi ha-i' tomāra vaśa'

SYNONYMS

rāghava paṇḍite—unto Rāghava Paṇḍita; *kahena*—says; *vacana*—words; *sarasa*—very relishable; *tomāra*—your; *śuddha preme*—by pure devotional service; *āmi ha-i'*—I become; *tomāra*—your; *vaśa*—under obligation.

TRANSLATION

Śrī Caitanya Mahāprabhu next spoke some relishable words to Rāghava Paṇḍita. He said, "I am obliged to you due to your pure love for Me."

TEXT 69

ইঁহার কৃষ্ণসেবার কথা শুন, সর্বজন ।
পরম-পবিত্র সেবা অতি সর্বোত্তম ॥ ৬৯ ॥

iṅhāra kṛṣṇa-sevāra kathā śuna, sarva-jana
parama-pavitra sevā ati sarvottama

SYNONYMS

iṅhāra—of him; *kṛṣṇa-sevāra*—of service to Lord Kṛṣṇa; *kathā*—stories; *śuna*—hear; *sarva-jana*—all people; *parama-pavitra*—supremely pure; *sevā*—service; *ati*—very much; *sarva-uttama*—well accomplished.

TRANSLATION

Śrī Caitanya Mahāprabhu then informed everyone, "Just hear about the pure devotional service rendered to Kṛṣṇa by Rāghava Paṇḍita. Indeed, Rāghava Paṇḍita's service is supremely pure and highly accomplished.

TEXT 70

আর দ্রব্য রহু—শুন নারিকেলের কথা ।
পাঁচ গণ্ডা করি' নারিকেল বিকায় তথা ॥ ৭০ ॥

āra dravya rahu——śuna nārikelera kathā
pāṅca gaṇḍā kari' nārikela vikāya tathā

SYNONYMS

āra dravya rahu—apart from the other commodities; *śuna*—just hear; *nārikelera kathā*—the incident of offering coconuts; *pāṅca gaṇḍā kari'*—at the price of five *gaṇḍās; nārikela*—coconut; *vikāya*—is sold; *tathā*—there.

TRANSLATION

"Apart from other commodities, just hear about his coconut offering. A coconut is sold at the rate of five gaṇḍās each.

TEXT 71

বাটিতে কত শত বৃক্ষে লক্ষ লক্ষ ফল।
তথাপি শুনেন যথা মিষ্ট নারিকেল ॥ ৭১ ॥

vāṭite kata śata vṛkṣe lakṣa lakṣa phala
tathāpi śunena yathā miṣṭa nārikela

SYNONYMS

vāṭite—in his garden; *kata śata*—how many hundreds of; *vṛkṣe*—trees; *lakṣa lakṣa phala*—millions of fruits; *tathāpi*—still; *śunena*—hears; *yathā*—where; *miṣṭa nārikela*—sweet coconut.

TRANSLATION

"Although he already has hundreds of trees and millions of fruits, he is still very eager to hear about the place where sweet coconut is available.

TEXT 72

এক এক ফলের মূল্য দিয়া চারিচারি পণ।
দশক্রোশ হৈতে আনায় করিয়া যতন ॥ ৭২ ॥

eka eka phalera mūlya diyā cāri-cāri paṇa
daśa-krośa haite ānāya kariyā yatana

SYNONYMS

eka eka phalera—of each and every fruit; *mūlya*—price; *diyā*—giving; *cāri-cāri paṇa*—four *paṇas* each (one *paṇa* equals twenty *gaṇḍās*); *daśa-krośa*—twenty miles away; *haite*—from; *ānāya*—brings; *kariyā yatana*—with great endeavor.

TRANSLATION

"He collects coconut with great endeavor from a place twenty miles away, and he gives four paṇas each for them.

TEXT 73

প্রতিদিন পাঁচ-সাত ফল ছোলাঞা।
সুশীতল করিতে রাখে জলে ডুবাইঞা ॥ ৭৩ ॥

prati-dina pāñca-sāta phala cholāñā
suśītala karite rākhe jale ḍubāiñā

SYNONYMS

prati-dina—each day; *pāñca-sāta*—five to seven; *phala*—fruits; *cholāñā*—clipping; *su-śītala karite*—to make it very cool; *rākhe*—keeps; *jale*—in water; *ḍubāiñā*—immersing.

TRANSLATION

"Every day five to seven coconuts are clipped and put into water to keep cool.

TEXT 74

ভোগের সময় পুনঃ ছুলি' সংস্করি'।
কৃষ্ণে সমর্পণ করে মুখ ছিদ্র করি' ॥ ৭৪ ॥

bhogera samaya punaḥ chuli' saṁskari'
kṛṣṇe samarpaṇa kare mukha chidra kari'

SYNONYMS

bhogera samaya—at the time of offering *bhoga; punaḥ*—again; *chuli'*—clipping; *saṁskari'*—cleansing; *kṛṣṇe*—unto Lord Kṛṣṇa; *samarpaṇa*—offering; *kare*—makes; *mukha*—at the top; *chidra kari'*—making a hole.

TRANSLATION

"At the time of offering bhoga, the coconuts are again clipped and cleansed. After holes are made in them, they are offered to Lord Kṛṣṇa.

TEXT 75

কৃষ্ণ সেই নারিকেল-জল পান করি'।
কভু শূন্য ফল রাখেন, কভু জল ভরি' ॥ ৭৫ ॥

kṛṣṇa sei nārikela-jala pāna kari'
kabhu śūnya phala rākhena, kabhu jala bhari'

SYNONYMS

kṛṣṇa—Lord Kṛṣṇa; *sei*—that; *nārikela-jala*—water of the coconut; *pāna kari'*—drinking; *kabhu*—sometimes; *śūnya*—vacant; *phala rākhena*—leaves the fruit; *kabhu*—sometimes; *jala bhari'*—being filled with water.

TRANSLATION

"Lord Kṛṣṇa used to drink the juice from these coconuts, and sometimes the coconuts were left drained of juice. At other times the coconuts were filled with juice.

TEXT 76

জলশূন্য ফল দেখি' পণ্ডিত—হরষিত।
ফল ভাঙ্গি' শস্যে করে সৎপাত্র পূরিত ॥ ৭৬ ॥

jala-śūnya phala dekhi' paṇḍita——haraṣita
phala bhāṅgi' śasye kare sat-pātra pūrita

SYNONYMS

jala-śūnya—without water; *phala*—fruit; *dekhi'*—by seeing; *paṇḍita*—Rāghava Paṇḍita; *haraṣita*—very pleased; *phala bhāṅgi'*—breaking the fruit; *śasye*—with the pulp; *kare*—makes; *sat-pātra*—another plate; *pūrita*—filled.

TRANSLATION

"When Rāghava Paṇḍita saw that the juice had been drunk from the coconuts, he was very pleased. He would then break the coconut, take out the pulp and put it on another plate.

TEXT 77

শস্য সমর্পণ করি' বাহিরে ধেয়ান।
শস্য খাঞা কৃষ্ণ করে শূন্য ভাজন ॥ ৭৭ ॥

śasya samarpaṇa kari' bāhire dheyāna
śasya khāñā kṛṣṇa kare śūnya bhājana

SYNONYMS

śasya—the pulp; *samarpaṇa kari'*—offering; *bāhire*—outside the temple room; *dheyāna*—meditates; *śasya khāñā*—eating the pulp; *kṛṣṇa*—Lord Kṛṣṇa; *kare*—makes; *śūnya*—vacant; *bhājana*—the plate.

TRANSLATION

"After offering the pulp, he would meditate outside the temple door. In the meantime, Lord Kṛṣṇa, having eaten the pulp, would leave the plate empty.

TEXT 78

কভু শস্য খাঞা পুনঃ পাত্র ভরে শাঁসে।
শ্রদ্ধা বাড়ে পণ্ডিতের, প্রেমসিন্ধু ভাসে ॥ ৭৮ ॥

kabhu śasya khāñā punaḥ pātra bhare śāṁse
śraddhā bāḍe paṇḍitera, prema-sindhu bhāse

SYNONYMS

kabhu—sometimes; *śasya khāñā*—eating the pulp; *punaḥ*—again; *pātra*—the plate; *bhare*—fills; *śāṁse*—with pulp; *śraddhā*—faith; *bāḍe*—increases; *paṇḍitera*—of Rāghava Paṇḍita; *prema-sindhu*—in the ocean of love; *bhāse*—floats.

TRANSLATION

"Sometimes, after eating the pulp, Kṛṣṇa would fill the plate again with new pulp. In this way, Rāghava Paṇḍita's faith increases, and he floats in an ocean of love.

TEXT 79

এক দিন ফল দশ সংস্কার করিয়া।
ভোগ লাগাইতে সেবক আইল লঞা ॥ ৭৯ ॥

eka dina phala daśa saṁskāra kariyā
bhoga lāgāite sevaka āila lañā

SYNONYMS

eka dina—one day; *phala*—fruits; *daśa*—ten; *saṁskāra kariyā*—after cleansing; *bhoga lāgāite*—to offer *bhoga; sevaka*—servant; *āila*—came; *lañā*—taking.

TRANSLATION

"One day it so happened that about ten coconuts were properly clipped and brought by a servant to offer to the Deity.

TEXT 80

অবসর নাহি হয়, বিলম্ব হইল।
ফল-পাত্র-হাতে সেবক দ্বারে ত' রহিল ॥ ৮০ ॥

avasara nāhi haya, vilamba ha-ila
phala-pātra-hāte sevaka dvāre ta' rahila

SYNONYMS

avasara nāhi haya—there was little time; *vilamba ha-ila*—it was late; *phala-pātra*—the pot of fruits; *hāte*—in the hands; *sevaka*—the servant; *dvāre*—at the door; *ta'*—indeed; *rahila*—remained.

TRANSLATION

"When the coconuts were brought, there was little time to offer them because it was already late. The servant, holding the container of coconuts, remained standing at the door.

TEXT 81

দ্বারের উপর ভিতে তেঁহো হাত দিল ।
সেই হাতে ফল ছুঁইল, পণ্ডিত দেখিল ॥ ৮১ ॥

dvārera upara bhite teṅho hāta dila
sei hāte phala chuṅila, paṇḍita dekhila

SYNONYMS

dvārera upara—above the door; *bhite*—on the ceiling; *teṅho*—he; *hāta dila*—brushed his hand; *sei hāte*—with that hand; *phala chuṅila*—touched the fruit; *paṇḍita*—Rāghava Paṇḍita; *dekhila*—saw.

TRANSLATION

"Rāghava Paṇḍita then saw that the servant touched the ceiling above the door and then touched the coconuts with the same hand.

TEXT 82

পণ্ডিত কহে,—দ্বারে লোক করে গতায়াতে ।
তার পদধূলি উড়ি' লাগে উপর ভিতে ॥ ৮২ ॥

paṇḍita kahe,——dvāre loka kare gatāyāte
tāra pada-dhūli uḍi' lāge upara bhite

SYNONYMS

paṇḍita kahe—Rāghava Paṇḍita said; *dvāre*—through the door; *loka*—people in general; *kare*—do; *gatāyāte*—coming and going; *tāra*—their; *pada-dhūli*—dust of the feet; *uḍi'*—being blown; *lāge*—touches; *upara*—upward; *bhite*—the ceiling.

TRANSLATION

"Rāghava Paṇḍita then said, 'People are always coming and going through that door. The dust from their feet blows up and touches the ceiling.

TEXT 83

সেই ভিতে হাত দিয়া ফল পরশিলা ।
কৃষ্ণ-যোগ্য নহে, ফল অপবিত্র হৈলা ॥ ৮৩ ॥

sei bhite hāta diyā phala paraśilā
kṛṣṇa-yogya nahe, phala apavitra hailā

SYNONYMS

sei bhite—on that ceiling; *hāta diyā*—touching your hand; *phala*—the fruit; *paraśilā*—touched; *kṛṣṇa-yogya nahe*—is not fit to be offered to Kṛṣṇa; *phala*—the fruit; *apavitra hailā* —has become contaminated.

TRANSLATION

" 'After touching the ceiling above the door, you have touched the coconuts. Now they are no longer fit to be offered to Kṛṣṇa because they are contaminated.'

PURPORT

Śrīla Bhaktisiddhānta Sarasvatī Ṭhākura states that Rāghava Paṇḍita was not simply a crazy fellow suffering from some cleansing phobia. He did not belong to the mundane world. In lower consciousness, accepting something to be spiritual when it is actually material is called *bhauma-ijya-dhīḥ*. Rāghava Paṇḍita was an eternal servant of Kṛṣṇa, and everything he saw was related to the service of the Lord. He was always absorbed in the transcendental thought of how he could always serve Kṛṣṇa with everything. Sometimes neophytes, devotees on the lower platform, try to imitate Rāghava Paṇḍita on the platform of material purity and impurity. Such imitation will not help anyone. As explained in *Caitanya-caritāmṛta*, (*Antya-līlā* 4.174): *bhadrābhadra-vastu-jñāna nāhika 'prākṛte'.* On the transcendental platform there is no higher or lower, pure or impure. On the material platform, distinction is made between good and bad, but on the spiritual platform everything is of the same quality.

'dvaite' bhadrābhadra-jñāna, saba——'manodharma'
'ei bhāla, ei manda',——ei saba 'bhrama'

"In the material world, conceptions of good and bad are all mental speculations. Therefore, saying, 'This is good, and this is bad, is all a mistake."(*Cc. Antya* 4.176)

TEXT 84

এত বলি' ফল ফেলে প্রাচীর লঙ্ঘিয়া ।
ঐছে পবিত্র প্রেম-সেবা জগৎ জিনিয়া ॥ ৮৪ ॥

eta bali' phala phele prācīra laṅghiyā
aiche pavitra prema-sevā jagat jiniyā

SYNONYMS

eta bali'—saying this; *phala phele*—throws away the fruits; *prācīra laṅghiyā*—across the boundary wall; *aiche*—such; *pavitra*—pure; *prema-sevā*—service in love; *jagat jiniyā*—conquering all the world.

TRANSLATION

"Such was the service of Rāghava Paṇḍita. He did not accept the coconuts but threw them over the wall. His service is purely based on unalloyed love, and it conquers the whole world.

TEXT 85

তবে আর নারিকেল সংস্কার করাইল ।
পরম পবিত্র করি' ভোগ লাগাইল ॥ ৮৫ ॥

tabe āra nārikela saṁskāra karāila
parama pavitra kari' bhoga lāgāila

SYNONYMS

tabe—thereafter; *āra*—other; *nārikela*—coconuts; *saṁskāra karāila*—made clipped and cleaned; *parama pavitra kari'*—with great attention to keep them pure; *bhoga lāgāila*—offered for eating.

TRANSLATION

"Thereafter, Rāghava Paṇḍita had other coconuts gathered, cleansed and clipped, and with great attention he offered them to the Deity to eat.

TEXT 86

এইমত কলা, আম্র, নারঙ্গ, কাঁঠাল ।
যাহা যাহা দূর-গ্রামে শুনিয়াছে ভাল ॥ ৮৬ ॥

ei-mata kalā, āmra, nāraṅga, kāṅṭhāla
yāhā yāhā dūra-grāme śuniyāche bhāla

SYNONYMS

ei-mata—in this way; *kalā*—bananas; *āmra*—mangoes; *nāraṅga*—oranges; *kāṅṭhāla*—jackfruit; *yāhā yāhā*—whatever; *dūra-grāme*—in distant villages; *śuniyāche*—he heard; *bhāla*—good.

TRANSLATION

"In this way he collected excellent bananas, mangoes, oranges, jackfruits and whatever first-class fruits from distant villages he had heard about.

TEXT 87

বহুমূল্য দিয়া আনি' করিয়া যতন ।
পবিত্র সংস্কার করি' করে নিবেদন ॥ ৮৭ ॥

bahu-mūlya diyā āni' kariyā yatana
pavitra saṁskāra kari' kare nivedana

SYNONYMS

bahu-mūlya—high price; *diyā*—offering; *āni'*—bringing; *kariyā yatana*—with great attention; *pavitra*—purified; *saṁskāra kari'*—trimming; *kare nivedana*—offers to the Deity.

TRANSLATION

"All these fruits were collected from distant places and were bought at a high price. After trimming them with great care and purity, Rāghava Paṇḍita offered them to the Deity.

TEXT 88

এই মত ব্যঞ্জনের শাক, মূল, ফল ।
এই মত চিড়া, হুড়ুম, সন্দেশ সকল ॥ ৮৮ ॥

ei mata vyañjanera śāka, mūla, phala
ei mata ciḍā, huḍuma, sandeśa sakala

SYNONYMS

ei mata—in this way; *vyañjanera*—of vegetables; *śāka*—spinach; *mūla*—radishes; *phala*—fruits; *ei mata*—in this way; *ciḍā*—chipped rice; *huḍuma*—powdered rice; *sandeśa*—sweetmeats; *sakala*—all.

TRANSLATION

"Thus with great care and attention Rāghava Paṇḍita would prepare spinach, other vegetables, radishes, fruits, chipped rice, powdered rice and sweetmeats.

TEXT 89

এইমত পিঠা-পানা, ক্ষীর-ওদন ।
পরম পবিত্র, আর করে সর্বোত্তম ॥ ৮৯ ॥

ei-mata piṭhā-pānā, kṣīra-odana
parama pavitra, āra kare sarvottama

SYNONYMS

ei-mata—in this way; *piṭhā-pānā*—cakes and sweet rice; *kṣīra-odana*—concentrated milk; *parama pavitra*—highly purified; *āra*—and; *kare*—he makes; *sarva-uttama*—first class, tasteful.

TRANSLATION

"He prepared cakes, sweet rice, concentrated milk and everything else with great attention, and the cooking conditions were purified so that the food was first class and tasteful.

TEXT 90

কাশমৃদি, আচার আদি অনেক প্রকার ।
গন্ধ, বস্ত্র, অলঙ্কার, সর্ব দ্রব্য-সার ॥ ৯০ ॥

kāśamdi, ācāra ādi aneka prakāra
gandha, vastra, alaṅkāra, sarva dravya-sāra

SYNONYMS

kāśamdi—a kind of pickle; *ācāra*—other pickles; *ādi*—and so on; *aneka prakāra*—of many varieties; *gandha*—scents; *vastra*—clothing; *alaṅkāra*—ornaments; *sarva*—all; *dravya*—of things; *sāra*—best.

TRANSLATION

"Rāghava Paṇḍita would also offer all kinds of pickles, such as kāśamdi. He offered various scents, garments, ornaments and the best of everything.

TEXT 91

এইমত প্রেমের সেবা করে অনুপম।
যাহা দেখি' সর্বলোকের জুড়ান নয়ন ॥ ৯১ ॥

ei-mata premera sevā kare anupama
yāhā dekhi' sarva-lokera juḍāna nayana

SYNONYMS

ei-mata—in this way; *premera sevā*—service in love; *kare*—performs; *anupama*—without comparison; *yāhā dekhi'*—seeing which; *sarva-lokera*—of all people; *juḍāna*—become pleased; *nayana*—the eyes.

TRANSLATION

"Thus Rāghava Paṇḍita would serve the Lord in an incomparable way. Everyone was very satisfied just to see him."

TEXT 92

এত বলি' রাঘবেরে কৈল আলিঙ্গনে।
এইমত সম্মানিল সর্ব ভক্তগণে ॥ ৯২ ॥

eta bali' rāghavere kaila āliṅgane
ei-mata sammānila sarva bhakta-gaṇe

SYNONYMS

eta bali'—saying this; *rāghavere*—Rāghava Paṇḍita; *kaila āliṅgane*—He embraced; *ei-mata*—in this way; *sammānila*—showed respect; *sarva*—all; *bhakta-gaṇe*—to the devotees.

TRANSLATION

Śrī Caitanya Mahāprabhu then mercifully embraced Rāghava Paṇḍita. The Lord also offered all the other devotees a reception with similar respect.

TEXT 93

শিবানন্দ সেনে কহে করিয়া সম্মান।
বাসুদেব-দত্তের তুমি করিহ সমাধান ॥ ৯৩ ॥

śivānanda sene kahe kariyā sammāna
vāsudeva-dattera tumi kariha samādhāna

SYNONYMS

śivānanda sene—unto Śivānanda Sena; *kahe*—says; *kariyā sammāna*—with great respect; *vāsudeva-dattera*—of Vāsudeva Datta; *tumi*—you; *kariha*—take; *samādhāna*—care.

TRANSLATION

The Lord also respectfully told Śivānanda Sena, "Take care of Vāsudeva Datta very nicely.

TEXT 94

পরম উদার ইঁহো, যে দিন যে আইসে।
সেই দিনে ব্যয় করে, নাহি রাখে শেষে ॥ ৯৪ ॥

parama udāra iṅho, ye dina ye āise
sei dine vyaya kare, nāhi rākhe śeṣe

SYNONYMS

parama udāra—very liberal; *iṅho*—he; *ye dina*—every day; *ye āise*—whatever he gets; *sei dine*—on that very day; *vyaya kare*—spends; *nāhi*—does not; *rākhe*—keep; *śeṣe*—any balance.

TRANSLATION

"Vāsudeva Datta is very liberal. Every day, whatever income he receives, he spends. He does not keep any balance.

TEXT 95

'গৃহস্থ' হয়েন ইঁহো, চাহিয়ে সঞ্চয়।
সঞ্চয় না কৈলে কুটুম্ব-ভরণ নাহি হয় ॥ ৯৫ ॥

'gṛhastha' hayena iṅho, cāhiye sañcaya
sañcaya nā kaile kuṭumba-bharaṇa nāhi haya

SYNONYMS

gṛhastha—householder; *hayena*—is; *iṅho*—he (Vāsudeva Datta); *cāhiye sañcaya*—requires to save some money; *sañcaya nā kaile*—without saving money; *kuṭumba-bharaṇa*—maintenance of a family; *nāhi haya*—is not possible.

TRANSLATION

"Being a householder, Vāsudeva Datta needs to save some money. Because he is not doing so, it is very difficult for him to maintain his family.

TEXT 96

ইহার ঘরের আয়-ব্যয় সব— তোমার স্থানে ।
'সরখেল' হঞা তুমি করিহ সমাধানে ॥ ৯৬ ॥

ihāra gharera āya-vyaya saba——tomāra sthāne
'sara-khela' hañā tumi kariha samādhāne

SYNONYMS

ihāra—of Vāsudeva Datta; *gharera*—of household affairs; *āya-vyaya*—income and expenditures; *saba*—all; *tomāra sthāne*—at your place; *sara-khela hañā*—being the manager; *tumi*—you; *kariha samādhāne*—arrange.

TRANSLATION

"Please take care of Vāsudeva Datta's family affairs. Become his manager and make the proper adjustments.

PURPORT

Both Vāsudeva Datta and Śivānanda Sena were living in the same neighborhood, which is presently called Kumārahaṭṭa or Hālisahara.

TEXT 97

প্রতিবর্ষে আমার সব ভক্তগণ লঞা ।
গুণ্ডিচায় আসিবে সবায় পালন করিয়া ॥ ৯৭ ॥

prati-varṣe āmāra saba bhakta-gaṇa lañā
guṇḍicāya āsibe sabāya pālana kariyā

SYNONYMS

prati-varṣe—each and every year; *āmāra*—My; *saba*—all; *bhakta-gaṇa lañā*—accompanied by the devotees; *guṇḍicāya*—to perform the Guṇḍicā cleansing festival; *āsibe*—you will come; *sabāya*—to everyone; *pālana kariyā*—providing maintenance.

TRANSLATION

"Come every year and bring all My devotees with you to the Guṇḍicā festival. I also request you to maintain all of them."

TEXT 98

কুলীনগ্রামীরে কহে সম্মান করিয়া।
প্রত্যব্দ আসিবে যাত্রায় পট্টডোরী লঞা॥ ৯৮॥

kulīna-grāmīre kahe sammāna kariyā
pratyabda āsibe yātrāya paṭṭa-ḍorī lañā

SYNONYMS

kulīna-grāmīre—unto the inhabitants of Kulīna-grāma; *kahe*—says; *sammāna kariyā*—with great respect; *prati-abda*—each year; *āsibe*—please come; *yātrāya*—during the Ratha-yātrā festival; *paṭṭa-ḍorī*—silken rope; *lañā*—taking.

TRANSLATION

The Lord then with great respect extended an invitation to all the inhabitants of Kulīna-grāma, asking them to come every year and bring silken rope to carry Lord Jagannātha during the Ratha-yātrā festival.

TEXT 99

গুণরাজ-খাঁন কৈল শ্রীকৃষ্ণবিজয়।
তাহাঁ একবাক্য তাঁর আছে প্রেমময়॥ ৯৯॥

guṇarāja-khāṅna kaila śrī-kṛṣṇa-vijaya
tāhāṅ eka-vākya tāṅra āche premamaya

SYNONYMS

guṇarāja-khāṅna—Guṇarāja Khān; *kaila*—compiled; *śrī-kṛṣṇa-vijaya*—the book named *Śrī Kṛṣṇa-vijaya; tāhāṅ*—there; *eka-vākya*—one sentence; *tāṅra*—of it; *āche*—is; *prema-maya*—full of love of Kṛṣṇa.

TRANSLATION

Śrī Caitanya Mahāprabhu then said, "Guṇarāja Khān of Kulīna-grāma compiled a book named Śrī Kṛṣṇa-vijaya in which there is a sentence revealing the author's ecstatic love of Kṛṣṇa."

PURPORT

Śrī Kṛṣṇa-vijaya is a book of poems considered to be the first poetry book written in Bengal. Śrīla Bhaktisiddhānta Sarasvatī Ṭhākura states that this book was compiled in the Bengali *śakābda* year 1395. After seven years, it was completed (1402 *śakābda*). This book was written in plain language, and even half-educated

Bengalis and women could read it very clearly. Even ordinary men with little knowledge of the alphabet could read this book and understand it. Its language is not very ornamental, and sometimes the poetry is not very sweet to hear. Although according to the sonnet style each line should contain fourteen syllables, there are sometimes sixteen, twelve and thirteen syllables in his verse. Many words used in those days could be understood only by local inhabitants, yet this book is still so popular that no book store is complete without it. It is very valuable for those who are interested in advancing in Kṛṣṇa consciousness.

Śrī Guṇarāja Khān was one of the topmost Vaiṣṇavas, and he has translated the Tenth and Eleventh Cantos of *Śrīmad-Bhāgavatam* for the understanding of the common man. The book *Śrī Kṛṣṇa-vijaya* was highly praised by Śrī Caitanya Mahāprabhu, and it is very valuable for all Vaiṣṇavas. Śrīla Bhaktisiddhānta Sarasvatī Ṭhākura gives a genealogical table and family history of Guṇarāja Khān. When a Bengali emperor named Ādiśūra first came from Kānyakubja, or Kānowj, he brought with him five *brāhmaṇas* and five *kāyasthas.* Since the king is supposed to be accompanied by his associates, the *brāhmaṇas* accompanied the King to help him in higher spiritual matters. The *kāyasthas* were to render other services. In the northern Indian high country, the *kāyasthas* are accepted as *śūdras,* but in Bengal the *kāyasthas* are considered among the higher castes. It is a fact that the *kāyasthas* came to Bengal from northern India, specifically from Kānyakubja, or Kānowj. Śrīla Bhaktisiddhānta Sarasvatī Ṭhākura says that the *kāyasthas* who came from Kānyakubja were high-class men. Of them, Daśaratha Vasu was a great personality, and the thirteenth generation of his family included Guṇarāja Khān.

His real name was Mālādhara Vasu, but the title Khān was given to him by the Emperor of Bengal. Thus he became known as Guṇarāja Khān. Bhaktisiddhānta Sarasvatī Ṭhākura gives the following genealogical table of Guṇarāja Khān: (1) Daśaratha Vasu; (2) Kuśala; (3) Śubhaśaṅkara; (4) Haṁsa; (5) Śaktirāma (Bāgāṇḍā), Muktirāma (Māinagara) and Alaṅkāra (Baṅgaja); (6) Dāmodara; (7) Anantarāma; (8) Guṇīnāyaka and Vīṇānāyaka. The twelfth generation included Bhagīratha, and the thirteenth Mālādhara Vasu, or Guṇarāja Khān. Śrī Guṇarāja Khān had fourteen sons, of whom the second son, Lakṣmīnāthavasu, received the title Satyarāja Khān. His son was Śrī Rāmānanda Vasu; therefore Rāmānanda Vasu belonged to the fifteenth generation. Guṇarāja Khān was a very well known and wealthy man. His palace, fort and temples are still existing, and from these we can deduce that the opulence of Guṇarāja Khān was certainly very great. Śrī Guṇarāja Khān never cared for the artificial aristocracy introduced by Ballāl Sena.

TEXT 100

“নন্দনন্দন কৃষ্ণ—মোর প্রাণনাথ” ।
এই বাক্যে বিকাইনু তাঁর বংশের হাত ॥ ১০০ ॥

"nandanandana kṛṣṇa——mora prāṇa-nātha"
ei vākye vikāinu tāṅra vaṁśera hāta

SYNONYMS

nanda-nandana kṛṣṇa—Kṛṣṇa, the son of Nanda Mahārāja; *mora prāṇa-nātha*—my life and soul; *ei vākye*—because of this statement; *vikāinu*—I became sold; *tāṅra*—of him; *vaṁśera hāta*—in the hands of the descendants.

TRANSLATION

Śrī Caitanya Mahāprabhu said, " 'Kṛṣṇa, the son of Nanda Mahārāja, is my life and soul.' By this statement I am sold into the hands of the descendants of Guṇarāja Khān.

PURPORT

The full verse referred to here is:

eka-bhāve vanda hari yoḍa kari' hāta
nandanandana kṛṣṇa——mora prāṇa-nātha

"With folded hands I offer my prayers unto Kṛṣṇa, the son of Nanda Mahārāja, who is my life and soul."

TEXT 101

তোমার কি কথা, তোমার গ্রামের কুক্কুর ।
সেহ মোর প্রিয়, অন্যজন রহু দূর ॥ ১০১ ॥

tomāra ki kathā, tomāra grāmera kukkura
sei mora priya, anya-jana rahu dūra

SYNONYMS

tomāra—of you; *ki kathā*—what to speak; *tomāra*—of your; *grāmera*—village; *kukkura*—a dog; *sei*—that; *mora*—to Me; *priya*—very dear; *anya-jana*—others; *rahu dūra*—apart from.

TRANSLATION

"To say nothing of you, even a dog living in your village is very dear to Me. What, then, to speak of others?"

TEXT 102

তবে রামানন্দ, আর সত্যরাজ খাঁন ।
প্রভুর চরণে কিছু কৈল নিবেদন ॥ ১০২ ॥

tabe rāmānanda, āra satyarāja khāṅna
prabhura caraṇe kichu kaila nivedana

SYNONYMS

tabe—after this; *rāmānanda*—Rāmānanda Vasu; *āra*—and; *satyarāja khāṅna*—Satyarāja Khān; *prabhura caraṇe*—at the lotus feet of Lord Śrī Caitanya Mahāprabhu; *kichu*—some; *kaila*—made; *nivedana*—submission.

TRANSLATION

After this, Rāmānanda Vasu and Satyarāja Khān both submitted questions at the lotus feet of Śrī Caitanya Mahāprabhu.

TEXT 103

গৃহস্থ বিষয়ী আমি, কি মোর সাধনে ।
শ্রীমুখে আজ্ঞা কর প্রভু—নিবেদি চরণে ॥১০৩ ॥

gṛhastha viṣayī āmi, ki mora sādhane
śrī-mukhe ājñā kara prabhu——nivedi caraṇe

SYNONYMS

gṛhastha—householder; *viṣayī*—materialistic man; *āmi*—I; *ki*—what; *mora sādhane*—the process of my advancement in spiritual life; *śrī-mukhe*—from Your own mouth; *ājñā kara*—please order; *prabhu*—my Lord; *nivedi caraṇe*—I submit unto Your lotus feet.

TRANSLATION

Satyarāja Khān said, "My dear Lord, being a householder and a materialistic man, I do not know the process of advancing in spiritual life. I therefore submit myself unto Your lotus feet and request You to give me orders."

TEXT 104

প্রভু কহেন,—'কৃষ্ণসেবা', 'বৈষ্ণব-সেবন' ।
'নিরন্তর কর কৃষ্ণনাম-সংকীর্তন' ॥ ১০৪ ॥

prabhu kahena,——'kṛṣṇa-sevā', 'vaiṣṇava-sevana'
'nirantara kara kṛṣṇa-nāma-saṅkīrtana'

SYNONYMS

prabhu kahena—the Lord replied; *kṛṣṇa-sevā*—serving Kṛṣṇa; *vaiṣṇava-sevana*—abiding by the orders of Vaiṣṇavas; *nirantara*—without cessation; *kara*—do; *kṛṣṇa-nāma-saṅkīrtana*—chanting of the holy name of Lord Kṛṣṇa.

TRANSLATION

Śrī Caitanya Mahāprabhu replied, "Without cessation continue chanting the holy name of Lord Kṛṣṇa. Whenever possible, serve Him and His devotees, the Vaiṣṇavas."

TEXT 105

সত্যরাজ বলে,—বৈষ্ণব চিনিব কেমনে ?
কে বৈষ্ণব, কহ তাঁর সামান্য লক্ষণে ॥ ১০৫ ॥

satyarāja bale,——vaiṣṇava ciniba kemane?
ke vaiṣṇava, kaha tāṅra sāmānya lakṣaṇe

SYNONYMS

satyarāja bale—Satyarāja Khān said; *vaiṣṇava*—a Vaiṣṇava; *ciniba kemane*—how shall I recognize; *ke vaiṣṇava*—who is a Vaiṣṇava; *kaha*—please say; *tāṅra*—of him; *sāmānya lakṣaṇe*—common symptoms.

TRANSLATION

Upon hearing this, Satyarāja said, "How can I recognize a Vaiṣṇava? Please let me know what a Vaiṣṇava is. What are his common symptoms?"

TEXT 106

প্রভু কহে,—"যাঁর মুখে শুনি একবার ।
কৃষ্ণনাম, সেই পূজ্য,— শ্রেষ্ঠ সবাকার ॥" ১০৬ ॥

prabhu kahe,——"yāṅra mukhe śuni eka-bāra
kṛṣṇa-nāma, sei pūjya,——śreṣṭha sabākāra"

SYNONYMS

prabhu kahe—Lord Śrī Caitanya Mahāprabhu replied; *yāṅra mukhe*—in whose mouth; *śuni*—I hear; *eka-bāra*—once; *kṛṣṇa-nāma*—the holy name of Lord Kṛṣṇa; *sei pūjya*—he is worshipable; *śreṣṭha sabākāra*—the best of all human beings.

TRANSLATION

Śrī Caitanya Mahāprabhu replied, "Whoever chants the holy name of Kṛṣṇa just once is worshipable and is the topmost human being.

PURPORT

Śrīla Bhaktisiddhānta Sarasvatī Ṭhākura says that simply by chanting the holy name of Kṛṣṇa once, a person becomes perfect. Such a person is understood to be a Vaiṣṇava. With such faith and belief, one may begin a life of Kṛṣṇa consciousness, but an ordinary person cannot chant the holy name of Kṛṣṇa with such faith. This is confirmed by Śrīla Rūpa Gosvāmī in his *Upadeśāmṛta: kṛṣṇeti yasya giri taṁ manasādriyeta.* One should accept the holy name of Kṛṣṇa to be identical with the Supreme Personality of Godhead, Transcendence Himself. The holy name of Kṛṣṇa is also identical with Kṛṣṇa and is also *cintāmaṇi.* The name Kṛṣṇa is the personification of sound perfectly transcendental and eternally liberated from material contamination. One should understand that the name Kṛṣṇa and Kṛṣṇa are identical. Having such faith, one must continue to chant the holy name. When one is situated on the neophyte platform, one cannot understand the devotional ingredients of a pure, unalloyed devotee. However, when the novice engages in devotional service—especially in Deity worship—and follows the order of a bona fide spiritual master, he becomes a pure devotee. Anyone can take advantage of hearing about Kṛṣṇa consciousness from a pure devotee and thus gradually become purified.

A devotee who believes that the holy name of the Lord is identical with the Lord is a pure devotee, even though he may be in the neophyte stage. By his association, others may also become Vaiṣṇavas.

One is known as a materialistic devotee if he simply worships the Deity of Hari with faith but does not show proper respect to the devotees and to others. This is confirmed in *Śrīmad-Bhāgavatam* (11.2.47):

arcāyām eva haraye
yaḥ pūjāṁ śraddhayehate
na tad-bhakteṣu cānyeṣu
sa bhaktaḥ prākṛtaḥ smṛtaḥ

"Anyone who engages with faith in the worship of the Deity of Hari but does not show proper respect to the devotees and to others is known as a materialistic devotee." However, by associating with a neophyte devotee who believes that the holy name of the Lord is identical with the Lord, one can become a devotee also. When Lord Caitanya was teaching Sanātana Gosvāmī, He said:

śraddhāvān jana haya bhakti-adhikārī
'uttama', 'madhyama', 'kaniṣṭha'——śraddhā-anusārī

yāhāra komala-śraddhā, se 'kaniṣṭha' jana
krame krame teṅho bhakta ha-ibe 'uttama'

rati-prema-tāratamye bhakta-taratama

"A person who has attained firm faith is a real candidate for advancing in Kṛṣṇa consciousness. According to the faith, there are first-class, second-class and neophyte devotees. One who has preliminary faith is called *kaniṣṭha,* or a neophyte. The neophyte, however, can become an advanced devotee if he strictly follows the regulative principles set down by the spiritual master. The pure devotee whose faith advances becomes a *madhyama-adhikārī* and *uttama-adhikārī.*" (*Cc. Madhya* 22.64,69-70)

It is thus concluded that even a neophyte devotee is superior to the *karmīs* and *jñānīs* because he has full faith in chanting the holy name of the Lord. A *karmī* or a *jñānī,* regardless of his greatness, has no faith in Lord Viṣṇu, His holy name or His devotional service. One may be advanced religiously, but if he is not trained in devotional service, he has very little credit on the transcendental platform. Even a neophyte devotee engaged in Deity worship in accordance with the regulations set forth by the spiritual master is in a position superior to that of the fruitive worker and speculative philosopher.

TEXT 107

"এক কৃষ্ণনামে করে সর্ব-পাপ ক্ষয় ।
নববিধা ভক্তি পূর্ণ নাম হৈতে হয় ॥ ১০৭ ॥

"eka kṛṣṇa-nāme kare sarva-pāpa kṣaya
nava-vidhā bhakti pūrṇa nāma haite haya

SYNONYMS

eka kṛṣṇa-nāme—one holy name of Kṛṣṇa; *kare*—can do; *sarva-pāpa*—of all sinful reactions; *kṣaya*—destruction; *nava-vidhā*—nine processes; *bhakti*—of devotional service; *pūrṇa*—complete; *nāma haite*—simply by chanting the holy name; *haya*—are.

TRANSLATION

"Simply by chanting the holy name of Kṛṣṇa, one is relieved from all the reactions of a sinful life. One can complete the nine processes of devotional service simply by chanting the holy name.

PURPORT

The nine types of devotional service are mentioned in *Śrīmad-Bhāgavatam* (7.5.23):

śravaṇaṁ kīrtanaṁ viṣṇoḥ
smaraṇaṁ pāda-sevanam
arcanaṁ vandanaṁ dāsyaṁ
sakhyam ātma-nivedanam

iti puṁsārpitā viṣṇau
bhaktiś cen nava-lakṣaṇā
kriyeta bhagavaty addhā
tan manye 'dhītam uttamam

These are the activities of hearing, chanting, remembering, serving, worshiping, praying, obeying, maintaining friendship and surrendering everything. As far as chanting the holy name of Kṛṣṇa is concerned, one can be freed from all sinful reactions by chanting the holy name without committing offenses. If one chants offenselessly, he may be saved from all sinful reactions. It is very important in devotional service to chant the holy name of the Lord without committing offenses. The nine devotional processes such as *śravaṇa* and *kīrtana* can all be attained at once if one simply chants the holy name of the Lord offenselessly.

In this regard, Śrīla Jīva Gosvāmī states in his book *Bhakti-sandarbha* (173): *yadyapi anyā bhaktiḥ kalau kartavyā, tada kīrtanākhya-bhakti-saṁyogenaiva.* Out of the nine processes of devotional service, *kīrtana* is very important. Śrīla Jīva Gosvāmī therefore instructs that the other processes, such as *arcana, vandana, dāsya* and *sakhya,* should be executed, but they must be preceded and followed by *kīrtana,* the chanting of the holy name. We have therefore introduced this system in all of our centers. *Arcana, ārati, bhoga* offering, Deity dressing and decoration are all preceded and followed by the chanting of the holy name of the Lord—Hare Kṛṣṇa, Hare Kṛṣṇa, Kṛṣṇa Kṛṣṇa, Hare Hare/ Hare Rāma, Hare Rāma, Rāma Rāma, Hare Hare.

TEXT 108

দীক্ষা-পুরশ্চর্যা-বিধি অপেক্ষা না করে ।
জিহ্বা-স্পর্শে আ-চণ্ডাল সবারে উদ্ধারে ॥ ১০৮ ॥

dīkṣā-puraścaryā-vidhi apekṣā nā kare
jihvā-sparśe ā-caṇḍāla sabāre uddhāre

SYNONYMS

dīkṣā—initiation; *puraścaryā*—activities before initiation; *vidhi*—regulative principles; *apekṣā*—reliance on; *nā*—not; *kare*—does; *jihvā*—the tongue;

sparśe—by touching; *ā-caṇḍāla*—even to the lowest of men, the *caṇḍāla; sabāre*—everyone; *uddhāre*—delivers.

TRANSLATION

"One does not have to undergo initiation or execute the activities required before initiation. One simply has to vibrate the holy name with his lips. Thus even a man in the lowest class [caṇḍāla] can be delivered.

PURPORT

Śrīla Jīva Gosvāmī explains *dīkṣā* in his *Bhakti-sandarbha* (283):

divyaṁ jñānaṁ yato dadyāt
kuryāt pāpasya saṅkṣayam
tasmāt dīkṣeti sā proktā
deśikais tattva-kovidaiḥ

"*Dīkṣā* is the process by which one can awaken his transcendental knowledge and vanquish all reactions caused by sinful activity. A person expert in the study of the revealed scriptures knows this process as *dīkṣā*." The regulative principles of *dīkṣā* are explained in the *Hari-bhakti-vilāsa* (*Vilāsa* 2.3,4) and in *Bhakti-sandarbha* (283). As stated:

dvijānām anupetānāṁ svakarmādhyayanādiṣu
yathādhikāro nāstīha syāc copanayanād anu
tathātrādīkṣitānāṁ tu mantra-devārcanādiṣu
nādhikāro 'sty ataḥ kuryād ātmānaṁ śiva-saṁstutam

"Even though born in a *brāhmaṇa* family, one cannot engage in Vedic rituals without being initiated and having a sacred thread. Although born in a *brāhmaṇa* family, one becomes a *brāhmaṇa* after initiation and the sacred thread ceremony. Unless one is initiated as a *brāhmaṇa,* he cannot worship the holy name properly."

According to the Vaiṣṇava regulative principles, one must be initiated as a *brāhmaṇa*. The *Hari-bhakti-vilāsa* (2.6) quotes the following injunction from the *Viṣṇu-yāmala:*

adīkṣitasya vāmoru
kṛtaṁ sarvaṁ nirarthakam
paśu-yonim avāpnoti
dīkṣā-virahito janaḥ

"Unless one is initiated by a bona fide spiritual master, all his devotional activities are useless. A person who is not properly initiated can descend again into the animal species."

Hari-bhakti-vilāsa (2.10) further quotes:

ato guruṁ praṇamyaivaṁ
sarva-svaṁ vinivedya ca
gṛhṇīyād vaiṣṇavaṁ mantraṁ
dīkṣā-pūrvaṁ vidhānataḥ

"It is the duty of every human being to surrender to a bona fide spiritual master. Giving him everything—body, mind and intelligence—one must take a Vaiṣṇava initiation from him."

The *Bhakti-sandarbha* (298) gives the following quotation from the *Tattva-sāgara:*

yathā kāñcanatāṁ yāti
kāsyaṁ rasa-vidhānataḥ
tathā dīkṣā-vidhānena
dvijatvaṁ jāyate nṛṇām

"By chemical manipulation, bell metal is turned into gold when touched by mercury; similarly, when a person is properly initiated, he can acquire the qualities of a *brāhmaṇa.*"

The *Hari-bhakti-vilāsa* (17.11,12) in discussing the *puraścaryā* process, quotes the following verses from *Agastya-saṁhitā:*

pūjā traikālikī nityaṁ
japas tarpaṇam eva ca
homo brāhmaṇa-bhuktiś ca
puraścaraṇam ucyate

guror labdhasya mantrasya
prasādena yathā-vidhi
pañcāṅgopāsanā-siddhyai
puraś caitad vidhīyate

"In the morning, afternoon and evening, one should worship the Deity, chant the Hare Kṛṣṇa *mantra,* offer oblations, perform a fire sacrifice, and feed the *brāhmaṇas.* These five activities constitute *puraścaryā.* To attain full success when taking initiation from the spiritual master, one should first perform these *puraścaryā* processes."

The word *puraḥ* means "before" and *caryā* means "activities." Due to the necessity of these activities, we do not immediately initiate disciples in the International Society for Krishna Consciousness. For six months, a candidate for initiation must first attend *ārati* and classes in the *śāstras,* practice the regulative principles and associate with other devotees. When one is actually advanced in the *puraścaryā-vidhi,* he is recommended by the local temple president for initiation. It is not that anyone can be suddenly initiated without meeting the requirements. When one is further advanced by chanting the Hare Kṛṣṇa *mantra* sixteen rounds daily, following the regulative principles and attending classes, he receives the sacred thread (brahminical recognition) after the second six months.

In the *Hari-bhakti-vilāsa* (17.4,5,7) it is stated:

vinā yena na siddhaḥ syān
mantro varṣa-śatair api
kṛtena yena labhate
sādhako vāñchitaṁ phalam

puraścaraṇa-sampanno
mantro hi phala-dhāyakaḥ
atah puraṣkriyāṁ kuryāt
mantravit siddhi-kaṅksayā

puraṣkriyā hi mantrāṇāṁ
pradhānaṁ vīryam ucyate
vīrya-hīno yathā dehī
sarva-karmasu na kṣamaḥ
puraścaraṇa-hīno hi
tathā mantraḥ prakīrtitaḥ

"Without performing the *puraścaryā* activities, one cannot become perfect even by chanting this *mantra* for hundreds of years. However, one who has undergone the *puraścaryā-vidhi* process can attain success very easily. If one wishes to perfect his initiation, he must first undergo the *puraścaryā* activities. The *puraścaryā* process is the life-force by which one is successful in chanting the *mantra.* Without the life-force, one cannot do anything; similarly, without the life force of *puraścaryā-vidhi,* no *mantra* can be perfected."

In his *Bhakti-sandarbha* (283), Śrīla Jīva Gosvāmī states:

yadyapi śrī-bhāgavata-mate pañcarātrādi-vat arcana-mārgasya āvaśyakatvaṁ nāsti, tad vināpi śaraṇāpattyādīnām ekatareṇāpi puruṣārtha-siddher abhihitatvāt, tathāpi śrī-nāradādi-vartmānusaradbhiḥ śrī-bhagavatā saha sambandha-viśeṣaṁ dīkṣā-vidhānena śrī-guru-caraṇa-sampāditaṁ cikīrṣadbhiḥ kṛtāyāṁ dīkṣāyām arcanam avaśyaṁ kriyetaiva.

Of similar importance is *dīkṣā,* which is explained as follows in *Bhakti-sandarbha* (284):

yadyapi svarūpato nāsti, tathāpi prāyaḥ svabhāvato
dehādi-sambandhena kardaya-śīlānāṁ vikṣipta-cittānāṁ
janānāṁ tat-tat-saṅkocī-karaṇāya śrīmad-ṛṣi-prabhṛtibhir
atrārcana-mārge kvacit kvacit kācit kācin maryādā sthāpitāsti.

Similarly in the *Rāmārcana-candrikā* it is stated:

vinaiva dīkṣāṁ viprendra
puraścaryāṁ vinaiva hi
vinaiva nyāsa-vidhinā
japa-mātreṇa siddhidā

In other words, the chanting of the Hare Kṛṣṇa *mahā-mantra* is so powerful that it does not depend on official initiation, but if one is initiated and engages in *pañcarātra-vidhi* (Deity worship), his Kṛṣṇa consciousness will awaken very soon, and his identification with the material world will be vanquished. The more one is freed from material identification, the more one can realize that the spirit soul is qualitatively as good as the Supreme Soul. At such a time, when one is situated on the absolute platform, he can understand that the holy name of the Lord and the Lord Himself are identical. At that stage of realization, the holy name of the Lord, the Hare Kṛṣṇa *mantra,* cannot be identified with any material sound. If one accepts the Hare Kṛṣṇa *mahā-mantra* as a material vibration, he falls down. One should worship and chant the holy name of the Lord by accepting it as the Lord Himself. One should therefore be initiated properly according to revealed scriptures under the direction of a bona fide spiritual master. Although chanting the holy name is good for both the conditioned and liberated soul, it is especially beneficial to the conditioned soul because by chanting it one is liberated. When a person who chants the holy name is liberated, he attains the ultimate perfection by returning home, back to Godhead. In the words of *Śrī Caitanya-caritāmṛta* (*Ādi* 7.73):

kṛṣṇa-mantra haite habe saṁsāra-mocana
kṛṣṇa-nāma haite pābe kṛṣṇera caraṇa

"Simply by chanting the holy name of Kṛṣṇa one can obtain freedom from material existence. Indeed, simply by chanting the Hare Kṛṣṇa *mantra* one will be able to see the lotus feet of the Lord."

The offenseless chanting of the holy name does not depend on the initiation process. Although initiation may depend on *puraścaryā* or *puraścaraṇa,* the actual chanting of the holy name does not depend on *puraścaryā-vidhi,* or the regulative principles. If one chants the holy name once without committing an offense, he attains all success. During the chanting of the holy name, the tongue must work. Simply by chanting the holy name, one is immediately delivered. The tongue is *sevonmukha-jihvā*—it is controlled by service. One whose tongue is engaged in tasting material things and also talking about them cannot use the tongue for absolute realization.

ataḥ śrī-kṛṣṇa-nāmādi
na bhaved grāhyam indriyaiḥ
sevonmukhe hi jihvādau
svayam eva sphuraty adaḥ

According to *Caitanya-caritāmṛta* (*Madhya* 17.134):

ataeva kṛṣṇera 'nāma', 'deha', 'vilāsa'
prākṛtendriya-grāhya nahe, haya sva-prakāśa

"With these material senses, one cannot understand the transcendental holy name of the Lord or His form, activities and pastimes. However, when one actually engages in devotional service, utilizing the tongue, the Lord is revealed."

TEXT 109

অনুষঙ্গ-ফলে করে সংসারের ক্ষয় ।
চিত্ত আকর্ষিয়া করায় কৃষ্ণে প্রেমোদয় ॥ ১০৯ ॥

anuṣaṅga-phale kare saṁsārera kṣaya
citta ākarṣiyā karāya kṛṣṇe premodaya

SYNONYMS

anuṣaṅga-phale—as a simultaneous result; *kare*—does; *saṁsārera kṣaya*—annihilation of entanglement in the material world; *citta*—thought; *ākarṣiyā*—attracting; *karāya*—causes; *kṛṣṇe*—unto Lord Kṛṣṇa; *prema-udaya*—arousal of transcendental love.

TRANSLATION

"By chanting the holy name of the Lord, one dissolves his entanglement in material activities. After this, one becomes very attracted to Kṛṣṇa, and thus dormant love for Kṛṣṇa is awakened.

TEXT 110

আকৃষ্টিঃ কৃতচেতসাং সুমনসামুচ্চাটনং চাংহসা-
মাচণ্ডালমমূকলোকসুলভো বশ্যশ্চ মুক্তিশ্রিয়ঃ ।
নো দীক্ষাং ন চ সৎক্রিয়াং ন চ পুরশ্চর্যাং মনাগীক্ষতে
মন্ত্রোঽয়ং রসনাস্পৃগেব ফলতি শ্রীকৃষ্ণ-নামাত্মকঃ ॥ ১১০ ॥

ākṛṣṭiḥ kṛta-cetasāṁ sumanasām uccāṭanaṁ cāṁhasām
ācaṇḍālam amūka-loka-sulabho vaśyaś ca mukti-śriyaḥ
no dīkṣāṁ na ca sat-kriyāṁ na ca puraścaryāṁ manāg īkṣate
mantro 'yaṁ rasanā-spṛg eva phalati śrī-kṛṣṇa-nāmātmakaḥ

SYNONYMS

ākṛṣṭiḥ—attraction; *kṛta-cetasām*—of saintly persons; *su-manasām*—of the most liberal-minded; *uccāṭanam*—annihilator; *ca*—also; *aṁhasām*—of sinful reactions; *ā-caṇḍālam*—even to the *caṇḍālas; amūka*—except the dumb; *loka-sulabhaḥ*—very easy to achieve for all persons; *vaśyaḥ*—full controller; *ca*—and; *mukti-śriyaḥ*—of the opulence of liberation; *no*—not; *dīkṣām*—initiation; *na*—not; *ca*—also; *sat-kriyām*—pious activities; *na*—not; *ca*—also; *puraścaryām*—regulative principles before initiation; *manāk*—slightly; *īkṣate*—depends upon; *mantraḥ*—*mantra; ayam*—this; *rasanā*—tongue; *spṛk*—touching; *eva*—simply; *phalati*—is fruitful; *śrī-kṛṣṇa-nāma-ātmakaḥ*—consisting of the holy name of Lord Kṛṣṇa.

TRANSLATION

" 'The holy name of Lord Kṛṣṇa is an attractive feature for many saintly, liberal people. It is the annihilator of all sinful reactions and is so powerful that save for the dumb who cannot chant it, it is readily available to everyone, including the lowest type of man, the caṇḍāla. The holy name of Kṛṣṇa is the controller of the opulence of liberation, and it is identical with Kṛṣṇa. Simply by touching the holy name with one's tongue, immediate effects are produced. Chanting the holy name does not depend on initiation, pious activities or the puraścaryā regulative principles generally observed before initiation. The holy name does not wait for all these activities. It is self-sufficient.' "

PURPORT

This verse is found in the *Padyāvalī* (29) by Śrīla Rūpa Gosvāmī.

TEXT 111

"অতএব যাঁর মুখে এক কৃষ্ণনাম ।
সেই ত' বৈষ্ণব, করিহ তাঁহার সম্মান ॥" ১১১ ॥

"ataeva yāṅra mukhe eka kṛṣṇa-nāma
sei ta' vaiṣṇava, kariha tāṅhāra sammāna"

SYNONYMS

ataeva—therefore; *yāṅra mukhe*—in whose mouth; *eka*—one; *kṛṣṇa-nāma*—the holy name of Kṛṣṇa; *sei ta' vaiṣṇava*—he is a Vaiṣṇava; *kariha*—offer; *tāṅhāra*—to him; *sammāna*—respect.

TRANSLATION

Śrī Caitanya Mahāprabhu then finally advised, "One who is chanting the Hare Kṛṣṇa mantra is understood to be a Vaiṣṇava; therefore you should offer all respects to him."

PURPORT

In his *Upadeśāmṛta,* Śrīla Rūpa Gosvāmī states: *kṛṣṇeti yasya giri taṁ manasādriyeta dīkṣāsti cet.* An advanced devotee should respect a person who has been initiated by a bona fide spiritual master and who is situated on the transcendental platform, chanting the holy name with faith and obeisances and following the instructions of the spiritual master. Śrīla Bhaktivinoda Ṭhākura comments that serving Vaiṣṇavas is most important for householders. Whether a Vaiṣṇava is properly initiated or not is not a subject for consideration. One may be initiated and yet contaminated by the Māyāvāda philosophy, but a person who chants the holy name of the Lord offenselessly will not be so contaminated. A properly initiated Vaiṣṇava may be imperfect, but one who chants the holy name of the Lord offenselessly is all-perfect. Although he may apparently be a neophyte, he still has to be considered a pure unalloyed Vaiṣṇava. It is the duty of the householder to offer respects to such an unalloyed Vaiṣṇava. This is Śrī Caitanya Mahāprabhu's instruction.

TEXT 112

খণ্ডের মুকুন্দদাস, শ্রীরঘুনন্দন।
শ্রীনরহরি,—এই মুখ্য তিন জন ॥ ১১২ ॥

khaṇḍera mukunda-dāsa, śrī-raghunandana
śrī-narahari,——ei mukhya tina jana

SYNONYMS

khaṇḍera—of the place known as Khaṇḍa; *mukunda-dāsa*—Mukunda dāsa; *śrī-raghunandana* —Śrī Raghunandana; *śrī-narahari* —Śrī Narahari; *ei*—these; *mukhya*—chief; *tina*—three; *jana*—persons.

TRANSLATION

Śrī Caitanya Mahāprabhu then turned His attention to three persons—Mukunda dāsa, Raghunandana and Śrī Narahari—inhabitants of the place called Khaṇḍa.

TEXT 113

মুকুন্দ দাসেরে পুছে শচীর নন্দন।
'তুমি—পিতা, পুত্র তোমার—শ্রীরঘুনন্দন? ১১৩ ॥

mukunda dāsere puche śacīra nandana
'tumi——pitā, putra tomāra——śrī-raghunandana?

SYNONYMS

mukunda dāsere—unto Mukunda dāsa; *puche*—inquired; *śacīra nandana*—the son of mother Śacī; *tumi*—you; *pitā*—father; *putra*—son; *tomāra*—your; *śrī-raghunandana*—Śrī Raghunandana.

TRANSLATION

Śrī Caitanya Mahāprabhu, the son of mother Śacī, next asked Mukunda dāsa, "You are the father, and your son is Raghunandana. Is that so?

TEXT 114

কিবা রঘুনন্দন—পিতা, তুমি—তার তনয়?
নিশ্চয় করিয়া কহ, যাউক সংশয় ॥' ১১৪ ॥

kibā raghunandana——pitā, tumi——tāra tanaya?
niścaya kariyā kaha, yāuka saṁśaya'

SYNONYMS

kibā—or; *raghunandana*—Raghunandana; *pitā*—father; *tumi*—you; *tāra*—his; *tanaya*—son; *niścaya kariyā*—making certain; *kaha*—just speak; *yāuka saṁśaya*—let My doubts be dissipated.

TRANSLATION

"Or is Śrīla Raghunandana your father whereas you are his son? Please let Me know the facts so that My doubts will go away."

TEXT 115

মুকুন্দ কহে,—রঘুনন্দন মোর 'পিতা' হয়।
আমি তার 'পুত্র',—এই আমার নিশ্চয় ॥ ১১৫ ॥

mukunda kahe,——raghunandana mora 'pitā' haya
āmi tāra 'putra',——ei āmāra niścaya

SYNONYMS

mukunda kahe—Mukunda dāsa replied; *raghunandana*—my son Raghunandana; *mora*—my; *pitā*—father; *haya*—is; *āmi*—I; *tāra*—his; *putra*—son; *ei*—this; *āmāra*—my; *niścaya*—decision.

TRANSLATION

Mukunda replied, "Raghunandana is my father, and I am his son. This is my decision.

TEXT 116

আমা সবার কৃষ্ণভক্তি রঘুনন্দন হৈতে।
অতএব পিতা —রঘুনন্দন আমার নিশ্চিতে ॥ ১১৬ ॥

āmā sabāra kṛṣṇa-bhakti raghunandana haite
ataeva pitā——raghunandana āmāra niścite

SYNONYMS

āmā sabāra—of all of us; *kṛṣṇa-bhakti*—devotion to Kṛṣṇa; *raghunandana haite*—because of Raghunandana; *ataeva*—therefore; *pitā*—father; *raghunandana*—Raghunandana; *āmāra niścite*—my decision.

TRANSLATION

"All of us have attained devotion to Kṛṣṇa due to Raghunandana. Therefore in my mind he is my father."

TEXT 117

শুনি' হর্ষে কহে প্রভু —"কহিলে নিশ্চয়।
যাঁহা হৈতে কৃষ্ণভক্তি সেই গুরু হয়" ॥ ১১৭ ॥

śuni' harṣe kahe prabhu——"kahile niścaya
yāṅhā haite kṛṣṇa-bhakti sei guru haya"

SYNONYMS

śuni'—hearing; *harṣe*—in great jubilation; *kahe prabhu*—Śrī Caitanya Mahāprabhu said; *kahile niścaya*—you have spoken correctly; *yāṅhā haite*—from whom; *kṛṣṇa-bhakti*—devotion to Kṛṣṇa; *sei*—that person; *guru haya*—is the spiritual master.

TRANSLATION

Hearing Mukunda dāsa give this proper decision, Śrī Caitanya Mahāprabhu confirmed it, saying, "Yes, it is correct. One who awakens devotion to Kṛṣṇa is certainly a spiritual master."

TEXT 118

ভক্তের মহিমা প্রভু কহিতে পায় সুখ ।
ভক্তের মহিমা কহিতে হয় পঞ্চমুখ ॥ ১১৮ ॥

bhaktera mahimā prabhu kahite pāya sukha
bhaktera mahimā kahite haya pañca-mukha

SYNONYMS

bhaktera mahimā—the glories of a devotee; *prabhu*—Śrī Caitanya Mahāprabhu; *kahite*—to speak; *pāya sukha*—gets happiness; *bhaktera mahimā*—the glories of a devotee; *kahite*—to speak; *haya*—becomes; *pañca-mukha*—five faced.

TRANSLATION

Śrī Caitanya Mahāprabhu became very happy just to speak of the glories of His devotees. Indeed, when He spoke of their glories, it was as if He had five faces.

TEXT 119

ভক্তগণে কহে,—শুন মুকুন্দের প্রেম ।
নিগূঢ় নির্মল প্রেম, যেন দগ্ধ হেম ॥ ১১৯ ॥

bhakta-gaṇe kahe,——śuna mukundera prema
nigūḍha nirmala prema, yena dagdha hema

SYNONYMS

bhakta-gaṇe kahe—Śrī Caitanya Mahāprabhu informed His devotees; *śuna*—please hear; *mukundera prema*—Mukunda's love of Godhead; *nigūḍha*—very deep; *nirmala*—pure; *prema*—ecstatic love; *yena*—as if; *dagdha*—clarified; *hema*—gold.

TRANSLATION

Śrī Caitanya Mahāprabhu then informed all His devotees, "Please hear about Mukunda's love of Godhead. It is a very deep and pure love and can only be compared with purified gold.

TEXT 120

বাহ্যে রাজবৈদ্য ইঁহো করে রাজ-সেবা ।
অন্তরে কৃষ্ণ-প্রেম ইঁহার জানিবেক কেবা ॥ ১২০ ॥

bāhye rāja-vaidya iṅho kare rāja-sevā
antare kṛṣṇa-prema iṅhāra jānibeka kebā

SYNONYMS

bāhye—externally; *rāja-vaidya*—royal physician; *iṅho*—he; *kare*—performs; *rāja-sevā*—government service; *antare*—within the heart; *kṛṣṇa-prema*—love of Kṛṣṇa; *iṅhāra*—of Mukunda dāsa; *jānibeka*—can know; *kebā*—who.

TRANSLATION

"Mukunda dāsa externally appears to be a royal physician engaged in governmental service, but internally he has a deep love for Kṛṣṇa. Who can understand his love?

PURPORT

Unless Śrī Kṛṣṇa Caitanya Mahāprabhu discloses the fact, no one can understand who is actually a great devotee of the Lord engaged in His service. It is therefore said in *Caitanya-caritāmṛta* (*Madhya* 23.39), *tāṅra vākya, kriyā, mudrā vijñeha nā bujhaya:* even the most perfect and learned scholar cannot understand a Vaiṣṇava's activities. A Vaiṣṇava may be engaged in governmental service or in a professional business so that externally one cannot understand his position. Internally, however, he may be a *nitya-siddha* Vaiṣṇava—that is, an eternally liberated Vaiṣṇava. Externally Mukunda dāsa was a royal physician, but internally he was the most liberated *paramahaṁsa* devotee. Śrī Caitanya Mahāprabhu knew this very well, but ordinary men could not understand it, for the activities and plans of a Vaiṣṇava cannot be understood by ordinary men. However, Śrī Caitanya Mahāprabhu and His representative understand everything about a devotee, even though the devotee may externally pretend to be an ordinary householder and professional businessman.

TEXT 121

এক দিন ম্লেচ্ছ-রাজার উচ্চ-টুঙ্গিতে ।
চিকিৎসার বাত্ কহে তাঁহার অগ্রেতে ॥ ১২১ ॥

eka dina mleccha-rājāra ucca-ṭuṅgite
cikitsāra vāt kahe tāṅhāra agrete

SYNONYMS

eka dina—one day; *mleccha-rājāra*—of the Mohammedan King; *ucca-ṭuṅgite*—on a high platform; *cikitsāra vāt*—talk of medical treatment; *kahe*—was speaking; *tāṅhāra agrete*—before him.

TRANSLATION

"One day Mukunda dāsa, the royal physician, was seated with the Mohammedan King on a high platform and was telling the King about medical treatment.

TEXT 122

হেনকালে এক ময়ূর-পুচ্ছের আড়ানী ।
রাজ-শিরোপরি ধরে এক সেবক আনি' ॥ ১২২ ॥

hena-kāle eka mayūra-pucchera āḍānī
rāja-śiropari dhare eka sevaka āni'

SYNONYMS

hena-kāle—at this time; *eka*—one; *mayūra-pucchera*—of peacock feathers; *āḍānī*—fan; *rāja-śira-upari*—above the head of the King; *dhare*—holds; *eka*—one; *sevaka*—servant; *āni'*—bringing.

TRANSLATION

"While the King and Mukunda dāsa were conversing, a servant brought a fan made of peacock feathers to shade the head of the King from the sun. Consequently he held the fan above the King's head.

TEXT 123

শিখিপিচ্ছ দেখি' মুকুন্দ প্রেমাবিষ্ট হৈলা ।
অতি-উচ্চ টুঙ্গি হৈতে ভূমিতে পড়িলা ॥ ১২৩ ॥

śikhi-piccha dekhi' mukunda premāviṣṭa hailā
ati-ucca ṭuṅgi haite bhūmite paḍilā

SYNONYMS

śikhi-piccha—peacock feathers; *dekhi'*—seeing; *mukunda*—Mukunda dāsa; *prema-āviṣṭa hailā*—became ecstatic in love of Godhead; *ati-ucca*—very high; *ṭuṅgi*—platform; *haite*—from; *bhūmite*—on the ground; *paḍilā*—fell down.

TRANSLATION

"Just by seeing the peacock-feathered fan, Mukunda dāsa became absorbed in ecstatic love of Godhead and fell from the high platform onto the ground.

TEXT 124

রাজার জ্ঞান,—রাজ-বৈদ্যের হইল মরণ ।
আপনে নামিয়া তবে করাইল চেতন ॥ ১২৪ ॥

rājāra jñāna,——rāja-vaidyera ha-ila maraṇa
āpane nāmiyā tabe karāila cetana

SYNONYMS

rājāra jñāna—the King thought; *rāja-vaidyera*—of the royal physician; *ha-ila maraṇa*—there was death; *āpane*—personally; *nāmiyā*—getting down; *tabe*—thereupon; *karāila cetana*—brought him to consciousness.

TRANSLATION

"The King, fearing that the royal physician was killed, personally descended and brought him to his consciousness.

TEXT 125

রাজা বলে—ব্যথা তুমি পাইলে কোন ঠাঞি ?
মুকুন্দ কহে,— অতিবড় ব্যথা পাই নাই ॥ ১২৫ ॥

rājā bale——vyathā tumi pāile kona ṭhāñi?
mukunda kahe,——ati-baḍa vyathā pāi nāi

SYNONYMS

rājā bale—the King said; *vyathā*—pain; *tumi pāile*—you have gotten; *kona ṭhāñi*—where; *mukunda kahe*—Mukunda replied; *ati-baḍa vyathā*—very much pain; *pāi nāi*—I have not gotten.

TRANSLATION

"When the King asked Mukunda, 'Where is it paining you?' Mukunda replied, 'I am not very much pained.'

TEXT 126

রাজা কহে, - মুকুন্দ, তুমি পড়িলা কি লাগি' ?
মুকুন্দ কহে, রাজা, মোর ব্যাধি আছে মৃগী ॥ ১২৬ ॥

rājā kahe,——mukunda, tumi paḍilā ki lāgi'?
mukunda kahe, rājā, mora vyādhi āche mṛgī

SYNONYMS

rājā kahe—the King inquired; *mukunda*—O Mukunda; *tumi paḍilā*—you fell; *ki lāgi'*—for what reason; *mukunda kahe*—Mukunda replied; *rājā*—my dear King; *mora*—of me; *vyādhi*—disease; *āche*—is; *mṛgī*—epilepsy.

TRANSLATION

"The King then inquired, 'Mukunda, why did you fall down?' Mukunda replied, 'My dear King, I have a disease that is like epilepsy.'

TEXT 127

মহাবিদগ্ধ রাজা, সেই সব জানে ।
মুকুন্দেরে হৈল তাঁর 'মহাসিদ্ধ'-জ্ঞানে ॥ ১২৭ ॥

mahā-vidagdha rājā, sei saba jāne
mukundere haila tāṅra 'mahā-siddha'-jñāne

SYNONYMS

mahā-vidagdha—highly intelligent; *rājā*—the King; *sei*—he; *saba jāne*—knows everything; *mukundere*—upon Mukunda; *haila*—was; *tāṅra*—his; *mahā-siddha-jñāne*—calculation as the most perfect devotee.

TRANSLATION

"Being extraordinarily intelligent, the King could understand the whole affair. In his estimation, Mukunda was a most uncommon, exalted, liberated personality.

TEXTS 128-129

রঘুনন্দন সেবা করে কৃষ্ণের মন্দিরে ।
দ্বারে পুষ্করিণী, তার ঘাটের উপরে ॥ ১২৮ ॥
কদম্বের এক বৃক্ষে ফুটে বারমাসে ।
নিত্য দুই ফুল হয় কৃষ্ণ-অবতংসে ॥ ১২৯ ॥

raghunandana sevā kare kṛṣṇera mandire
dvāre puṣkariṇī, tāra ghāṭera upare

kadambera eka vṛkṣe phuṭe bāra-māse
nitya dui phula haya kṛṣṇa-avataṁse

SYNONYMS

raghunandana—Raghunandana; *sevā kare*—serves; *kṛṣṇera mandire*—in the temple of Lord Kṛṣṇa; *dvāre*—near the door; *puṣkariṇī*—a lake; *tāra*—of it; *ghāṭera upare*—on the bank; *kadambera*—of *kadamba* flowers; *eka vṛkṣe*—on one tree; *phuṭe*—blossom; *bāra-māse*—all year around; *nitya*—daily; *dui phala*—two flowers; *haya*—become; *kṛṣṇa-avataṁse*—decoration for Lord Kṛṣṇa.

TRANSLATION

"Raghunandana is constantly engaged in serving the temple of Lord Kṛṣṇa. Beside the entrance of the temple is a lake, and on its banks is a kadamba tree, which daily delivers two flowers to be used for Kṛṣṇa's service."

TEXT 130

মুকুন্দেরে কহে পুনঃ মধুর বচন ।
'তোমার কার্য—ধর্মে ধন-উপার্জন ॥ ১৩০ ॥

mukundere kahe punaḥ madhura vacana
'tomāra kārya——dharme dhana-upārjana

SYNONYMS

mukundere—to Mukunda; *kahe*—Lord Caitanya Mahāprabhu says; *punaḥ*—again; *madhura vacana*—sweet words; *tomāra kārya*—your duty; *dharme dhana-upārjana*—to earn both material and spiritual wealth.

TRANSLATION

Śrī Caitanya Mahāprabhu again spoke to Mukunda with sweet words: "Your duty is to earn both material and spiritual wealth.

TEXT 131

রঘুনন্দনের কার্য—কৃষ্ণের সেবন ।
কৃষ্ণ-সেবা বিনা ইঁহার অন্য নাহি মন ॥ ১৩১ ॥

raghunandanera kārya——kṛṣṇera sevana
kṛṣṇa-sevā vinā iṅhāra anya nāhi mana

SYNONYMS

raghunandanera kārya—the duty of Raghunandana; *kṛṣṇera sevana*—worshiping Lord Kṛṣṇa; *kṛṣṇa-sevā vinā*—except for worshiping Kṛṣṇa; *iṅhāra*—of him; *anya*—other; *nāhi*—there is not; *mana*—intention.

TRANSLATION

"Furthermore it is the duty of Raghunandana to always engage in Lord Kṛṣṇa's service. He has no other intention but the service of Lord Kṛṣṇa."

TEXT 132

নরহরি রহু আমার ভক্তগণ-সনে ।
এই তিন কার্য সদা করহ তিন জনে ॥' ১৩২ ॥

narahari rahu āmāra bhakta-gaṇa-sane
ei tina kārya sadā karaha tina jane'

SYNONYMS

narahari—Narahari; *rahu*—let him remain; *āmāra*—My; *bhakta-gaṇa-sane*—along with other devotees; *ei tina kārya*—these three divisions of duty; *sadā*—always; *karaha*—execute; *tina jane*—you three persons.

TRANSLATION

Śrī Caitanya Mahāprabhu then ordered Narahari: "I wish you to remain here with My devotees. In this way the three of you should always execute these three duties for the service of the Lord."

PURPORT

Śrī Caitanya Mahāprabhu set forth three duties for three different people. Mukunda was to earn money and follow the religious principles, whereas Narahari was to remain with the Lord's devotees, and Raghunandana was to engage in the Lord's service in the temple. Thus one person worships in the temple, another earns money honestly by executing his professional duty, and yet another preaches Kṛṣṇa consciousness with the devotees. Apparently these three types of service appear separate, but actually they are not. When Kṛṣṇa or Śrī Caitanya Mahāprabhu is the center, everyone can engage in different activities for the service of the Lord. That is the verdict of Śrī Caitanya Mahāprabhu.

TEXT 133

সার্বভৌম, বিদ্যাবাচস্পতি,—দুই ভাই ।
দুইজনে কৃপা করি' কহেন গোসাঞি ॥ ১৩৩ ॥

sārvabhauma, vidyā-vācaspati,——dui bhāi
dui-jane kṛpā kari' kahena gosāñi

SYNONYMS

sārvabhauma—Sārvabhauma Bhaṭṭācārya; *vidyā-vācaspati*—Vidyā-vācaspati; *dui bhāi*—two brothers; *dui-jane*—unto the two; *kṛpā kari'*—out of His causeless mercy; *kahena*—says; *gosāñi*—Śrī Caitanya Mahāprabhu.

TRANSLATION

Out of His causeless mercy, Śrī Caitanya Mahāprabhu gave the following directions to the brothers Sārvabhauma Bhaṭṭācārya and Vidyā-vācaspati.

TEXT 134

'দারু'-'জল'-রূপে কৃষ্ণ প্রকট সম্প্রতি ।
'দরশন'-স্নানে' করে জীবের মুকতি ॥ ১৩৪ ॥

'dāru'-'jala'-rūpe kṛṣṇa prakaṭa samprati
'daraśana'-'snāne' kare jīvera mukati

SYNONYMS

dāru—wood; *jala*—water; *rūpe*—in the forms of; *kṛṣṇa*—Lord Kṛṣṇa; *prakaṭa*—manifested; *samprati*—at the present moment; *daraśana*—by seeing; *snāne*—by bathing; *kare*—does; *jīvera mukati*—the deliverance of the conditioned souls.

TRANSLATION

Śrī Caitanya Mahāprabhu said, "In this age of Kali, Kṛṣṇa is manifest in two forms—wood and water. Thus He helps conditioned souls to become liberated by seeing the wood and bathing in the water.

TEXT 135

'দারুব্রহ্ম'-রূপে—সাক্ষাৎ শ্রীপুরুষোত্তম ।
ভাগীরথী হন সাক্ষাৎ 'জলব্রহ্ম'-সম ॥ ১৩৫ ॥

'dāru-brahma'-rūpe——sākṣāt śrī-puruṣottama
bhāgīrathī hana sākṣāt 'jala-brahma'-sama

SYNONYMS

dāru-brahma-rūpe—in the form of Brahman as wood; *sākṣāt*—directly; *śrī-puruṣottama*—Lord Jagannātha; *bhāgīrathī*—the River Ganges; *hana*—is; *sākṣāt*—directly; *jala-brahma-sama*—the Supreme in the form of water.

TRANSLATION

"Lord Jagannātha is the Supreme Lord Himself in the form of wood, and the River Ganges is the Supreme Lord Himself in the form of water.

PURPORT

The *Vedas* enjoin, *sarvaṁ khalv idaṁ brahma:* everything is the energy of the Supreme Personality of Godhead, the Supreme Brahman or Paraṁ Brahman. *Parasya brahmaṇaḥ śaktis tathedam akhilaṁ jagat:* everything is a manifestation of the energy of the Supreme Brahman. Since the energy and energetic are identical, actually everything is Kṛṣṇa, Paraṁ Brahman. *Bhagavad-gītā* (9.4) confirms this:

mayā tatam idaṁ sarvaṁ
jagad avyakta-mūrtinā
mat-sthāni sarva-bhūtāni
na cāhaṁ teṣv avasthitaḥ

"By Me, in My unmanifested form, this entire universe is pervaded. All beings are in Me, but I am not in them."

Kṛṣṇa is spread throughout the whole universe in His impersonal form. Since everything is a manifestation of the Lord's energy, the Lord can manifest Himself through any energy. In this age, the Lord is manifest through wood as Lord Jagannātha, and He is manifest through water as the River Ganges. Therefore Śrī Caitanya Mahāprabhu ordered the two brothers—Sārvabhauma Bhaṭṭācārya and Vidyā-vācaspati—to worship Lord Jagannātha and the River Ganges.

TEXT 136

সার্বভৌম, কর 'দারুব্রহ্ম'-আরাধন ।
বাচস্পতি, কর জলব্রহ্মের সেবন ॥ ১৩৬ ॥

sārvabhauma, kara 'dāru-brahma'-ārādhana
vācaspati, kara jala-brahmera sevana

SYNONYMS

sārvabhauma—O Sārvabhauma; *kara*—be engaged in; *dāru-brahma*—of wooden Brahman; *ārādhana*—worship; *vācaspati*—and you, Vācaspati; *kara*—do; *jala-brahmera*—of Paraṁ Brahman manifested in water; *sevana*—worship.

TRANSLATION

"Sārvabhauma Bhaṭṭācārya, you should engage in the worship of Lord Jagannātha Puruṣottama, and Vācaspati should worship mother Ganges."

TEXT 137

মুরারি-গুপ্তেরে প্রভু করি' আলিঙ্গন।
তাঁর ভক্তিনিষ্ঠা কহেন, শুনে ভক্তগণ ॥ ১৩৭ ॥

murāri-guptere prabhu kari' āliṅgana
tāṅra bhakti-niṣṭhā kahena, śune bhakta-gaṇa

SYNONYMS

murāri-guptere—Murāri Gupta; *prabhu*—Lord Śrī Caitanya Mahāprabhu; *kari' āliṅgana*—embracing; *tāṅra*—his; *bhakti-niṣṭhā*—faith in devotional service; *kahena*—says; *śune bhakta-gaṇa*—all the devotees hear.

TRANSLATION

Śrī Caitanya Mahāprabhu then embraced Murāri Gupta and began to speak about his firm faith in devotional service. This was heard by all the devotees.

TEXT 138

পূর্বে আমি ইঁহারে লোভাইল বার বার।
পরম মধুর, গুপ্ত, ব্রজেন্দ্রকুমার ॥ ১৩৮ ॥

pūrve āmi iṅhāre lobhāila bāra bāra
parama madhura, gupta, vrajendra-kumāra

SYNONYMS

pūrve—previously; *āmi*—I; *iṅhāre*—him; *lobhāila*—induced to be allured; *bāra bāra*—again and again; *parama madhura*—very sweet; *gupta*—O Gupta; *vrajendra-kumāra*—Lord Kṛṣṇa, the son of Nanda Mahārāja.

TRANSLATION

Śrī Caitanya Mahāprabhu said, "Previously I induced Murāri Gupta again and again to be allured by Lord Kṛṣṇa. I said to him, 'My dear Gupta, Lord Śrī Kṛṣṇa, Vrajendra-kumāra, is the supreme sweetness.

TEXT 139

স্বয়ং ভগবান্ কৃষ্ণ—সর্বাংশী, সর্বাশ্রয়।
বিশুদ্ধ-নির্মল-প্রেম, সর্বরসময় ॥ ১৩৯ ॥

svayaṁ bhagavān kṛṣṇa——sarvāṁśī, sarvāśraya
viśuddha-nirmala-prema, sarva-rasamaya

SYNONYMS

svayam bhagavān kṛṣṇa—Lord Kṛṣṇa is the Supreme Personality of Godhead; *sarva-aṁśī*—the source of all others; *sarva-āśraya*—the reservoir of all energies; *viśuddha*—transcendental; *nirmala*—free from all material contamination; *prema*—love; *sarva-rasa-maya*—the reservoir of all pleasure.

TRANSLATION

" 'Kṛṣṇa is the Supreme Personality of Godhead, the origin of all incarnations and the source of everything. He is pure transcendental love itself, and He is the reservoir of all pleasure.

TEXT 140

সকল-সদ্‌গুণ-বৃন্দ-রত্ন-রত্নাকর ।
বিদগ্ধ, চতুর, ধীর, রসিক-শেখর ॥ ১৪০ ॥

sakala-sadguṇa-vṛnda-ratna-ratnākara
vidagdha, catura, dhīra, rasika-śekhara

SYNONYMS

sakala—all; *sat-guṇa*—transcendental qualities; *vṛnda*—multitude; *ratna*—of gems; *ratna-ākara*—the mine; *vidagdha*—intelligent; *catura*—expert; *dhīra*—sober; *rasika-śekhara*—master of all humor.

TRANSLATION

" 'Kṛṣṇa is the reservoir of all transcendental qualities. He is like a mine of gems. He is expert at everything, very intelligent and sober, and He is the summit of all humors.

TEXT 141

মধুর-চরিত্র কৃষ্ণের মধুর-বিলাস ।
চাতুর্য-বৈদগ্ধ্য করে যাঁর লীলারস ॥ ১৪১ ॥

madhura-caritra kṛṣṇera madhura-vilāsa
cāturya-vaidagdhya kare yāṅra līlā-rasa

SYNONYMS

madhura-caritra—pleasing character; *kṛṣṇera*—of Lord Kṛṣṇa; *madhura-vilāsa*—melodious pastimes; *cāturya*—expertise; *vaidagdhya*—intelligence; *kare*—manifests; *yāṅra*—whose; *līlā*—of pastimes; *rasa*—mellows.

TRANSLATION

" 'His character is very sweet, and His pastimes are melodious. He is expert in intelligence, and thus He enjoys all His pastimes and mellows.'

TEXT 142

সেই কৃষ্ণ ভজ তুমি, হও কৃষ্ণাশ্রয় ।
কৃষ্ণ বিনা অন্য-উপাসনা মনে নাহি লয় ॥ ১৪২ ॥

sei kṛṣṇa bhaja tumi, hao kṛṣṇāśraya
kṛṣṇa vinā anya-upāsanā mane nāhi laya

SYNONYMS

sei kṛṣṇa—that Lord Kṛṣṇa; *bhaja tumi*—engage yourself in His service; *hao kṛṣṇa-āśraya*—take shelter of Kṛṣṇa; *kṛṣṇa vinā*—except for Kṛṣṇa; *anya-upāsanā*—any other worship; *mane nāhi laya*—does not appeal to the mind.

TRANSLATION

"I then requested Murāri Gupta, 'Worship Kṛṣṇa and take shelter of Him. But for His service, nothing appeals to the mind.'

TEXT 143

এইমত বার বার শুনিয়া বচন ।
আমার গৌরবে কিছু ফিরি' গেল মন ॥ ১৪৩ ॥

ei-mata bāra bāra śuniyā vacana
āmāra gaurave kichu phiri' gela mana

SYNONYMS

ei-mata—in this way; *bāra bāra*—again and again; *śuniyā vacana*—hearing these words; *āmāra gaurave*—because of My influence; *kichu*—somewhat; *phiri' gela*—transformed; *mana*—his mind.

TRANSLATION

"In this way, he heard from Me again and again. By My influence, his mind was a little converted.

TEXT 144

আমারে কহেন,—আমি তোমার কিঙ্কর ।
তোমার আজ্ঞাকারী আমি নহি স্বতন্তর ॥ ১৪৪ ॥

āmāre kahena,——āmi tomāra kiṅkara
tomāra ājñākārī āmi nāhi svatantara

SYNONYMS

āmāre kahena—he said unto Me; *āmi*—I; *tomāra kiṅkara*—Your servant; *tomāra ājñā-kārī*—Your order carrier; *āmi*—I; *nāhi*—am not; *svatantara*—independent.

TRANSLATION

"Murāri Gupta then replied, 'I am Your servant and Your order carrier. I have no independent existence.'

TEXT 145

এত বলি' ঘরে গেল, চিন্তি' রাত্রিকালে ।
রঘুনাথ-ত্যাগ-চিন্তায় হইল বিকলে ॥ ১৪৫ ॥

eta bali' ghare gela, cinti' rātri-kāle
raghunātha-tyāga-cintāya ha-ila vikale

SYNONYMS

eta bali'—saying this; *ghare gela*—went to his house; *cinti'*—thinking; *rātri-kāle*—at night; *raghunātha*—Lord Rāmacandra; *tyāga*—giving up; *cintāya*—by thoughts of; *ha-ila vikale*—became overwhelmed.

TRANSLATION

"After this, Murāri Gupta went home and spent the whole night thinking how he would be able to give up the association of Raghunātha, Lord Rāmacandra. Thus he was overwhelmed.

TEXT 146

কেমনে ছাড়িব রঘুনাথের চরণ ।
আজি রাত্র্যে প্রভু মোর করাহ মরণ ॥ ১৪৬ ॥

kemane chāḍiba raghunāthera caraṇa
āji rātrye prabhu mora karāha maraṇa

SYNONYMS

kemane chāḍiba—how shall I give up; *raghunāthera caraṇa*—the lotus feet of Lord Raghunātha; *āji rātrye*—this night; *prabhu*—O Lord Raghunātha; *mora*—my; *karāha maraṇa*—please cause death.

TRANSLATION

"Murāri Gupta then began to pray at the lotus feet of Lord Rāmacandra. He prayed that death would come that night because it was not possible for him to give up the service of the lotus feet of Raghunātha.

TEXT 147

এই মত সর্ব-রাত্রি করেন ক্রন্দন ।
মনে সোয়াস্তি নাহি, রাত্রি কৈল জাগরণ ॥ ১৪৭ ॥

ei mata sarva-rātri karena krandana
mane soyāsti nāhi, rātri kaila jāgaraṇa

SYNONYMS

ei mata—in this way; *sarva-rātri*—the whole night; *karena krandana*—cried; *mane*—in the mind; *soyāsti nāhi*—there is no rest; *rātri*—the whole night; *kaila*—kept; *jāgaraṇa*—awake.

TRANSLATION

"Thus Murāri Gupta cried the entire night. There was no rest for his mind; therefore he could not sleep but stayed awake the entire night.

TEXT 148

প্রাতঃকালে আসি' মোর ধরিল চরণ ।
কান্দিতে কান্দিতে কিছু করে নিবেদন ॥ ১৪৮ ॥

prātaḥ-kāle āsi' mora dharila caraṇa
kāndite kāndite kichu kare nivedana

SYNONYMS

prātaḥ-kāle—in the morning; *āsi'*—coming; *mora*—My; *dharila*—caught hold of; *caraṇa*—feet; *kāndite kāndite*—continuously crying; *kichu kare nivedana*—submits some appeals.

TRANSLATION

"In the morning Murāri Gupta came to see Me. Catching hold of My feet and crying, he submitted an appeal.

TEXT 149

রঘুনাথের পায় মুঞি বেচিয়াছোঁ মাথা।
কাঢ়িতে না পারি মাথা, মনে পাই ব্যথা ॥ ১৪৯ ॥

raghunāthera pāya muñi veciyāchoṅ māthā
kāḍhite nā pāri māthā, mane pāi vyathā

SYNONYMS

raghunāthera pāya—unto the lotus feet of Lord Raghunātha; *muñi*—I; *veciyāchoṅ*—sold; *māthā*—head; *kāḍhite*—to cut off; *nā pāri*—I am unable; *māthā*—my head; *mane*—in my mind; *pāi vyathā*—I get too much pain.

TRANSLATION

"Murāri Gupta said, 'I have sold my head to the lotus feet of Raghunātha. I cannot withdraw my head, for that would give me too much pain.

TEXT 150

শ্রীরঘুনাথ-চরণ ছাড়ান না যায়।
তব আজ্ঞা-ভঙ্গ হয়, কি করোঁ উপায় ॥ ১৫০ ॥

śrī-raghunātha-caraṇa chāḍāna nā yāya
tava ājñā-bhaṅga haya, ki karoṅ upāya

SYNONYMS

śrī-raghunātha-caraṇa—the lotus feet of Lord Rāmacandra; *chāḍāna nā yāya*—cannot be given up; *tava*—Your; *ājñā*—order; *bhaṅga*—broken; *haya*—is; *ki*—what; *karoṅ*—shall I do; *upāya*—remedy.

TRANSLATION

" 'It is not possible for me to give up the service of Raghunātha's lotus feet. At the same time, if I do not do so I shall break your order. What can I do?'

TEXT 151

তাতে মোরে এই কৃপা কর, দয়াময়।
তোমার আগে মৃত্যু হউক, যাউক সংশয় ॥ ১৫১ ॥

tāte more ei kṛpā kara, dayāmaya
tomāra āge mṛtyu ha-uka, yāuka saṁśaya

SYNONYMS

tāte—therefore; *more*—unto me; *ei*—this; *kṛpā*—mercy; *kara*—bestow; *dayā-maya*—O merciful one; *tomāra āge*—before You; *mṛtyu ha-uka*—let me die; *yāuka saṁśaya*—and let all doubts go away.

TRANSLATION

"In this way Murāri Gupta appealed to Me, saying, 'Kindly grant me this mercy because You are all-merciful. Let me die before You so that all my doubts will be finished.'

TEXT 152

এত শুনি' আমি বড় মনে সুখ পাইলুঁ ।
ইঁহারে উঠাঞা তবে আলিঙ্গন কৈলুঁ ॥ ১৫২ ॥

eta śuni' āmi baḍa mane sukha pāiluṅ
iṅhāre uṭhāñā tabe āliṅgana kailuṅ

SYNONYMS

eta śuni'—hearing this; *āmi*—I; *baḍa*—very great; *mane*—in the mind; *sukha*—happiness; *pāiluṅ*—got; *iṅhāre*—him; *uṭhāñā*—raising; *tabe*—at that time; *āliṅgana kailuṅ*—I embraced.

TRANSLATION

"Hearing this, I became very happy. I then raised Murāri Gupta and embraced him.

TEXT 153

সাধু সাধু, গুপ্ত, তোমার সুদৃঢ় ভজন ।
আমার বচনেহ তোমার না টলিল মন ॥ ১৫৩ ॥

sādhu sādhu, gupta, tomāra sudṛḍha bhajana
āmāra vacaneha tomāra nā ṭalila mana

SYNONYMS

sādhu sādhu—all glories unto you; *gupta*—Murāri Gupta; *tomāra*—your; *su-dṛḍha*—firmly fixed; *bhajana*—method of worship; *āmāra*—My; *vacaneha*—even on the request; *tomāra*—your; *nā ṭalila*—did not budge; *mana*—mind.

TRANSLATION

"I said to him, 'All glories to you, Murāri Gupta! Your method of worship is very firmly fixed—so much so that even upon My request your mind did not turn.

TEXT 154

এইমত সেবকের প্রীতি চাহি প্রভু-পায় ।
প্রভু ছাড়াইলেহ, পদ ছাড়ান না যায় ॥ ১৫৪ ॥

ei-mata sevakera prīti cāhi prabhu-pāya
prabhu chāḍāileha, pada chāḍāna nā yāya

SYNONYMS

ei-mata—like this; *sevakera*—of the servitor; *prīti*—love; *cāhi*—is wanted; *prabhu-pāya*—unto the lotus feet of the Lord; *prabhu chāḍāileha*—even though the Lord causes separation; *pada*—the lotus feet of the Lord; *chāḍāna nā yāya*—cannot be given up.

TRANSLATION

" 'The servitor must have love and affection for the lotus feet of the Lord exactly like this. Even if the Lord wants separation, a devotee cannot abandon the shelter of His lotus feet.

PURPORT

The word *prabhu,* or master, indicates that the Lord is to be continuously served by His devotee. The original *prabhu* is the Lord, Śrī Kṛṣṇa. Nonetheless, there are many devotees attached to Lord Rāmacandra, and Murāri Gupta is a vivid example of such unalloyed devotion. He never agreed to give up Lord Rāmacandra's worship, not even upon Śrī Caitanya Mahāprabhu's request. Such is the chastity of devotional service, as stated in the *Antya-līlā* of *Caitanya-caritāmṛta* (4.46-47):

sei bhakta dhanya, ye nā chāḍe prabhura caraṇa
sei prabhu dhanya, ye nā chāḍe nija-jana

durdaive sevaka yadi yāya anya sthāne
sei ṭhākura dhanya tāre cule dhari' āne

In a firm relationship with the Lord, the devotee does not give up the Lord's service under any circumstance. As far as the Lord Himself is concerned, if the devotee chooses to leave, the Lord brings him back again, dragging him by the hair.

TEXT 155

এইমত তোমার নিষ্ঠা জানিবার তরে।
তোমারে আগ্রহ আমি কৈলুঁ বারে বারে ॥ ১৫৫ ॥

ei-mata tomāra niṣṭhā jānibāra tare
tomāre āgraha āmi kailuṅ bāre bāre

SYNONYMS

ei-mata—in this way; *tomāra*—your; *niṣṭhā*—firm faith; *jānibāra tare*—to understand; *tomāre*—unto you; *āgraha*—persistence; *āmi kailuṅ*—I did; *bāre bāre*—again and again.

TRANSLATION

" 'Just to test your firm faith in your Lord, I requested you again and again to change your worship from Lord Rāmacandra to Kṛṣṇa.'

TEXT 156

সাক্ষাৎ হনুমান্ তুমি শ্রীরাম-কিঙ্কর।
তুমি কেনে ছাড়িবে তাঁর চরণ-কমল ॥ ১৫৬ ॥

sākṣāt hanumān tumi śrī-rāma-kiṅkara
tumi kene chāḍibe tāṅra caraṇa-kamala

SYNONYMS

sākṣāt—directly; *hanumān*—Hanumān; *tumi*—you; *śrī-rāma-kiṅkara*—the servant of Śrī Rāma; *tumi*—you; *kene*—why; *chāḍibe*—should give up; *tāṅra*—His; *caraṇa-kamala*—lotus feet.

TRANSLATION

"In this way, I congratulated Murāri Gupta, saying, 'Indeed, you are the incarnation of Hanumān. Consequently you are the eternal servant of Lord Rāmacandra. Why should you give up the worship of Lord Rāmacandra and His lotus feet?' "

TEXT 157

সেই মুরারি-গুপ্ত এই—মোর প্রাণ সম।
ইঁহার দৈন্য শুনি' মোর ফাটয়ে জীবন ॥ ১৫৭ ॥

sei murāri-gupta ei——mora prāṇa sama
iṅhāra dainya śuni' mora phāṭaye jīvana

SYNONYMS

sei murāri-gupta—that Murāri Gupta; *ei*—this; *mora prāṇa sama*—not different from My life and soul; *iṅhāra*—of him; *dainya*—humility; *śuni'*—hearing; *mora*—My; *phāṭaye*—perturbs; *jīvana*—life.

TRANSLATION

Śrī Caitanya Mahāprabhu continued, "I accept this Murāri Gupta as My life and soul. When I hear of his humility, it perturbs My very life."

TEXT 158

তবে বাসুদেবে প্রভু করি' আলিঙ্গন ।
তাঁর গুণ কহে হঞা সহস্র-বদন ॥ ১৫৮ ॥

tabe vāsudeve prabhu kari' āliṅgana
tāṅra guṇa kahe hañā sahasra-vadana

SYNONYMS

tabe—then; *vāsudeve*—Vāsudeva; *prabhu*—Śrī Caitanya Mahāprabhu; *kari' āliṅgana*—embracing; *tāṅra guṇa*—his good qualities; *kahe*—began to explain; *hañā*—becoming; *sahasra-vadana*—possessing thousands of mouths.

TRANSLATION

Śrī Caitanya Mahāprabhu then embraced Vāsudeva Datta and began to speak of his glories as if He had a thousand mouths.

TEXT 159

নিজ-গুণ শুনি' দত্ত মনে লজ্জা পাঞা ।
নিবেদন করে প্রভুর চরণে ধরিয়া ॥ ১৫৯ ॥

nija-guṇa śuni' datta mane lajjā pāñā
nivedana kare prabhura caraṇe dhariyā

SYNONYMS

nija-guṇa—his personal qualities; *śuni'*—hearing; *datta*—Vāsudeva Datta; *mane*—in the mind; *lajjā pāñā*—being ashamed; *nivedana kare*—submits; *prabhura*—of Lord Śrī Caitanya Mahāprabhu; *caraṇe dhariyā*—catching the lotus feet.

TRANSLATION

When Caitanya Mahāprabhu glorified him, Vāsudeva Datta immediately became very embarrassed and shy. He then submitted himself, touching the Lord's lotus feet.

TEXT 160

জগৎ তারিতে প্রভু তোমার অবতার ।
মোর নিবেদন এক করহ অঙ্গীকার ॥ ১৬০ ॥

jagat tārite prabhu tomāra avatāra
mora nivedana eka karaha aṅgīkāra

SYNONYMS

jagat tārite—to deliver the whole world; *prabhu*—my Lord; *tomāra*—Your; *avatāra*—incarnation; *mora*—my; *nivedana*—petition; *eka*—one; *karaha aṅgīkāra*—please accept.

TRANSLATION

Vāsudeva Datta told Caitanya Mahāprabhu, "My dear Lord, You incarnate just to deliver all conditioned souls. I have now one petition, which I wish You would accept.

TEXT 161

করিতে সমর্থ তুমি হও, দয়াময় ।
তুমি মন কর, তবে অনায়াসে হয় ॥ ১৬১ ॥

karite samartha tumi hao, dayāmaya
tumi mana kara, tabe anāyāse haya

SYNONYMS

karite—to execute; *samartha*—capable; *tumi*—You; *hao*—are; *dayā-maya*—O merciful one; *tumi mana kara*—if You so desire; *tabe*—then; *anāyāse*—without difficulty; *haya*—it becomes possible.

TRANSLATION

"My Lord, You are certainly capable of doing whatever You like, and You are indeed merciful. If You so desire, You can very easily do whatever You want.

TEXT 162

জীবের দুঃখ দেখি' মোর হৃদয় বিদরে ।
সর্বজীবের পাপ প্রভু দেহ' মোর শিরে ॥ ১৬২ ॥

jīvera duḥkha dekhi' mora hṛdaya bidare
sarva-jīvera pāpa prabhu deha' mora śire

SYNONYMS

jīvera—of all conditioned souls; *duḥkha dekhi'*—by seeing the sufferings; *mora*—my; *hṛdaya*—heart; *bidare*—breaks; *sarva-jīvera*—of all living entities; *pāpa*—the sinful reactions; *prabhu*—My dear Lord; *deha'*—just put; *mora śire*—upon my head.

TRANSLATION

"My Lord, my heart breaks to see the sufferings of all conditioned souls; therefore I request You to transfer the karma of their sinful lives upon my head.

TEXT 163

জীবের পাপ লঞা মুঞি করোঁ নরক ভোগ ।
সকল জীবের, প্রভু, ঘুচাহ ভবরোগ ॥ ১৬৩ ॥

jīvera pāpa lañā muñi karoṅ naraka bhoga
sakala jīvera, prabhu, ghucāha bhava-roga

SYNONYMS

jīvera—of all conditioned souls; *pāpa lañā*—accepting the sinful reactions; *muñi*—I; *karoṅ*—do; *naraka*—hellish life; *bhoga*—suffering; *sakala jīvera*—of all living entities; *prabhu*—my dear Lord; *ghucāha*—please finish; *bhava-roga*—the material disease.

TRANSLATION

"My dear Lord, let me suffer perpetually in a hellish condition, accepting all the sinful reactions of all living entities. Please finish their diseased material life."

PURPORT

Śrīla Bhaktisiddhānta Sarasvatī Ṭhākura gives the following commentary on this verse. In the Western countries, Christians believe that Lord Jesus Christ, their spiritual master, appeared in order to eradicate all the sins of his disciples. To this end, Lord Jesus Christ appeared and disappeared. Here, however, we find Śrī Vāsudeva Datta Ṭhākura and Śrīla Haridāsa Ṭhākura to be many millions of times more advanced even when compared to Lord Jesus Christ. Jesus Christ relieved only his followers from all sinful reactions, but Vāsudeva Datta is here prepared to accept the sins of everyone in the universe. A Vaiṣṇava is so liberal that he is prepared to risk everything to rescue conditioned souls from material existence. Śrīla Vāsudeva Datta Ṭhākura is universal love itself, for he was willing to sacrifice everything and fully engage in the service of the Supreme.

Śrīla Vāsudeva Datta knew very well that Śrī Caitanya Mahāprabhu was the original Personality of Godhead. He was transcendence itself, above the material conception of illusion and *māyā.* Lord Jesus Christ certainly finished the sinful reactions of his followers by his mercy, but that does not mean that he completely delivered them from the pangs of material existence. A person may be relieved from sins once, but it is a practice among Christians to confess sins and yet commit them again. By getting freed from sins and again engaging in them, one cannot attain freedom from the pangs of material existence. A diseased person may go to a physician for relief, but after he leaves the hospital he may again be infected due to his unclean habits. Thus material existence continues. Śrīla Vāsudeva Datta wanted to completely relieve the conditioned souls from material existence so that they would no longer have an opportunity to commit sinful acts. This is the difference between Śrīla Vāsudeva Datta and Lord Jesus Christ. It is a great offense to receive pardon for sins and then commit the same sins again. Such an offense is more dangerous than the sinful activity itself. Vāsudeva Datta was so liberal that he requested Śrī Caitanya Mahāprabhu to transfer all offensive activity upon him so the conditioned souls might be purified. This prayer was certainly without duplicity.

Vāsudeva Datta's example is unique not only within this world but within the universe. It is beyond the conception of fruitive actors or the speculation of mundane philosophers. Due to being illusioned by the external energy and due to a poor fund of knowledge, people tend to envy one another. Because of this they are entangled in fruitive activity, and they try to escape this fruitive activity by mental speculation. Consequently neither *karmīs* nor *jñānīs* are purified. In the words of Śrīla Bhaktisiddhānta Ṭhākura, they are *kukarmīs* and *kujñānīs*—bad actors and bad speculators. The Māyāvādīs and *karmīs* should therefore turn their attention to the magnanimous Vāsudeva Datta, who wanted to suffer for others in a hellish condition. Nor should one consider Vāsudeva Datta a mundane philanthropist or welfare worker. He was not interested in merging into the Brahman effulgence, nor was he interested in material honor or reputation. He was far above philanthropists, philosophers and fruitive actors. He was a most exalted personality who wanted to show mercy upon conditioned souls. This is not an exaggeration of his transcendental qualities. It is perfectly true. Actually there cannot be any comparison to Vāsudeva Datta. He was a Vaiṣṇava—*para-duḥkha-duḥkhī*—very much aggrieved to see others suffer. The entire world is purified simply by the appearance of such a great devotee. By his presence the whole world is glorified, and all conditioned souls—due to his transcendental presence—are also glorified. As Narottama dāsa Ṭhākura confirms, Vāsudeva Datta is the ideal devotee of Śrī Caitanya Mahāprabhu.

gaurāṅgera saṅgi-gaṇe, nitya-siddha kari' māne,
se yāya vrajendrasuta-pāśa

One who executes Śrī Caitanya Mahāprabhu's mission must be considered to be eternally liberated. He is a transcendental person and does not belong to this material world. Such a devotee engaging in the deliverance of the total population is as magnanimous as Śrī Caitanya Mahāprabhu Himself.

namo mahā-vadānyāya
kṛṣṇa-prema-pradāya te
kṛṣṇāya kṛṣṇa-caitanya-
nāmne gaura-tviṣe namaḥ

Such a personality factually represents Śrī Caitanya Mahāprabhu because his heart is always filled with compassion for conditioned souls.

TEXT 164

এত শুনি' মহাপ্রভুর চিত্ত দ্রবিলা।
অশ্রু-কম্প-স্বরভঙ্গে কহিতে লাগিলা ॥ ১৬৪ ॥

eta śuni' mahāprabhura citta dravilā
aśru-kampa-svarabhaṅge kahite lāgilā

SYNONYMS

eta śuni'—hearing this; *mahāprabhura*—of Śrī Caitanya Mahāprabhu; *citta*—heart; *dravilā*—became softened; *aśru*—tears; *kampa*—trembling; *svara-bhaṅge*—with faltering of the voice; *kahite*—to speak; *lāgilā*—began.

TRANSLATION

When Śrī Caitanya Mahāprabhu heard Vāsudeva Datta's statement, His heart became very soft. Tears flowed from His eyes, and He began to tremble. In a faltering voice He spoke as follows.

TEXT 165

"তোমার বিচিত্র নহে, তুমি—সাক্ষাৎ প্রহ্লাদ।
তোমার উপরে কৃষ্ণের সম্পূর্ণ প্রসাদ॥ ১৬৫॥

"tomāra vicitra nahe, tumi——sākṣāt prahlāda
tomāra upare kṛṣṇera sampūrṇa prasāda

SYNONYMS

tomāra—in you; *vicitra nahe*—this is not extraordinary; *tumi*—you; *sākṣāt prahlāda*—incarnation of Prahlāda Mahārāja; *tomāra upare*—upon you; *kṛṣṇera*—of Lord Kṛṣṇa; *sampūrṇa*—complete; *prasāda*—mercy.

TRANSLATION

Accepting Vāsudeva Datta as a great devotee, the Lord said, "Such a statement is not at all astonishing because you are the incarnation of Prahlāda Mahārāja. It appears that Lord Kṛṣṇa has bestowed complete mercy upon you. There is no doubt about it.

TEXT 166

কৃষ্ণ সেই সত্য করে, যেই মাগে ভৃত্য।
ভৃত্য-বাঞ্ছা-পূর্তি বিনু নাহি অন্য কৃত্য॥ ১৬৬॥

kṛṣṇa sei satya kare, yei māge bhṛtya
bhṛtya-vāñchā-pūrti vinu nāhi anya kṛtya

SYNONYMS

kṛṣṇa—Lord Kṛṣṇa; *sei*—that; *satya kare*—fulfills as true; *yei*—whatever; *māge*—wants; *bhṛtya*—servant; *bhṛtya-vāñchā*—the desire of His servant; *pūrti*—fulfilling; *vinu*—without; *nāhi*—there is not; *anya*—other; *kṛtya*—duty.

TRANSLATION

"Whatever a pure devotee wants from his master, Lord Kṛṣṇa doubtlessly grants because He has no duty other than to fulfill the desire of His devotee.

TEXT 167

ব্রহ্মাণ্ড জীবের তুমি বাঞ্ছিলে নিস্তার।
বিনা পাপ-ভোগে হবে সবার উদ্ধার॥ ১৬৭॥

brahmāṇḍa jīvera tumi vāñchile nistāra
vinā pāpa-bhoge habe sabāra uddhāra

SYNONYMS

brahmāṇḍa—of the universe; *jīvera*—of all living entities; *tumi vāñchile*—if you desire; *nistāra*—deliverance; *vinā*—without; *pāpa-bhoge*—undergoing tribulations of sinful activities; *habe*—there will be; *sabāra*—everyone's; *uddhāra*—liberation.

TRANSLATION

"If you desire the deliverance of all living entities within the universe, then all of them can be delivered even without your undergoing the tribulations of sinful activity.

TEXT 168

অসমর্থ নহে কৃষ্ণ, ধরে সর্ব বল।
তোমাকে বা কেনে ভুঞ্জাইবে পাপ-ফল? ১৬৮ ॥

asamartha nahe kṛṣṇa, dhare sarva bala
tomāke vā kene bhuñjāibe pāpa-phala?

SYNONYMS

asamartha nahe—is not unable; *kṛṣṇa*—Lord Kṛṣṇa; *dhare*—possesses; *sarva bala*—all potencies; *tomāke*—you; *vā*—then; *kene*—why; *bhuñjāibe*—would cause to suffer; *pāpa-phala*—results of sinful reactions.

TRANSLATION

"Kṛṣṇa is not incapable, for He has all potencies. Why would He induce you to suffer the sinful reactions of other living entities?

TEXT 169

তুমি যাঁর হিত বাঞ্ছ', সে হৈল 'বৈষ্ণব'।
বৈষ্ণবের পাপ কৃষ্ণ দূর করে সব ॥ ১৬৯ ॥

tumi yāṅra hita vāñcha', se haila 'vaiṣṇava'
vaiṣṇavera pāpa kṛṣṇa dūra kare saba

SYNONYMS

tumi—you; *yāṅra*—of whom; *hita vāñcha'*—desire the welfare; *se*—such a person; *haila*—immediately becomes; *vaiṣṇava*—a devotee; *vaiṣṇavera*—of a

Vaiṣṇava; *pāpa*—the accidental sinful life; *kṛṣṇa*—Lord Kṛṣṇa; *dūra kare*—vanquishes; *saba*—all.

TRANSLATION

"Whosever welfare you desire immediately becomes a Vaiṣṇava, and Kṛṣṇa delivers all Vaiṣṇavas from the reactions of their past sinful activities.

PURPORT

Śrī Caitanya Mahāprabhu here informed Vāsudeva Datta that since Kṛṣṇa is all-powerful, He can immediately deliver all conditioned souls from material existence. In essence, Śrī Caitanya Mahāprabhu said, "You desire the liberation of all kinds of living entities without discrimination. You are very anxious for their good fortune, and I say that simply by your prayer all living entities within the universe can be liberated. You do not even have to take up the burden of their sinful activities. Thus there is no need for you to suffer for their sinful lives. Whoever receives your compassion becomes a Vaiṣṇava immediately, and Kṛṣṇa delivers all Vaiṣṇavas from the reactions to their past sinful activities." This is also promised in *Bhagavad-gītā* (18.66):

sarva-dharmān parityajya
mām ekaṁ śaraṇaṁ vraja
ahaṁ tvāṁ sarva-pāpebhyo
mokṣayiṣyāmi mā śucaḥ

"Abandon all varieties of religion and just surrender unto Me. I shall deliver you from all sinful reaction. Do not fear."

As soon as one fully surrenders to Kṛṣṇa, he becomes a Vaiṣṇava. In this verse from *Bhagavad-gītā,* Kṛṣṇa promises to relieve His devotee from all the reactions to sinful life. It is a fact that a fully surrendered Vaiṣṇava is completely out of the range of material infection. This is to say that he does not suffer the results of pious or impious actions. Unless one is freed from a sinful life, he cannot become a Vaiṣṇava. In other words, if one is a Vaiṣṇava, his sinful life is certainly ended. According to *Padma Purāṇa:*

aprārabdha-phalaṁ pāpaṁ
kūṭaṁ bījaṁ phalonmukham
krameṇaiva pralīyeta
viṣṇu-bhakti-ratātmanām

"There are different stages of dormant reactions to sinful activities to be observed in a sinful life. Sinful reactions may be just waiting to take effect [*phalonmukha*], reactions may be still further dormant [*kūṭa*], or the reactions may be in a seedlike state [*bīja*]. In any case, all types of sinful reactions are vanquished one after another if a person engages in the devotional service of Lord Viṣṇu."

TEXT 170

যস্ত্বিন্দ্রগোপমথবেন্দ্রমহো স্বকর্ম-
বন্ধানুরূপফলভাজনমাতনোতি ।
কর্মাণি নির্দহতি কিন্তু চ ভক্তিভাজাং
গোবিন্দমাদিপুরুষং তমহং ভজামি ॥ ১৭০ ॥

yas tv indra-gopam athavendram aho sva-karma-
bandhānurūpa-phala-bhājanam ātanoti
karmāṇi nirdahati kintu ca bhakti-bhājāṁ
govindam ādi-puruṣaṁ tam ahaṁ bhajāmi

SYNONYMS

yaḥ—He who (Govinda); *tu*—but; *indra-gopam*—to the small red insect called *indra-gopa; athavā*—or even; *indram*—to Indra, King of heaven; *aho*—oh; *sva-karma*—of one's own fruitive activities; *bandha*—bondage; *anurūpa*—according to; *phala*—of reactions; *bhājanam*—enjoying or suffering; *ātanoti*—bestows; *karmāṇi*—all fruitive activities and their reactions; *nirdahati*—destroys; *kintu*—but; *ca*—certainly; *bhakti-bhājām*—of persons engaged in devotional service; *govindam*—unto Lord Govinda; *ādi-puruṣam*—the original person; *tam*—unto Him; *aham*—I; *bhajāmi*—offer my obeisances.

TRANSLATION

" 'Let me offer my respectful obeisances unto the original Personality of Godhead, Govinda, who regulates the sufferings and enjoyments of fruitive activity for everyone—from the heavenly King Indra down to the smallest insect [indra-gopa]. That very Personality of Godhead destroys the fruitive karma of one engaged in devotional service.'

PURPORT

This is a quotation from *Brahma-saṁhitā* (5.54).

TEXT 171

তোমার ইচ্ছা-মাত্রে হবে ব্রহ্মাণ্ড-মোচন ।
সর্ব মুক্ত করিতে কৃষ্ণের নাহি কিছু শ্রম ॥ ১৭১ ॥

tomāra icchā-mātre habe brahmāṇḍa-mocana
sarva mukta karite kṛṣṇera nāhi kichu śrama

SYNONYMS

tomāra icchā-mātre—simply by your desire; *habe*—there will be; *brahmāṇḍa-mocana*—deliverance of the universe; *sarva*—everyone; *mukta karite*—to liberate; *kṛṣṇera*—of Lord Kṛṣṇa; *nāhi*—there is not; *kichu*—even a little; *śrama*—labor.

TRANSLATION

"Because of your honest desire, all living entities within the universe will be delivered, for Kṛṣṇa does not have to do anything to deliver all the living entities of the universe.

TEXT 172

এক উড়ুম্বর বৃক্ষে লাগে কোটি-ফলে।
কোটি যে ব্রহ্মাণ্ড ভাসে বিরজার জলে ॥ ১৭২ ॥

eka uḍumbara vṛkṣe lāge koṭi-phale
koṭi ye brahmāṇḍa bhāse virajāra jale

SYNONYMS

eka uḍumbara vṛkṣe—in one *uḍumbara* tree; *lāge*—there are; *koṭi-phale*—millions of fruits; *koṭi*—millions; *ye*—which; *brahmāṇḍa*—of universes; *bhāse*—float; *virajāra*—of the Virajā River; *jale*—in the water.

TRANSLATION

"Just as there are millions of fruits on the uḍumbara tree, millions of universes float on the waters of the River Virajā.

PURPORT

Virajā is a river that divides the material world from the spiritual world. On one side of the River Virajā is the effulgence of Brahmaloka and innumerable Vaikuṇṭha planets, and on the other side is this material world. It is to be understood that this side of the Virajā River is filled with material planets floating in the Causal Ocean. The name Virajā indicates a marginal position between the spiritual and material worlds, but this Virajā River is not under the control of material energy. Consequently it is devoid of the three *guṇas*.

TEXT 173

তার এক ফল পড়ি' যদি নষ্ট হয়।
তথাপি বৃক্ষ নাহি জানে নিজ-অপচয়॥ ১৭৩॥

tāra eka phala paḍi' yadi naṣṭa haya
tathāpi vṛkṣa nāhi jāne nija-apacaya

SYNONYMS

tāra—of the tree; *eka phala*—one fruit; *paḍi'*—falling down; *yadi*—if; *naṣṭa haya*—becomes destroyed; *tathāpi*—still; *vṛkṣa*—the tree; *nāhi jāne*—does not know; *nija-apacaya*—its loss.

TRANSLATION

"The uḍumbara tree is filled with millions of fruits, and if one falls down and is destroyed, the tree does not even consider the loss.

TEXT 174

তৈছে এক ব্রহ্মাণ্ড যদি মুক্ত হয়।
তবু অল্প-হানি কৃষ্ণের মনে নাহি লয়॥ ১৭৪॥

taiche eka brahmāṇḍa yadi mukta haya
tabu alpa-hāni kṛṣṇera mane nāhi laya

SYNONYMS

taiche—similarly; *eka brahmāṇḍa*—one universe; *yadi*—if; *mukta haya*—becomes liberated; *tabu*—still; *alpa-hāni*—very little loss; *kṛṣṇera*—of Lord Kṛṣṇa; *mane*—the mind; *nāhi laya*—does not take it very seriously.

TRANSLATION

"In the same way, if one universe is vacated due to the living entities' having been liberated, that is a very little thing for Kṛṣṇa. He does not take it very seriously.

TEXT 175

অনন্ত ঐশ্বর্য কৃষ্ণের বৈকুণ্ঠাদি-ধাম।
তার গড়খাই—কারণাব্ধি যার নাম॥ ১৭৫॥

ananta aiśvarya kṛṣṇera vaikuṇṭhādi-dhāma
tāra gaḍa-khāi——kāraṇābdhi yāra nāma

SYNONYMS

ananta—unlimited; *aiśvarya*—opulence; *kṛṣṇera*—of Lord Kṛṣṇa; *vaikuṇṭha-ādi-dhāma*—innumerable Vaikuṇṭha planets; *tāra*—of Vaikuṇṭhaloka; *gaḍa-khāi*—surrounding water; *kāraṇa-abdhi*—Causal Ocean; *yāra*—of which; *nāma*—name.

TRANSLATION

"The entire spiritual world constitutes the unlimited opulence of Kṛṣṇa, and there are innumerable Vaikuṇṭha planets there. The Causal Ocean is considered the surrounding waters of Vaikuṇṭhaloka.

TEXT 176

তাতে ভাসে মায়া লঞা অনন্ত ব্রহ্মাণ্ড ।
গড়খাইতে ভাসে যেন রাই-পূর্ণ ভাণ্ড ॥ ১৭৬ ॥

tāte bhāse māyā lañā ananta brahmāṇḍa
gaḍa-khāite bhāse yena rāi-pūrṇa bhāṇḍa

SYNONYMS

tāte—in that water; *bhāse*—floats; *māyā*—the material energy; *lañā*—taking; *ananta*—unlimited; *brahmāṇḍa*—universes; *gaḍa-khāite*—in the surrounding water; *bhāse*—floats; *yena*—as if; *rāi-pūrṇa bhāṇḍa*—a pot filled with mustard seeds.

TRANSLATION

"Māyā and her unlimited material universes are situated in that Causal Ocean. Indeed, māyā appears to be floating like a pot filled with mustard seeds.

TEXT 177

তার এক রাই-নাশে হানি নাহি মানি ।
ঐছে এক অণ্ড-নাশে কৃষ্ণের নাহি হানি ॥ ১৭৭ ॥

tāra eka rāi-nāśe hāni nāhi māni
aiche eka aṇḍa-nāśe kṛṣṇera nāhi hāni

SYNONYMS

tāra—of it; *eka*—one; *rāi-nāśe*—loss of a mustard seed; *hāni*—loss; *nāhi*—does not; *māni*—notice; *aiche*—in that way; *eka*—one; *aṇḍa*—universe; *nāśe*—being lost; *kṛṣṇera*—of Kṛṣṇa; *nāhi hāni*—there is no loss.

TRANSLATION

"Of the millions of mustard seeds floating in that pot, if one seed is lost, the loss is not at all significant. Similarly, if one universe is lost, it is not significant to Lord Kṛṣṇa.

TEXT 178

সব ব্রহ্মাণ্ড সহ যদি 'মায়া'র হয় ক্ষয় ।
তথাপি না মানে কৃষ্ণ কিছু অপচয় ॥ ১৭৮ ॥

saba brahmāṇḍa saha yadi 'māyā'ra haya kṣaya
tathāpi nā māne kṛṣṇa kichu apacaya

SYNONYMS

saba brahmāṇḍa—all the universes; *saha*—with; *yadi*—if; *māyāra*—of the material energy; *haya kṣaya*—there is destruction; *tathāpi*—still; *nā*—not; *māne*—considers; *kṛṣṇa*—Lord Kṛṣṇa; *kichu*—any; *apacaya*—lost.

TRANSLATION

"To say nothing of one universal mustard seed, even if all the universes and the material energy [māyā] are destroyed, Kṛṣṇa does not even consider the loss.

TEXT 179

কোটি-কামধেনু-পতির ছাগী যৈছে মরে ।
ষড়ৈশ্বর্যপতি কৃষ্ণের মায়া কিবা করে ? ১৭৯ ॥

koṭi-kāmadhenu-patira chāgī yaiche mare
ṣaḍ-aiśvarya-pati kṛṣṇera māyā kibā kare?

SYNONYMS

koṭi—of millions; *kāma-dhenu*—of desire cows; *patira*—of the master; *chāgī*—one she-goat; *yaiche*—as; *mare*—dies; *ṣaṭ-aiśvarya-pati*—the master of six opulences; *kṛṣṇera*—of Kṛṣṇa; *māyā*—external energy; *kibā*—what; *kare*—can do.

TRANSLATION

"If a person possessing millions of wish-fulfilling cows loses one she-goat, he does not consider the loss. Kṛṣṇa owns all six opulences in full. If the entire material energy is destroyed, what does He lose?"

PURPORT

Śrīla Bhaktivinoda Ṭhākura, in clarifying verses 171-179, states that the meaning of these stanzas is very simple but that the purport is a little difficult to understand. Generally, conditioned souls forget Kṛṣṇa when they are enticed by the material, external energy. Consequently they are called *kṛṣṇa-bahirmukha*—bereft of their relationship with Kṛṣṇa. When such a living entity comes under the jurisdiction of the material energy, he is sent into one of the innumerable material universes created by the material energy to give a chance to conditioned souls to enjoy their desires in the material world. Being very eager to enjoy the fruits of their activities, conditioned souls become involved in the actions and reactions of material life. Consequently one has to enjoy and suffer the results of *karma.* However, if a conditioned soul becomes Kṛṣṇa conscious, the *karma* of his pious and impious activities is completely destroyed. Simply by becoming a devotee, one is bereft of all the reactions of *karma.* Similarly, simply by the desire of a devotee, a conditioned soul can attain liberation and transcend the results of *karma.* If everyone is liberated in this way, one may conclude that according to the sweet will of the devotee, the material world exists or does not exist. Ultimately, however, it is not the sweet will of the devotee but the will of the Supreme Personality of Godhead, who, if He so desires, can completely annihilate the material creation. There is no loss on His part. The owner of millions of cows does not consider the loss of one she-goat. Similarly, Lord Kṛṣṇa is the proprietor of both material and spiritual universes. The material world constitutes only one-fourth of His creative energy. If, according to the desire of the devotee, the Lord completely destroys the creation, He is so opulent that He will not mind the loss.

TEXT 180

জয় জয় জহ্যজামজিত দোষগৃভীতগুণাং
ত্বমসি যদাত্মনা সমবরুদ্ধসমস্তভগঃ ।
অগজগদোকসামখিলশক্ত্যববোধক তে
ক্বচিদজয়াত্মনা চ চরতোঽনুচরেন্নিগমঃ ॥" ১৮০ ॥

jaya jaya jahy ajām ajita doṣa-gṛbhīta-guṇāṁ
tvam asi yad ātmanā samavaruddha-samasta-bhagaḥ
aga-jagad-okasām akhila-śakty-avabodhaka te
kvacid ajayātmanā ca carato 'nucaren nigamaḥ"

SYNONYMS

jaya jaya—kindly exhibit Your glory; *jahi*—please conquer; *ajām*—nescience, *māyā; ajita*—O unconquerable one; *doṣa*—faulty; *gṛbhīta-guṇām*—by which the qualities are accepted; *tvam*—You; *asi*—are; *yat*—because; *ātmanā*—by Your internal potency; *samavaruddha*—possessing; *samasta-bhagaḥ*—all kinds of opulences; *aga*—nonmoving; *jagat*—moving; *okasām*—of the embodied living entities; *akhila*—all; *śakti*—of potencies; *avabodhaka*—master; *te*—You; *kvacit*—sometimes; *ajayā*—by the external energy; *ātmanā*—of Your self; *ca*—also; *carataḥ*—manifesting pastimes (by Your glance); *anucaret*—confirm; *nigamaḥ*—all the *Vedas.*

TRANSLATION

Śrī Caitanya Mahāprabhu continued, " 'O my Lord, O unconquerable one, O master of all potencies, please exhibit Your internal potency to conquer the nescience of all moving and inert living entities. Due to nescience, they accept all kinds of faulty things, thus provoking a fearful situation. O Lord, please show Your glories! You can do this very easily, for Your internal potency is beyond the external potency, and You are the reservoir of all opulence. You are also the demonstrator of the material potency. You are also always engaged in Your pastimes in the spiritual world. You exhibit Your reserved internal potency and sometimes exhibit the external potency by glancing over it. Thus You manifest Your pastimes. The Vedas confirm Your two potencies and accept both types of pastimes due to them.' "

PURPORT

This verse is taken from *Śrīmad-Bhāgavatam* (10.87.14). It is from the prayers of the *śruti-gaṇa,* the personified *Vedas* who glorify the Lord.

The almighty Personality of Godhead has three potencies—internal, external and marginal. When the conditioned souls are condemned due to forgetfulness, the external potency creates the material world and puts the living entities under its control. The three modes of material nature keep the living entity in a constant state of fear. *Bhayaṁ dvitīyābhiniveśataḥ.* The controlled conditioned soul is always fearful due to being controlled by the external potency; therefore the conditioned soul should always pray to the almighty Lord to conquer the external potency (*māyā*) so that she will no longer manifest her powers, which bind all living entities, moving and inert.

TEXT 181

এই মত সর্বভক্তের কহি' সব গুণ ।
সবারে বিদায় দিল করি' আলিঙ্গন ॥ ১৮১ ॥

ei mata sarva-bhaktera kahi' saba guṇa
sabāre vidāya dila kari' āliṅgana

SYNONYMS

ei mata—in this way; *sarva-bhaktera*—of all the devotees; *kahi'*—describing; *saba guṇa*—all the good qualities; *sabāre*—unto everyone; *vidāya dila*—bade farewell; *kari' āliṅgana*—embracing.

TRANSLATION

In this way, Śrī Caitanya Mahāprabhu described the good qualities of His devotees one after the other. He then embraced them and bade them farewell.

TEXT 182

প্রভুর বিচ্ছেদে ভক্ত করেন রোদন ।
ভক্তের বিচ্ছেদে প্রভুর বিষণ্ণ হৈল মন ॥ ১৮২ ॥

prabhura vicchede bhakta karena rodana
bhaktera vicchede prabhura viṣaṇṇa haila mana

SYNONYMS

prabhura—from Lord Śrī Caitanya Mahāprabhu; *vicchede*—by separation; *bhakta*—all the devotees; *karena*—do; *rodana*—crying; *bhaktera*—of the devotees; *vicchede*—by the separation; *prabhura*—of Lord Caitanya Mahāprabhu; *viṣaṇṇa*—morose; *haila*—became; *mana*—the mind.

TRANSLATION

Due to the impending separation from Śrī Caitanya Mahāprabhu, all the devotees began to cry. The Lord was also morose due to separation from the devotees.

TEXT 183

গদাধর-পণ্ডিত রহিলা প্রভুর পাশে ।
যমেশ্বরে প্রভু যাঁরে করাইলা আবাসে ॥ ১৮৩ ॥

gadādhara-paṇḍita rahilā prabhura pāśe
yameśvare prabhu yāṅre karāilā āvāse

SYNONYMS

gadādhara-paṇḍita—Gadādhara Paṇḍita; *rahilā*—remained; *prabhura pāśe*—along with Śrī Caitanya Mahāprabhu; *yameśvare*—at Yameśvara; *prabhu*—Śrī

Caitanya Mahāprabhu; *yāṅre*—unto whom; *karāilā*—made to take; *āvāse*—residence.

TRANSLATION

Gadādhara Paṇḍita remained with Śrī Caitanya Mahāprabhu, and he was given a place to live at Yameśvara.

PURPORT

Yameśvara is on the southwest side of the Jagannātha temple. Gadādhara Paṇḍita resided there, and there was a small garden and a sandy beach known as Yameśvara-ṭoṭā.

TEXTS 184-185

পুরী-গোসাঞি, জগদানন্দ, স্বরূপ-দামোদর।
দামোদর-পণ্ডিত, আর গোবিন্দ, কাশীশ্বর ॥ ১৮৪ ॥
এইসব-সঙ্গে প্রভু বৈসে নীলাচলে।
জগন্নাথ-দরশন নিত্য করে প্রাতঃকালে ॥ ১৮৫ ॥

purī-gosāñi, jagadānanda, svarūpa-dāmodara
dāmodara-paṇḍita, āra govinda, kāśīśvara

ei-saba-saṅge prabhu vaise nīlācale
jagannātha-daraśana nitya kare prātaḥ-kāle

SYNONYMS

purī-gosāñi—Paramānanda Purī; *jagadānanda*—Jagadānanda; *svarūpa-dāmodara*—Svarūpa Dāmodara; *dāmodara-paṇḍita*—Dāmodara Paṇḍita; *āra*—and; *govinda*—Govinda; *kāśīśvara*—Kāśīśvara; *ei-saba*—all these personalities; *saṅge*—accompanied by; *prabhu*—Śrī Caitanya Mahāprabhu; *vaise*—stays; *nīlācale*—at Jagannātha Purī; *jagannātha-daraśana*—seeing Lord Jagannātha; *nitya*—daily; *kare*—does; *prātaḥ-kāle*—in the morning.

TRANSLATION

Śrī Caitanya Mahāprabhu remained at Jagannātha Purī, Nīlācala, with Paramānanda Purī, Jagadānanda, Svarūpa Dāmodara, Dāmodara Paṇḍita, Govinda and Kāśīśvara. It was Śrī Caitanya Mahāprabhu's daily business to see Lord Jagannātha in the morning.

TEXT 186

প্রভু-পাশ আসি' সার্বভৌম এক দিন।
যোড়হাত করি' কিছু কৈল নিবেদন ॥ ১৮৬ ॥

prabhu-pāśa āsi' sārvabhauma eka dina
yoḍa-hāta kari' kichu kaila nivedana

SYNONYMS

prabhu-pāśa—in the presence of Śrī Caitanya Mahāprabhu; *āsi'*—coming; *sārvabhauma*—Sārvabhauma Bhaṭṭācārya; *eka dina*—one day; *yoḍa-hāta kari'*—with folded hands; *kichu*—some; *kaila*—did; *nivedana*—submission.

TRANSLATION

One day Sārvabhauma Bhaṭṭācārya came before Śrī Caitanya Mahāprabhu with folded hands and submitted a request.

TEXT 187

এবে সব বৈষ্ণব গৌড়দেশে চলি' গেল ।
এবে প্রভুর নিমন্ত্রণে অবসর হৈল ॥ ১৮৭ ॥

ebe saba vaiṣṇava gauḍa-deśe cali' gela
ebe prabhura nimantraṇe avasara haila

SYNONYMS

ebe—now; *saba*—all; *vaiṣṇava*—devotees; *gauḍa-deśe*—to Bengal; *cali' gela*—have returned; *ebe*—now; *prabhura*—of Lord Śrī Caitanya Mahāprabhu; *nimantraṇe*—for invitations; *avasara haila*—there is a chance.

TRANSLATION

Since all the Vaiṣṇavas had returned to Bengal, there was a good chance that the Lord would accept an invitation.

TEXT 188

এবে মোর ঘরে ভিক্ষা করহ 'মাস' ভরি' ।
প্রভু কহে,—ধর্ম নহে, করিতে না পারি ॥ ১৮৮ ॥

ebe mora ghare bhikṣā karaha 'māsa' bhari'
prabhu kahe,—dharma nahe, karite nā pāri

SYNONYMS

ebe—now; *mora ghare*—at my place; *bhikṣā*—lunch; *karaha*—accept; *māsa bhari'*—for one month; *prabhu kahe*—Śrī Caitanya Mahāprabhu replied; *dharma*—religious principle; *nahe*—it is not; *karite*—to do; *nā pāri*—I am unable.

TRANSLATION

Sārvabhauma Bhaṭṭācārya said, "Please accept my invitation for lunch for one month." The Lord replied, "That is not possible because it is against the religious principles of a sannyāsī."

TEXT 189

সার্বভৌম কহে,—ভিক্ষা করহ বিশ দিন ।
প্রভু কহে,—এহ নহে যতিধর্ম-চিহ্ন ॥ ১৮৯ ॥

sārvabhauma kahe,——bhikṣā karaha viśa dina
prabhu kahe,——eha nahe yati-dharma-cihna

SYNONYMS

sārvabhauma kahe—Sārvabhauma Bhaṭṭācārya said; *bhikṣā karaha*—accept lunch; *viśa dina*—for twenty days; *prabhu kahe*—Lord Śrī Caitanya Mahāprabhu said; *eha nahe*—this is not; *yati-dharma-cihna*—the symptom of a person in the renounced order of life.

TRANSLATION

Sārvabhauma then said, "Please accept the invitation for twenty days," but Śrī Caitanya Mahāprabhu replied, "It is not a religious principle of the renounced order."

TEXT 190

সার্বভৌম কহে পুনঃ,—দিন 'পঞ্চদশ' ।
প্রভু কহে,—তোমার ভিক্ষা 'এক' দিবস ॥ ১৯০ ॥

sārvabhauma kahe punaḥ,——dina 'pañca-daśa'
prabhu kahe,——tomāra bhikṣā 'eka' divasa

SYNONYMS

sārvabhauma kahe—Sārvabhauma Bhaṭṭācārya said; *punaḥ*—again; *dina pañca-daśa*—fifteen days; *prabhu kahe*—the Lord replied; *tomāra bhikṣā*—lunch at your place; *eka divasa*—only one day.

TRANSLATION

When Sārvabhauma requested Caitanya Mahāprabhu to accept lunch for fifteen days, the Lord said, "I shall accept lunch at your place for one day only."

TEXT 191

তবে সার্বভৌম প্রভুর চরণে ধরিয়া ।
'দশদিন ভিক্ষা কর' কহে বিনতি করিয়া ॥ ১৯১ ॥

tabe sārvabhauma prabhura caraṇe dhariyā
'daśa-dina bhikṣā kara' kahe vinati kariyā

SYNONYMS

tabe—thereafter; *sārvabhauma*—Sārvabhauma Bhaṭṭācārya; *prabhura*—of Lord Śrī Caitanya Mahāprabhu; *caraṇe dhariyā*—catching the lotus feet; *daśa-dina*—for ten days; *bhikṣā kara*—accept lunch; *kahe*—says; *vinati kariyā*—with great submission.

TRANSLATION

Sārvabhauma Bhaṭṭācārya then caught hold of the Lord's lotus feet and submissively begged, "Please accept lunch for at least ten days."

TEXT 192

প্রভু ক্রমে ক্রমে পাঁচ-দিন ঘাটাইল ।
পাঁচ-দিন তাঁর ভিক্ষা নিয়ম করিল ॥ ১৯২ ॥

prabhu krame krame pāṅca-dina ghāṭāila
pāṅca-dina tāṅra bhikṣā niyama karila

SYNONYMS

prabhu—Śrī Caitanya Mahāprabhu; *krame krame*—gradually; *pāṅca-dina*—to five days; *ghāṭāila*—reduced; *pāñca-dina*—for five days; *tāṅra*—his; *bhikṣā*—invitation for lunch; *niyama karila*—accepted regularly.

TRANSLATION

In this way, by and by, Śrī Caitanya Mahāprabhu reduced the duration to five days. Thus for five days He regularly accepted the invitation to lunch.

TEXT 193

তবে সার্বভৌম করে আর নিবেদন ।
তোমার সঙ্গে সন্ন্যাসী আছে দশজন ॥ ১৯৩ ॥

tabe sārvabhauma kare āra nivedana
tomāra saṅge sannyāsī āche daśa-jana

SYNONYMS

tabe—thereafter; *sārvabhauma*—Sārvabhauma Bhaṭṭācārya; *kare*—does; *āra*—another; *nivedana*—submission; *tomāra saṅge*—with You; *sannyāsī*—in the renounced order of life; *āche*—there are; *daśa-jana*—ten persons.

TRANSLATION

After this, Sārvabhauma Bhaṭṭācārya said, "My Lord, there are ten sannyāsīs with You."

PURPORT

A *sannyāsī* should not cook food for himself or accept an invitation to eat at a devotee's house continuously for many days. Śrī Caitanya Mahāprabhu was very kind and affectionate toward His devotees, yet He would not accept a long invitation at Sārvabhauma's house. Out of affection, He accepted only five days in the month. The ten *sannyāsīs* living with the Lord were (1) Paramānanda Purī, (2) Svarūpa Dāmodara, (3) Brahmānanda Purī, (4) Brahmānanda Bhāratī, (5) Viṣṇu Purī, (6) Keśava Purī, (7) Kṛṣṇānanda Purī, (8) Nṛsiṁha Tīrtha, (9) Sukhānanda Purī and (10) Satyānanda Bhāratī.

TEXT 194

পুরী-গোসাঞির ভিক্ষা পাঁচদিন মোর ঘরে ।
পূর্বে আমি কহিয়াছোঁ তোমার গোচরে ॥ ১৯৪ ॥

purī-gosāñira bhikṣā pāṅca-dina mora ghare
pūrve āmi kahiyāchoṅ tomāra gocare

SYNONYMS

purī-gosāñira—of Paramānanda Purī; *bhikṣā*—invitation for lunch; *pāṅca-dina*—five days; *mora ghare*—at my home; *pūrve*—previously; *āmi*—I; *kahiyāchoṅ*—mentioned; *tomāra gocare*—it is known to you.

TRANSLATION

Sārvabhauma Bhaṭṭācārya then submitted that Paramānanda Purī Gosvāmī should accept a five-day invitation at his place. This was settled before the Lord.

TEXT 195

দামোদর-স্বরূপ, এই বান্ধব আমার ।
কভু তোমার সঙ্গে যাবে, কভু একেশ্বর ॥ ১৯৫ ॥

dāmodara-svarūpa,——ei bāndhava āmāra
kabhu tomāra saṅge yābe, kabhu ekeśvara

SYNONYMS

dāmodara-svarūpa—Svarūpa Dāmodara Gosvāmī; *ei*—this; *bāndhava āmāra*—my very intimate friend; *kabhu*—sometimes; *tomāra saṅge*—with You; *yābe*—will come; *kabhu*—sometimes; *ekeśvara*—alone.

TRANSLATION

Sārvabhauma Bhaṭṭācārya said, "Dāmodara Svarūpa is my intimate friend. He will come sometimes with You and sometimes alone.

TEXT 196

আর অষ্ট সন্ন্যাসীর ভিক্ষা দুই দুই দিবসে ।
এক একদিন, এক এক জনে পূর্ণ হইল মাসে ॥১৯৬॥

āra aṣṭa sannyāsīra bhikṣā dui dui divase
eka eka-dina, eka eka jane pūrṇa ha-ila māse

SYNONYMS

āra—other; *aṣṭa*—eight; *sannyāsīra*—of *sannyāsīs; bhikṣā*—invitation for lunch; *dui dui divase*—two days each; *eka eka-dina*—on each day; *eka eka jane*—one person; *pūrṇa*—filled; *ha-ila*—will be; *māse*—the month.

TRANSLATION

"The other eight sannyāsīs will accept invitations for two days each. In this way there will be engagements for each and every day during the entire month.

PURPORT

For the entire month consisting of thirty days, Śrī Caitanya Mahāprabhu would visit five days, Paramānanda Purī Gosvāmī five days, Svarūpa Dāmodara four days, and the eight other *sannyāsīs* two days each. In this way the thirty days of the month were completed.

TEXT 197

বহুত সন্ন্যাসী যদি আইসে এক ঠাঞি ।
সম্মান করিতে নারি, অপরাধ পাই ॥ ১৯৭ ॥

bahuta sannyāsī yadi āise eka ṭhāñi
sammāna karite nāri, aparādha pāi

SYNONYMS

bahuta sannyāsī—many *sannyāsīs; yadi*—if; *āise*—come; *eka ṭhāñi*—together; *sammāna karite nāri*—I cannot receive them properly; *aparādha pāi*—I shall be an offender.

TRANSLATION

"If all the sannyāsīs come together, it would not be possible for me to pay them proper respects. Therefore I would be an offender.

TEXT 198

তুমিহ নিজ-ছায়ে আসিবে মোর ঘর ।
কভু সঙ্গে আসিবেন স্বরূপ-দামোদর ॥ ১৯৮ ॥

tumiha nija-chāye āsibe mora ghara
kabhu saṅge āsibena svarūpa-dāmodara

SYNONYMS

tumiha—You; *nija-chāye*—alone; *āsibe*—will come; *mora ghara*—to my place; *kabhu*—sometimes; *saṅge*—with You; *āsibena*—will come; *svarūpa-dāmodara*—Svarūpa Dāmodara Gosvāmī.

TRANSLATION

"Sometimes You will come alone to my place, and sometimes You will be accompanied by Svarūpa Dāmodara."

TEXT 199

প্রভুর ইঙ্গিত পাঞা আনন্দিত মন ।
সেই দিন মহাপ্রভুর কৈল নিমন্ত্রণ ॥ ১৯৯ ॥

prabhura iṅgita pāñā ānandita mana
sei dina mahāprabhura kaila nimantraṇa

SYNONYMS

prabhura—of Śrī Caitanya Mahāprabhu; *iṅgita*—acceptance; *pāñā*—receiving; *ānandita*—very happy; *mana*—mind; *sei dina*—on that day; *mahāprabhura*—of Śrī Caitanya Mahāprabhu; *kaila*—made; *nimantraṇa*—invitation.

TRANSLATION

Having this arrangement confirmed by Śrī Caitanya Mahāprabhu, the Bhaṭṭācārya became very glad and immediately invited the Lord to his house on that very day.

TEXT 200

'ষাঠীর মাতা' নাম, ভট্টাচার্যের গৃহিণী ।
প্রভুর মহাভক্ত তেঁহো, স্নেহেতে জননী ॥ ২০০ ॥

'ṣāṭhīra mātā' nāma, bhaṭṭācāryera gṛhiṇī
prabhura mahā-bhakta teṅho, snehete jananī

SYNONYMS

ṣāṭhīra mātā—the mother of Ṣāṭhī; *nāma*—named; *bhaṭṭācāryera gṛhiṇī*—the wife of Sārvabhauma Bhaṭṭācārya; *prabhura*—of Śrī Caitanya Mahāprabhu; *mahā-bhakta*—a great devotee; *teṅho*—she; *snehete*—in affection; *jananī*—just like a mother.

TRANSLATION

Sārvabhauma Bhaṭṭācārya's wife was known as the mother of Ṣāṭhī. She was a great devotee of Śrī Caitanya Mahāprabhu, and she was affectionate like a mother.

TEXT 201

ঘরে আসি' ভট্টাচার্য তাঁরে আজ্ঞা দিল ।
আনন্দে ষাঠীর মাতা পাক চড়াইল ॥ ২০১ ॥

ghare āsi' bhaṭṭācārya tāṅre ājñā dila
ānande ṣāṭhīra mātā pāka caḍāila

SYNONYMS

ghare āsi'—coming home; *bhaṭṭācārya*—Sārvabhauma Bhaṭṭācārya; *tāṅre*—her; *ājñā dila*—ordered; *ānande*—with great satisfaction; *ṣāṭhīra mātā*—the mother of Ṣāṭhī; *pāka caḍāila*—began cooking.

TRANSLATION

After returning to his home, Sārvabhauma Bhaṭṭācārya gave orders to his wife, and his wife, known as Ṣāṭhīra Mātā, the mother of Ṣāṭhī, began cooking with great pleasure.

TEXT 202

ভট্টাচার্যের গৃহে সব দ্রব্য আছে ভরি'।
যেবা শাকফলাদিক, আনাইল আহরি' ॥ ২০২ ॥

bhaṭṭācāryera gṛhe saba dravya āche bhari'
yebā śāka-phalādika, ānāila āhari'

SYNONYMS

bhaṭṭācāryera gṛhe—at the house of Sārvabhauma Bhaṭṭācārya; *saba dravya*—all kinds of ingredients; *āche*—there are; *bhari'*—filling; *yebā*—whatever; *śāka*—spinach; *phala-ādika*—fruits and so on; *ānāila*—he brought; *āhari'*—collecting.

TRANSLATION

At Sārvabhauma Bhaṭṭācārya's house, there was always a full stock of food. Whatever spinach, vegetables, fruit and so on were required, he collected and brought back home.

TEXT 203

আপনি ভট্টাচার্য করে পাকের সব কর্ম।
ষাঠীর মাতা– বিচক্ষণা, জানে পাক-মর্ম ॥ ২০৩ ॥

āpani bhaṭṭācārya kare pākera saba karma
ṣāṭhīra mātā——vicakṣaṇā, jāne pāka-marma

SYNONYMS

āpani—personally; *bhaṭṭācārya*—Sārvabhauma Bhaṭṭācārya; *kare*—arranges; *pākera*—of cooking; *saba karma*—all activities; *ṣāṭhīra mātā*—the mother of Ṣāṭhī; *vicakṣaṇā*—very experienced; *jāne*—knows; *pāka-marma*—how to cook.

TRANSLATION

Sārvabhauma Bhaṭṭācārya personally began to help his wife cook. His wife, the mother of Ṣāṭhī, was very experienced, and she knew how to cook nicely.

TEXT 204

পাকশালার দক্ষিণে—দুই ভোগালয়।
এক-ঘরে শালগ্রামের ভোগ-সেবা হয় ॥ ২০৪ ॥

pāka-śālāra dakṣiṇe——dui bhogālaya
eka-ghare śālagrāmera bhoga-sevā haya

SYNONYMS

pāka-śālāra dakṣiṇe—on the southern side of the kitchen; *dui bhoga-ālaya*—two rooms for offering food; *eka-ghare*—in one room; *śālagrāmera*—of Lord Śālagrāma; *bhoga-sevā*—offering of food; *haya*—there is.

TRANSLATION

On the southern side of the kitchen were two rooms for offering food, and in one of them the food was offered to Śālagrāma Nārāyaṇa.

PURPORT

Among the followers of the Vedic way, *śālagrāma-śilā,* the *vigraha* of Nārāyaṇa, is worshiped in the form of a stone ball. In India, every *brāhmaṇa* still worships the *śālagrāma-śilā* in his home. The *vaiśyas* and *kṣatriyas* may also engage in this worship, but it is compulsory in the house of a *brāhmaṇa.*

TEXT 205

আর ঘর মহাপ্রভুর ভিক্ষার লাগিয়া।
নিভৃতে করিয়াছে ভট্ট নূতন করিয়া॥ ২০৫ ॥

āra ghara mahāprabhura bhikṣāra lāgiyā
nibhṛte kariyāche bhaṭṭa nūtana kariyā

SYNONYMS

āra ghara—the other room; *mahāprabhura*—of Śrī Caitanya Mahāprabhu; *bhikṣāra lāgiyā*—for taking lunch; *nibhṛte kariyāche*—constructed in a solitary place; *bhaṭṭa*—Sārvabhauma Bhaṭṭācārya; *nūtana kariyā*—newly done.

TRANSLATION

The other room was for Śrī Caitanya Mahāprabhu's lunch. The Lord's lunch room was very secluded, and it was newly constructed by Bhaṭṭācārya.

TEXT 206

বাহ্যে এক দ্বার তার, প্রভু প্রবেশিতে।
পাকশালার এক দ্বার অন্ন পরিবেশিতে॥ ২০৬॥

bāhye eka dvāra tāra, prabhu praveśite
pāka-śālāra eka dvāra anna pariveśite

SYNONYMS

bāhye—outside; *eka dvāra*—one door; *tāra*—of this room; *prabhu praveśite*—for the entrance of Lord Śrī Caitanya Mahāprabhu; *pāka-śālāra*—of the kitchen; *eka dvāra*—another door; *anna*—food; *pariveśite*—to serve.

TRANSLATION

The room was so constructed that there was only one door as an entrance from the outside for Śrī Caitanya Mahāprabhu. There was another door attached to the kitchen, and it was through this door that the food was brought.

TEXT 207

বত্তিশা-আঠিয়া কলার আঙ্গটিয়া পাতে ।
তিন-মান তণ্ডুলের উভারিল ভাতে ॥ ২০৭ ॥

battiśā-āṭhiyā kalāra āṅgaṭiyā pāte
tina-māna taṇḍulera ubhārila bhāte

SYNONYMS

battiśā-āṭhiyā—named *battiśā-āṭhiyā; kalāra*—of the banana tree; *āṅgaṭiyā*—without being divided; *pāte*—on a leaf; *tina*—three; *māna*—*mānas* (a certain weight); *taṇḍulera*—of rice; *ubhārila*—poured; *bhāte*—cooked rice.

TRANSLATION

First, three mānas of cooked rice—almost six pounds—was poured on a big banana leaf.

PURPORT

This is the beginning of a description of the food prepared for Śrī Caitanya Mahāprabhu. This description is given by Kavirāja Gosvāmī, who, it is assumed, was an expert cook who knew both how to prepare and how to serve food.

TEXT 208

পীত-সুগন্ধি-ঘৃতে অন্ন সিক্ত কৈল ।
চারিদিকে পাতে ঘৃত বহিয়া চলিল ॥ ২০৮ ॥

pīta-sugandhi-ghṛte anna sikta kaila
cāri-dike pāte ghṛta vahiyā calila

SYNONYMS

pīta—yellowish; *su-gandhi*—fragrant; *ghṛte*—with clarified butter; *anna*—rice; *sikta*—mixed; *kaila*—made; *cāri-dike*—on all sides; *pāte*—the leaf; *ghṛta*—the clarified butter; *vahiyā calila*—began to flood.

TRANSLATION

Then, the whole stack of rice was mixed with so much yellowish and fragrant clarified butter that it began to overflow the leaf.

TEXT 209

কেয়াপত্র-কলাখোলা-ডোঙ্গা সারি সারি ।
চারিদিকে ধরিয়াছে নানা ব্যঞ্জন ভরি' ॥ ২০৯ ॥

keyāpatra-kalākholā-ḍoṅgā sāri sāri
cāri-dike dhariyāche nānā vyañjana bhari'

SYNONYMS

keyā-patra—the leaf of the *keyā* plant; *kalā-kholā*—the skin of the banana tree; *ḍoṅgā*—pots; *sāri sāri*—one after another; *cāri-dike*—on all sides; *dhariyāche*—were holding; *nānā*—various; *vyañjana*—cooked vegetables; *bhari'*—filled.

TRANSLATION

There were a number of pots made of the bark of banana trees and the leaves of the keyā plant. These pots were filled with various cooked vegetables and placed on all sides of the leaf.

TEXT 210

দশপ্রকার শাক, নিম্ব-তিক্ত-সুখ্‌ত-ঝোল ।
মরিচের ঝাল, ছানাবড়া, বড়ি ঘোল ॥ ২১০ ॥

daśa-prakāra śāka, nimba-tikta-sukhta-jhola
maricera jhāla, chānā-baḍā, baḍi ghola

SYNONYMS

daśa-prakāra śāka—spinach of ten varieties; *nimba-tikta-sukhta-jhola*—a soup called *sukhta,* made with bitter *nimba* leaf; *maricera jhāla*—a pungent preparation made with black pepper; *chānā-baḍā*—a mild cake made of fried curd; *baḍi ghola*—buttermilk with small pieces of fried *dahl.*

TRANSLATION

There were about ten kinds of spinach, a soup called sukhta, which was made with bitter nimba leaves, a pungent preparation made with black pepper, a mild cake made of fried curd, and buttermilk mixed with small fried pieces of dahl.

TEXT 211

দুগ্ধতুম্বী, দুগ্ধকুষ্মাণ্ড, বেসর, লাফ্‌রা ।
মোচাঘণ্ট, মোচাভাজা, বিবিধ শাক্‌রা ॥ ২১১ ॥

dugdha-tumbī, dugdha-kuṣmāṇḍa, vesara, lāphrā
mocā-ghaṇṭa, mocā-bhājā, vividha śākrā

SYNONYMS

dugdha-tumbī—squash cooked with milk; *dugdha-kuṣmāṇḍa*—pumpkin cooked with milk; *vesara*—a preparation made from chick-pea flour; *lāphrā*—a combination of several vegetables; *mocā-ghaṇṭa*—boiled banana flowers; *mocā-bhājā*—fried banana flowers; *vividha*—various; *śākrā*—vegetables.

TRANSLATION

There were preparations of dugdha-tumbī, dugdha-kuṣmāṇḍa, vesara, lāphrā, mocā-ghaṇṭa, mocā-bhājā and other vegetables.

TEXT 212

বৃদ্ধকুষ্মাণ্ডবড়ীর ব্যঞ্জন অপার ।
ফুলবড়ী-ফল-মূল বিবিধ প্রকার ॥ ২১২ ॥

vṛddha-kuṣmāṇḍa-baḍīra vyañjana apāra
phulabaḍī-phala-mūla vividha prakāra

SYNONYMS

vṛddha-kuṣmāṇḍa-baḍīra—of small pieces of fried dahl mixed with ripe pumpkin; *vyañjana*—vegetables; *apāra*—unlimited; *phula-baḍī*—small fried pieces of another kind of *dahl; phala*—fruits; *mūla*—roots; *vividha prakāra*—of different varieties.

TRANSLATION

There were unlimited quantities of vṛddha-kuṣmāṇḍa-baḍī, phula-baḍī, fruits and various roots.

TEXT 213

নব-নিম্বপত্র-সহ ভৃষ্ট-বার্তাকী ।
ফুলবড়ী, পটোল-ভাজা, কুষ্মাণ্ড-মান-চাকী ॥ ২১৩ ॥

nava-nimbapatra-saha bhṛṣṭa-vārtākī
phula-baḍī, paṭola-bhājā, kuṣmāṇḍa-māna-cākī

SYNONYMS

nava—newly grown; *nimba-patra*—*nimba* leaves; *saha*—along with; *bhṛṣṭa-vārtākī*—fried eggplant; *phula-baḍī*—light *baḍī; paṭola-bhājā*—fried *paṭola* vegetable; *kuṣmāṇḍa*—of pumpkin; *māna*—of squash; *cākī*—rounds.

TRANSLATION

Other preparations included eggplant mixed with newly grown nimba leaves fried together, light baḍī, fried paṭola, and fried rounds of squash and pumpkin.

TEXT 214

ভৃষ্ট-মাষ-মুদ্গ-সূপ অমৃত নিন্দয় ।
মধুরাম্ল, বড়াম্লাদি অম্ল পাঁচ ছয় ॥ ২১৪ ॥

bhṛṣṭa-māṣa-mudga-sūpa amṛta nindaya
madhurāmla, baḍāmlādi amla pāṅca chaya

SYNONYMS

bhṛṣṭa—fried; *māṣa*—urd *dahl; mudga*—mung *dahl; sūpa*—soup; *amṛta*—nectar; *nindaya*—defeating; *madhura-amla*—sweet chutney; *baḍa-amla*—sour preparation made with fried *dahl; ādi*—and so on; *amla*—sour; *pāṅca chaya*—five or six kinds.

TRANSLATION

There was a soup made with fried urad dahl and mung dahl, defeating nectar. There were also sweet chutney and five or six kinds of sour preparations, beginning with baḍāmla.

TEXT 215

মুদ্গবড়া, মাষবড়া, কলাবড়া মিষ্ট ।
ক্ষীরপুলি, নারিকেল-পুলী আর যত পিষ্ট ॥ ২১৫ ॥

mudga-baḍā, māṣa-baḍā, kalā-baḍā miṣṭa
kṣīra-puli, nārikela-pulī āra yata piṣṭa

SYNONYMS

mudga-baḍā—fried cakes made of mung *dahl; māṣa-baḍā*—fried cakes made of *urd dahl; kalā-baḍā*—fried cakes made of banana; *miṣṭa*—very sweet; *kṣīra-puli*—cakes made with sweet rice; *nārikela-pulī*—coconut cake; *āra*—and; *yata*—varieties of; *piṣṭa*—cakes.

TRANSLATION

There were bharats made of mung dahl, of urd dahl and of sweet bananas, and there was sweet rice cake, coconut cake and various other cakes.

TEXT 216

কাঁজিবড়া, দুগ্ধ-চিড়া, দুগ্ধ-লক্লকী ।
আর যত পিঠা কৈল, কহিতে না শকি ॥ ২১৬ ॥

kāṅji-baḍā, dugdha-ciḍā, dugdha-laklakī
āra yata piṭhā kaila, kahite nā śaki

SYNONYMS

kāñji-baḍā—cakes made with sour rice-water; *dugdha-ciḍā*—sweet rice mixed with milk; *dugdha-laklakī*—another preparation of milk and cakes to be licked up; *āra*—and; *yata*—various types of; *piṭhā*—cakes; *kaila*—made; *kahite*—to describe; *nā śaki*—I am not able.

TRANSLATION

There was kāṅji-baḍā, dugdha-ciḍā, dugdha-laklakī and various cakes, which I am unable to describe.

TEXT 217

ঘৃত-সিক্ত পরমান্ন, মৃৎকুণ্ডিকা ভরি' ।
চাঁপাকলা-ঘনদুগ্ধ-আম্র তাহা ধরি ॥ ২১৭ ॥

ghṛta-sikta paramānna, mṛt-kuṇḍikā bhari'
cāṅpākalā-ghanadugdha-āmra tāhā dhari

SYNONYMS

ghṛta-sikta parama-anna—sweet rice mixed with ghee; *mṛt-kuṇḍikā bhari'*—filling an earthen pot; *cāṅpā-kalā*—a kind of banana; *ghana-dugdha*—condensed milk; *āmra*—mango pulp; *tāhā*—that; *dhari*—including.

TRANSLATION

Sweet rice mixed with ghee was poured into an earthen pot and mixed with cāṅpā-kalā, condensed milk and mango.

TEXT 218

রসালা-মথিত দধি, সন্দেশ অপার ।
গৌড়ে উৎকলে যত ভক্ষ্যের প্রকার ॥ ২১৮ ॥

rasālā-mathita dadhi, sandeśa apāra
gauḍe utkale yata bhakṣyera prakāra

SYNONYMS

rasālā—delicious; *mathita*—churned; *dadhi*—curd; *sandeśa*—a sweetmeat; *apāra*—unlimited; *gauḍe*—in Bengal; *utkale*—in Orissa; *yata*—all; *bhakṣyera*—of eatables; *prakāra*—kinds.

TRANSLATION

Other preparations included a very delicious churned curd and a variety of sandeśa sweetmeats. Indeed, all the various eatables available in Bengal and Orissa were prepared.

TEXT 219

শ্রদ্ধা করি' ভট্টাচার্য সব করাইল ।
শুভ্র-পীঠোপরি সূক্ষ্ম বসন পাতিল ॥ ২১৯ ॥

śraddhā kari' bhaṭṭācārya saba karāila
śubhra-pīṭhopari sūkṣma vasana pātila

SYNONYMS

śraddhā kari'—with great respect; *bhaṭṭācārya*—Sārvabhauma Bhaṭṭācārya; *saba karāila*—had them all prepared; *śubhra*—white; *pīṭha*—a wooden platform; *upari*—over; *sūkṣma*—fine; *vasana*—cloth; *pātila*—spread.

TRANSLATION

Thus Bhaṭṭācārya prepared a great variety of food and spread a fine cloth over a white wooden platform.

TEXT 220

দুই পাশে সুগন্ধি শীতল জল-ঝারী ।
অন্ন-ব্যঞ্জনোপরি দিল তুলসী-মঞ্জরী ॥ ২২০ ॥

dui pāśe sugandhi śītala jala-jhārī
anna-vyañjanopari dila tulasī-mañjarī

SYNONYMS

dui pāśe—on two sides; *su-gandhi*—nicely scented; *śītala*—cold; *jala-jhārī*—pitchers of water; *anna-vyañjana-upari*—over the rice and vegetables; *dila*—placed; *tulasī-mañjarī*—flowers of *tulasī.*

TRANSLATION

On two sides of the stack of food were pitchers filled with scented cold water. The flowers of the tulasī tree were placed above the mound of rice.

TEXT 221

অমৃত-গুটিকা, পিঠা-পানা আনাইল।
জগন্নাথ-প্রসাদ সব পৃথক্ ধরিল ॥ ২২১ ॥

amṛta-guṭikā, piṭhā-pānā ānāila
jagannātha-prasāda saba pṛthak dharila

SYNONYMS

amṛta-guṭikā—the sweet named *amṛta-guṭikā; piṭhā-pānā*—cakes and sweet rice; *ānāila*—brought; *jagannātha-prasāda*—remnants of the food of Lord Jagannātha; *saba*—all; *pṛthak dharila*—kept separately.

TRANSLATION

Sārvabhauma Bhaṭṭācārya also included several types of food that had been offered to Lord Jagannātha. This included sweetballs known as amṛta-guṭikā, sweet rice and cakes. All these were kept separately.

PURPORT

Although the remnants of food left by Jagannātha were brought into Bhaṭṭācārya's house, they were kept separate from the preparations he had made at his home. It sometimes happens that *prasāda* is mixed with a larger quantity of food and then distributed, but in this case we find that Sārvabhauma Bhaṭṭācārya kept the *jagannātha-prasāda* separate. He kept it aside particularly for the satisfaction of Śrī Caitanya Mahāprabhu.

TEXT 222

হেনকালে মহাপ্রভু মধ্যাহ্ন করিয়া।
একলে আইল তাঁর হৃদয় জানিয়া ॥ ২২২ ॥

hena-kāle mahāprabhu madhyāhna kariyā
ekale āila tāṅra hṛdaya jāniyā

SYNONYMS

hena-kāle—at this time; *mahāprabhu*—Śrī Caitanya Mahāprabhu; *madhyāhna kariyā*—finishing His midday duties; *ekale*—alone; *āila*—came; *tāṅra*—of Sārvabhauma Bhaṭṭācārya; *hṛdaya*—the heart; *jāniyā*—knowing.

TRANSLATION

When everything was ready, Śrī Caitanya Mahāprabhu came there alone after finishing His midday duties. He knew the heart of Sārvabhauma Bhaṭṭācārya.

TEXT 223

ভট্টাচার্য কৈল তবে পাদ প্রক্ষালন ।
ঘরের ভিতরে গেলা করিতে ভোজন ॥ ২২৩ ॥

bhaṭṭācārya kaila tabe pāda prakṣālana
gharera bhitare gelā karite bhojana

SYNONYMS

bhaṭṭācārya—Sārvabhauma Bhaṭṭācārya; *kaila*—performed; *tabe*—thereafter; *pāda prakṣālana*—washing the feet; *gharera bhitare*—within the room; *gelā*—entered; *karite bhojana*—to take lunch.

TRANSLATION

After Sārvabhauma Bhaṭṭācārya washed the Lord's feet, the Lord entered the room to take His lunch.

TEXT 224

অন্নাদি দেখিয়া প্রভু বিস্মিত হঞা ।
ভট্টাচার্যে কহে কিছু ভঙ্গি করিয়া ॥ ২২৪ ॥

annādi dekhiyā prabhu vismita hañā
bhaṭṭācārye kahe kichu bhaṅgi kariyā

SYNONYMS

anna-ādi dekhiyā—seeing the arrangement of food; *prabhu*—Śrī Caitanya Mahāprabhu; *vismita hañā*—being astonished; *bhaṭṭācārye kahe*—said to Bhaṭṭācārya; *kichu*—some; *bhaṅgi*—gesture; *kariyā*—making.

TRANSLATION

Śrī Caitanya Mahāprabhu was a little astonished to see the gorgeous arrangement, and, gesturing, He spoke to Sārvabhauma Bhaṭṭācārya.

TEXT 225

অলৌকিক এই সব অন্ন-ব্যঞ্জন ।
দুই প্রহর ভিতরে কৈছে হইল রন্ধন ? ২২৫ ॥

alaukika ei saba anna-vyañjana
dui prahara bhitare kaiche ha-ila randhana?

SYNONYMS

alaukika—uncommon; *ei*—this; *saba*—all; *anna-vyañjana*—rice and vegetables; *dui prahara bhitare*—within six hours; *kaiche*—how; *ha-ila randhana*—cooking was finished.

TRANSLATION

"This is most uncommon! How was this arrangement of rice and vegetables finished within six hours?

TEXT 226

শত চুলায় শত জন পাক যদি করে ।
তবু শীঘ্র এত দ্রব্য রান্ধিতে না পারে ॥ ২২৬ ॥

śata culāya śata jana pāka yadi kare
tabu śīghra eta dravya rāndhite nā pāre

SYNONYMS

śata culāya—in one hundred ovens; *śata jana*—one hundred men; *pāka yadi kare*—if engaged in cooking; *tabu*—still; *śīghra*—so soon; *eta dravya*—so many preparations; *rāndhite nā pāre*—could not cook.

TRANSLATION

"Even a hundred men cooking on a hundred ovens could not possibly finish all these preparations within so short a time.

TEXT 227

কৃষ্ণের ভোগ লাগাঞাছ,—অনুমান করি ।
উপরে দেখিয়ে যাতে তুলসী-মঞ্জরী ॥ ২২৭ ॥

kṛṣṇera bhoga lāgāñācha,——anumāna kari
upare dekhiye yāte tulasī-mañjarī

SYNONYMS

kṛṣṇera bhoga lāgāñācha—you have offered to Kṛṣṇa; *anumāna kari*—I hope; *upare*—upon the food; *dekhiye*—I see; *yāte*—since; *tulasī-mañjarī*—flowers of the *tulasī* tree.

TRANSLATION

"I hope the food has already been offered to Kṛṣṇa, since I see there are tulasī flowers over the plates.

TEXT 228

ভাগ্যবান্ তুমি, সফল তোমার উদ্যোগ ।
রাধাকৃষ্ণে লাগাঞাছ এতাদৃশ ভোগ ॥ ২২৮ ॥

bhāgyavān tumi, saphala tomāra udyoga
rādhā-kṛṣṇe lāgāñācha etādṛśa bhoga

SYNONYMS

bhāgyavān tumi—you are fortunate; *sa-phala*—successful; *tomāra*—your; *udyoga*—endeavor; *rādhā-kṛṣṇe*—unto Their Lordships Rādhā and Kṛṣṇa; *lāgāñācha*—you offered; *etādṛśa*—such; *bhoga*—food.

TRANSLATION

"You are most fortunate, and your endeavor is successful, for you have offered such wonderful food to Rādhā-Kṛṣṇa.

TEXT 229

অন্নের সৌরভ্য, বর্ণ—অতি মনোরম ।
রাধাকৃষ্ণ সাক্ষাৎ ইহঁা করিয়াছেন ভোজন ॥ ২২৯ ॥

annera saurabhya, varṇa——ati manorama
rādhā-kṛṣṇa sākṣāt ihāṅ kariyāchena bhojana

SYNONYMS

annera saurabhya—the flavor of the cooked rice; *varṇa*—color; *ati manorama*—very attractive; *rādhā-kṛṣṇa*—Lord Kṛṣṇa and Rādhārāṇī; *sākṣāt*—directly; *ihāṅ*—all this; *kariyāchena bhojana*—have eaten.

TRANSLATION

"The color of the rice is so attractive and its aroma so good that it appears Rādhā and Kṛṣṇa have directly taken it.

TEXT 230

তোমার বহুত ভাগ্য কত প্রশংসিব ।
আমি—ভাগ্যবান্, ইহার অবশেষ পাব ॥ ২৩০ ॥

tomāra bahuta bhāgya kata praśaṁsiba
āmi——bhāgyavān, ihāra avaśeṣa pāba

SYNONYMS

tomāra—your; *bahuta*—great; *bhāgya*—fortune; *kata*—how much; *praśaṁsiba*—shall I praise; *āmi*—I; *bhāgyavān*—fortunate; *ihāra*—of this; *avaśeṣa*—remnants; *pāba*—shall get.

TRANSLATION

"My dear Bhaṭṭācārya, your fortune is very great. How much shall I praise you? I also am very fortunate to be able to take the remnants of this food.

TEXT 231

কৃষ্ণের আসন-পীঠ রাখহ উঠাঞা ।
মোরে প্রসাদ দেহ' ভিন্ন পাত্রেতে করিয়া ॥ ২৩১ ॥

kṛṣṇera āsana-pīṭha rākhaha uṭhāñā
more prasāda deha' bhinna pātrete kariyā

SYNONYMS

kṛṣṇera—of Lord Kṛṣṇa; *āsana-pīṭha*—the sitting place; *rākhaha*—keep aside; *uṭhāñā*—raising; *more*—unto Me; *prasāda*—*prasāda;* *deha'*—give; *bhinna*—separate; *pātrete*—on a plate; *kariyā*—putting.

TRANSLATION

"Take away Kṛṣṇa's sitting place and put it aside. Then give me prasāda on a different plate."

TEXT 232

ভট্টাচার্য বলে,—প্রভু না করহ বিস্ময় ।
যেই খাবে, তাঁহার শক্ত্যে ভোগ সিদ্ধ হয় ॥ ২৩২ ॥

bhaṭṭācārya bale,——prabhu nā karaha vismaya
yei khābe, tāṅhāra śaktye bhoga siddha haya

SYNONYMS

bhaṭṭācārya bale—Bhaṭṭācārya said; *prabhu*—my Lord; *nā karaha vismaya*—do not become astonished; *yei khābe*—whoever shall eat; *tāṅhāra śaktye*—by His grace; *bhoga*—the food; *siddha haya*—has been prepared.

TRANSLATION

Sārvabhauma Bhaṭṭācārya said, "It is not so wonderful, my Lord. Everything has been made possible by the energy and mercy of He who will eat the food.

TEXT 233

উদ্‌যোগ না ছিল মোর গৃহিণীর রন্ধনে ।
যাঁর শক্ত্যে ভোগ সিদ্ধ, সেই তাহা জানে ॥ ২৩৩ ॥

udyoga nā chila mora gṛhiṇīra randhane
yāṅra śaktye bhoga siddha, sei tāhā jāne

SYNONYMS

udyoga—exertion; *nā chila*—there was not; *mora*—of me; *gṛhiṇīra*—of my wife; *randhane*—in cooking; *yāṅra śaktye*—by whose potency; *bhoga siddha*—the food has been prepared; *sei*—He; *tāhā jāne*—knows that.

TRANSLATION

"My wife and I did not especially exert ourselves in the cooking. He by whose power the food has been prepared knows everything.

TEXT 234

এইত আসনে বসি' করহ ভোজন ।
প্রভু কহে,—পূজ্য এই কৃষ্ণের আসন ॥ ২৩৪ ॥

eita āsane vasi' karaha bhojana
prabhu kahe,——pūjya ei kṛṣṇera āsana

SYNONYMS

eita āsane—on this sitting place; *vasi'*—sitting; *karaha bhojana*—take Your lunch; *prabhu kahe*—Śrī Caitanya Mahāprabhu said; *pūjya*—worshipable; *ei*—this; *kṛṣṇera āsana*—sitting place of Kṛṣṇa.

TRANSLATION

"Now please sit in this place and take Your lunch." Caitanya Mahāprabhu replied, "This place is worshipable because it was used by Kṛṣṇa."

PURPORT

According to etiquette, things used by Kṛṣṇa should not be used by anyone else. Similarly, things used by the spiritual master should also not be used by anyone else. That is etiquette. Whatever is used by Kṛṣṇa or the spiritual master is worshipable. In particular, their sitting or eating places should not be used by anyone else. A devotee must be very careful to observe this.

TEXT 235

ভট্ট কহে,—অন্ন, পীঠ,—সমান প্রসাদ ।
অন্ন খাবে, পীঠে বসিতে কাহাঁ অপরাধ ? ২৩৫ ॥

bhaṭṭa kahe,——anna, pīṭha,——samāna prasāda
anna khābe, pīṭhe vasite kāhāṅ aparādha?

SYNONYMS

bhaṭṭa kahe—Sārvabhauma Bhaṭṭācārya said; *anna*—food; *pīṭha*—sitting place; *samāna*—equal; *prasāda*—mercy remnants of the Lord; *anna khābe*—You will eat the food; *pīṭhe vasite*—to sit on the place; *kāhāṅ aparādha*—where is the offense.

TRANSLATION

Bhaṭṭācārya said, "Both the food and the sitting place are the Lord's mercy. If You can eat the remnants of the food, what is the offense in Your sitting in this place?"

TEXT 236

প্রভু কহে,—ভাল কৈলে, শাস্ত্র-আজ্ঞা হয় ।
কৃষ্ণের সকল শেষ ভৃত্য আস্বাদয় ॥ ২৩৬ ॥

prabhu kahe,——bhāla kaile, śāstra-ājñā haya
kṛṣṇera sakala śeṣa bhṛtya āsvādaya

SYNONYMS

prabhu kahe—Lord Śrī Caitanya Mahāprabhu replied; *bhāla kaile*—you have spoken correctly; *śāstra-ājñā haya*—there is such an order in the revealed scripture; *kṛṣṇera sakala śeṣa*—everything left by Kṛṣṇa; *bhṛtya*—the servant; *āsvādaya*—partakes of.

TRANSLATION

Caitanya Mahāprabhu then said, "Yes, you have spoken correctly. The śāstras enjoin that the devotee can partake of everything left by Kṛṣṇa.

TEXT 237

ত্বয়োপযুক্তস্রগ্‌গন্ধবাসোঽলঙ্কারচর্চিতাঃ ।
উচ্ছিষ্টভোজিনো দাসাস্তব মায়াং জয়েম হি ॥ ২৩৭ ॥

tvayopayukta-srag-gandha-
vāso 'laṅkāra-carcitāḥ
ucchiṣṭa-bhojino dāsās
tava māyāṁ jayema hi

SYNONYMS

tvayā—by You; *upayukta*—used; *srak*—flower garlands; *gandha*—scented substances like sandalwood pulp; *vāsaḥ*—garments; *alaṅkāra*—ornaments; *carcitāḥ*—being decorated with; *ucchiṣṭa*—remnants of food; *bhojinaḥ*—eating; *dāsāḥ*—servants; *tava*—Your; *māyām*—illusory energy; *jayema*—can conquer over; *hi*—certainly.

TRANSLATION

" 'My dear Lord, the garlands, scented substances, garments, ornaments and other such things that have been offered to You may later be used by Your servants. By partaking of these things and eating the remnants of food You have left, we will be able to conquer the illusory energy.' "

PURPORT

This is a quotation from *Śrīmad-Bhāgavatam* (11.6.46). In the Hare Kṛṣṇa movement, the chanting of the Hare Kṛṣṇa *mahā-mantra,* the dancing in ecstasy and the eating of the remnants of food offered to the Lord are very, very important. One may be illiterate or incapable of understanding the philosophy, but if he partakes of these three items, he will certainly be liberated without delay.

This verse was spoken by Uddhava to Lord Kṛṣṇa. This was during the time when the *Uddhava-gītā* was spoken. At that time there was some disturbance in Dvārakā, and Lord Kṛṣṇa had to leave the material world and enter the spiritual world. Uddhava could understand the situation, and he talked with the Supreme Personality of Godhead. The verse quoted above is an excerpt from their conversations. Śrī Kṛṣṇa's pastimes in this material world are called *prakaṭa-līlā* (manifested pastimes), and His pastimes in the spiritual world are called *aprakaṭa-līlā* (unmanifested pastimes). By unmanifested we mean that they are not present before our eyes. It is not that Lord Kṛṣṇa's pastimes are unmanifest. They are going on exactly as the sun is going on perpetually, but when the sun is present before our eyes, we call it daytime (manifest), and when it is not present, we call it night (unmanifest). Those who are above the jurisdiction of night are always in the spiritual world, where the Lord's pastimes are constantly manifest to them. As the *Brahma-saṁhitā* confirms:

ānanda-cinmaya-rasa-pratibhāvitābhis
tābhir ya eva nija-rūpatayā kalābhiḥ
goloka eva nivasaty akhilātma-bhūto
govindam ādi-puruṣaṁ tam ahaṁ bhajāmi

premāñjana-cchurita-bhakti-vilocanena
santaḥ sadaiva hṛdayeṣu vilokayanti
yaṁ śyāmasundaram acintya-guṇa-svarūpaṁ
govindam ādi-puruṣaṁ tam ahaṁ bhajāmi

"I worship Govinda, the primeval Lord, who resides in His own realm, Goloka, with Rādhā, who resembles His own spiritual figure and who embodies the ecstatic potency [*hlādinī*]. Their companions are Her confidantes, who embody extensions of Her bodily form and who are imbued and permeated with ever-blissful spiritual rasa. I worship Govinda, the primeval Lord, who is Śyāmasundara, Kṛṣṇa Himself with inconceivable innumerable attributes, whom the pure devotees see in their heart of hearts with the eye of devotion tinged with the salve of love." (Bs. 5.37-38)

TEXT 238

তথাপি এতেক অন্ন খাওন না যায় ।
ভট্ট কহে,—জানি, খাও যতেক যুয়ায় ॥ ২৩৮ ॥

tathāpi eteka anna khāona nā yāya
bhaṭṭa kahe,——jāni, khāo yateka yuyāya

SYNONYMS

tathāpi—still; *eteka*—so much; *anna*—food; *khāona*—eating; *nā yāya*—is not possible; *bhaṭṭa kahe*—Bhaṭṭācārya said; *jāni*—I know; *khāo*—You can eat; *yateka*—how much; *yuyāya*—is possible.

TRANSLATION

Śrī Caitanya Mahāprabhu then said, "There is so much food here that it is impossible to eat." Bhaṭṭācārya replied, "I know how much You can eat.

TEXT 239

নীলাচলে ভোজন তুমি কর বায়ান্ন বার ।
এক এক ভোগের অন্ন শত শত ভার ॥ ২৩৯ ॥

nīlācale bhojana tumi kara bāyānna bāra
eka eka bhogera anna śata śata bhāra

SYNONYMS

nīlācale—at Jagannātha Purī; *bhojana*—accepting lunch; *tumi*—You; *kara*—do; *bāyānna bāra*—fifty-two times; *eka eka bhogera*—of each and every offering; *anna*—eatables; *śata śata bhāra*—hundreds of buckets.

TRANSLATION

"After all, at Jagannātha Purī You eat fifty-two times a day, and each time You eat hundreds of buckets filled with prasāda.

TEXT 240

দ্বারকাতে ষোল-সহস্র মহিষী-মন্দিরে ।
অষ্টাদশ মাতা, আর যাদবের ঘরে ॥ ২৪০ ॥

dvārakāte ṣola-sahasra mahiṣī-mandire
aṣṭādaśa mātā, āra yādavera ghare

SYNONYMS

dvārakāte—at Dvārakā-dhāma; *ṣola-sahasra*—sixteen thousand; *mahiṣī*—queens; *mandire*—palaces; *aṣṭādaśa mātā*—eighteen mothers; *āra*—and; *yādavera ghare*—in the house of the Yadu dynasty.

TRANSLATION

"At Dvārakā, You keep sixteen thousand queens in sixteen thousand palaces. Also, there are eighteen mothers and numerous friends and relatives of the Yadu dynasty.

TEXT 241

ব্রজে জ্যেঠা, খুড়া, মামা, পিসাদি গোপগণ ।
সখাবৃন্দ সবার ঘরে দ্বিসন্ধ্যা-ভোজন ॥ ২৪১ ॥

vraje jyeṭhā, khuḍā, māmā, pisādi gopa-gaṇa
sakhā-vṛnda sabāra ghare dvisandhyā-bhojana

SYNONYMS

vraje—at Vṛndāvana; *jyeṭhā*—the father's elder brothers; *khuḍā*—the father's younger brothers; *māmā*—the mother's brothers; *pisā*—the husbands of aunts; *ādi*—and so on; *gopa-gaṇa*—cowherd men; *sakhā-vṛnda*—hundreds of friends; *sabāra*—of all of them; *ghare*—in the houses; *dvi-sandhyā*—twice a day; *bhojana*—eating.

TRANSLATION

"In Vṛndāvana You also have Your father's elder brothers, Your father's younger brothers, maternal uncles, husbands of Your father's sisters and many cowherd men. There are also cowherd boy friends, and You eat twice a day, morning and evening, in the house of each and every one.

PURPORT

In Dvārakā, Lord Kṛṣṇa had eighteen mothers like Devakī, Rohiṇī and others. Besides these was His foster mother Yaśodā in Vṛndāvana. Lord Kṛṣṇa also had two uncles, who were brothers of Nanda Mahārāja. As stated by Śrīla Rūpa Gosvāmī in his *Śrī-kṛṣṇa-gaṇoddeśa-dīpikā, upanando 'bhinandaś ca pitṛvyau pūrva-jau pituḥ:* "The elder brothers of Nanda Mahārāja were Upananda and Abhinanda." Similarly, in the same book the names of the younger brothers of Nanda Mahārāja are given. *Pitṛvyau tu kanīyāṁsau syātāṁ sannanda-nandanau:* "Sannanda and Nandana, or Sunanda and Pāṇḍava, were the younger brothers of Kṛṣṇa's father, Nanda Mahārāja." Śrī Kṛṣṇa's maternal uncles were also described there. *Yaśodhara-yaśodeva-sudevādyās tu mātulāḥ:* "Yaśodhara, Yaśodeva and Sudeva were the maternal uncles of Kṛṣṇa." Kṛṣṇa's uncles are also mentioned. *Mahānīlaḥ sunīlaś ca ramaṇāv etayoḥ kramāt:* "Mahānīla and Sunīla are the husbands of Kṛṣṇa's aunts."

TEXT 242

গোবর্ধন-যজ্ঞে অন্ন খাইলা রাশি রাশি ।
তার লেখায় এই অন্ন নহে এক গ্রাসী ॥ ২৪২ ॥

govardhana-yajñe anna khāilā rāśi rāśi
tāra lekhāya ei anna nahe eka grāsī

SYNONYMS

govardhana-yajñe—in the Govardhana-pūjā sacrifice; *anna*—food; *khāilā*—You ate; *rāśi rāśi*—stacks; *tāra*—to that; *lekhāya*—in comparison; *ei*—this; *anna*—food; *nahe*—not; *eka grāsī*—one morsel.

TRANSLATION

"Indeed," Sārvabhauma Bhaṭṭācārya continued, "at the Govardhana-pūjā ceremony You ate stacks of rice. In comparison to that, this small quantity is not even a morsel for You.

TEXT 243

তুমি ত' ঈশ্বর, মুঞি—ক্ষুদ্র জীব ছার।
এক-গ্রাস মাধুকরী করহ অঙ্গীকার ॥ ২৪৩ ॥

tumi ta' īśvara, muñi——kṣudra jīva chāra
eka-grāsa mādhukarī karaha aṅgīkāra

SYNONYMS

tumi—You; *ta'*—certainly; *īśvara*—the Supreme Personality of Godhead; *muñi*—I; *kṣudra jīva*—insignificant living being; *chāra*—worthless; *eka-grāsa*—one small quantity; *mādhu-karī*—as collected by the bees; *karaha*—please do; *aṅgīkāra*—accept.

TRANSLATION

"You are the Supreme Personality of Godhead, whereas I am a most insignificant living being. Therefore You may accept a little quantity of food from my house."

PURPORT

A *sannyāsī* is expected to collect a little food from each and every householder. That is to say, he should take whatever he requires to eat. This system is called *mādhukarī.* The word *mādhukarī* comes from the word *mādhukara* and means "honey-collecting bees." Bees collect a little honey from each flower, but all these small quantities of honey accumulate to become a beehive. *Sannyāsīs* should collect a little from each and every householder and should eat simply what is necessary to maintain the body. Being a *sannyāsī,* Lord Caitanya Mahāprabhu could collect a little food from the house of Sārvabhauma Bhaṭṭācārya, and this was the Bhaṭṭācārya's request. Compared to the food eaten by the Lord on other occasions, Bhaṭṭācārya's feast was not even a morsel. This is what Bhaṭṭācārya is pointing out to the Lord.

TEXT 244

এত শুনি' হাসি' প্রভু বসিলা ভোজনে।
জগন্নাথের প্রসাদ ভট্ট দেন হর্ষ-মনে ॥ ২৪৪ ॥

eta śuni' hāsi' prabhu vasilā bhojane
jagannāthera prasāda bhaṭṭa dena harṣa-mane

SYNONYMS

eta śuni'—hearing this; *hāsi'*—smiling; *prabhu*—Lord Śrī Caitanya Mahāprabhu; *vasilā bhojane*—sat down to eat; *jagannāthera*—of Lord Jagannātha; *prasāda*—remnants of food; *bhaṭṭa*—Sārvabhauma Bhaṭṭācārya; *dena harṣa-mane*—delivers in great happiness.

TRANSLATION

Hearing this, Śrī Caitanya Mahāprabhu smiled and sat down to eat. Bhaṭṭācārya, with great pleasure, first offered Him the prasāda from the Jagannātha temple.

TEXT 245

হেনকালে 'অমোঘ',—ভট্টাচার্যের জামাতা ।
কুলীন, নিন্দক তেঁহো ষাঠী-কন্যার ভর্তা ॥ ২৪৫ ॥

hena-kāle 'amogha,'——bhaṭṭācāryera jāmātā
kulīna, nindaka teṅho ṣāṭhī-kanyāra bhartā

SYNONYMS

hena-kāle—exactly at this time; *amogha*—Amogha; *bhaṭṭācāryera jāmātā*—the son-in-law of Bhaṭṭācārya; *kulīna*—of aristocratic birth; *nindaka*—blasphemer; *teṅho*—he; *ṣāṭhī-kanyāra bhartā*—the husband of Sārvabhauma Bhaṭṭācārya's daughter named Ṣāṭhī.

TRANSLATION

At this time Bhaṭṭācārya had a son-in-law named Amogha, who was the husband of his daughter named Ṣāṭhī. Although born in an aristocratic brāhmaṇa family, this Amogha was a great faultfinder and blasphemer.

TEXT 246

ভোজন দেখিতে চাহে, আসিতে না পারে ।
লাঠী-হাতে ভট্টাচার্য আছেন দুয়ারে ॥ ২৪৬ ॥

bhojana dekhite cāhe, āsite nā pāre
lāṭhī-hāte bhaṭṭācārya āchena duyāre

SYNONYMS

bhojana—the eating; *dekhite cāhe*—he wanted to see; *āsite nā pāre*—could not come; *lāṭhī-hāte*—with a stick in his hand; *bhaṭṭācārya*—Sārvabhauma Bhaṭṭācārya; *āchena*—was; *duyāre*—on the threshold.

TRANSLATION

Amogha wanted to see Śrī Caitanya Mahāprabhu eat, but he was not allowed to enter. Indeed, Bhaṭṭācārya guarded the threshold of his house with a stick in his hand.

TEXT 247

তেঁহো যদি প্রসাদ দিতে হৈলা আন-মন ।
অমোঘ আসি' অন্ন দেখি' করয়ে নিন্দন ॥ ২৪৭ ॥

teṅho yadi prasāda dite hailā āna-mana
amogha āsi' anna dekhi' karaye nindana

SYNONYMS

teṅho—he (Bhaṭṭācārya); *yadi*—when; *prasāda dite*—supplying the *prasāda; hailā*—became; *āna-mana*—inattentive; *amogha*—Amogha; *āsi'*—coming; *anna dekhi'*—seeing the food; *karaye nindana*—began blaspheming.

TRANSLATION

However, as soon as Bhaṭṭācārya began distributing prasāda and was a little inattentive, Amogha came in. Seeing the quantity of food, he began to blaspheme.

TEXT 248

এই অন্নে তৃপ্ত হয় দশ বার জন ।
একেলা সন্ন্যাসী করে এতেক ভক্ষণ ! ২৪৮ ॥

ei anne tṛpta haya daśa bāra jana
ekelā sannyāsī kare eteka bhakṣaṇa!

SYNONYMS

ei anne—with so much food; *tṛpta haya*—can be satisfied; *daśa bāra jana*—at least ten to twelve men; *ekelā*—alone; *sannyāsī*—this person in the renounced order; *kare*—does; *eteka*—so much; *bhakṣaṇa*—eating.

TRANSLATION

"This much food is sufficient to satisfy ten or twelve men, but this sannyāsī alone is eating so much!"

TEXT 249

শুনিতেই ভট্টাচার্য উলটি' চাহিল ।
তাঁর অবধান দেখি' অমোঘ পলাইল ॥ ২৪৯ ॥

śunitei bhaṭṭācārya ulaṭi' cāhila
tāṅra avadhāna dekhi' amogha palāila

SYNONYMS

śunitei—hearing; *bhaṭṭācārya*—Sārvabhauma Bhaṭṭācārya; *ulaṭi' cāhila*—turned his eyes upon him; *tāṅra*—his; *avadhāna*—attention; *dekhi'*—seeing; *amogha*—Amogha; *palāila*—left.

TRANSLATION

As soon as Amogha said this, Sārvabhauma Bhaṭṭācārya turned his eyes upon him. Seeing Bhaṭṭācārya's attitude, Amogha immediately left.

TEXT 250

ভট্টাচার্য লাঠি লঞা মারিতে ধাইল ।
পলাইল অমোঘ, তার লাগ না পাইল ॥ ২৫০ ॥

bhaṭṭācārya lāṭhi lañā mārite dhāila
palāila amogha, tāra lāga nā pāila

SYNONYMS

bhaṭṭācārya—Sārvabhauma Bhaṭṭācārya; *lāṭhi lañā*—taking a stick; *mārite*—to strike; *dhāila*—ran; *palāila*—fled; *amogha*—Amogha; *tāra*—him; *lāga nā pāila*—could not catch.

TRANSLATION

Bhaṭṭācārya ran after him to strike him with a stick, but Amogha fled so fast that Bhaṭṭācārya could not catch him.

TEXT 251

তবে গালি, শাপ দিতে ভট্টাচার্য আইলা ।
নিন্দা শুনি' মহাপ্রভু হাসিতে লাগিলা ॥ ২৫১ ॥

tabe gāli, śāpa dite bhaṭṭācārya āilā
nindā śuni' mahāprabhu hāsite lāgilā

SYNONYMS

tabe—at that time; *gāli*—calling by ill names; *śāpa dite*—cursing; *bhaṭṭācārya*—Sārvabhauma Bhaṭṭācārya; *āilā*—came back; *nindā śuni'*—hearing the criticism; *mahāprabhu*—Śrī Caitanya Mahāprabhu; *hāsite lāgilā*—began to laugh.

TRANSLATION

Bhaṭṭācārya then began to curse and call his son-in-law ill names. When Bhaṭṭācārya returned, he saw that Śrī Caitanya Mahāprabhu was laughing to hear him criticize Amogha.

TEXT 252

শুনি' ষাঠীর মাতা শিরে-বুকে ঘাত মারে ।
'ষাঠী রাণ্ডী হউক'—ইহা বলে বারে বারে ॥ ২৫২ ॥

śuni' ṣāṭhīra mātā śire-buke ghāta māre
'ṣāṭhī rāṇḍī ha-uka'——ihā bale bāre bāre

SYNONYMS

śuni'—hearing; *ṣāṭhīra mātā*—the mother of Ṣāṭhī; *śire*—on the head; *buke*—on the chest; *ghāta māre*—strikes; *ṣāṭhī rāṇḍī ha-uka*—let Ṣāṭhī become a widow; *ihā bale*—says this; *bāre bāre*—again and again.

TRANSLATION

When Ṣāṭhī's mother, Bhaṭṭācārya's wife, heard of this incident, she immediately began to strike her head and chest, saying again, "Let Ṣāṭhī become a widow!"

TEXT 253

দুঁহার দুঃখ দেখি' প্রভু দুঁহা প্রবোধিয়া ।
দুঁহার ইচ্ছাতে ভোজন কৈল তুষ্ট হঞা ॥ ২৫৩ ॥

duṅhāra duḥkha dekhi' prabhu duṅhā prabodhiyā
duṅhāra icchāte bhojana kaila tuṣṭa hañā

SYNONYMS

duṅhāra duḥkha dekhi'—seeing the lamentation of both; *prabhu*—Lord Śrī Caitanya Mahāprabhu; *duṅhā prabodhiyā*—pacifying them; *duṅhāra icchāte*—by the will of both of them; *bhojana kaila*—took His lunch; *tuṣṭa hañā*—with great satisfaction.

TRANSLATION

Seeing the lamentation of both husband and wife, Śrī Caitanya Mahāprabhu tried to pacify them. According to their desire, He ate the prasāda and was very satisfied.

TEXT 254

আচমন করাঞা ভট্ট দিল মুখবাস ।
তুলসী-মঞ্জরী, লবঙ্গ, এলাচি রসবাস ॥ ২৫৪ ॥

ācamana karāñā bhaṭṭa dila mukha-vāsa
tulasī-mañjarī, lavaṅga, elāci rasa-vāsa

SYNONYMS

ācamana karāñā—washing the mouth, hands and legs of Śrī Caitanya Mahāprabhu; *bhaṭṭa*—Sārvabhauma Bhaṭṭācārya; *dila mukha-vāsa*—gave some flavored spices; *tulasī-mañjarī*—the flowers of *tulasī; lavaṅga*—cloves; *elāci*—cardamom; *rasa-vāsa*—that which brings saliva.

TRANSLATION

After Śrī Caitanya Mahāprabhu finished eating, Bhaṭṭācārya washed His mouth, hands and legs and offered Him flavored spices, tulasī-mañjarī, cloves, and cardamom.

TEXT 255

সর্বাঙ্গে পরাইল প্রভুর মাল্যচন্দন ।
দণ্ডবৎ হঞা বলে সদৈন্য বচন ॥ ২৫৫ ॥

sarvāṅge parāila prabhura mālya-candana
daṇḍavat hañā bale sadainya vacana

SYNONYMS

sarva-aṅge—all over the body; *parāila*—put; *prabhura*—of the Lord; *mālya-candana*—a flower garland and sandalwood pulp; *daṇḍavat hañā*—offering obeisances; *bale*—says; *sa-dainya*—humble; *vacana*—statement.

TRANSLATION

The Bhaṭṭācārya then placed a flower garland over Śrī Caitanya Mahāprabhu and smeared His body with sandalwood pulp. After offering obeisances, the Bhaṭṭācārya submitted the following humble statement.

TEXT 256

নিন্দা করাইতে তোমা আনিনু নিজ-ঘরে ।
এই অপরাধ, প্রভু, ক্ষমা কর মোরে ॥ ২৫৬ ॥

nindā karāite tomā āninu nija-ghare
ei aparādha, prabhu, kṣamā kara more

SYNONYMS

nindā karāite—just to cause blasphemy; *tomā*—You; *āninu*—I brought; *nija-ghare*—to my place; *ei aparādha*—this offense; *prabhu*—my Lord; *kṣamā kara*—please pardon; *more*—me.

TRANSLATION

"I brought You to my home just to have You blasphemed. This is a great offense. Please excuse me. I beg Your pardon."

TEXT 257

প্রভু কহে,—নিন্দা নহে, 'সহজ' কহিল ।
ইহাতে তোমার কিবা অপরাধ হৈল ? ২৫৭ ॥

prabhu kahe,——nindā nahe, 'sahaja' kahila
ihāte tomāra kibā aparādha haila?

SYNONYMS

prabhu kahe—Lord Śrī Caitanya Mahāprabhu said; *nindā nahe*—not blasphemy; *sahaja*—rightly; *kahila*—he spoke; *ihāte*—in this; *tomāra*—your; *kibā*—what; *aparādha*—offense; *haila*—was there.

TRANSLATION

Śrī Caitanya Mahāprabhu said, "What Amogha has said is correct; therefore it is not blasphemy. What is your offense?"

TEXT 258

এত বলি' মহাপ্রভু চলিলা ভবনে ।
ভট্টাচার্য তাঁর ঘরে গেলা তাঁর সনে ॥ ২৫৮ ॥

eta bali' mahāprabhu calilā bhavane
bhaṭṭācārya tāṅra ghare gelā tāṅra sane

SYNONYMS

eta bali'—saying this; *mahāprabhu*—Śrī Caitanya Mahāprabhu; *calilā bhavane*—returned to His residence; *bhaṭṭācārya*—Sārvabhauma Bhaṭṭācārya; *tāṅra ghare*—to His place; *gelā*—went; *tāṅra sane*—with Him.

TRANSLATION

After saying this, Śrī Caitanya Mahāprabhu left and returned to His residence. Sārvabhauma Bhaṭṭācārya also followed Him.

TEXT 259

প্রভু-পদে পড়ি' বহু আত্মনিন্দা কৈল ।
তাঁরে শান্ত করি' প্রভু ঘরে পাঠাইল ॥ ২৫৯ ॥

prabhu-pade paḍi' bahu ātma-nindā kaila
tāṅre śānta kari' prabhu ghare pāṭhāila

SYNONYMS

prabhu-pade—at the feet of Lord Śrī Caitanya Mahāprabhu; *paḍi'*—falling down; *bahu*—much; *ātma-nindā kaila*—made self-reproach; *tāṅre*—him; *śānta kari'*—making pacified; *prabhu*—Śrī Caitanya Mahāprabhu; *ghare pāṭhāila*—sent back to his home.

TRANSLATION

Falling down at the Lord's feet, Sārvabhauma Bhaṭṭācārya said many things in self-reproach. The Lord then pacified him and sent him back to his home.

TEXT 260

ঘরে আসি' ভট্টাচার্য ষাঠীর মাতা-সনে ।
আপনা নিন্দিয়া কিছু বলেন বচনে ॥ ২৬০ ॥

ghare āsi' bhaṭṭācārya ṣāṭhīra mātā-sane
āpanā nindiyā kichu balena vacane

SYNONYMS

ghare āsi'—returning home; *bhaṭṭācārya*—Sārvabhauma Bhaṭṭācārya; *ṣāṭhīra mātā-sane*—with the mother of Ṣāṭhī; *āpanā nindiyā*—condemning himself; *kichu*—some; *balena vacane*—speaks words.

TRANSLATION

After returning to his home, Sārvabhauma Bhaṭṭācārya consulted with his wife, the mother of Ṣāṭhī. After personally condemning himself, he began to speak as follows.

TEXT 261

চৈতন্য-গোসাঞির নিন্দা শুনিল যাহা হৈতে ।
তারে বধ কৈলে হয় পাপ-প্রায়শ্চিত্তে ॥ ২৬১ ॥

caitanya-gosāñira nindā śunila yāhā haite
tāre vadha kaile haya pāpa-prāyaścitte

SYNONYMS

caitanya-gosāñira—of Śrī Caitanya Mahāprabhu; *nindā*—blasphemy; *śunila*—I have heard; *yāhā haite*—from whom; *tāre vadha kaile*—if he is killed; *haya*—there is; *pāpa-prāyaścitte*—atonement for the sinful act.

TRANSLATION

"If the man who blasphemed Śrī Caitanya Mahāprabhu is killed, his sinful action may be atoned."

PURPORT

The *Hari-bhakti-vilāsa* cites the following quotation from *Skanda Purāṇa* concerning the blaspheming of a Vaiṣṇava:

yo hi bhāgavataṁ lokam
upahāsaṁ nṛpottama
karoti tasya naśyanti
artha-dharma-yaśaḥ-sutāḥ

nindāṁ kurvanti ye mūḍhā
vaiṣṇavānāṁ mahātmanām
patanti pitṛbhiḥ sārdhaṁ
mahā-raurava-saṁjñite

hanti nindati vai dveṣṭi
vaiṣṇavān nābhinandati
krudhyate yāti no harṣaṁ
darśane patanāni ṣaṭ

In this conversation between Mārkaṇḍeya and Bhagīratha, it is said: "My dear King, if one derides an exalted devotee, he loses the results of his pious activities, his opulence, his reputation and his sons. Vaiṣṇavas are all great souls. Whoever blasphemes them falls down to the hell known as Mahāraurava. He is also accompanied by his forefathers. Whoever kills or blasphemes a Vaiṣṇava and whoever is envious of a Vaiṣṇava or angry with him, or whoever does not offer him obeisances or feel joy upon seeing a Vaiṣṇava, certainly falls into a hellish condition."

The *Hari-bhakti-vilāsa* (10.314) also gives the following quotation from *Dvārakā-māhātmya:*

kara-patraiś ca phālyante
sutīvrair yama-śāsanaiḥ
nindāṁ kurvanti ye pāpā
vaiṣṇavānāṁ mahātmanām

In a conversation between Prahlāda Mahārāja and Bali Mahārāja, it is said, "Those sinful people who blaspheme Vaiṣṇavas, who are all great souls, are subjected very severely to the punishment offered by Yamarāja."

In the *Bhakti-sandarbha* (313) there is a statement concerning the blaspheming of Lord Viṣṇu.

ye nindanti hṛṣīkeśaṁ
tad-bhaktaṁ puṇya-rūpiṇam
śata-janmārjitaṁ puṇyaṁ
teṣāṁ naśyati niścitam

te pacyante mahā-ghore
kumbhīpāke bhayānake
bhakṣitāḥ kīṭa-saṅghena
yāvac candra-divākarau
śrī-viṣṇor avamānanād
gurutaraṁ śrī-vaiṣṇavollaṅghanam

tadīya-dūṣaka-janān
na paśyet puruṣādhamān
taiḥ sārdhaṁ vañcaka-janaiḥ
saha-vāsaṁ na kārayet

"One who criticizes Lord Viṣṇu and His devotees loses all the benefits accrued in a hundred pious births. Such a person rots in the Kumbhīpāka hell and is bitten by worms as long as the sun and moon exist. One should therefore not even see the face of a person who blasphemes Lord Viṣṇu and His devotees. Never try to associate with such persons."

In his *Bhakti-sandarbha* (265), Jīva Gosvāmī further quotes from *Śrīmad-Bhāgavatam* (10.74.40):

nindāṁ bhagavataḥ śṛṇvan
tat-parasya janasya vā
tato nāpaiti yaḥ so 'pi
yāty adhaḥ sukṛtāc cyutaḥ

"If one does not immediately leave upon hearing the Lord or the Lord's devotee blasphemed, he falls down from devotional service." Similarly, Lord Śiva's wife Satī states in *Śrīmad-Bhāgavatam* (4.4.17):

karṇau pidhāya nirayād yad akalpa īśe
dharmāvitary asṛṇibhir nṛbhir asyamāne
chindyāt prasahya ruśatīm asatīṁ prabhuś cej
jihvām asūn api tato visṛjet sa dharmaḥ

"If one hears an irresponsible person blaspheme the master and controller of religion, he should block his ears and go away if unable to punish him. But if one is able to kill, then one should by force cut out the blasphemer's tongue and kill the offender, and after that he should give up his own life."

TEXT 262

কিম্বা নিজ-প্রাণ যদি করি বিমোচন ।
দুই যোগ্য নহে, দুই শরীর ব্রাহ্মণ ॥ ২৬২ ॥

kimvā nija-prāṇa yadi kari vimocana
dui yogya nahe, dui śarīra brāhmaṇa

SYNONYMS

kimvā—or; *nija-prāṇa*—my own life; *yadi*—if; *kari vimocana*—I give up; *dui*—both such actions; *yogya nahe*—are not befitting; *dui śarīra*—both the bodies; *brāhmaṇa*—*brāhmaṇas.*

TRANSLATION

Sārvabhauma Bhaṭṭācārya continued, "Or, if I give up my own life, this sinful action may be atoned. However, neither of these ideas are befitting because both bodies belong to brāhmaṇas.

TEXT 263

পুনঃ সেই নিন্দকের মুখ না দেখিব ।
পরিত্যাগ কৈলুঁ, তার নাম না লইব ॥ ২৬৩ ॥

punaḥ sei nindakera mukha nā dekhiba
parityāga kailuṅ, tāra nāma nā la-iba

SYNONYMS

punaḥ—again; *sei*—that; *nindakera*—of the blasphemer; *mukha*—face; *nā*—not; *dekhiba*—I shall see; *parityāga*—giving up; *kailuṅ*—I do; *tāra*—his; *nāma*—name; *nā*—not; *la-iba*—I shall take.

TRANSLATION

"Instead, I shall never see the face of that blasphemer. I reject him and give up his relationship. I shall never even speak his name.

TEXT 264

ষাঠীরে কহ—তারে ছাড়ুক, সে হইল 'পতিত' ।
'পতিত' হইলে ভর্তা ত্যজিতে উচিত ॥ ২৬৪ ॥

ṣāṭhīre kaha——tāre chāḍuka, se ha-ila 'patita'
'patita' ha-ile bhartā tyajite ucita

SYNONYMS

ṣāṭhīre kaha—inform Ṣāṭhī; *tāre chāḍuka*—let her give him up; *se ha-ila*—he has become; *patita*—fallen; *patita ha-ile*—when one has fallen; *bhartā*—such a husband; *tyajite*—to give up; *ucita*—is the duty.

TRANSLATION

"Inform my daughter Ṣāṭhī to abandon her relationship with her husband because he has fallen down. When the husband falls down, it is the wife's duty to relinquish the relationship.

PURPORT

Śrīla Sārvabhauma Bhaṭṭācārya considered that if Amogha were killed, one would suffer sinful reactions for killing the body of a *brāhmaṇa.* For the same reason, it would have been undesirable for Bhaṭṭācārya to commit suicide because he also was a *brāhmaṇa.* Since neither course could be accepted, Bhaṭṭācārya decided to give up his relationship with Amogha and never see his face.

As far as killing the body of a *brāhmaṇa* is concerned, *Śrīmad-Bhāgavatam* (1.7.53) gives the following injunction:

śrī bhagavān uvāca
brahma-bandhur na hantavya
ātatāyī vadhār-haṇaḥ
mayaivobhayam āmnātaṁ
paripāhy anuśāsanam

"The Personality of Godhead Śrī Kṛṣṇa said: A friend of a *brāhmaṇa* is not to be killed, but if he is an aggressor, he must be killed. All these rulings are in the scriptures, and you should act accordingly."

Quoting from the *smṛti,* Śrīla Śrīdhara Svāmī comments on this quotation from *Śrīmad-Bhāgavatam:*

ātatāyinam āyāntam
api vedānta-pāragam
jighāṁ-santaṁ jighāṁsīyān
na tena brahmahā bhavet

"Even though an aggressor may be a very learned scholar of Vedānta, he should be killed because of his envy in killing others. In such a case, it is not sinful to kill a *brāhmaṇa.*"

It is also stated in *Śrīmad-Bhāgavatam* (1.7.57):

vapanaṁ draviṇādānaṁ
sthānān niryāpaṇaṁ tathā
eṣa hi brahma-bandhūnāṁ
vadho nānyo 'sti daihikaḥ

"Cutting the hair from his head, depriving him of his wealth and driving him from his residence are the prescribed punishments for the relative of a *brāhmaṇa.* There is no injunction for killing the body."

Such punishment is sufficient for a *brahma-bandhu.* There is no need to personally kill his body. As far as Ṣāṭhī, the daughter of Sārvabhauma Bhaṭṭācārya, was concerned, she was advised to give up her relationship with her husband. Concerning this, the *Śrīmad-Bhāgavatam* (5.5.18) states, *na patiś ca sa syān na mocayed yaḥ samupeta-mṛtyum:* "One cannot be a husband if he cannot liberate his dependents from inevitable death." If a person is not in Kṛṣṇa consciousness and is bereft of spiritual power, he cannot protect his wife from the path of repeated birth and death. Consequently such a person cannot be accepted as a husband. A wife should dedicate her life and everything to Kṛṣṇa for further advancement in Kṛṣṇa consciousness. If she gives up her connection with her husband, who abandons Kṛṣṇa consciousness, she follows in the footsteps of the *dvija-patnī,* the wives of the *brāhmaṇas* who were engaged in performing sacrifices. The wife is not to be condemned for cutting off such a relationship. In this regard, Śrī Kṛṣṇa states in *Śrīmad-Bhāgavatam* (10.23.31-32):

patayo nābhyasūyeran
pitṛ-bhrātṛ-sutādayaḥ
lokāś ca vo mayopetā
devā apy anumanvate

na prītaye 'nurāgāya
hy aṅga-saṅgo nṛṇām iha
tan mano mayi yuñjānā
acirān mām avāpsyatha

Such a separation is never condemned by the supreme will. No one should be envious of the order of Kṛṣṇa. Even demigods support such action. In this material world, one does not become beloved simply by maintaining a bodily relationship. However, one can attain complete perfection by associating in Kṛṣṇa consciousness.

TEXT 265

পতিঞ্চ পতিতং ত্যজেৎ ॥ ২৬৫ ॥

patiṁ ca patitaṁ tyajet

SYNONYMS

patim—husband; *ca*—and; *patitam*—fallen; *tyajet*—one should give up.

TRANSLATION

"When a husband is fallen, his relationship must be given up."

PURPORT

This is a quotation from *smṛti-śāstra.* As stated in *Śrīmad-Bhāgavatam* (7.11.28):

santuṣṭālolupā dakṣā
dharma-jñā priya-satya-vāk
apramattā śuciḥ snigdhā
patiṁ tv apatitaṁ bhajet

"A wife who is satisfied, who is not greedy, who is expert and knows religious principles, who speaks what is dear and truthful and is not bewildered, who is always clean and affectionate, should be very devoted to her husband who is not fallen."

TEXT 266

সেই রাত্রে অমোঘ কাহাঁ পলাঞা গেল।
প্রাতঃকালে তার বিসূচিকা-ব্যাধি হৈল ॥ ২৬৬ ॥

sei rātre amogha kāhāṅ palāñā gela
prātaḥ-kāle tāra visūcikā-vyādhi haila

SYNONYMS

sei rātre—that night; *amogha*—the son-in-law of Sārvabhauma Bhaṭṭācārya; *kāhāṅ*—where; *palāñā gela*—fled; *prātaḥ-kāle*—in the morning; *tāra*—his; *visūcikā-vyādhi*—infection of cholera; *haila*—there was.

TRANSLATION

That night Amogha, Sārvabhauma Bhaṭṭācārya's son-in-law, fled, and in the morning he immediately fell sick with cholera.

TEXT 267

অমোঘ মরেন—শুনি' কহে ভট্টাচার্য।
সহায় হইয়া দৈব কৈল মোর কার্য ॥২৬৭ ॥

amogha marena——śuni' kahe bhaṭṭācārya
sahāya ha-iyā daiva kaila mora kārya

SYNONYMS

amogha marena—Amogha is dying; *śuni'*—hearing; *kahe bhaṭṭācārya*—Bhaṭṭācārya said; *sahāya ha-iyā*—helping; *daiva*—Providence; *kaila*—did; *mora*—my; *kārya*—duty.

TRANSLATION

When Bhaṭṭācārya heard that Amogha was dying of cholera, he thought, "It is the favor of Providence that He is doing what I want to do.

TEXT 268

ঈশ্বরে ত' অপরাধ ফলে ততক্ষণ।
এত বলি' পড়ে দুই শাস্ত্রের বচন ॥ ২৬৮ ॥

īśvare ta' aparādha phale tata-kṣaṇa
eta bali' paḍe dui śāstrera vacana

SYNONYMS

īśvare—unto the Supreme Personality of Godhead; *ta'*—indeed; *aparādha*—offense; *phale*—brings results; *tata-kṣaṇa*—immediately; *eta bali'*—saying this; *paḍe*—recites; *dui*—two; *śāstrera vacana*—quotations from revealed scriptures.

TRANSLATION

"When one offends the Supreme Personality of Godhead, karma immediately takes effect." After saying this, he recited two verses from revealed scripture.

TEXT 269

মহতা হি প্রযত্নেন হস্ত্যশ্বরথপত্তিভিঃ ।
অস্মাভির্যদনুষ্ঠেয়ং গন্ধর্বৈস্তদনুষ্ঠিতম্ ॥ ২৬৯ ॥

mahatā hi prayatnena
hasty-aśva-ratha-pattibhiḥ
asmābhir yad anuṣṭheyaṁ
gandharvais tad anuṣṭhitam

SYNONYMS

mahatā—very great; *hi*—certainly; *prayatnena*—by endeavor; *hasti*—elephants; *aśva*—horses; *ratha*—chariots; *pattibhiḥ*—and by infantry soldiers; *asmābhiḥ*—by ourselves; *yat*—whatever; *anuṣṭheyaṁ*—has to be arranged; *gandharvaiḥ*—by the Gandharvas; *tat*—that; *anuṣṭhitam*—done.

TRANSLATION

"'What we have had to arrange with great endeavor by collecting elephants, horses, chariots and infantry soldiers has already been accomplished by the Gandharvas.'

PURPORT

This is a quotation from the *Mahābhārata* (*Vana-parva* 241.15). Bhīmasena made this statement when all the Pāṇḍavas were living incognito. At that time there was a fight between the Kauravas and the Gandharvas. The Kaurava soldiers were under the command of Karṇa, but the commander-in-chief of the Gandharvas was able to arrest all the Kauravas by virtue of superior military strength. At that time Duryodhana's ministers and commanders, who were living in the forest, requested Mahārāja Yudhiṣṭhira to help. After being thus petitioned, Bhīmasena spoke the verse given above, remembering Duryodhana's former nefarious and atrocious activities against them. Indeed, Bhīmasena felt it very fitting that Duryodhana and his company were arrested. This could have been accomplished by the Pāṇḍavas only with great endeavor.

TEXT 270

আয়ুঃ শ্রিয়ং যশো ধর্মং লোকানাশিষ এব চ।
হন্তি শ্রেয়াংসি সর্বাণি পুংসো মহদতিক্রমঃ ॥ ২৭০ ॥

āyuḥ śriyaṁ yaśo dharmaṁ
lokān āśiṣa eva ca
hanti śreyāṁsi sarvāṇi
puṁso mahad-atikramaḥ

SYNONYMS

āyuḥ—duration of life; *śriyam*—opulence; *yaśaḥ*—reputation; *dharmam*—religion; *lokān*—possessions; *āśiṣaḥ*—benedictions; *eva*—certainly; *ca*—and; *hanti*—destroys; *śreyāṁsi*—good fortune; *sarvāṇi*—all; *puṁsaḥ*—of a person; *mahat*—of great souls; *atikramaḥ*—violation.

TRANSLATION

" 'When a person mistreats great souls, his life span, opulence, reputation, religion, possessions and good fortune are all destroyed.'

PURPORT

This is a statement made by Śukadeva Gosvāmī, who was relating *Śrīmad-Bhāgavatam* (10.4.46) to Mahārāja Parīkṣit. This quotation concerns the attempted killing of Kṛṣṇa's sister (Yogamāyā), who appeared before Kṛṣṇa's birth as the daughter of mother Yaśodā. This daughter Yogamāyā and Kṛṣṇa were born simultaneously, and Vasudeva replaced Kṛṣṇa by taking Yogamāyā away. When she was brought to Mathurā and Kaṁsa attempted to kill her, Yogamāyā slipped out of his hands. She could not be killed. She then informed Kaṁsa about the birth of his enemy, Kṛṣṇa, and being thus baffled, Kaṁsa consulted his associates, who were all demons. When this big conspiracy was taking place, this verse was spoken by Śukadeva Gosvāmī. He points out that a demon can lose everything because of his nefarious activities.

The word *mahad-atikramaḥ,* meaning "envy of Lord Viṣṇu and His devotees," is significant in this verse. The word *mahat* indicates a great personality, a devotee or the Supreme Personality of Godhead Himself. Being always engaged in the

Lord's service, the devotees themselves are as great as the Supreme Personality of Godhead. The word *mahat* is also explained in *Bhagavad-gītā* (9.13):

mahātmānas tu māṁ pārtha
daivīṁ prakṛtim āśritāḥ
bhajanty ananya-manaso
jñātvā bhūtādim avyayam

"O son of Pṛthā, those who are not deluded, the great souls, are under the protection of the divine nature. They are fully engaged in devotional service because they know Me as the Supreme Personality of Godhead, original and inexhaustible."

Being envious of the Lord and His devotees is not at all auspicious for a demon. By such envy, a demon loses everything considered beneficial.

TEXT 271

গোপীনাথাচার্য গেলা প্রভু-দরশনে ।
প্রভু তাঁরে পুছিল ভট্টাচার্য-বিবরণে ॥ ২৭১ ॥

gopīnāthācārya gelā prabhu-daraśane
prabhu tāṅre puchila bhaṭṭācārya-vivaraṇe

SYNONYMS

gopīnāthācārya—Gopīnātha Ācārya; *gelā*—went; *prabhu-daraśane*—to see Lord Śrī Caitanya Mahāprabhu; *prabhu*—Lord Śrī Caitanya Mahāprabhu; *tāṅre*—unto Him; *puchila*—inquired; *bhaṭṭācārya-vivaraṇe*—the affairs in the house of Sārvabhauma Bhaṭṭācārya.

TRANSLATION

At this time, Gopīnātha Ācārya went to see Śrī Caitanya Mahāprabhu, and the Lord asked him about the events taking place in Sārvabhauma Bhaṭṭācārya's house.

TEXT 272

আচার্য কহে,—উপবাস কৈল দুই জন ।
বিসূচিকা-ব্যাধিতে অমোঘ ছাড়িছে জীবন ॥ ২৭২ ॥

ācārya kahe,——upavāsa kaila dui jana
visūcikā-vyādhite amogha chāḍiche jīvana

SYNONYMS

ācārya kahe—Gopīnātha Ācārya informed; *upavāsa*—fasting; *kaila*—observed; *dui jana*—the two persons; *visūcikā-vyādhite*—by the disease of cholera; *amogha*—Amogha; *chāḍiche jīvana*—is going to die.

TRANSLATION

Gopīnātha Ācārya informed the Lord that both the husband and wife were fasting and that their son-in-law Amogha was dying of cholera.

TEXT 273

শুনি' কৃপাময় প্রভু আইলা ধাঞা ।
অমোঘেরে কহে তার বুকে হস্ত দিয়া ॥ ২৭৩ ॥

śuni' kṛpāmaya prabhu āilā dhāñā
amoghere kahe tāra buke hasta diyā

SYNONYMS

śuni'—hearing; *kṛpā-maya*—merciful; *prabhu*—Lord Śrī Caitanya Mahāprabhu; *āilā*—came; *dhāñā*—running; *amoghere*—unto Amogha; *kahe*—He says; *tāra*—His; *buke*—on the chest; *hasta diyā*—keeping His hand.

TRANSLATION

As soon as Caitanya Mahāprabhu heard that Amogha was going to die, He immediately ran to him in great haste. Placing His hand on Amogha's chest, He spoke as follows.

TEXT 274

সহজে নির্মল এই 'ব্রাহ্মণ'-হৃদয় ।
কৃষ্ণের বসিতে এই যোগ্যস্থান হয় ॥ ২৭৪ ॥

sahaje nirmala ei 'brāhmaṇa'-hṛdaya
kṛṣṇera vasite ei yogya-sthāna haya

SYNONYMS

sahaje—by nature; *nirmala*—without contamination; *ei*—this; *brāhmaṇa-hṛdaya*—heart of a *brāhmaṇa; kṛṣṇera*—of Lord Kṛṣṇa; *vasite*—to sit down; *ei*—this; *yogya-sthāna*—proper place; *haya*—is.

TRANSLATION

"The heart of a brāhmaṇa is by nature very clean; therefore it is a proper place for Kṛṣṇa to sit.

TEXT 275

'মাৎসর্য'-চণ্ডাল কেনে ইহাঁ বসাইলে ।
পরম পবিত্র স্থান অপবিত্র কৈলে ॥ ২৭৫ ॥

'mātsarya'-caṇḍāla kene ihāṅ vasāile
parama pavitra sthāna apavitra kaile

SYNONYMS

mātsarya—jealousy; *caṇḍāla*—the lowest of the men; *kene*—why; *ihāṅ*—here; *vasāile*—you allowed to sit; *parama pavitra*—most purified; *sthāna*—place; *apavitra*—impure; *kaile*—you have made.

TRANSLATION

"Why have you allowed jealousy to sit here also? Because of this, you have become like a caṇḍāla, the lowest of men, and you have also contaminated a most purified place—your heart.

TEXT 276

সার্বভৌম-সঙ্গে তোমার 'কলুষ' হৈল ক্ষয় ।
'কল্মষ' ঘুচিলে জীব 'কৃষ্ণনাম' লয় ॥ ২৭৬ ॥

sārvabhauma-saṅge tomāra 'kaluṣa' haila kṣaya
'kalmaṣa' ghucile jīva 'kṛṣṇa-nāma' laya

SYNONYMS

sārvabhauma-saṅge—by the association of Sārvabhauma; *tomāra*—your; *kaluṣa*—contamination; *haila kṣaya*—is now vanquished; *kalmaṣa*—contamination; *ghucile*—when dispelled; *jīva*—the living entity; *kṛṣṇa-nāma*—the Hare Kṛṣṇa *mahā-mantra; laya*—can chant.

TRANSLATION

"However, due to the association of Sārvabhauma Bhaṭṭācārya, all your contamination is now vanquished. When a person's heart is cleansed of all contamination, he is able to chant the mahā-mantra, Hare Kṛṣṇa.

TEXT 277

উঠহ, অমোঘ, তুমি লও কৃষ্ণনাম ।
অচিরে তোমারে কৃপা করিবে ভগবান্ ॥ ২৭৭ ॥

uṭhaha, amogha, tumi lao kṛṣṇa-nāma
acire tomāre kṛpā karibe bhagavān

SYNONYMS

uṭhaha—get up; *amogha*—Amogha; *tumi*—you; *lao*—chant; *kṛṣṇa-nāma*—the holy name of Lord Kṛṣṇa; *acire*—very soon; *tomāre*—unto you; *kṛpā*—mercy; *karibe*—will bestow; *bhagavān*—the Supreme Personality of Godhead.

TRANSLATION

"Therefore, Amogha, get up and chant the Hare Kṛṣṇa mahā-mantra! If you do so, Kṛṣṇa will unfailingly bestow mercy upon you."

PURPORT

The Absolute Truth is realized in three phases—impersonal Brahman, Paramātmā and the Supreme Personality of Godhead, Bhagavān. All of these are one and the same truth, but Brahman, Paramātmā and Bhagavān constitute three different features. Whoever understands Brahman is called a *brāhmaṇa,* and when a *brāhmaṇa* engages in the Lord's devotional service, he is called a Vaiṣṇava. Unless one comes to understand the Supreme Personality of Godhead, his realization of impersonal Brahman is imperfect. A *brāhmaṇa* can chant the Hare Kṛṣṇa *mantra* on the platform of *nāmābhāsa,* but not on the platform of pure vibration. When a *brāhmaṇa* engages in the Lord's service, fully understanding his eternal relationship, his devotional service is called *abhidheya.* When one attains that stage, he is called a *bhāgavata* or a Vaiṣṇava. This indicates that he is free from contamination and material attachment. This is confirmed by *Bhagavad-gītā* (7.28):

yeṣāṁ tv anta-gataṁ pāpaṁ
janānāṁ puṇya-karmaṇām
te dvandva-moha-nirmuktā
bhajante māṁ dṛḍha-vratāḥ

"Persons who have acted piously in previous lives and in this life, whose sinful actions are completely eradicated and who are freed from the duality of delusion, engage themselves in My service with determination."

A *brāhmaṇa* may be a very learned scholar, but this does not mean that he is free from material contamination. A *brāhmaṇa's* contamination, however, is in the mode of goodness. In the material world, the three modes are goodness, passion and ignorance, and all of these are simply different gradations of contamination. Unless a *brāhmaṇa* transcends such contamination and approaches the platform of unalloyed devotional service, he cannot be accepted as a Vaiṣṇava. An impersonalist may be aware of the impersonal Brahman feature of the Absolute Truth, but his activities are on the impersonal platform. Sometimes he imagines a form of the Lord (*saguṇa-upāsanā*), but such an attempt is never successful in helping one attain complete realization. The impersonalist may consider himself a *brāhmaṇa* and may be situated in the mode of goodness, but nonetheless he is conditioned by one of the modes of material nature. This means that he is not yet liberated, for liberation cannot be attained unless one is completely free from the modes. In any case, the Māyāvāda philosophy keeps one conditioned. If one becomes a Vaiṣṇava through proper initiation, he automatically becomes a *brāhmaṇa*. There is no doubt about it. The *Garuḍa Purāṇa* confirms this:

brāhmaṇānāṁ sahasrebhyaḥ
satra-yājī viśiṣyate
satra-yāji-sahasrebhyaḥ
sarva-vedānta-pāragaḥ
sarva-vedānta-vit-koṭyā
viṣṇu-bhakto viśiṣyate

"Out of many thousands of *brāhmaṇas,* one may become qualified to perform *yajña.* Out of many thousands of such qualified *brāhmaṇas,* one may be fully aware of the Vedānta philosophy. Out of many millions of learned Vedānta scholars, there may be one *viṣṇu-bhakta,* or devotee of Lord Viṣṇu. It is he who is most exalted."

Unless one is a fully qualified *brāhmaṇa,* he cannot advance in the spiritual science. A real *brāhmaṇa* is never envious of Vaiṣṇavas. If he is, he is considered an imperfect neophyte. Impersonalist *brāhmaṇas* are always opposed to Vaiṣṇava principles. They are envious of Vaiṣṇavas because they do not know the goal of life. *Na te viduḥ svārtha-gatiṁ hi viṣṇum.* However, when a *brāhmaṇa* becomes a Vaiṣṇava, there is no duality. If a *brāhmaṇa* does not become a Vaiṣṇava, he certainly falls down from the *brāhmaṇa* platform. This is confirmed by *Śrīmad-Bhāgavatam* (11.5.3): *na bhajanty avajānanti sthānād bhraṣṭāḥ patanty adhaḥ.*

We can actually see that in this age of Kali many so-called *brāhmaṇas* are envious of Vaiṣṇavas. The Kali-contaminated *brāhmaṇas* consider Deity worship to be imaginative: *arcye viṣṇau śilā-dhīr guruṣu nara-matir vaiṣṇave jāti-buddhiḥ.* Such a contaminated *brāhmaṇa* may superficially imagine a form of the Lord, but actually he considers the Deity in the temple to be made of stone or wood. Similarly, such a contaminated *brāhmaṇa* considers the *guru* to be an ordinary human being, and he objects when a Vaiṣṇava is created by the Kṛṣṇa consciousness movement. Many so-called *brāhmaṇas* attempt to fight us, saying, "How can you create a *brāhmaṇa* out of a European or American? A *brāhmaṇa* can be born only in a *brāhmaṇa* family." They do not consider that this is never stated in any revealed scripture. It is specifically stated in *Bhagavad-gītā* (4.13): *cāturvarṇyaṁ mayā sṛṣṭaṁ guṇa-karma-vibhāgaśaḥ*. "According to the three modes of material nature and the work ascribed to them, the four divisions of human society were created by Me."

Thus a *brāhmaṇa* is not a result of the caste system. He becomes a *brāhmaṇa* only by qualification. Similarly, a Vaiṣṇava does not belong to a particular caste; rather, his designation is determined by the rendering of devotional service.

TEXT 278

শুনি' 'কৃষ্ণ' 'কৃষ্ণ' বলি' অমোঘ উঠিলা।
প্রেমোন্মাদে মত্ত হঞা নাচিতে লাগিলা ২৭৮ ॥

śuni' 'kṛṣṇa' 'kṛṣṇa' bali' amogha uṭhilā
premonmāde matta hañā nācite lāgilā

SYNONYMS

śuni'—hearing; *kṛṣṇa kṛṣṇa*—the holy name of Kṛṣṇa; *bali'*—speaking; *amogha uṭhilā*—Amogha stood up; *premonmāde*—in ecstatic love of Kṛṣṇa; *matta hañā*—becoming maddened; *nācite lāgilā*—began to dance.

TRANSLATION

After hearing Śrī Caitanya Mahāprabhu and being touched by Him, Amogha, who was on his deathbed, immediately stood up and began to chant the holy name of Kṛṣṇa. Thus he became mad with ecstatic love and began to dance emotionally.

TEXT 279

কম্প, অশ্রু, পুলক, স্তম্ভ, স্বেদ, স্বরভঙ্গ।
প্রভু হাসে দেখি' তার প্রেমের তরঙ্গ ॥ ২৭৯ ॥

kampa, aśru, pulaka, stambha, sveda, svara-bhaṅga
prabhu hāse dekhi' tāra premera taraṅga

SYNONYMS

kampa—trembling; *aśru*—tears; *pulaka*—jubilation; *stambha*—being stunned; *sveda*—perspiration; *svara-bhaṅga*—faltering of the voice; *prabhu hāse*—Śrī

Caitanya Mahāprabhu began to laugh; *dekhi'*—seeing; *tāra*—Amogha's; *premera taraṅga*—waves of ecstatic love.

TRANSLATION

While Amogha danced in ecstatic love, he manifested all the ecstatic symptoms—trembling, tears, jubilation, trance, perspiration and a faltering voice. Seeing these waves of ecstatic emotion, Śrī Caitanya Mahāprabhu began to laugh.

TEXT 280

প্রভুর চরণে ধরি' করয়ে বিনয়।
অপরাধ ক্ষম মোরে, প্রভু, দয়াময় ॥ ২৮০॥

prabhura caraṇe dhari' karaye vinaya
aparādha kṣama more, prabhu, dayāmaya

SYNONYMS

prabhura caraṇe—the lotus feet of Lord Śrī Caitanya Mahāprabhu; *dhari'*—catching; *karaye*—does; *vinaya*—submission; *aparādha*—offense; *kṣama*—kindly excuse; *more*—me; *prabhu*—O Lord; *dayā-maya*—merciful.

TRANSLATION

Amogha then fell before the Lord's lotus feet and submissively said, "O merciful Lord, please excuse my offense."

TEXT 281

এই ছার মুখে তোমার করিনু নিন্দনে।
এত বলি' আপন গালে চড়ায় আপনে ॥ ২৮১ ॥

ei chāra mukhe tomāra karinu nindane
eta bali' āpana gāle caḍāya āpane

SYNONYMS

ei chāra mukhe—in this abominable mouth; *tomāra*—Your; *karinu*—I did; *nindane*—blaspheming; *eta bali'*—saying this; *āpana*—his own; *gāle*—cheeks; *caḍāya*—he slapped; *āpane*—himself.

TRANSLATION

Not only did Amogha beg the Lord's pardon, but he also began slapping his own cheeks, saying, "By this mouth I have blasphemed You."

TEXT 282

চড়াইতে চড়াইতে গাল ফুলাইল ।
হাতে ধরি' গোপীনাথাচার্য নিষেধিল ॥ ২৮২ ॥

caḍāite caḍāite gāla phulāila
hāte dhari' gopīnāthācārya niṣedhila

SYNONYMS

caḍāite caḍāite—slapping over and over again; *gāla*—the cheeks; *phulāila*—he made them swollen; *hāte dhari'*—catching his hands; *gopīnātha-ācārya*—Gopīnātha Ācārya; *niṣedhila*—forbade.

TRANSLATION

Indeed, Amogha continued slapping his face over and over until his cheeks were swollen. Finally Gopīnātha Ācārya stopped him by catching hold of his hands.

TEXT 283

প্রভু আশ্বাসন করে স্পর্শি' তার গাত্র ।
সার্বভৌম-সম্বন্ধে তুমি মোর স্নেহপাত্র ॥ ২৮৩ ॥

prabhu āśvāsana kare sparśi' tāra gātra
sārvabhauma-sambandhe tumi mora sneha-pātra

SYNONYMS

prabhu—Śrī Caitanya Mahāprabhu; *āśvāsana kare*—pacifies; *sparśi'*—touching; *tāra*—his; *gātra*—body; *sārvabhauma-sambandhe*—because of a relation to Sārvabhauma Bhaṭṭācārya; *tumi*—you; *mora*—My; *sneha-pātra*—object of affection.

TRANSLATION

After this, Śrī Caitanya Mahāprabhu pacified Amogha by touching his body and saying, "You are the object of My affection because you are the son-in-law of Sārvabhauma Bhaṭṭācārya.

TEXT 284

সার্বভৌম-গৃহে দাস-দাসী, যে কুক্কুর।
সেহ মোর প্রিয়, অন্য জন রহু দূর ॥ ২৮৪ ॥

sārvabhauma-gṛhe dāsa-dāsī, ye kukkura
seha mora priya, anya jana rahu dūra

SYNONYMS

sārvabhauma-gṛhe—at the house of Sārvabhauma Bhaṭṭācārya; *dāsa-dāsī*—servants and maidservants; *ye kukkura*—even a dog; *seha*—all of them; *mora*—to Me; *priya*—very dear; *anya jana*—others; *rahu dūra*—what to speak of.

TRANSLATION

"Everyone in Sārvabhauma Bhaṭṭācārya's house is very dear to Me, including his maids and servants and even his dog. And what to speak of his relatives?

TEXT 285

অপরাধ' নাহি, সদা লও কৃষ্ণনাম।
এত বলি' প্রভু আইলা সার্বভৌম-স্থান॥ ২৮৫ ॥

aparādha' nāhi, sadā lao kṛṣṇa-nāma
eta bali' prabhu āilā sārvabhauma-sthāna

SYNONYMS

aparādha' nāhi—do not commit offenses; *sadā*—always; *lao*—chant; *kṛṣṇa-nāma*—the Hare Kṛṣṇa *mahā-mantra; eta bali'*—saying this; *prabhu*—Śrī Caitanya Mahāprabhu; *āilā*—came; *sārvabhauma-sthāna*—to the place of Sārvabhauma Bhaṭṭācārya.

TRANSLATION

"Amogha, always chant the Hare Kṛṣṇa mahā-mantra and do not commit any further offenses." After giving Amogha this instruction, Śrī Caitanya Mahāprabhu went to Sārvabhauma's house."

TEXT 286

প্রভু দেখি' সার্বভৌম ধরিলা চরণে।
প্রভু তাঁরে আলিঙ্গিয়া বসিলা আসনে॥ ২৮৬ ॥

prabhu dekhi' sārvabhauma dharilā caraṇe
prabhu tāṅre āliṅgiyā vasilā āsane

SYNONYMS

prabhu dekhi'—seeing Lord Śrī Caitanya Mahāprabhu; *sārvabhauma*—Sārvabhauma Bhaṭṭācārya; *dharilā caraṇe*—caught hold of His feet; *prabhu*—Śrī Caitanya Mahāprabhu; *tāṅre*—him; *āliṅgiyā*—embracing; *vasilā āsane*—sat down on the seat.

TRANSLATION

Upon seeing the Lord, Sārvabhauma Bhaṭṭācārya immediately caught hold of His lotus feet. The Lord also embraced him and sat down.

TEXT 287

প্রভু কহে,—অমোঘ শিশু, কিবা তার দোষ।
কেনে উপবাস কর, কেনে কর রোষ॥ ২৮৭ ॥

prabhu kahe,——amogha śiśu, kibā tāra doṣa
kene upavāsa kara, kene kara roṣa

SYNONYMS

prabhu kahe—Śrī Caitanya Mahāprabhu said; *amogha śiśu*—Amogha is a child; *kibā*—what; *tāra doṣa*—his fault; *kene*—why; *upavāsa kara*—are you fasting; *kene*—why; *kara roṣa*—are you angry.

TRANSLATION

Śrī Caitanya Mahāprabhu pacified Sārvabhauma, saying, "After all, Amogha, your son-in-law, is a child. So what is his fault? Why are you fasting, and why are you angry?

TEXT 288

উঠ, স্নান কর, দেখ জগন্নাথ-মুখ।
শীঘ্র আসি, ভোজন কর, তবে মোর সুখ॥ ২৮৮ ॥

uṭha, snāna kara, dekha jagannātha-mukha
śīghra āsi, bhojana kara, tabe mora sukha

SYNONYMS

uṭha—get up; *snāna kara*—take your bath; *dekha*—see; *jagannātha-mukha*—Lord Jagannātha's face; *śīghra āsi*—coming back very soon; *bhojana kara*—take your lunch; *tabe mora sukha*—then I shall be very happy.

TRANSLATION

"Just get up and take your bath and go see the face of Lord Jagannātha. Then return here to eat your lunch. In this way I shall be happy.

TEXT 289

তাবৎ রহিব আমি এথায় বসিয়া ।
যাবৎ না খাইবে তুমি প্রসাদ আসিয়া ॥ ২৮৯ ॥

tāvat rahiba āmi ethāya vasiyā
yāvat nā khāibe tumi prasāda āsiyā

SYNONYMS

tāvat—as long as; *rahiba*—shall stay; *āmi*—I; *ethāya*—here; *vasiyā*—sitting; *yāvat*—as long as; *nā khāibe*—will not eat; *tumi*—you; *prasāda*—remnants of the food of Jagannātha; *āsiyā*—coming here.

TRANSLATION

"I shall stay here until you return to take Lord Jagannātha's remnants for your lunch."

TEXT 290

প্রভু-পদ ধরি' ভট্ট কহিতে লাগিলা ।
মরিত' অমোঘ, তারে কেনে জীয়াইলা ॥ ২৯০ ॥

prabhu-pada dhari' bhaṭṭa kahite lāgilā
marita' amogha, tāre kene jīyāilā

SYNONYMS

prabhu-pada—Śrī Caitanya Mahāprabhu's lotus feet; *dhari'*—catching hold of; *bhaṭṭa*—Sārvabhauma Bhaṭṭācārya; *kahite lāgilā*—began to speak; *marita' amogha*—Amogha would have died; *tāre*—him; *kene*—why; *jīyāilā*—have You brought to life.

TRANSLATION

Catching hold of Śrī Caitanya Mahāprabhu's lotus feet, Bhaṭṭācārya said, "Why did You bring Amogha back to life? It would have been better had he died."

TEXT 291

প্রভু কহে,—অমোঘ শিশু, তোমার বালক ।
বালক-দোষ না লয় পিতা, তাহাতে পালক ॥ ২৯১ ॥

prabhu kahe,——amogha śiśu, tomāra bālaka
bālaka-doṣa nā laya pitā, tāhāte pālaka

SYNONYMS

prabhu kahe—Śrī Caitanya Mahāprabhu said; *amogha śiśu*—Amogha is a child; *tomāra bālaka*—your son; *bālaka-doṣa*—the offense of a child; *nā laya*—does not accept; *pitā*—the father; *tāhāte*—unto him; *pālaka*—the maintainer.

TRANSLATION

Śrī Caitanya Mahāprabhu said, "Amogha is a child and your son. The father does not take the faults of his son seriously, especially when he is maintaining him.

TEXT 292

এবে 'বৈষ্ণব' হৈল, তার গেল 'অপরাধ' ।
তাহার উপরে এবে করহ প্রসাদ ॥ ২৯২ ॥

ebe 'vaiṣṇava' haila, tāra gela 'aparādha'
tāhāra upare ebe karaha prasāda

SYNONYMS

ebe—now; *vaiṣṇava haila*—has become a Vaiṣṇava; *tāra*—his; *gela*—went away; *aparādha*—offenses; *tāhāra upare*—upon him; *ebe*—now; *karaha prasāda*—show mercy.

TRANSLATION

"Now that he has become a Vaiṣṇava, he is offenseless. You can bestow your mercy upon him without hesitation."

TEXT 293

ভট্ট কহে,—চল, প্রভু, ঈশ্বর-দরশনে ।
স্নান করি' তাঁহা মুঞি আসিছোঁ এখনে ॥ ২৯৩ ॥

bhaṭṭa kahe,——cala, prabhu, īśvara-daraśane
snāna kari' tāṅhā muñi āsichoṅ ekhane

SYNONYMS

bhaṭṭa kahe—Bhaṭṭācārya said; *cala*—go; *prabhu*—my Lord; *īśvara-daraśane*—to see Lord Jagannātha, the Personality of Godhead; *snāna kari'*—taking my bath; *tāṅhā*—there; *muñi*—I; *āsichoṅ*—shall come back; *ekhane*—here.

TRANSLATION

Sārvabhauma Bhaṭṭācārya said, "Please go, my Lord, to see Lord Jagannātha. After taking my bath, I shall go there and then return."

TEXT 294

প্রভু কহে,—গোপীনাথ, ইহাঞি রহিবা ।
ইঁহো প্রসাদ পাইলে, বার্তা আমাকে কহিবা ॥২৯৪॥

prabhu kahe,——gopīnātha, ihāñi rahibā
iṅho prasāda pāile, vārtā āmāke kahibā

SYNONYMS

prabhu kahe—Śrī Caitanya Mahāprabhu said; *gopīnātha*—Gopīnātha; *ihāñi rahibā*—please stay here; *iṅho*—Sārvabhauma Bhaṭṭācārya; *prasāda pāile*—when he takes his lunch; *vārtā*—the news; *āmāke kahibā*—inform Me.

TRANSLATION

Śrī Caitanya Mahāprabhu then told Gopīnātha, "Stay here and inform Me when Sārvabhauma Bhaṭṭācārya has taken his prasāda."

TEXT 295

এত বলি' প্রভু গেলা ঈশ্বর-দরশনে ।
ভট্ট স্নান দর্শন করি' করিলা ভোজনে ॥ ২৯৫ ॥

eta bali' prabhu gelā īśvara-daraśane
bhaṭṭa snāna darśana kari' karilā bhojane

SYNONYMS

eta bali'—saying this; *prabhu*—Śrī Caitanya Mahāprabhu; *gelā*—went; *īśvara-daraśane*—to see Lord Jagannātha; *bhaṭṭa*—Sārvabhauma Bhaṭṭācārya; *snāna darśana kari'*—finishing his bathing and seeing of Lord Jagannātha; *karilā bhojane*—accepted food.

TRANSLATION

After saying this, Śrī Caitanya Mahāprabhu went to see Lord Jagannātha. Sārvabhauma Bhaṭṭācārya completed his bath, went to see Lord Jagannātha and then returned to his house to accept food.

TEXT 296

সেই অমোঘ হৈল প্রভুর ভক্ত 'একান্ত'।
প্রেমে নাচে, কৃষ্ণনাম লয় মহাশান্ত ॥ ২৯৬ ॥

sei amogha haila prabhura bhakta 'ekānta'
preme nāce, kṛṣṇa-nāma laya mahā-śānta

SYNONYMS

sei amogha—that same Amogha; *haila*—became; *prabhura*—of Lord Śrī Caitanya Mahāprabhu; *bhakta*—devotee; *ekānta*—unflinching; *preme nāce*—dances in ecstasy; *kṛṣṇa-nāma laya*—chants the Hare Kṛṣṇa *mahā-mantra; mahā-śānta*—very peaceful.

TRANSLATION

Thereafter, Amogha became an unalloyed devotee of Śrī Caitanya Mahāprabhu. He danced in ecstasy and peacefully chanted the holy name of Lord Kṛṣṇa.

TEXT 297

ঐছে চিত্র-লীলা করে শচীর নন্দন।
যেই দেখে, শুনে, তাঁর বিস্ময় হয় মন ॥ ২৯৭ ॥

aiche citra-līlā kare śacīra nandana
yei dekhe, śune, tāṅra vismaya haya mana

SYNONYMS

aiche—in this way; *citra-līlā*—varieties of pastimes; *kare*—performs; *śacīra nandana*—the son of mother Śacī; *yei dekhe*—anyone who sees; *śune*—hears; *tāṅra*—his; *vismaya*—astonished; *haya*—becomes; *mana*—mind.

TRANSLATION

In this way, Śrī Caitanya Mahāprabhu performed His various pastimes. Whoever sees them or hears of them becomes truly astonished.

TEXT 298

ঐছে ভট্ট-গৃহে করে ভোজন-বিলাস।
তার মধ্যে নানা চিত্র-চরিত্র-প্রকাশ ॥ ২৯৮ ॥

aiche bhaṭṭa-gṛhe kare bhojana-vilāsa
tāra madhye nānā citra-caritra-prakāśa

SYNONYMS

aiche—in this way; *bhaṭṭa-gṛhe*—in the house of Sārvabhauma Bhaṭṭācārya; *kare*—performs; *bhojana-vilāsa*—pastime of eating; *tāra madhye*—within that pastime; *nānā*—various; *citra-caritra*—of varieties of activities; *prakāśa*—manifestation.

TRANSLATION

Thus Śrī Caitanya Mahāprabhu enjoyed eating in Sārvabhauma Bhaṭṭācārya's house. Within that one pastime, many wonderful pastimes were manifest.

TEXT 299

সার্বভৌম-ঘরে এই ভোজন-চরিত ।
সার্বভৌম-প্রেম যাঁহা হইলা বিদিত ॥ ২৯৯ ॥

sārvabhauma-ghare ei bhojana-carita
sārvabhauma-prema yāṅhā ha-ilā vidita

SYNONYMS

sārvabhauma-ghare—in the house of Sārvabhauma Bhaṭṭācārya; *ei*—these; *bhojana-carita*—eating affairs; *sārvabhauma-prema*—love of Sārvabhauma Bhaṭṭācārya; *yāṅhā*—where; *ha-ilā*—became; *vidita*—well known.

TRANSLATION

These are the peculiar characteristics of Śrī Caitanya Mahāprabhu's pastimes. Thus the Lord ate in Sārvabhauma Bhaṭṭācārya's house, and in this way Sārvabhauma's love for the Lord has become very well known.

PURPORT

As stated in the *Śākhā-nirṇayāmṛta:*

amogha-paṇḍitaṁ vande
śrī-gaureṇātma-sātkṛtam
prema-gadgada-sāndrāṅgaṁ
pulakākula-vigraham

"I offer my obeisances unto Amogha Paṇḍita, who was accepted by Lord Śrī Caitanya Mahāprabhu. As a result of this acceptance, he was always merged in ecstatic love, and he manifested ecstatic symptoms such as choking of the voice and standing of the hairs on his body."

TEXT 300

ষাঠীর মাতার প্রেম, আর প্রভুর প্রসাদ।
ভক্ত-সম্বন্ধে যাহা ক্ষমিল অপরাধ ॥ ৩০০ ॥

ṣāṭhīra mātāra prema, āra prabhura prasāda
bhakta-sambandhe yāhā kṣamila aparādha

SYNONYMS

ṣāṭhīra mātāra prema—the love of the mother of Ṣāṭhī; *āra*—and; *prabhura prasāda*—the mercy of Śrī Caitanya Mahāprabhu; *bhakta-sambandhe*—because of a relationship with a devotee; *yāhā*—where; *kṣamila aparādha*—Śrī Caitanya Mahāprabhu excused the offense.

TRANSLATION

Thus I have related the ecstatic love of Sārvabhauma's wife, who is known as the mother of Ṣāṭhī. I have also related Śrī Caitanya Mahāprabhu's great mercy, which He manifested by excusing Amogha's offense. He did so due to Amogha's relationship with a devotee.

PURPORT

Amogha was an offender because he blasphemed the Lord. As a result, he was about to die of cholera. Amogha did not receive an opportunity to be freed from all offenses after being attacked by the disease, but Sārvabhauma Bhaṭṭācārya and his wife were very dear to the Lord. Because of their relationship, Śrī Caitanya Mahāprabhu excused Amogha. Instead of being punished by the Lord, he was saved by the Lord's mercy. All this was due to the unflinching love of Sārvabhauma Bhaṭṭācārya for Śrī Caitanya Mahāprabhu. Externally, Amogha was Sārvabhauma Bhaṭṭācārya's son-in-law, and he was being maintained by Sārvabhauma. Consequently if Amogha were not excused, his punishment would have directly affected Sārvabhauma. Amogha's death would have indirectly brought about the death of Sārvabhauma Bhaṭṭācārya.

TEXT 301

শ্রদ্ধা করি' এই লীলা শুনে যেই জন।
অচিরাৎ পায় সেই চৈতন্য-চরণ ॥ ৩০১ ॥

śraddhā kari' ei līlā śune yei jana
acirāt pāya sei caitanya-caraṇa

SYNONYMS

śraddhā kari'—with faith and love; *ei līlā*—this pastime; *śune*—hears; *yei jana*—whoever; *acirāt*—very soon; *pāya*—attains; *sei*—he; *caitanya-caraṇa*—the lotus feet of Lord Caitanya.

TRANSLATION

Whoever hears these pastimes of Śrī Caitanya Mahāprabhu with faith and love will attain the shelter of the Lord's lotus feet very soon.

TEXT 302

শ্রীরূপ-রঘুনাথ-পদে যার আশ ।
চৈতন্যচরিতামৃত কহে কৃষ্ণদাস ॥ ৩০২ ॥

śrī-rūpa-raghunātha-pade yāra āśa
caitanya-caritāmṛta kahe kṛṣṇadāsa

SYNONYMS

śrī-rūpa—Śrī Rūpa Gosvāmī; *raghunātha*—Śrīla Raghunātha dāsa Gosvāmī; *pade*—at the lotus feet; *yāra*—whose; *āśa*—expectation; *caitanya-caritāmṛta*—the book named *Caitanya-caritāmṛta; kahe*—describes; *kṛṣṇadāsa*—Śrīla Kṛṣṇadāsa Kavirāja Gosvāmī.

TRANSLATION

Praying at the lotus feet of Śrī Rūpa and Śrī Raghunātha, always desiring their mercy, I, Kṛṣṇadāsa, narrate Śrī Caitanya-caritāmṛta, following in their footsteps.

Thus end the Bhaktivedanta purports to the Śrī Caitanya-caritāmṛta, Madhya-līlā, *Fifteenth Chapter, describing the Lord's eating at the house of Sārvabhauma Bhaṭṭācārya.*

CHAPTER 16

The Lord's Attempt to Go to Vṛndāvana

Śrīla Bhaktivinoda Ṭhākura gives the following summary of this chapter in his *Amṛta-pravāha-bhāṣya.* When Śrī Caitanya Mahāprabhu wanted to go to Vṛndāvana, Rāmānanda Rāya and Sārvabhauma Bhaṭṭācārya indirectly presented many obstructions. In due course of time, all the devotees of Bengal visited Jagannātha Purī for the third year. This time, all the wives of the Vaiṣṇavas brought many types of food, intending to extend invitations to Śrī Caitanya Mahāprabhu at Jagannātha Purī. When the devotees arrived, Caitanya Mahāprabhu sent his blessings in the form of garlands. In that year also, the Guṇḍicā temple was cleansed, and when the Cāturmāsya period was over, all the devotees returned to their homes in Bengal. Caitanya Mahāprabhu forbade Nityānanda to visit Nīlācala every year. Questioned by the inhabitants of Kulīna-grāma, Caitanya Mahāprabhu again repeated the symptoms of a Vaiṣṇava. Vidyānidhi also came to Jagannātha Purī and saw the festival of Oḍana-ṣaṣṭhī. When the devotees bade farewell to the Lord, the Lord was determined to go to Vṛndāvana, and on the day of Vijayā-daśamī, He departed.

Mahārāja Pratāparudra made various arrangements for Śrī Caitanya Mahāprabhu's trip to Vṛndāvana. When He crossed the River Citrotpalā, Rāmānanda Rāya, Mardarāja and Haricandana went with Him. Śrī Caitanya Mahāprabhu requested Gadādhara Paṇḍita to go to Nīlācala, Jagannātha Purī, but he did not abide by this order. From Kaṭaka, Śrī Caitanya Mahāprabhu again requested Gadādhara Paṇḍita to return to Nīlācala, and He bade farewell to Rāmānanda Rāya from Bhadraka. After this, Śrī Caitanya Mahāprabhu crossed the border of Orissa state, and He arrived at Pānihāṭi by boat. Thereafter He visited the house of Rāghava Paṇḍita, and from there He went to Kumārahaṭṭa and eventually to Kuliyā, where He excused many offenders. From there He went to Rāmakeli, where He saw Śrī Rūpa and Sanātana and accepted them as His chief disciples. Returning from Rāmakeli, He met Raghunātha dāsa and after giving him instructions sent him back home. Thereafter the Lord returned to Nīlācala and began to make plans to go to Vṛndāvana without a companion.

TEXT 1

গৌড়োদ্যানং গৌরমেঘঃ সিঞ্চন্ স্বালোকনামৃতৈঃ ।
ভবাগ্নিদগ্ধজনতা-বীরুধঃ সমজীবয়ৎ ॥ ১ ॥

gauḍodyānaṁ gaura-meghaḥ
siñcan svālokanāmṛtaiḥ
bhavāgni-dagdha-janatā-
vīrudhaḥ samajīvayat

SYNONYMS

gauḍa-udyānam—upon the garden known as Gauḍa-deśa; *gaura-meghaḥ*—the cloud known as Gaura; *siñcan*—pouring water; *sva*—His own; *ālokana-amṛtaiḥ*—with the nectar of the glance; *bhava-agni*—by the blazing fire of material existence; *dagdha*—having been burnt; *janatā*—the people in general; *vīrudhaḥ*—who are like creepers and plants; *samajīvayat*—revived.

TRANSLATION

By the nectar of His personal glance, the cloud known as Śrī Caitanya Mahāprabhu poured water upon the garden of Gauḍa-deśa and revived the people, who were like creepers and plants burning in the forest fire of material existence.

TEXT 2

জয় জয় গৌরচন্দ্র জয় নিত্যানন্দ ।
জয়াদ্বৈতচন্দ্র জয় গৌরভক্তবৃন্দ ॥ ২ ॥

jaya jaya gauracandra jaya nityānanda
jayādvaita-candra jaya gaura-bhakta-vṛnda

SYNONYMS

jaya jaya—all glories; *gauracandra*—to Lord Śrī Caitanya Mahāprabhu; *jaya*—all glories; *nityānanda*—to Nityānanda Prabhu; *jaya*—all glories; *advaita-candra*—to Advaita Ācārya; *jaya*—all glories; *gaura-bhakta-vṛnda*—to the devotees of Lord Śrī Caitanya Mahāprabhu.

TRANSLATION

All glories to Śrī Caitanya Mahāprabhu! All glories to Lord Nityānanda! All glories to Advaitacandra! All glories to all the devotees of the Lord!

TEXT 3

প্রভুর হইল ইচ্ছা যাইতে বৃন্দাবন ।
শুনিয়া প্রতাপরুদ্র হইলা বিমন ॥ ৩ ॥

prabhura ha-ila icchā yāite vṛndāvana
śuniyā pratāparudra ha-ilā vimana

SYNONYMS

prabhura—of Lord Śrī Caitanya Mahāprabhu; *ha-ila*—there was; *icchā*—the desire; *yāite*—to go; *vṛndāvana*—to Vṛndāvana; *śuniyā*—hearing; *pratāparudra*—Mahārāja Pratāparudra; *ha-ilā vimana*—became morose.

TRANSLATION

Śrī Caitanya Mahāprabhu decided to go to Vṛndāvana, and Mahārāja Pratāparudra became very morose upon hearing this news.

TEXT 4

সার্বভৌম, রামানন্দ, আনি' দুই জন ।
দুঁহাকে কহেন রাজা বিনয়-বচন ॥ ৪ ॥

sārvabhauma, rāmānanda, āni' dui jana
duṅhāke kahena rājā vinaya-vacana

SYNONYMS

sārvabhauma—Sārvabhauma; *rāmānanda*—Rāmānanda; *āni'*—calling; *dui jana*—two persons; *duṅhāke*—unto both of them; *kahena*—said; *rājā*—the King; *vinaya-vacana*—submissive words.

TRANSLATION

The King therefore called for Sārvabhauma Bhaṭṭācārya and Rāmānanda Rāya, and he spoke the following submissive words to them.

TEXT 5

নীলাদ্রি ছাড়ি' প্রভুর মন অন্যত্র যাইতে ॥
তোমরা করহ যত্ন তাঁহারে রাখিতে ॥ ৫ ॥

nīlādri chāḍi' prabhura mana anyatra yāite
tomarā karaha yatna tāṅhāre rākhite

SYNONYMS

nīlādri—Jagannātha Purī; *chāḍi'*—giving up; *prabhura*—of Śrī Caitanya Mahāprabhu; *mana*—the mind; *anyatra*—elsewhere; *yāite*—to go; *tomarā*—both of you; *karaha*—make; *yatna*—endeavor; *tāṅhāre*—Him; *rākhite*—to keep.

TRANSLATION

Pratāparudra Mahārāja said, "Please endeavor to keep Śrī Caitanya Mahāprabhu here at Jagannātha Purī, for now He is thinking of going elsewhere.

TEXT 6

তাঁহা বিনা এই রাজ্য মোরে নাহি ভায়।
গোসাঞি রাখিতে করহ নানা উপায় ॥ ৬ ॥

tāṅhā vinā ei rājya more nāhi bhāya
gosāñi rākhite karaha nānā upāya

SYNONYMS

tāṅhā vinā—without Him; *ei rājya*—this kingdom; *more*—to me; *nāhi bhāya*—is not very pleasing; *gosāñi*—Śrī Caitanya Mahāprabhu; *rākhite*—to keep; *karaha*—do; *nānā upāya*—various sorts of devices.

TRANSLATION

"Without Śrī Caitanya Mahāprabhu, this kingdom is not pleasing to me. Therefore please try to devise some plan to enable the Lord to stay here."

TEXT 7

রামানন্দ, সার্বভৌম, দুইজনা-স্থানে।
তবে যুক্তি করে প্রভু—'যাব বৃন্দাবনে' ॥ ৭ ॥

rāmānanda, sārvabhauma, dui-janā-sthāne
tabe yukti kare prabhu——'yāba vṛndāvane'

SYNONYMS

rāmānanda—Rāmānanda; *sārvabhauma*—Sārvabhauma; *dui-janā-sthāne*—before the two persons; *tabe*—then; *yukti kare*—consulted; *prabhu*—Śrī Caitanya Mahāprabhu; *yāba vṛndāvane*—I shall go to Vṛndāvana.

TRANSLATION

After this, Śrī Caitanya Mahāprabhu Himself consulted Rāmānanda Rāya and Sārvabhauma Bhaṭṭācārya, saying, "I shall go to Vṛndāvana."

TEXT 8

দুঁহে কহে,—রথযাত্রা কর দরশন।
কার্তিক আইলে, তবে করিহ গমন॥ ৮॥

duṅhe kahe,——ratha-yātrā kara daraśana
kārtika āile, tabe kariha gamana

SYNONYMS

duṅhe kahe—both of them said; *ratha-yātrā*—the Ratha-yātrā festival; *kara daraśana*—please see; *kārtika āile*—when the month of Kārttika arrives; *tabe*—at that time; *kariha gamana*—You can go.

TRANSLATION

Rāmānanda Rāya and Sārvabhauma Bhaṭṭācārya requested the Lord to observe first the Ratha-yātrā festival. Then when the month of Kārttika arrived, He could go to Vṛndāvana.

TEXT 9

কার্তিক আইলে কহে—এবে মহাশীত।
দোলযাত্রা দেখি' যাও—এই ভাল রীত॥ ৯॥

kārtika āile kahe——ebe mahā-śīta
dola-yātrā dekhi' yāo——ei bhāla rīta

SYNONYMS

kārtika āile—when the month of Kārttika arrived; *kahe*—both of them said; *ebe*—now; *mahā-śīta*—very cold; *dola-yātrā dekhi'*—after seeing the Dola-yātrā ceremony; *yāo*—You go; *ei*—this; *bhāla rīta*—a very nice program.

TRANSLATION

However, when the month of Kārttika came, they both told the Lord, "Now it is very cold. It is better that You wait to see the Dola-yātrā festival and then go. That will be very nice."

TEXT 10

আজি-কালি করি' উঠায় বিবিধ উপায়।
যাইতে সম্মতি না দেয় বিচ্ছেদের ভয়॥ ১০॥

āji-kāli kari' uṭhāya vividha upāya
yāite sammati nā deya vicchedera bhaya

SYNONYMS

āji-kāli kari'—delaying today and tomorrow; *uṭhāya*—they put forward; *vividha upāya*—many devices; *yāite*—to go; *sammati*—permission; *nā deya*—did not give; *vicchedera bhaya*—because of fearing separation.

TRANSLATION

In this way they both presented many impediments, indirectly not granting the Lord permission to go to Vṛndāvana. They did this because they were afraid of separation from Him.

TEXT 11

যদ্যপি স্বতন্ত্র প্রভু নহে নিবারণ ।
ভক্ত-ইচ্ছা বিনা প্রভু না করে গমন ॥ ১১ ॥

yadyapi svatantra prabhu nahe nivāraṇa
bhakta-icchā vinā prabhu nā kare gamana

SYNONYMS

yadyapi—although; *svatantra*—fully independent; *prabhu*—Śrī Caitanya Mahāprabhu; *nahe nivāraṇa*—there is no checking Him; *bhakta-icchā vinā*—without the permission of devotees; *prabhu*—Śrī Caitanya Mahāprabhu; *nā kare gamana*—does not go.

TRANSLATION

Although the Lord is completely independent and incapable of being checked by anyone, He still did not go without the permission of His devotees.

TEXT 12

তৃতীয় বৎসরে সব গৌড়ের ভক্তগণ ।
নীলাচলে চলিতে সবার হৈল মন ॥ ১২ ॥

tṛtīya vatsare saba gauḍera bhakta-gaṇa
nīlācale calite sabāra haila mana

SYNONYMS

tṛtīya vatsare—in the third year; *saba*—all; *gauḍera bhakta-gaṇa*—devotees from Bengal; *nīlācale*—to Jagannātha Purī; *calite*—to go; *sabāra*—of everyone; *haila*—there was; *mana*—the mind.

TRANSLATION

Then, for the third year, all the devotees of Bengal wanted to return again to Jagannātha Purī.

TEXT 13

সবে মেলি' গেলা অদ্বৈত আচার্যের পাশে ।
প্রভু দেখিতে আচার্য চলিলা উল্লাসে ॥ ১৩ ॥

sabe meli' gelā advaita ācāryera pāśe
prabhu dekhite ācārya calilā ullāse

SYNONYMS

sabe—everyone; *meli'*—after assembling together; *gelā*—went; *advaita*—Advaita; *ācāryera*—of the leader of Navadvīpa; *pāśe*—in the presence; *prabhu dekhite*—to see Lord Śrī Caitanya Mahāprabhu; *ācārya*—Advaita Ācārya; *calilā*—departed; *ullāse*—in great jubilation.

TRANSLATION

All the Bengali devotees gathered around Advaita Ācārya, and in great jubilation Advaita Ācārya departed to Jagannātha Purī to see Śrī Caitanya Mahāprabhu.

TEXTS 14-15

যদ্যপি প্রভুর আজ্ঞা গৌড়েতে রহিতে ।
নিত্যানন্দ-প্রভুকে প্রেমভক্তি প্রকাশিতে ॥ ১৪ ॥
তথাপি চলিলা মহাপ্রভুরে দেখিতে ।
নিত্যানন্দের প্রেম-চেষ্টা কে পারে বুঝিতে ॥ ১৫ ॥

yadyapi prabhura ājñā gauḍete rahite
nityānanda-prabhuke prema-bhakti prakāśite

tathāpi calilā mahāprabhure dekhite
nityānandera prema-ceṣṭā ke pāre bujhite

SYNONYMS

yadyapi—although; *prabhura*—of Śrī Caitanya Mahāprabhu; *ājñā*—the order; *gauḍete rahite*—to stay in Bengal; *nityānanda-prabhuke*—unto Nityānanda Prabhu; *prema-bhakti*—ecstatic love of Godhead; *prakāśite*—to preach; *tathāpi*—still; *calilā*—departed; *mahāprabhure*—Śrī Caitanya Mahāprabhu; *dekhite*—to see; *nityānandera*—of Lord Nityānanda Prabhu; *prema-ceṣṭā*—the activities of ecstatic love; *ke*—who; *pāre*—is able; *bujhite*—to understand.

TRANSLATION

Although the Lord told Nityānanda Prabhu to stay in Bengal and spread ecstatic love of God, Nityānanda left to go see Caitanya Mahāprabhu. Who can understand Nityānanda Prabhu's ecstatic love?

TEXTS 16-17

আচার্যরত্ন, বিদ্যানিধি, শ্রীবাস, রামাই ।
বাসুদেব, মুরারি, গোবিন্দাদি তিন ভাই ॥ ১৬ ॥
রাঘব পণ্ডিত নিজ-ঝালি সাজাঞা ।
কুলীন-গ্রামবাসী চলে পট্টডোরী লঞা ॥ ১৭ ॥

ācāryaratna, vidyānidhi, śrīvāsa, rāmāi
vāsudeva, murāri, govindādi tina bhāi

rāghava paṇḍita nija-jhāli sājāñā
kulīna-grāma-vāsī cale paṭṭa-ḍorī lañā

SYNONYMS

ācāryaratna—Ācāryaratna; *vidyānidhi*—Vidyānidhi; *śrīvāsa*—Śrīvāsa; *rāmāi*—Rāmāi; *vāsudeva*—Vāsudeva; *murāri*—Murāri; *govinda-ādi tina bhāi*—Govinda and his two brothers; *rāghava paṇḍita*—Rāghava Paṇḍita; *nija-jhāli*—his own bags; *sājāñā*—assorting; *kulīna-grāma-vāsī*—the inhabitants of Kulīna-grāma; *cale*—went; *paṭṭa-ḍorī lañā*—taking silken ropes.

TRANSLATION

All the devotees of Navadvīpa departed, including Ācāryaratna, Vidyānidhi, Śrīvāsa, Rāmāi, Vāsudeva, Murāri, Govinda and his two brothers and Rāghava Paṇḍita, who took bags of assorted foods. The inhabitants of Kulīna-grāma, carrying silken ropes, also departed.

TEXT 18

খণ্ডবাসী নরহরি, শ্রীরঘুনন্দন ।
সর্ব-ভক্ত চলে, তার কে করে গণন ॥ ১৮ ॥

khaṇḍa-vāsī narahari, śrī-raghunandana
sarva-bhakta cale, tāra ke kare gaṇana

SYNONYMS

khaṇḍa-vāsī narahari—Narahari, a resident of the village Khaṇḍa; *śrī-raghunandana*—Śrī Raghunandana; *sarva-bhakta*—all the devotees; *cale*—went; *tāra*—of that; *ke*—who; *kare gaṇana*—can count.

TRANSLATION

Narahari and Śrī Raghunandana, who were from the village of Khaṇḍa, and many other devotees also departed. Who can count them?

TEXT 19

শিবানন্দ-সেন করে ঘাটি সমাধান ।
সবারে পালন করি' সুখে লঞা যান ॥ ১৯ ॥

śivānanda-sena kare ghāṭi samādhāna
sabāre pālana kari' sukhe lañā yāna

SYNONYMS

śivānanda-sena—Śivānanda Sena; *kare*—made; *ghāṭi samādhāna*—arrangements for expenditures to clear the tax collecting centers; *sabāre*—everyone; *pālana*—maintaining; *kari'*—doing; *sukhe*—in happiness; *lañā*—taking; *yāna*—goes.

TRANSLATION

Śivānanda Sena, who was in charge of the party, made arrangements to clear the tax collecting centers. He took care of all the devotees and happily traveled with them.

TEXT 20

সবার সর্বকার্য করেন, দেন বাসা-স্থান ।
শিবানন্দ জানে উড়িয়া-পথের সন্ধান ॥ ২০ ॥

sabāra sarva-kārya karena, dena vāsā-sthāna
śivānanda jāne uḍiyā-pathera sandhāna

SYNONYMS

sabāra—of all of them; *sarva-kārya*—everything necessary to be done; *karena*—he does; *dena*—gives; *vāsā-sthāna*—residential places; *śivānanda*—Śivānanda; *jāne*—knows; *uḍiyā-pathera*—of the roads in Orissa; *sandhāna*—the junctions.

TRANSLATION

Śivānanda Sena took care of all the necessities the devotees required. In particular, he made arrangements for residential quarters, and he knew the roads of Orissa.

TEXT 21

সে বৎসর প্রভু দেখিতে সব ঠাকুরাণী।
চলিলা আচার্য-সঙ্গে অচ্যুত-জননী ॥ ২১ ॥

se vatsara prabhu dekhite saba ṭhākurāṇī
calilā ācārya-saṅge acyuta-jananī

SYNONYMS

se vatsara—that year; *prabhu*—Śrī Caitanya Mahāprabhu; *dekhite*—to see; *saba ṭhākurāṇī*—all the wives of the devotees; *calilā*—went; *ācārya-saṅge*—with Advaita Ācārya; *acyuta-jananī*—the mother of Acyutānanda.

TRANSLATION

That year also all the wives of the devotees [ṭhākurāṇīs] also went to see Śrī Caitanya Mahāprabhu. Sītādevī, the mother of Acyutānanda, went with Advaita Ācārya.

TEXT 22

শ্রীবাস পণ্ডিত-সঙ্গে চলিলা মালিনী।
শিবানন্দ-সঙ্গে চলে তাঁহার গৃহিণী ॥ ২২ ॥

śrīvāsa paṇḍita-saṅge calilā mālinī
śivānanda-saṅge cale tāṅhāra gṛhiṇī

SYNONYMS

śrīvāsa paṇḍita-saṅge—with Śrīvāsa Paṇḍita; *calilā*—went; *mālinī*—his wife, Mālinī; *śivānanda-saṅge*—with Śivānanda Sena; *cale*—goes; *tāṅhāra*—his; *gṛhiṇī*—wife.

TRANSLATION

Śrīvāsa Paṇḍita also took his wife, Mālinī, and the wife of Śivānanda Sena also went with her husband.

TEXT 23

শিবানন্দের বালক, নাম—চৈতন্য-দাস ।
তেঁহো চলিয়াছে প্রভুরে দেখিতে উল্লাস ॥ ২৩ ॥

śivānandera bālaka, nāma——caitanya-dāsa
teṅho caliyāche prabhure dekhite ullāsa

SYNONYMS

śivānandera bālaka—the son of Śivānanda; *nāma*—named; *caitanya-dāsa*—Caitanya dāsa; *teṅho*—he; *caliyāche*—was going; *prabhure*—Śrī Caitanya Mahāprabhu; *dekhite*—to see; *ullāsa*—jubilantly.

TRANSLATION

Caitanya dāsa, the son of Śivānanda Sena, also jubilantly accompanied them as they went to see the Lord.

TEXT 24

আচার্যরত্ন-সঙ্গে চলে তাঁহার গৃহিণী ।
তাঁহার প্রেমের কথা কহিতে না জানি ॥ ২৪ ॥

ācāryaratna-saṅge cale tāṅhāra gṛhiṇī
tāṅhāra premera kathā kahite nā jāni

SYNONYMS

ācāryaratna-saṅge—with Candraśekhara; *cale*—goes; *tāṅhāra*—his; *gṛhiṇī*—wife; *tāṅhāra*—his; *premera kathā*—the description of the ecstatic love; *kahite*—to speak; *nā jāni*—I do not know how.

TRANSLATION

The wife of Candraśekhara [Ācāryaratna] also went. I cannot speak of the greatness of Candraśekhara's love for the Lord.

TEXT 25

সব ঠাকুরাণী মহাপ্রভুকে ভিক্ষা দিতে ।
প্রভুর নানা প্রিয় দ্রব্য নিল ঘর হৈতে ॥ ২৫ ॥

saba ṭhākurāṇī mahāprabhuke bhikṣā dite
prabhura nānā priya dravya nila ghara haite

SYNONYMS

saba ṭhākurāṇī—all the wives of the great devotees; *mahāprabhuke*—to Śrī Caitanya Mahāprabhu; *bhikṣā dite*—to offer food; *prabhura*—of Śrī Caitanya Mahāprabhu; *nānā*—various; *priya dravya*—pleasing foods; *nila*—took; *ghara haite*—from home.

TRANSLATION

To offer Śrī Caitanya Mahāprabhu various types of food, all the wives of the great devotees brought from home various things that pleased Caitanya Mahāprabhu.

TEXT 26

শিবানন্দ-সেন করে সব সমাধান ।
ঘাটিয়াল প্রবোধি' দেন সবারে বাসা-স্থান ॥ ২৬ ॥

śivānanda-sena kare saba samādhāna
ghāṭiyāla prabodhi' dena sabāre vāsā-sthāna

SYNONYMS

śivānanda-sena—Śivānanda Sena; *kare*—does; *saba samādhāna*—all arrangements; *ghāṭiyāla*—the men in charge of levying taxes; *prabodhi'*—satisfying; *dena*—gives; *sabāre*—to everyone; *vāsā-sthāna*—resting places.

TRANSLATION

As stated, Śivānanda Sena used to make all arrangements for the party's necessities. In particular, he used to pacify the men in charge of levying taxes, and he found resting places for everyone.

TEXT 27

ভক্ষ্য দিয়া করেন সবার সর্বত্র পালনে ।
পরম আনন্দে যান প্রভুর দরশনে ॥ ২৭ ॥

bhakṣya diyā karena sabāra sarvatra pālane
parama ānande yāna prabhura daraśane

SYNONYMS

bhakṣya diyā—supplying food; *karena*—he does; *sabāra*—of everyone; *sarvatra*—everywhere; *pālane*—maintenance; *parama ānande*—in great pleasure; *yāna*—he goes; *prabhura daraśane*—to see Śrī Caitanya Mahāprabhu.

TRANSLATION

Śivānanda Sena also supplied food to all the devotees and took care of them along the way. In this way, feeling great happiness he went to see Śrī Caitanya Mahāprabhu at Jagannātha Purī.

TEXT 28

রেমুণায় আসিয়া কৈল গোপীনাথ দরশন ।
আচার্য করিল তাহাঁ কীর্তন, নর্তন ॥ ২৮ ॥

remuṇāya āsiyā kaila gopīnātha daraśana
ācārya karila tāhāṅ kīrtana, nartana

SYNONYMS

remuṇāya—to Remuṇā; *āsiyā*—after coming; *kaila*—performed; *gopīnātha daraśana*—visiting the temple of Gopīnātha; *ācārya*—Advaita Ācārya; *karila*—performed; *tāhāṅ*—there; *kīrtana*—chanting; *nartana*—dancing.

TRANSLATION

When they all arrived at Remuṇā, they went to see Lord Gopīnātha. In the temple there, Advaita Ācārya danced and chanted.

TEXT 29

নিত্যানন্দের পরিচয় সব সেবক সনে ।
বহুত সম্মান আসি' কৈল সেবকগণে ॥ ২৯ ॥

nityānandera paricaya saba sevaka sane
bahuta sammāna āsi' kaila sevaka-gaṇe

SYNONYMS

nityānandera—of Lord Nityānanda Prabhu; *paricaya*—there was acquaintance; *saba*—all; *sevaka sane*—with the priests of the temple; *bahuta sammāna*—great respect; *āsi'*—coming; *kaila*—offered; *sevaka-gaṇe*—all the priests.

TRANSLATION

All the priests of the temple had been previously acquainted with Śrī Nityānanda Prabhu; therefore they all came to offer great respects to the Lord.

TEXT 30

সেই রাত্রি সব মহান্ত তাহাঞি রহিলা ।
বার ক্ষীর আনি' আগে সেবক ধরিলা ॥ ৩০ ॥

sei rātri saba mahānta tāhāñi rahilā
bāra kṣīra āni' āge sevaka dharilā

SYNONYMS

sei rātri—that night; *saba mahānta*—all the great devotees; *tāhāñi rahilā*—remained there; *bāra*—twelve pots; *kṣīra*—condensed milk; *āni'*—bringing; *āge*—in front of Nityānanda Prabhu; *sevaka*—the priests; *dharilā*—placed.

TRANSLATION

That night, all the great devotees remained in the temple, and the priests brought twelve pots of condensed milk, which they placed before Lord Nityānanda Prabhu.

TEXT 31

ক্ষীর বাঁটি' সবারে দিল প্রভু-নিত্যানন্দ ।
ক্ষীর-প্রসাদ পাঞা সবার বাড়িল আনন্দ ॥ ৩১ ॥

kṣīra bāṅṭi' sabāre dila prabhu-nityānanda
kṣīra-prasāda pāñā sabāra bāḍila ānanda

SYNONYMS

kṣīra—the condensed milk; *bāṅṭi'*—dividing; *sabāre*—unto everyone; *dila*—gave; *prabhu-nityānanda*—Nityānanda Prabhu; *kṣīra-prasāda*—remnants of condensed milk from the Deity; *pāñā*—getting; *sabāra*—of everyone; *bāḍila*—increased; *ānanda*—the transcendental bliss.

TRANSLATION

When the condensed milk was placed before Nityānanda Prabhu, He distributed the prasāda to everyone, and thus everyone's transcendental bliss increased.

TEXT 32

মাধবপুরীর কথা, গোপাল-স্থাপন ।
তাঁহারে গোপাল যৈছে মাগিল চন্দন ॥ ৩২ ॥

mādhava-purīra kathā, gopāla-sthāpana
tāṅhāre gopāla yaiche māgila candana

SYNONYMS

mādhava-purīra kathā—the narration of Mādhavendra Purī; *gopāla-sthāpana*—installation of the Deity of Gopāla; *tāṅhāre*—unto him; *gopāla*—Lord Gopāla; *yaiche*—just as; *māgila*—He begged; *candana*—sandalwood.

TRANSLATION

They then all discussed the story of Śrī Mādhavendra Purī's installation of the Gopāla Deity, and they discussed how Gopāla begged sandalwood from him.

TEXT 33

তাঁর লাগি' গোপীনাথ ক্ষীর চুরি কৈল ।
মহাপ্রভুর মুখে আগে এ কথা শুনিল ॥ ৩৩ ॥

tāṅra lāgi' gopīnātha kṣīra curi kaila
mahāprabhura mukhe āge e kathā śunila

SYNONYMS

tāṅra lāgi'—for him (Mādhavendra Purī); *gopīnātha*—the Deity named Gopīnātha; *kṣīra*—condensed milk; *curi*—stealing; *kaila*—performed; *mahāprabhura mukhe*—from the mouth of Śrī Caitanya Mahāprabhu; *āge*—previously; *e kathā*—this incident; *śunila*—heard.

TRANSLATION

It was Gopīnātha who stole condensed milk for the sake of Mādhavendra Purī. This incident had been previously related by Śrī Caitanya Mahāprabhu Himself.

TEXT 34

সেই কথা সবার মধ্যে কহে নিত্যানন্দ ।
শুনিয়া বৈষ্ণব-মনে বাড়িল আনন্দ ॥ ৩৪ ॥

sei kathā sabāra madhye kahe nityānanda
śuniyā vaiṣṇava-mane bāḍila ānanda

SYNONYMS

sei kathā—that incident; *sabāra madhye*—among all of them; *kahe*—says; *nityānanda*—Lord Nityānanda Prabhu; *śuniyā*—hearing; *vaiṣṇava-mane*—in the minds of all the Vaiṣṇavas; *bāḍila*—increased; *ānanda*—the transcendental bliss.

TRANSLATION

This same narration was again related by Lord Nityānanda to all the devotees, and their transcendental bliss increased as they heard the story again.

PURPORT

The words *mahāprabhura mukhe,* "from the mouth of Śrī Caitanya Mahāprabhu," are significant because Śrī Caitanya Mahāprabhu first heard the story of Mādhavendra Purī from His spiritual master, Śrīpāda Īśvara Purī. For this story refer to *Madhya-līlā,* Chapter Four, verse eighteen. After staying at Śrī Advaita's house in Śāntipura for some time, the Lord narrated the story of Mādhavendra Purī to Nityānanda Prabhu, Jagadānanda Prabhu, Dāmodara Paṇḍita and Mukunda dāsa. When they went to Remuṇā to the temple of Gopīnātha, He described Mādhavendra Purī's installation of the Gopāla Deity as well as Gopīnātha's stealing condensed milk. Due to this incident, Lord Gopīnātha became well known as Kṣīracorā, the thief who stole condensed milk.

TEXT 35

এইমত চলি' চলি' কটক আইলা ।
সাক্ষিগোপাল দেখি' সবে সে দিন রহিলা ॥ ৩৫ ॥

ei-mata cali' cali' kaṭaka āilā
sākṣi-gopāla dekhi' sabe se dina rahilā

SYNONYMS

ei-mata—in this way; *cali' cali'*—walking and walking; *kaṭaka āilā*—they reached the town known as Kaṭaka; *sākṣi-gopāla dekhi'*—after seeing the Deity known as Sākṣi-gopāla; *sabe*—all the devotees; *se dina*—that day; *rahilā*—stayed.

TRANSLATION

Walking and walking in this way, the devotees arrived at the city of Kaṭaka, where they remained for a day and saw the temple of Sākṣi-gopāla.

TEXT 36

সাক্ষিগোপালের কথা কহে নিত্যানন্দ ।
শুনিয়া বৈষ্ণব-মনে বাড়িল আনন্দ ॥ ৩৬ ॥

sākṣi-gopālera kathā kahe nityānanda
śuniyā vaiṣṇava-mane bāḍila ānanda

SYNONYMS

sākṣi-gopālera—of the Deity known as Sākṣi-gopāla; *kathā*—the narration; *kahe*—describes; *nityānanda*—Nityānanda Prabhu; *śuniyā*—hearing; *vaiṣṇava-mane*—in the minds of all the Vaiṣṇavas; *bāḍila*—increased; *ānanda*—the transcendental bliss.

TRANSLATION

When Nityānanda Prabhu described all the activities of Sākṣi-gopāla, transcendental bliss increased in the minds of all the Vaiṣṇavas.

PURPORT

For these activities refer to *Madhya-līlā,* Chapter Five, verses 8-138.

TEXT 37

প্রভুকে মিলিতে সবার উৎকণ্ঠা অন্তরে ।
শীঘ্র করি' আইলা সবে শ্রীনীলাচলে ॥ ৩৭ ॥

prabhuke milite sabāra utkaṇṭhā antare
śīghra kari' āilā sabe śrī-nīlācale

SYNONYMS

prabhuke milite—to see Śrī Caitanya Mahāprabhu; *sabāra*—of everyone; *utkaṇṭhā*—anxiety; *antare*—within the heart; *śīghra kari'*—making great haste; *āilā*—reached; *sabe*—all of them; *śrī-nīlācale*—Jagannātha Purī.

TRANSLATION

Everyone in the party was very anxious at heart to see Caitanya Mahāprabhu; therefore they hastily went on to Jagannātha Purī.

TEXT 38

আঠারনালাকে আইলা গোসাঞি শুনিয়া ।
দুইমালা পাঠাইলা গোবিন্দ-হাতে দিয়া ॥ ৩৮ ॥

āṭhāranālāke āilā gosāñi śuniyā
dui-mālā pāṭhāilā govinda-hāte diyā

SYNONYMS

āṭhāranālāke—Āṭhāranālā; *āilā*—they have reached; *gosāñi*—Śrī Caitanya Mahāprabhu; *śuniyā*—hearing; *dui-mālā*—two garlands; *pāṭhāilā*—sent; *govinda-hāte diyā*—through the hands of Govinda.

TRANSLATION

When they all arrived at a bridge called Āṭhāranālā, Śrī Caitanya Mahāprabhu, hearing the news of their arrival, sent two garlands with Govinda.

TEXT 39

দুই মালা গোবিন্দ দুইজনে পরাইল ।
অদ্বৈত, অবধূত-গোসাঞি বড় সুখ পাইল ॥ ৩৯ ॥

dui mālā govinda dui-jane parāila
advaita, avadhūta-gosāñi baḍa sukha pāila

SYNONYMS

dui mālā—the two garlands; *govinda*—Govinda; *dui-jane parāila*—placed on the necks of two personalities; *advaita*—Advaita Ācārya; *avadhūta-gosāñi*—Nityānanda Prabhu; *baḍa sukha pāila*—became very happy.

TRANSLATION

Govinda offered the two garlands to Advaita Ācārya and Nityānanda Prabhu, and They both became very happy.

TEXT 40

তাহাঞি আরম্ভ কৈল কৃষ্ণ-সংকীর্তন ।
নাচিতে নাচিতে চলি' আইলা দুইজন ॥ ৪০ ॥

tāhāñi ārambha kaila kṛṣṇa-saṅkīrtana
nācite nācite cali' āilā dui-jana

SYNONYMS

tāhāñi—on that very spot; *ārambha kaila*—began; *kṛṣṇa-saṅkīrtana*—chanting the holy name of Lord Kṛṣṇa; *nācite nācite*—dancing and dancing; *cali'*—going; *āilā*—reached; *dui-jana*—both of Them.

TRANSLATION

Indeed, They began chanting the holy name of Kṛṣṇa on that very spot, and, dancing and dancing, both Advaita Ācārya and Nityānanda Prabhu reached Jagannātha Purī.

TEXT 41

পুনঃ মালা দিয়া স্বরূপাদি নিজগণ ।
আগু বাড়ি' পাঠাইল শচীর নন্দন ॥ ৪১ ॥

punaḥ mālā diyā svarūpādi nija-gaṇa
āgu bāḍi' pāṭhāila śacīra nandana

SYNONYMS

punaḥ—again; *mālā*—garlands; *diyā*—offering; *svarūpa-ādi*—Svarūpa Dāmodara Gosvāmī and others; *nija-gaṇa*—personal associates; *āgu bāḍi'*—going forward; *pāṭhāila*—sent; *śacīra nandana*—the son of mother Śacī.

TRANSLATION

Then, for the second time, Śrī Caitanya Mahāprabhu sent garlands through Svarūpa Dāmodara and other personal associates. Thus they went forward, sent by the son of mother Śacī.

TEXT 42

নরেন্দ্র আসিয়া তাহাঁ সবারে মিলিলা ।
মহাপ্রভুর দত্ত মালা সবারে পরাইলা ॥ ৪২ ॥

narendra āsiyā tāhāṅ sabāre mililā
mahāprabhura datta mālā sabāre parāilā

SYNONYMS

narendra—to the lake named Narendra; *āsiyā*—coming; *tāhāṅ*—there; *sabāre*—everyone; *mililā*—met; *mahāprabhura*—by Śrī Caitanya Mahāprabhu; *datta*—given; *mālā*—garlands; *sabāre parāilā*—offered to everyone.

TRANSLATION

When the devotees from Bengal reached Lake Narendra, Svarūpa Dāmodara and the others met them and offered them the garlands given by Śrī Caitanya Mahāprabhu.

TEXT 43

সিংহদ্বার-নিকটে আইলা শুনি' গৌররায় ।
আপনে আসিয়া প্রভু মিলিলা সবায় ॥ ৪৩ ॥

siṁha-dvāra-nikaṭe āilā śuni' gaurarāya
āpane āsiyā prabhu mililā sabāya

SYNONYMS

siṁha-dvāra—the lion gate; *nikaṭe*—near; *āilā*—arrived; *śuni'*—hearing; *gaurarāya*—Lord Śrī Caitanya Mahāprabhu; *āpane*—personally; *āsiyā*—coming; *prabhu*—Lord Śrī Caitanya Mahāprabhu; *mililā sabāya*—met them all.

TRANSLATION

When the devotees finally reached the lion gate, Śrī Caitanya Mahāprabhu heard the news and personally went to meet them.

TEXT 44

সবা লঞা কৈল জগন্নাথ-দরশন ।
সবা লঞা আইলা পুনঃ আপন-ভবন ॥ ৪৪ ॥

sabā lañā kaila jagannātha-daraśana
sabā lañā āilā punaḥ āpana-bhavana

SYNONYMS

sabā lañā—taking all of them; *kaila*—performed; *jagannātha-daraśana*—seeing Lord Jagannātha; *sabā lañā*—taking them all; *āilā*—went back; *punaḥ*—again; *āpana-bhavana*—to His own residence.

TRANSLATION

Then Śrī Caitanya Mahāprabhu and all His devotees visited Lord Jagannātha. Finally, accompanied by them all, He returned to His own residence.

TEXT 45

বাণীনাথ, কাশীমিশ্র প্রসাদ আনিল।
স্বহস্তে সবারে প্রভু প্রসাদ খাওয়াইল ॥ ৪৫ ॥

vāṇīnātha, kāśī-miśra prasāda ānila
svahaste sabāre prabhu prasāda khāoyāila

SYNONYMS

vāṇīnātha—Vāṇīnātha; *kāśī-miśra*—Kāśī Miśra; *prasāda ānila*—brought all kinds of *prasāda; sva-haste*—with His own hand; *sabāre*—unto everyone; *prabhu*—Śrī Caitanya Mahāprabhu; *prasāda*—the remnants of the food of Jagannātha; *khāoyāila*—fed.

TRANSLATION

Vāṇīnātha Rāya and Kāśī Miśra then brought a large quantity of prasāda, and Śrī Caitanya Mahāprabhu distributed it with His own hand and fed them all.

TEXT 46

পূর্ব বৎসরে যাঁর যেই বাসা-স্থান।
তাহাঁ সবা পাঠাঞা করাইল বিশ্রাম ॥ ৪৬ ॥

pūrva vatsare yāṅra yei vāsā-sthāna
tāhāṅ sabā pāṭhāñā karāila viśrāma

SYNONYMS

pūrva vatsare—in the previous year; *yāṅra*—of whom; *yei*—wherever; *vāsā-sthāna*—place to stay; *tāhāṅ*—there; *sabā*—all of them; *pāṭhāñā*—sending; *karāila viśrāma*—made them rest.

TRANSLATION

In the previous year, everyone had his own particular residence, and the same residences were again offered. Thus they all went to take rest.

TEXT 47

এইমত ভক্তগণ রহিলা চারি মাস।
প্রভুর সহিত করে কীর্তন-বিলাস ॥ ৪৭ ॥

ei-mata bhakta-gaṇa rahilā cāri māsa
prabhura sahita kare kīrtana-vilāsa

SYNONYMS

ei-mata—in this way; *bhakta-gaṇa*—the devotees; *rahilā*—remained; *cāri māsa*—for four months; *prabhura sahita*—with Śrī Caitanya Mahāprabhu; *kare*—performed; *kīrtana-vilāsa*—the pastimes of *saṅkīrtana.*

TRANSLATION

For four continuous months all the devotees remained there and enjoyed chanting the Hare Kṛṣṇa mahā-mantra with Śrī Caitanya Mahāprabhu.

TEXT 48

পূর্ব্ববৎ রথযাত্রা-কাল যবে আইল ।
সবা লঞা গুণ্ডিচা-মন্দির প্রক্ষালিল ॥ ৪৮ ॥

pūrvavat ratha-yātrā-kāla yābe āila
sabā lañā guṇḍicā-mandira prakṣālila

SYNONYMS

pūrva-vat—as in the previous year; *ratha-yātrā-kāla*—the time for Ratha-yātrā festival; *yābe*—when; *āila*—arrived; *sabā lañā*—taking all of them; *guṇḍicā-mandira*—the temple of Guṇḍicā; *prakṣālila*—washed.

TRANSLATION

As in the previous year, they all washed the Guṇḍicā temple when the time for Ratha-yātrā arrived.

TEXT 49

কুলীনগ্রামী পট্টডোরী জগন্নাথে দিল ।
পূর্ব্ববৎ রথ-অগ্রে নর্ত্তন করিল ॥ ৪৯ ॥

kulīna-grāmī paṭṭa-ḍorī jagannāthe dila
pūrvavat ratha-agre nartana karila

SYNONYMS

kulīna-grāmī—the residents of Kulīna-grāma; *paṭṭa-ḍorī*—silken ropes; *jagannāthe dila*—offered to Lord Jagannātha; *pūrva-vat*—like the previous year; *ratha-agre*—in front of the car; *nartana karila*—danced.

TRANSLATION

The inhabitants of Kulīna-grāma delivered silken ropes to Lord Jagannātha, and as previously they all danced before the Lord's car.

TEXT 50

বহু নৃত্য করি' পুনঃ চলিল উদ্যানে।
বাপী-তীরে তাহাঁ যাই' করিল বিশ্রামে ॥ ৫০ ॥

bahu nṛtya kari' punaḥ calila udyāne
vāpī-tīre tāhāṅ yāi' karila viśrāme

SYNONYMS

bahu nṛtya kari'—after dancing a great deal; *punaḥ*—again; *calila*—started for; *udyāne*—the garden; *vāpī-tīre*—on the bank of the lake; *tāhāṅ yāi'*—going there; *karila viśrāme*—took rest.

TRANSLATION

After dancing a great deal, they all went to a nearby garden and took rest beside a lake.

TEXT 51

রাঢ়ী এক বিপ্র, তেঁহো—নিত্যানন্দ দাস।
মহা-ভাগ্যবান্ তেঁহো, নাম—কৃষ্ণদাস ॥ ৫১ ॥

rāḍhī eka vipra, teṅho——nityānanda dāsa
mahā-bhāgyavān teṅho, nāma——kṛṣṇadāsa

SYNONYMS

rāḍhī eka vipra—one *brāhmaṇa* resident of Rāḍha-deśa (where the Ganges does not flow); *teṅho*—he; *nityānanda dāsa*—servant of Lord Nityānanda; *mahā-bhāgyavān*—greatly fortunate; *teṅho*—he; *nāma*—named; *kṛṣṇadāsa*—Kṛṣṇadāsa.

TRANSLATION

One brāhmaṇa named Kṛṣṇadāsa, who was a resident of Rāḍha-deśa and a servant of Lord Nityānanda's, was a very fortunate person.

TEXT 52

ঘট ভরি' প্রভুর তেঁহো অভিষেক কৈল।
তাঁর অভিষেকে প্রভু মহা-তৃপ্ত হৈল ॥ ৫২ ॥

ghaṭa bhari' prabhura teṅho abhiṣeka kaila
tāṅra abhiṣeke prabhu mahā-tṛpta haila

SYNONYMS

ghaṭa bhari'—filling one waterpot; *prabhura*—of Lord Caitanya Mahāprabhu; *teṅho*—he; *abhiṣeka kaila*—performed the bathing; *tāṅra*—his; *abhiṣeke*—by the act of bathing the Lord; *prabhu*—Śrī Caitanya Mahāprabhu; *mahā-tṛpta haila*—became very satisfied.

TRANSLATION

It was Kṛṣṇadāsa who filled a great waterpot and poured it over the Lord while He was taking His bath. The Lord was greatly satisfied by this.

TEXT 53

বলগণ্ডি-ভোগের বহু প্রসাদ আইল ।
সবা সঙ্গে মহাপ্রভু প্রসাদ খাইল ॥ ৫৩ ॥

balagaṇḍi-bhogera bahu prasāda āila
sabā saṅge mahāprabhu prasāda khāila

SYNONYMS

balagaṇḍi-bhogera—of the food offered at Balagaṇḍi; *bahu prasāda*—a great quantity of *prasāda; āila*—arrived; *sabā saṅge*—with all the devotees; *mahāprabhu*—Śrī Caitanya Mahāprabhu; *prasāda*—remnants of the food of Jagannātha; *khāila*—ate.

TRANSLATION

The remnants of food offered to the Lord at Balagaṇḍi then arrived in great quantity, and Śrī Caitanya Mahāprabhu and all His devotees ate it.

PURPORT

In reference to Balagaṇḍi, see *Madhya-līlā* (13.193).

TEXT 54

পূর্ব্ববৎ রথযাত্রা কৈল দরশন ।
হেরাপঞ্চমী-যাত্রা দেখে লঞা ভক্তগণ ॥ ৫৪ ॥

pūrvavat ratha-yātrā kaila daraśana
herā-pañcamī-yātrā dekhe lañā bhakta-gaṇa

SYNONYMS

pūrva-vat—as in the previous year; *ratha-yātrā*—the car festival; *kaila daraśana*—saw; *herā-pañcamī-yātrā*—the festival of Herā-pañcamī; *dekhe*—He sees; *lañā bhakta-gaṇa*—with all the devotees.

TRANSLATION

As in the previous year, the Lord, with all the devotees, saw the Ratha-yātrā festival and the Herā-pañcamī festival as well.

TEXT 55

আচার্য-গোসাঞি প্রভুর কৈল নিমন্ত্রণ ।
তার মধ্যে কৈল যৈছে ঝড়-বরিষণ ॥ ৫৫ ॥

ācārya-gosāñi prabhura kaila nimantraṇa
tāra madhye kaila yaiche jhaḍa-variṣaṇa

SYNONYMS

ācārya-gosāñi—Advaita Ācārya; *prabhura*—of Śrī Caitanya Mahāprabhu; *kaila*—made; *nimantraṇa*—invitation; *tāra madhye*—within that episode; *kaila*—occurred; *yaiche*—just as; *jhaḍa-variṣaṇa*—rainstorm.

TRANSLATION

Advaita Ācārya then extended an invitation to Śrī Caitanya Mahāprabhu, and there was a great rainstorm connected with that incident.

TEXT 56

বিস্তারি' বর্ণিয়াছেন দাস-বৃন্দাবন ।
শ্রীবাস প্রভুরে তবে কৈল নিমন্ত্রণ ॥ ৫৬ ॥

vistāri' varṇiyāchena dāsa-vṛndāvana
śrīvāsa prabhure tabe kaila nimantraṇa

SYNONYMS

vistāri'—elaborating; *varṇiyāchena*—has described; *dāsa-vṛndāvana*—Vṛndāvana dāsa Ṭhākura; *śrīvāsa*—Śrīvāsa; *prabhure*—to Śrī Caitanya Mahāprabhu; *tabe*—then; *kaila nimantraṇa*—gave an invitation.

TRANSLATION

All these episodes have been elaborately described by Śrīla Vṛndāvana dāsa Ṭhākura. Then one day Śrīvāsa Ṭhākura extended an invitation to the Lord.

PURPORT

Caitanya-bhāgavata (*Antya-līlā,* Chapter Eight) gives the following description. One day Śrīla Advaita Ācārya, having extended an invitation to Caitanya Mahāprabhu, thought that if the Lord came alone He would feed Him to His great satisfaction. It then so happened that when the other *sannyāsīs* were going to Advaita Ācārya's to take lunch, there was a big rainstorm, and they could not reach His house. Thus, according to Advaita Ācārya's desires, Śrī Caitanya Mahāprabhu came alone and accepted the *prasāda*.

TEXT 57

প্রভুর প্রিয়-ব্যঞ্জন সব রান্ধেন মালিনী ।
'ভক্ত্যে দাসী'-অভিমান, 'স্নেহেতে জননী' ॥ ৫৭ ॥

prabhura priya-vyañjana saba rāndhena mālinī
'bhaktye dāsī'-abhimāna, 'snehete jananī'

SYNONYMS

prabhura—of Lord Śrī Caitanya Mahāprabhu; *priya-vyañjana*—favorite vegetables; *saba*—all; *rāndhena*—cooks; *mālinī*—the wife of Śrīvāsa Ṭhākura; *bhaktye dāsī*—in devotion she was just like a maidservant; *abhimāna*—it was her conception; *snehete*—in affection; *jananī*—exactly like a mother.

TRANSLATION

The Lord's favorite vegetables were cooked by Mālinīdevī, the wife of Śrīvāsa Ṭhākura. She devotedly considered herself a maidservant of Śrī Caitanya Mahāprabhu's, but in affection she was just like a mother.

TEXT 58

আচার্যরত্ন-আদি যত মুখ্য ভক্তগণ ।
মধ্যে মধ্যে প্রভুরে করেন নিমন্ত্রণ ॥ ৫৮ ॥

ācāryaratna-ādi yata mukhya bhakta-gaṇa
madhye madhye prabhure karena nimantraṇa

SYNONYMS

ācāryaratna—Candraśekhara; *ādi*—and others; *yata*—all; *mukhya bhakta-gaṇa*—chief devotees; *madhye madhye*—at intervals; *prabhure*—to Śrī Caitanya Mahāprabhu; *karena nimantraṇa*—gave invitations.

TRANSLATION

All the chief devotees, headed by Candraśekhara [Ācāryaratna] used to extend invitations to Śrī Caitanya Mahāprabhu periodically.

TEXT 59

চাতুর্মাস্য-অন্তে পুনঃ নিত্যানন্দে লঞা।
কিবা যুক্তি করে নিত্য নিভৃতে বসিয়া ॥ ৫৯ ॥

cāturmāsya-ante punaḥ nityānande lañā
kibā yukti kare nitya nibhṛte vasiyā

SYNONYMS

cāturmāsya-ante—at the end of Cāturmāsya; *punaḥ*—again; *nityānande*—Śrī Nityānanda Prabhu; *lañā*—taking into confidence; *kibā*—what; *yukti kare*—They consult; *nitya*—daily; *nibhṛte*—in a solitary place; *vasiyā*—sitting.

TRANSLATION

At the end of the four-month Cāturmāsya period, Caitanya Mahāprabhu again consulted with Nityānanda Prabhu daily in a solitary place. No one could understand what Their consultation was about.

TEXT 60

আচার্য-গোসাঞি প্রভুকে কহে ঠারে-ঠোরে।
আচার্য তর্জা পড়ে, কেহ বুঝিতে না পারে ॥ ৬০ ॥

ācārya-gosāñi prabhuke kahe ṭhāre-ṭhore
ācārya tarjā paḍe, keha bujhite nā pāre

SYNONYMS

ācārya-gosāñi—Advaita Ācārya; *prabhuke*—unto Śrī Caitanya Mahāprabhu; *kahe*—speaks; *ṭhāre-ṭhore*—by indications; *ācārya*—Advaita Ācārya; *tarjā paḍe*—reads some poetic passages; *keha*—anyone; *bujhite*—to understand; *nā pāre*—was not able.

TRANSLATION

Then Śrīla Advaita Ācārya said something to Caitanya Mahāprabhu through gestures and read some poetic passages, which no one understood.

TEXT 61

তাঁর মুখ দেখি' হাসে শচীর নন্দন ।
অঙ্গীকার জানি' আচার্য করেন নর্তন ॥ ৬১ ॥

tāṅra mukha dekhi' hāse śacīra nandana
aṅgīkāra jāni' ācārya karena nartana

SYNONYMS

tāṅra mukha—His face; *dekhi'*—seeing; *hāse*—smiles; *śacīra nandana*—Lord Śrī Caitanya Mahāprabhu; *aṅgīkāra jāni'*—understanding the acceptance; *ācārya*—Advaita Ācārya; *karena*—performed; *nartana*—dancing.

TRANSLATION

Seeing the face of Advaita Ācārya, Lord Śrī Caitanya Mahāprabhu smiled. Understanding that the Lord had accepted the proposal, Advaita Ācārya started to dance.

TEXT 62

কিবা প্রার্থনা, কিবা আজ্ঞা—কেহ না বুঝিল ।
আলিঙ্গন করি' প্রভু তাঁরে বিদায় দিল ॥ ৬২ ॥

kibā prārthanā, kibā ājñā——keha nā bujhila
āliṅgana kari' prabhu tāṅre vidāya dila

SYNONYMS

kibā—what; *prārthanā*—the request; *kibā*—what; *ājnā*—the order; *keha*—anyone; *nā bujhila*—did not know; *āliṅgana kari'*—embracing; *prabhu*—Śrī Caitanya Mahāprabhu; *tāṅre*—to Him; *vidāya dila*—bade farewell.

TRANSLATION

No one knew what Advaita Ācārya requested or what the Lord ordered. After embracing the Ācārya, Śrī Caitanya Mahāprabhu bade Him farewell.

TEXT 63

নিত্যানন্দে কহে প্রভু,—শুনহ, শ্রীপাদ ।
এই আমি মাগি, তুমি করহ প্রসাদ ॥ ৬৩ ॥

nityānande kahe prabhu,——śunaha, śrīpāda
ei āmi māgi, tumi karaha prasāda

SYNONYMS

nityānande—unto Śrī Nityānanda Prabhu; *kahe*—says; *prabhu*—Śrī Caitanya Mahāprabhu; *śunaha*—please hear; *śrī-pāda*—O holy man; *ei*—this; *āmi*—I; *māgi*—request; *tumi*—You; *karaha*—kindly show; *prasāda*—mercy.

TRANSLATION

Śrī Caitanya Mahāprabhu then told Nityānanda Prabhu, "Please hear Me, O holy man: I now request something of You. Kindly grant My request.

TEXT 64

প্রতিবর্ষ নীলাচলে তুমি না আসিবা।
গৌড়ে রহি' মোর ইচ্ছা সফল করিবা॥ ৬৪॥

prati-varṣa nīlācale tumi nā āsibā
gauḍe rahi' mora icchā saphala karibā

SYNONYMS

prati-varṣa—every year; *nīlācale*—to Jagannātha Purī; *tumi*—You; *nā āsibā*—do not come; *gauḍe rahi'*—staying in Bengal; *mora icchā*—My desire; *sa-phala karibā*—make successful.

TRANSLATION

"Do not come to Jagannātha Purī every year, but stay in Bengal and fulfill My desire."

PURPORT

The mission of Śrī Caitanya Mahāprabhu is to spread the only medicine effective in this fallen age of Kali—the chanting of the Hare Kṛṣṇa *mahā-mantra.* Following the orders of His mother, Śrī Caitanya Mahāprabhu was residing at Jagannātha Purī, and the devotees were coming to see Him. However, the Lord felt that this message must be spread very elaborately in Bengal, and in His absence there was not a second person capable of doing it. Consequently the Lord requested Nityānanda Prabhu to stay there and broadcast the message of Kṛṣṇa consciousness. The Lord also entrusted a similar preaching responsibility to Rūpa and Sanātana. Nityānanda Prabhu was requested not to come every year to Jagannātha Purī, although seeing Lord Jagannātha greatly benefits everyone. Does this mean that the Lord was refusing Nityānanda Prabhu a fortunate opportunity? No. One who is a faithful servant of Śrī Caitanya Mahāprabhu must execute His order, even if one has to sacrifice going to Jagannātha Purī to see Lord Jagannātha there. In other words, it is a greater fortune to carry out Śrī Caitanya Mahāprabhu's order than to satisfy one's senses by seeing Lord Jagannātha.

Preaching Caitanya Mahāprabhu's cult throughout the world is more important than staying in Vṛndāvana or Jagannātha Purī for one's own personal satisfaction. Spreading Kṛṣṇa consciousness is Śrī Caitanya Mahāprabhu's mission; therefore His sincere devotees must carry out His desire.

pṛthivīte āche yata nagarādi grāma
sarvatra pracāra haibe mora nāma

The devotees of Lord Caitanya must preach Kṛṣṇa consciousness in every village and town in the world. That will satisfy the Lord. It is not that one should act whimsically for his own personal satisfaction. This order comes down through the *paramparā* system, and the spiritual master presents these orders to the disciple so that he can spread the message of Śrī Caitanya Mahāprabhu. It is the duty of every disciple to carry out the order of the bona fide spiritual master and spread Lord Caitanya's message all over the world.

TEXT 65

তাহাঁ সিদ্ধি করে—হেন অন্যে না দেখিয়ে ।
আমার 'দুষ্কর' কর্ম, তোমা হৈতে হয়ে ॥ ৬৫ ॥

tāhāṅ siddhi kare——hena anye nā dekhiye
āmāra 'duṣkara' karma, tomā haite haye

SYNONYMS

tāhāṅ—there; *siddhi*—success; *kare*—makes; *hena*—such; *anye*—other person; *nā*—not; *dekhiye*—I see; *āmāra*—My; *duṣkara*—difficult to perform; *karma*—work; *tomā*—You; *haite*—from; *haye*—becomes successful.

TRANSLATION

Śrī Caitanya Mahāprabhu continued, "You can perform a task that even I cannot do. But for You, I cannot find anyone in Gauḍa-deśa who can fulfill My mission there."

PURPORT

Lord Caitanya's mission is to deliver the fallen souls of this age. In this age of Kali, practically cent percent of the population is fallen. Śrī Caitanya Mahāprabhu certainly delivered many fallen souls, but His disciples mainly came from the upper classes. For example, He delivered Śrīla Rūpa Gosvāmī, Sanātana Gosvāmī, Sārvabhauma Bhaṭṭācārya and many others who were socially elevated but fallen from the spiritual point of view. Śrīla Rūpa and Sanātana Gosvāmīs were situated in government service, and Sārvabhauma Bhaṭṭācārya was the topmost scholar of India. Similarly, Prakāśānanda Sarasvatī was a leader of many thousands of Māyāvādī *sannyāsīs.* It was Śrīla Nityānanda Prabhu, however, who delivered persons like Jagāi and Mādhāi. Therefore, Lord Caitanya says, *āmāra 'duṣkara' karma, tomā haite haye.* Jagāi and Mādhāi were delivered solely by Nityānanda Prabhu's mercy. When they injured Nityānanda Prabhu, Lord Caitanya became angry and decided to kill them with His Sudarśana *cakra,* but Nityānanda Prabhu saved them from the Lord's wrath and delivered them. In the incarnation of Gaura-Nitāi, the Lord is not supposed to kill demons but deliver them by preaching Kṛṣṇa consciousness. In the case of Jagāi and Mādhāi, Śrī Caitanya Mahāprabhu was so angry that He would have immediately killed them, but Nityānanda Prabhu was so kind that He not only saved them from death but elevated them to the transcendental position. Thus what was not possible for Śrī Caitanya Mahāprabhu was carried out by Nityānanda Prabhu.

Similarly, if one is true to Gaura-Nitāi's service in the disciplic succession, he can even excel Nityānanda Prabhu's service. This is the process of disciplic succession. Nityānanda Prabhu delivered Jagāi and Mādhāi, but a servant of Nityānanda Prabhu, by His grace, can deliver many thousands of Jagāi's and Mādhāi's. That is the special benediction of the disciplic succession. One who is situated in the disciplic succession can be understood by the result of his activities. This is always true as far as the activities of the Lord and His devotees are concerned. Therefore Lord Śiva says:

ārādhanānāṁ sarveṣāṁ
viṣṇor ārādhanaṁ paraṁ
tasmāt parataraṁ devi
tadīyānāṁ samarcanam

"Of all types of worship, worship of Lord Viṣṇu is best, and better than the worship of Lord Viṣṇu is the worship of His devotee, the Vaiṣṇava." (*Padma Purāṇa*)

By the grace of Viṣṇu, a Vaiṣṇava can render better service than Viṣṇu; that is the special prerogative of a Vaiṣṇava. The Lord actually wants to see His servants work more gloriously than Himself. For instance, on the Battlefield of Kurukṣetra, Śrī Kṛṣṇa provoked Arjuna to fight because all the warriors on the battlefield were to die by Kṛṣṇa's plan. Kṛṣṇa Himself did not want to take credit; rather, He wanted Arjuna to take credit. Therefore He asked him to fight and win fame.

tasmāt tvam uttiṣṭha yaśo labhasva
jitvā śatrūn bhuṅkṣva rājyaṁ samṛddham

mayaivaite nihatāḥ pūrvam eva
nimitta-mātraṁ bhava savyasācin

"Therefore get up and prepare to fight. After conquering your enemies, you will enjoy a flourishing kingdom. They are already put to death by My arrangement, and you, O Savyasācin, can be but an instrument in the fight." (Bg. 11.33)

Thus the Supreme Personality of Godhead gives credit to a devotee who performs any heavy task perfectly. Hanumānjī, or Vajrāṅgajī, the servant of Lord Rāmacandra, also serves as another example. It was Hanumānjī who jumped over the sea in one leap and reached the shore of Laṅkā from the shore of Bhārata-varṣa. When Lord Rāmacandra chose to go there, He paved the way with stones, although by His will the stones were able to float on the sea. If we simply follow Śrī Caitanya Mahāprabhu's instructions and follow in the footsteps of Śrī Nityānanda Prabhu, this Kṛṣṇa consciousness movement can advance, and even more difficult tasks can be performed by the preachers remaining faithful to the service of the Lord.

TEXT 66

নিত্যানন্দ কহে,—আমি 'দেহ' তুমি'প্রাণ' ।
'দেহ' 'প্রাণ' ভিন্ন নহে,—এই ত প্রমাণ ॥ ৬৬ ॥

nityānanda kahe,——āmi 'deha' tumi 'prāṇa'
'deha' 'prāṇa' bhinna nahe,——ei ta pramāṇa

SYNONYMS

nityānanda kahe—Lord Nityānanda Prabhu said; *āmi*—I; *deha*—the body; *tumi*—You; *prāṇa*—the life; *deha*—the body; *prāṇa*—the life; *bhinna nahe*—not separate; *ei ta pramāṇa*—this is the evidence.

TRANSLATION

Nityānanda Prabhu replied, "O Lord, You are the life, and I am the body. There is no difference between the body and life itself, but life is more important than the body.

TEXT 67

অচিন্ত্যশক্ত্যে কর তুমি তাহার ঘটন ।
যে করাহ, সেই করি, নাহিক নিয়ম ॥ ৬৭ ॥

acintya-śaktye kara tumi tāhāra ghaṭana
ye karāha, sei kari, nāhika niyama

SYNONYMS

acintya-śaktye—by inconceivable energy; *kara*—do; *tumi*—You; *tāhāra*—of that relationship; *ghaṭana*—the operation; *ye*—whatever; *karāha*—You make Me do; *sei*—that; *kari*—I do; *nāhika*—there is not; *niyama*—restriction.

TRANSLATION

"By Your inconceivable energy, You can do whatever You like, and whatever You make Me do, I do without restriction."

PURPORT

As stated in the beginning of *Śrīmad-Bhāgavatam: tene brahma hṛdā ya ādi-kavaye.* Lord Brahmā is the first living creature within this universe, and he is also the creator of this universe. How is this possible? Although he is the first living entity, Lord Brahmā is not in the category of *viṣṇu-tattva.* Rather, he is part of the *jīva-tattva.* Nonetheless, by the grace of the Lord, who instructed him through the heart (*tene brahma hṛdā*), Lord Brahmā could create a huge universe. Those who are actually pure devotees of the Lord are instructed by the Lord through the heart, where the Lord is always situated. *Īśvaraḥ sarva-bhūtānāṁ hṛd-deśe 'rjuna tiṣṭhati* (Bg. 18.61). If he follows the instructions of the Supreme Personality of Godhead, the living entity, even though an insignificant creature, can perform the most difficult tasks by the Lord's grace. This also is confirmed in *Bhagavad-gītā:*

teṣāṁ satata-yuktānāṁ
bhajatāṁ prīti-pūrvakam
dadāmi buddhi-yogaṁ taṁ
yena māṁ upayānti te

"To those who are constantly devoted and worship Me with love, I give the understanding by which they can come to Me." (Bg. 10.10)

Everything is possible for a pure devotee because he acts under the instructions of the Supreme Personality of Godhead. Through His inconceivable energy, a pure devotee can perform tasks that are supposed to be very, very difficult. He can perform tasks not even previously performed by the Lord Himself. Therefore Nityānanda Prabhu told Śrī Caitanya Mahāprabhu, *ye karāha, sei kari, nāhika niyama:* "I do not know by what regulative principle I am carrying out this wonderful work, but I know for certain that I will do whatever You desire." Although the Lord wants to give all credit to His devotee, the devotee himself never takes credit, for he acts only under the Lord's direction. Consequently all credit goes to the Lord. This is the nature of the relationship between the Lord and His devotee. The Lord wants to give all credit to His servant, but the servant does not take any credit, for he knows that everything is carried out by the Lord.

TEXT 68

তাঁরে বিদায় দিল প্রভু করি' আলিঙ্গন।
এইমত বিদায় দিল সব ভক্তগণ ॥ ৬৮ ॥

tāṅre vidāya dila prabhu kari' āliṅgana
ei-mata vidāya dila saba bhakta-gaṇa

SYNONYMS

tāṅre—unto Him (Nityānanda Prabhu); *vidāya dila*—bade farewell; *prabhu*—Lord Śrī Caitanya Mahāprabhu; *kari'*—doing; *āliṅgana*—embracing; *ei-mata*—in this way; *vidāya dila*—bade farewell; *saba*—to all; *bhakta-gaṇa*—the devotees.

TRANSLATION

In this way, Śrī Caitanya Mahāprabhu embraced Nityānanda Prabhu and bade Him farewell. He then bade farewell to all the other devotees.

TEXT 69

কুলীনগ্রামী পূর্ব্ববৎ কৈল নিবেদন।
"প্রভু, আজ্ঞা কর,—আমার কর্তব্য সাধন" ॥ ৬৯ ॥

kulīna-grāmī pūrvavat kaila nivedana
"prabhu, ājñā kara,——āmāra kartavya sādhana"

SYNONYMS

kulīna-grāmī—one of the residents of Kulīna-grāma; *pūrva-vat*—like last year; *kaila*—submitted; *nivedana*—petition; *prabhu*—my Lord; *ājñā kara*—order; *āmāra*—my; *kartavya*—necessary; *sādhana*—performance.

TRANSLATION

As in the previous year, one of the inhabitants of Kulīna-grāma submitted a petition to the Lord, saying, "My Lord, kindly tell me what my duty is and how I should execute it."

TEXT 70

প্রভু কহে,—"বৈষ্ণব-সেবা, নাম-সংকীর্তন।
দুই কর, শীঘ্র পাবে শ্রীকৃষ্ণ-চরণ ॥" ৭০ ॥

prabhu kahe,——"vaiṣṇava-sevā, nāma-saṅkīrtana
dui kara, śīghra pābe śrī-kṛṣṇa-caraṇa"

SYNONYMS

prabhu kahe—the Lord replied; *vaiṣṇava-sevā*—service to the Vaiṣṇavas; *nāma-saṅkīrtana*—chanting the holy name of the Lord; *dui kara*—you perform these two things; *śīghra*—very soon; *pābe*—you will get; *śrī-kṛṣṇa-caraṇa*—shelter at the lotus feet of the Lord, Śrī Kṛṣṇa.

TRANSLATION

The Lord replied, "You should engage yourself in the service of the servants of Kṛṣṇa and always chant the holy name of Kṛṣṇa. If you do these two things, you will very soon attain shelter at Kṛṣṇa's lotus feet."

TEXT 71

তেঁহো কহে,—"কে বৈষ্ণব, কি তাঁর লক্ষণ ?"
তবে হাসি' কহে প্রভু জানি' তাঁর মন ॥ ৭১ ॥

teṅho kahe,——"ke vaiṣṇava, ki tāṅra lakṣaṇa?"
tabe hāsi' kahe prabhu jāni' tāṅra mana

SYNONYMS

teṅho kahe—he said; *ke*—who; *vaiṣṇava*—a Vaiṣṇava; *ki*—what; *tāṅra*—of him; *lakṣaṇa*—the symptoms; *tabe*—thereafter; *hāsi'*—smiling; *kahe*—says; *prabhu*—Śrī Caitanya Mahāprabhu; *jāni'*—knowing; *tāṅra mana*—his mind.

TRANSLATION

The inhabitant of Kulīna-grāma said, "Please let me know who is actually a Vaiṣṇava and what his symptoms are." Understanding his mind, Śrī Caitanya Mahāprabhu smiled and gave the following reply.

TEXT 72

"কৃষ্ণনাম নিরন্তর যাঁহার বদনে ।
সেই বৈষ্ণব-শ্রেষ্ঠ, ভজ তাঁহার চরণে ॥ ৭২ ॥

"kṛṣṇa-nāma nirantara yāṅhāra vadane
sei vaiṣṇava-śreṣṭha, bhaja tāṅhāra caraṇe

SYNONYMS

kṛṣṇa-nāma—the holy name of Lord Kṛṣṇa; *nirantara*—incessantly; *yāṅhāra*—whose; *vadane*—in the mouth; *sei*—such a person; *vaiṣṇava-śreṣṭha*—a first-class Vaiṣṇava; *bhaja*—worship; *tāṅhāra caraṇe*—his lotus feet.

TRANSLATION

"A person who is always chanting the holy name of the Lord is to be considered a first-class Vaiṣṇava, and your duty is to serve his lotus feet."

PURPORT

Śrīla Bhaktisiddhānta Sarasvatī Ṭhākura says that any Vaiṣṇava who is constantly chanting the holy name of the Lord should be considered to have attained the second platform of Vaiṣṇavism. Such a devotee is superior to a neophyte Vaiṣṇava who has just learned to chant the holy name of the Lord. A neophyte devotee simply tries to chant the holy name, whereas the advanced devotee is accustomed to chanting and takes pleasure in it. Such an advanced devotee is called *madhyama-bhāgavata,* which indicates that he has attained the intermediate stage between the neophyte and the perfect devotee. Generally a devotee in the intermediate stage becomes a preacher. A neophyte devotee or an ordinary person should worship the *madhyama-bhāgavata,* who is a via medium.

In his *Upadeśāmṛta* Śrīla Rūpa Gosvāmī says: *praṇatibhiś ca bhajantam īśam.* This means that *madhyama-adhikārī* devotees should exchange obeisances between themselves.

The word *nirantara,* meaning "without cessation, continuously, constantly," is very important in this verse. The word *antara* means "interval." If one has desires other than a desire to perform devotional service—in other words, if one sometimes engages in devotional service and sometimes strives for sense gratification—his service will be interrupted. A pure devotee, therefore, should have no other desire than to serve Kṛṣṇa. He should be above fruitive activity and speculative knowledge. In his *Bhakti-rasāmṛta-sindhu,* Śrīla Rūpa Gosvāmī says:

anyābhilāṣitā-śūnyaṁ
jñāna-karmādy-anāvṛtam
ānukūlyena kṛṣṇānu-
śīlanaṁ bhaktir uttamā

This is the platform of pure devotional service. One should not be motivated by fruitive activity or mental speculation but should simply serve Kṛṣṇa favorably. That is first-class devotion.

Another meaning of *antara* is "this body." The body is an impediment to self-realization because it is always engaged in sense gratification. Similarly, *antara* means "money." If money is not used in Kṛṣṇa's service, it is also an impediment. *Antara* also means *janatā,* "people in general." The association of ordinary persons may destroy the principles of devotional service. Similarly, *antara* may mean "greed," greed to acquire more money or enjoy more sense gratification. Finally, the word *antara* may also mean "atheistic ideas" by which one considers the temple Deity to be made of stone, wood or gold. All of these are impediments. The Deity in the temple is not material—He is the Supreme Personality of Godhead Himself. Similarly, considering the spiritual master an ordinary human being (*guruṣu nara-matiḥ*) is also an impediment. Nor should one consider a Vaiṣṇava a member of a particular caste or nation. Nor should a Vaiṣṇava be considered material. *Caraṇāmṛta* should not be considered ordinary drinking water, and the holy name of the Lord should not be considered an ordinary sound vibration. Nor should one look on Lord Kṛṣṇa as an ordinary human being, for He is the origin of all *viṣṇu-tattvas;* nor should one regard the Supreme Lord as a demigod. Intermingling the spiritual with the material causes one to look on transcendence as material and the mundane as spiritual. This is all due to a poor fund of knowledge. One should not consider Lord Viṣṇu and things related to him as being different. All this is offensive.

In the *Bhakti-sandarbha* (265), Śrīla Jīva Gosvāmī writes: *nāmaikaṁ yasya vāci smaraṇa-patha-gatam ityādau deha-draviṇādi-nimittaka-'pāṣaṇḍa'-śabdena ca daśa aparādhā lakṣyante, pāṣaṇḍamayatvāt teṣām.*

The Māyāvādīs look on Viṣṇu and Vaiṣṇavas imperfectly due to their poor fund of knowledge, and this is condemned. In *Śrīmad-Bhāgavatam* (11.2.46), the intermediate Vaiṣṇava is described as follows:

īśvare tad-adhīneṣu
bāliśeṣu dviṣatsu ca
prema-maitrī-kṛpopekṣā
yaḥ karoti sa madhyamaḥ

"The intermediate Vaiṣṇava has to love God, make friends with the devotees, instruct the innocent and reject jealous people." These are the four functions of the Vaiṣṇava in the intermediate stage. In *Caitanya-caritāmṛta* (*Madhya* 22.64) Śrī Sanātana Gosvāmī is taught:

śraddhāvān jana haya bhakti-adhikārī
'uttama', 'madhyama', 'kaniṣṭha'——sraddhā-anusārī

"One who is faithful is a proper candidate for devotional service. In terms of one's degree of faith in devotional service, one is a first-class, second-class or neophyte Vaiṣṇava."

śāstra-yukti nāhi jāne dṛḍha, śraddhāvān
'madhyama-adhikārī' sei mahā-bhāgyavān

"One who has attained the intermediate stage is not very advanced in śāstric knowledge, but he has firm faith in the Lord. Such a person is very fortunate to be situated on the intermediate platform." (Cc. *Madhya* 22.67)

rati-prema-tāratamye bhakta——tara-tama

"Attraction and love are the ultimate goal of devotional service. The degrees of such attraction and love for God distinguish the different stages of devotion—neophyte, intermediate and perfectional." (Cc. *Madhya* 22.71) An intermediate devotee is greatly attracted to chanting the holy name, and by chanting he is elevated to the platform of love. If one chants the holy name of the Lord with great attachment, he can understand his position as an eternal servant of the spiritual master, other Vaiṣṇavas and Kṛṣṇa Himself. Thus the intermediate Vaiṣṇava considers himself *kṛṣṇa-dāsa,* Kṛṣṇa's servant. He therefore preaches Kṛṣṇa consciousness to innocent neophytes and stresses the importance of chanting the Hare Kṛṣṇa *mahā-mantra.* An intermediate devotee can identify the nondevotee or motivated devotee. The motivated devotee or the nondevotee are on the material platform, and they are called *prākṛta.* The intermediate devotee does not mix with such materialistic people. However, he understands that the Supreme Personality of Godhead and everything related to Him are on the same transcendental platform. Actually none of them are mundane.

TEXT 73

বর্ষান্তরে পুনঃ তাঁরা ঐছে প্রশ্ন কৈল ।
বৈষ্ণবের তারতম্য প্রভু শিখাইল ॥ ৭৩ ॥

varṣāntare punaḥ tāṅrā aiche praśna kaila
vaiṣṇavera tāratamya prabhu śikhāila

SYNONYMS

varṣāntare—after one year; *punaḥ*—again; *tāṅrā*—they (the inhabitants of Kulīna-grāma); *aiche*—such; *praśna*—a question; *kaila*—made; *vaiṣṇavera*—of Vaiṣṇavas; *tāratamya*—upper and lower gradations; *prabhu*—Śrī Caitanya Mahāprabhu; *śikhāila*—taught.

TRANSLATION

The following year, the inhabitants of Kulīna-grāma again asked the Lord the same question. Hearing this question, Śrī Caitanya Mahāprabhu again taught them about the different types of Vaiṣṇavas.

TEXT 74

যাঁহার দর্শনে মুখে আইসে কৃষ্ণনাম ।
তাঁহারে জানিহ তুমি 'বৈষ্ণব-প্রধান' ॥ ৭৪ ॥

yāṅhāra darśane mukhe āise kṛṣṇa-nāma
tāṅhāre jāniha tumi 'vaiṣṇava-pradhāna'

SYNONYMS

yāṅhāra darśane—by the sight of whom; *mukhe*—in the mouth; *āise*—automatically awakens; *kṛṣṇa-nāma*—the holy name of Kṛṣṇa; *tāṅhāre*—him; *jāniha*—must know; *tumi*—you; *vaiṣṇava-pradhāna*—the first-class Vaiṣṇava.

TRANSLATION

Śrī Caitanya Mahāprabhu said, "A first-class Vaiṣṇava is he whose very presence makes others chant the holy name of Kṛṣṇa."

PURPORT

Śrīla Bhaktisiddhānta Sarasvatī Ṭhākura says that if an observer immediately remembers the holy name of Kṛṣṇa upon seeing a Vaiṣṇava, that Vaiṣṇava should be considered a *mahā-bhāgavata,* a first-class devotee. Such a Vaiṣṇava is always aware of his Kṛṣṇa conscious duty, and he is enlightened in self-realization. He is always in love with the Supreme Personality of Godhead, Kṛṣṇa, and this love is without adulteration. Because of this love, he is always awake to transcendental realization. Because he knows that Kṛṣṇa consciousness is the basis of knowledge and action, he sees everything connected with Kṛṣṇa. Such a person is able to chant the holy name of Kṛṣṇa perfectly. Such a *mahā-bhāgavata* Vaiṣṇava has the transcendental eyes to see who is sleeping under the spell of *māyā,* and he engages himself in awakening sleeping conditioned beings by spreading the knowledge of Kṛṣṇa consciousness. He opens eyes that are closed by forgetfulness of Kṛṣṇa. Thus the living entity is liberated from the dullness of material energy and is engaged fully in the service of the Lord. The *madhyama-adhikārī* Vaiṣṇava can awaken others to Kṛṣṇa consciousness and engage them in duties whereby they can advance. It is therefore said in *Caitanya-caritāmṛta* (*Madhya-līlā,* Chapter Six, verse 279):

lohāke yāvat sparśi' hema nāhi kare
tāvat sparśa-maṇi keha cinite nā pāre

"One cannot understand the value of touchstone until it turns iron into gold." One should judge by action, not by promises. A *mahā-bhāgavata* can turn a living entity from abominable material life to the Lord's service. This is the test of a *mahā-bhāgavata.* Although preaching is not meant for a *mahā-bhāgavata,* a *mahā-bhāgavata* can descend to the platform of *madhyama-bhāgavata* just to convert others to Vaiṣṇavism. Actually a *mahā-bhāgavata* is fit to spread Kṛṣṇa consciousness, but he does not distinguish where Kṛṣṇa consciousness should be spread from where it should not. He thinks that everyone is competent to accept Kṛṣṇa consciousness if the chance is provided. A neophyte and intermediate devotee should always be anxious to hear the *mahā-bhāgavata* and serve him in every respect. The neophyte and intermediate devotees can gradually rise to the platform of *uttama-adhikārī* and become first-class devotees. Symptoms of a first-class devotee are given in *Śrīmad-Bhāgavatam* (11.2.45):

sarva-bhūteṣu yaḥ paśyed
bhagavad-bhāvam ātmanaḥ
bhūtāni bhagavaty ātmany
eṣa bhāgavatottamaḥ

When teaching Sanātana Gosvāmī, the Lord further said:

śāstra-yuktye sunipuṇa, dṛḍha-śraddhā yāṅra
'uttama-adhikārī' se tāraye saṁsāra

"If one is expert in Vedic literature and has full faith in the Supreme Lord, then he is an *uttama-adhikārī*, a first-class Vaiṣṇava, a topmost Vaiṣṇava who can deliver the whole world and turn everyone to Kṛṣṇa consciousness." (Cc. *Madhya* 22.65) With great love and affection, the *mahā-bhāgavata* observes the Supreme Personality of Godhead, devotional service and the devotee. He observes nothing beyond Kṛṣṇa, Kṛṣṇa consciousness and Kṛṣṇa's devotees. The *mahā-bhāgavata* knows that everyone is engaged in the Lord's service in different ways. He therefore descends to the middle platform to elevate everyone to the Kṛṣṇa conscious position.

TEXT 75

ক্রম করি' কহে প্রভু 'বৈষ্ণব'-লক্ষণ ।
'বৈষ্ণব', 'বৈষ্ণবতর', আর 'বৈষ্ণবতম' ॥ ৭৫ ॥

krama kari' kahe prabhu 'vaiṣṇava'-lakṣaṇa
'vaiṣṇava', 'vaiṣṇavatara', āra 'vaiṣṇavatama'

SYNONYMS

krama kari'—dividing according to grades; *kahe prabhu*—Śrī Caitanya Mahāprabhu spoke; *vaiṣṇava-lakṣaṇa*—the symptoms of Vaiṣṇavas; *vaiṣṇava*—the ordinary Vaiṣṇava (the positive platform); *vaiṣṇava-tara*—the better Vaiṣṇava (the comparative platform); *āra*—and; *vaiṣṇava-tama*—the best Vaiṣṇava (the superlative platform).

TRANSLATION

In this way, Śrī Caitanya Mahāprabhu instructed different types of Vaiṣṇavas—the Vaiṣṇava, Vaiṣṇavatara and Vaiṣṇavatama. He thus successively explained all the symptoms of a Vaiṣṇava to the inhabitants of Kulīna-grāma.

TEXT 76

এইমত সব বৈষ্ণব গৌড়ে চলিলা ।
বিদ্যানিধি সে বৎসর নীলাদ্রি রহিলা ॥ ৭৬ ॥

ei-mata saba vaiṣṇava gauḍe calilā
vidyānidhi se vatsara nīlādri rahilā

SYNONYMS

ei-mata—in this way; *saba*—all; *vaiṣṇava*—devotees; *gauḍe calilā*—returned to Bengal; *vidyānidhi*—Puṇḍarīka Vidyānidhi; *se vatsara*—that year; *nīlādri rahilā*—remained at Nīlādri, Jagannātha Purī.

TRANSLATION

Finally all the Vaiṣṇavas returned to Bengal, but that year Puṇḍarīka Vidyānidhi remained at Jagannātha Purī.

TEXT 77

স্বরূপ-সহিত তাঁর হয় সখ্য-প্রীতি ।
দুই-জনায় কৃষ্ণ-কথায় একত্রই স্থিতি ॥ ৭৭ ॥

svarūpa-sahita tāṅra haya sakhya-prīti
dui-janāya kṛṣṇa-kathāya ekatra-i sthiti

SYNONYMS

svarūpa-sahita—with Svarūpa Dāmodara Gosvāmī; *tāṅra*—his; *haya*—there is; *sakhya-prīti*—very intimate friendship; *dui-janāya*—both of them; *kṛṣṇa-kathāya*—in topics of Kṛṣṇa; *ekatra-i*—on the same level; *sthiti*—position.

TRANSLATION

Svarūpa Dāmodara Gosvāmī and Puṇḍarīka Vidyānidhi had a friendly, intimate relationship, and as far as discussing topics about Kṛṣṇa, they were situated on the same platform.

TEXT 78

গদাধর-পণ্ডিতে তেঁহো পুনঃ মন্ত্র দিল ।
ওড়ন-ষষ্ঠীর দিনে যাত্রা যে দেখিল ॥ ৭৮ ॥

gadādhara-paṇḍite teṅho punaḥ mantra dila
oḍana-ṣaṣṭhīra dine yātrā ye dekhila

SYNONYMS

gadādhara-paṇḍite—unto Gadādhara Paṇḍita; *teṅho*—Puṇḍarīka Vidyānidhi; *punaḥ*—again, the second; *mantra*—initiation; *dila*—gave; *oḍana-ṣaṣṭhīra dine*—on the day of performing the Oḍana-ṣaṣṭhī function; *yātrā*—festival; *ye*—indeed; *dekhila*—he saw.

TRANSLATION

Puṇḍarīka Vidyānidhi initiated Gadādhara Paṇḍita for the second time, and on the day of Oḍana-ṣaṣṭhī he saw the festival.

PURPORT

At the beginning of winter, there is a ceremony known as the Oḍana-ṣaṣṭhī. This ceremony indicates that from that day forward, a winter covering should be given to Lord Jagannātha. That covering is directly purchased from a weaver. According to the *arcana-mārga,* a cloth should first be washed to remove all the starch, and then it can be used to cover the Lord. Puṇḍarīka Vidyānidhi saw that the priest neglected to wash the cloth before covering Lord Jagannātha. Since he wanted to find some fault in the devotees, he became indignant.

TEXT 79

জগন্নাথ পরেন তথা 'মাড়ুয়া' বসন ।
দেখিয়া সঘৃণ হৈল বিদ্যানিধির মন ॥ ৭৯ ॥

jagannātha parena tathā 'māḍuyā' vasana
dekhiyā saghṛṇa haila vidyānidhira mana

SYNONYMS

jagannātha—Lord Jagannātha; *parena*—puts on; *tathā*—there; *māḍuyā vasana*—cloth with starch; *dekhiyā*—seeing; *sa-ghṛṇa*—with hatred; *haila*—was; *vidyānidhira mana*—the mind of Vidyānidhi.

TRANSLATION

When Puṇḍarīka Vidyānidhi saw that Lord Jagannātha was given a starched garment, he became a little hateful. In this way his mind was polluted.

TEXT 80

সেই রাত্রে্য জগন্নাথ-বলাই আসিয়া।
দুই-ভাই চড়া'ন তাঁরে হাসিয়া হাসিয়া॥ ৮০ ॥

sei rātrye jagannātha-balāi āsiyā
dui-bhāi caḍā'na tāṅre hāsiyā hāsiyā

SYNONYMS

sei rātrye—on that night; *jagannātha*—Lord Jagannātha; *balāi*—Lord Balarāma; *āsiyā*—coming; *dui-bhāi*—both brothers; *caḍā'na*—slapped; *tāṅre*—him; *hāsiyā hāsiyā*—smiling.

TRANSLATION

That night the brothers Lord Jagannātha and Balarāma came to Puṇḍarīka Vidyānidhi and, smiling, began to slap him.

TEXT 81

গাল ফুলিল, আচার্য অন্তরে উল্লাস।
বিস্তারি' বর্ণিয়াছেন বৃন্দাবন-দাস॥ ৮১ ॥

gāla phulila, ācārya antare ullāsa
vistāri' varṇiyāchena vṛndāvana-dāsa

SYNONYMS

gāla—the cheeks; *phulila*—became swollen; *ācārya*—Puṇḍarīka Vidyānidhi; *antare*—within the heart; *ullāsa*—very happy; *vistāri'*—elaborating; *varṇiyāchena*—has narrated; *vṛndāvana-dāsa*—Śrīla Vṛndāvana dāsa Ṭhākura.

TRANSLATION

Although his cheeks were swollen from the slapping, Puṇḍarīka Vidyānidhi was very happy within. This incident has been elaborately described by Ṭhākura Vṛndāvana dāsa.

TEXT 82

এইমত প্রত্যব্দ আইসে গৌড়ের ভক্তগণ।
প্রভু-সঙ্গে রহি' করে যাত্রা-দরশন॥ ৮২ ॥

ei-mata pratyabda āise gauḍera bhakta-gaṇa
prabhu-saṅge rahi' kare yātrā-daraśana

SYNONYMS

ei-mata—in this way; *prati-abda*—every year; *āise*—come; *gauḍera*—of Bengal; *bhakta-gaṇa*—the devotees; *prabhu-saṅge*—with Lord Śrī Caitanya Prabhu; *rahi'*—residing; *kare*—do; *yātrā-daraśana*—observing the Ratha-yātrā festival.

TRANSLATION

Every year the devotees of Bengal would come and stay with Śrī Caitanya Mahāprabhu to see the Ratha-yātrā festival.

TEXT 83

তার মধ্যে যে যে বর্ষে আছয়ে বিশেষ।
বিস্তারিয়া আগে তাহা কহিব নিঃশেষ ॥ ৮৩ ॥

tāra madhye ye ye varṣe āchaye viśeṣa
vistāriyā āge tāhā kahiba niḥśeṣa

SYNONYMS

tāra madhye—within those episodes; *ye ye*—whatever; *varṣe*—in years; *āchaye*—there is; *viśeṣa*—particular occurrence; *vistāriyā*—elaborating; *āge*—ahead; *tāhā*—that; *kahiba*—I shall say; *niḥśeṣa*—completely.

TRANSLATION

Whatever happened during those years that is worth noting shall be described later.

TEXT 84

এইমত মহাপ্রভুর চারি বৎসর গেল।
দক্ষিণ যাঞা আসিতে দুই বৎসর লাগিল ॥ ৮৪ ॥

ei-mata mahāprabhura cāri vatsara gela
dakṣiṇa yāñā āsite dui vatsara lāgila

SYNONYMS

ei-mata—in this way; *mahāprabhura*—of Śrī Caitanya Mahāprabhu; *cāri*—four; *vatsara*—years; *gela*—passed; *dakṣiṇa yāñā*—after touring southern India; *āsite*—to come back; *dui vatsara lāgila*—He took two years.

TRANSLATION

Thus Śrī Caitanya Mahāprabhu passed four years. He spent the first two years on His tour in South India.

TEXT 85

আর দুই বৎসর চাহে বৃন্দাবন যাইতে ।
রামানন্দ-হঠে প্রভু না পারে চলিতে ॥ ৮৫ ॥

āra dui vatsara cāhe vṛndāvana yāite
rāmānanda-haṭhe prabhu nā pāre calite

SYNONYMS

āra dui vatsara—another two years; *cāhe*—He wanted; *vṛndāvana yāite*—to go to Vṛndāvana; *rāmānanda-haṭhe*—by the tricks of Rāmānanda Rāya; *prabhu*—Lord Śrī Caitanya Mahāprabhu; *nā pāre*—was not able; *calite*—to go.

TRANSLATION

The other two years, Śrī Caitanya Mahāprabhu wanted to go to Vṛndāvana, but He could not leave Jagannātha Purī because of Rāmānanda Rāya's tricks.

TEXT 86

পঞ্চম বৎসরে গৌড়ের ভক্তগণ আইলা ।
রথ দেখি' না রহিলা, গৌড়েরে চলিলা ॥ ৮৬ ॥

pañcama vatsare gauḍera bhakta-gaṇa āilā
ratha dekhi' nā rahilā, gauḍere calilā

SYNONYMS

pañcama vatsare—on the fifth year; *gauḍera*—of Bengal; *bhakta-gaṇa*—the devotees; *āilā*—came; *ratha dekhi'*—seeing the Ratha-yātrā festival; *nā rahilā*—did not stay; *gauḍere calilā*—returned to Bengal.

TRANSLATION

During the fifth year, the devotees from Bengal came to see the Ratha-yātrā festival. After seeing it, they did not stay but returned to Bengal.

TEXT 87

তবে প্রভু সার্বভৌম-রামানন্দ-স্থানে ।
আলিঙ্গন করি' কহে মধুর বচনে ॥ ৮৭ ॥

tabe prabhu sārvabhauma-rāmānanda-sthāne
āliṅgana kari' kahe madhura vacane

SYNONYMS

tabe—then; *prabhu*—Śrī Caitanya Mahāprabhu; *sārvabhauma-rāmānanda-sthāne*—before Sārvabhauma Bhaṭṭācārya and Rāmānanda Rāya; *āliṅgana kari'*—embracing; *kahe*—says; *madhura vacane*—sweet words.

TRANSLATION

Then Śrī Caitanya Mahāprabhu placed a proposal before Sārvabhauma Bhaṭṭācārya and Rāmānanda Rāya. He embraced them and spoke sweet words.

TEXT 88

বহুত উৎকণ্ঠা মোর যাইতে বৃন্দাবন।
তোমার হঠে দুই বৎসর না কৈলুঁ গমন॥ ৮৮॥

bahuta utkaṇṭhā mora yāite vṛndāvana
tomāra haṭhe dui vatsara nā kailuṅ gamana

SYNONYMS

bahuta utkaṇṭhā—great anxiety; *mora*—My; *yāite vṛndāvana*—to go to Vṛndāvana; *tomāra haṭhe*—by your tricks; *dui vatsara*—for two years; *nā kailuṅ*—I did not do; *gamana*—going.

TRANSLATION

Caitanya Mahāprabhu said, "My desire to go to Vṛndāvana has very much increased. Because of your tricks, I have not been able to go there for the past two years.

TEXT 89

অবশ্য চলিব, দুঁহে করহ সম্মতি।
তোমা-দুঁহা বিনা মোর নাহি অন্য গতি॥ ৮৯॥

avaśya caliba, duṅhe karaha sammati
tomā-duṅhā vinā mora nāhi anya gati

SYNONYMS

avaśya—certainly; *caliba*—I shall go; *duṅhe*—both of you; *karaha sammati*—kindly agree to this proposal; *tomā-duṅhā vinā*—except you two; *mora*—My; *nāhi*—there is not; *anya gati*—other resort.

TRANSLATION

"This time I must go. Will you please give Me permission? Save for you two, I have no other resort.

TEXT 90

গৌড়-দেশে হয় মোর 'দুই সমাশ্রয়'।
'জননী' 'জাহ্নবী',—এই দুই দয়াময় ॥ ৯০ ॥

gauḍa-deśe haya mora 'dui samāśraya'
'jananī' 'jāhnavī',——ei dui dayāmaya

SYNONYMS

gauḍa-deśe—in Bengal; *haya*—there are; *mora*—My; *dui*—two; *samāśraya*—shelters; *jananī*—the mother; *jāhnavī*—mother Ganges; *ei dui*—these two; *dayā-maya*—very merciful.

TRANSLATION

"In Bengal I have two shelters—my mother and the River Ganges. Both of them are very merciful.

TEXT 91

গৌড়-দেশ দিয়া যাব তাঁ-সবা দেখিয়া।
তুমি দুঁহে আজ্ঞা দেহ' পরসন্ন হঞা ॥ ৯১ ॥

gauḍa-deśa diyā yāba tāṅ-sabā dekhiyā
tumi duṅhe ājñā deha' parasanna hañā

SYNONYMS

gauḍa-deśa—the country known as Bengal; *diyā*—through; *yāba*—I shall go; *tāṅ-sabā*—both of them; *dekhiyā*—seeing; *tumi duṅhe*—both of you; *ājñā deha'*—give Me permission; *parasanna hañā*—being very pleased.

TRANSLATION

"I shall go to Vṛndāvana through Bengal and see both My mother and the River Ganges. Now would you two be pleased to give Me permission?"

TEXT 92

শুনিয়া প্রভুর বাণী মনে বিচারয়।
প্রভু-সনে অতি হঠ কভু ভাল নয় ॥ ৯২ ॥

śuniyā prabhura vāṇī mane vicāraya
prabhu-sane ati haṭha kabhu bhāla naya

SYNONYMS

śuniyā—hearing; *prabhura*—of Lord Śrī Caitanya Mahāprabhu; *vāṇī*—the words; *mane*—in their minds; *vicāraya*—considered; *prabhu-sane*—with Lord Caitanya Mahāprabhu; *ati*—very much; *haṭha*—tricks; *kabhu*—at any time; *bhāla naya*—is not very good.

TRANSLATION

When Sārvabhauma Bhaṭṭācārya and Rāmānanda Rāya heard these words, they began to consider that it was not at all good that they played so many tricks on the Lord.

TEXT 93

দুঁহে কহে,—এবে বর্ষা, চলিতে নারিবা।
বিজয়া-দশমী আইলে অবশ্য চলিবা ॥ ৯৩ ॥

duṅhe kahe,——ebe varṣā, calite nāribā
vijayā-daśamī āile avaśya calibā

SYNONYMS

duṅhe kahe—both of them said; *ebe*—now; *varṣā*—rainy season; *calite nāribā*—You will not be able to go; *vijayā-daśamī*—the Vijayā-daśamī day; *āile*—when it arrives; *avaśya*—certainly; *calibā*—You will go.

TRANSLATION

They both said, "Now that the rainy season is here, it will be difficult for You to travel. It is better to wait for Vijayā-daśamī before departing for Vṛndāvana."

TEXT 94

আনন্দে মহাপ্রভু বর্ষা কৈল সমাধান।
বিজয়া-দশমী-দিনে করিল পয়ান ॥ ৯৪ ॥

ānande mahāprabhu varṣā kaila samādhāna
vijayā-daśamī-dine karila payāna

SYNONYMS

ānande—in great pleasure; *mahāprabhu*—Śrī Caitanya Mahāprabhu; *varṣā*—the rainy season; *kaila samādhāna*—passed; *vijayā-daśamī-dine*—on Vijayā-daśamī, the day when the victory was won by Lord Rāmacandra; *karila payāna*—He departed.

TRANSLATION

Śrī Caitanya Mahāprabhu was very pleased to thus receive their permission. He waited until the rainy season passed, and when the day of Vijayā-daśamī arrived, He departed for Vṛndāvana.

TEXT 95

জগন্নাথের প্রসাদ প্রভু যত পাঞাছিল।
কড়ার, চন্দন, ডোর, সব সঙ্গে লৈল ॥ ৯৫ ॥

jagannāthera prasāda prabhu yata pāñāchila
kaḍāra, candana, ḍora, saba saṅge laila

SYNONYMS

jagannāthera—of Lord Jagannātha; *prasāda*—the remnants of food; *prabhu*—Śrī Caitanya Mahāprabhu; *yata*—all; *pāñāchila*—had obtained; *kaḍāra*—a kind of *tilaka; candana*—sandalwood; *ḍora*—ropes; *saba*—all; *saṅge laila*—He took with Him.

TRANSLATION

The Lord collected whatever remnants of food were left by Lord Jagannātha. He also took remnants of the Lord's kaḍāra ointment, sandalwood and ropes with Him.

TEXT 96

জগন্নাথে আজ্ঞা মাগি' প্রভাতে চলিলা।
উড়িয়া-ভক্তগণ সঙ্গে পাছে চলি' আইলা ॥ ৯৬ ॥

jagannāthe ājñā māgi' prabhāte calilā
uḍiyā-bhakta-gaṇa saṅge pāche cali' āilā

SYNONYMS

jagannāthe—from Lord Jagannātha; *ājñā māgi'*—taking permission; *prabhāte*—early in the morning; *calilā*—departed; *uḍiyā-bhakta-gaṇa*—all the devotees of Orissa; *saṅge*—with Him; *pāche*—following; *cali' āilā*—went.

TRANSLATION

After taking Lord Jagannātha's permission early in the morning, Śrī Caitanya Mahāprabhu departed, and all the devotees of Orissa began following Him.

TEXT 97

উড়িয়া-ভক্তগণে প্রভু যত্নে নিবারিলা ।
নিজগণ-সঙ্গে প্রভু 'ভবানীপুর' আইলা ॥ ৯৭ ॥

uḍiyā-bhakta-gaṇe prabhu yatne nivārilā
nija-gaṇa-saṅge prabhu 'bhavānīpura' āilā

SYNONYMS

uḍiyā-bhakta-gaṇe—the devotees of Orissa; *prabhu*—Śrī Caitanya Mahāprabhu; *yatne*—with great care; *nivārilā*—stopped; *nija-gaṇa-saṅge*—with His personal associates; *prabhu*—Śrī Caitanya Mahāprabhu; *bhavānīpura āilā*—came to Bhavānīpura.

TRANSLATION

It was with great care that Caitanya Mahāprabhu forbade the Orissa devotees to follow Him. Accompanied by personal associates, He first went to Bhavānīpura.

PURPORT

One goes through Bhavānīpura before reaching a well-known place named Jānkādei-pura, or Jānakīdevī-pura.

TEXT 98

রামানন্দ আইলা পাছে দোলায় চড়িয়া ।
বাণীনাথ বহু প্রসাদ দিল পাঠাঞা ॥ ৯৮ ॥

rāmānanda āilā pāche dolāya caḍiyā
vāṇīnātha bahu prasāda dila pāṭhāñā

SYNONYMS

rāmānanda—Rāmānanda Rāya; *āilā*—came; *pāche*—behind; *dolāya caḍiyā*—riding on a palanquin; *vāṇīnātha*—Vāṇīnātha Rāya; *bahu*—a large quantity of; *prasāda*—remnants of the food of Jagannātha; *dila*—gave; *pāṭhāñā*—sending.

TRANSLATION

After Lord Caitanya reached Bhavānīpura, Rāmānanda Rāya arrived on his palanquin, and Vāṇīnātha Rāya had a large quantity of prasāda sent to the Lord.

TEXT 99

প্রসাদ ভোজন করি' তথায় রহিলা ।
প্রাতঃকালে চলি' প্রভু 'ভুবনেশ্বর' আইলা ॥ ৯৯ ॥

prasāda bhojana kari' tathāya rahilā
prātaḥ-kāle cali' prabhu 'bhuvaneśvara' āilā

SYNONYMS

prasāda bhojana kari'—after taking the *prasāda; tathāya rahilā*—He stayed there; *prātaḥ-kāle*—early in the morning; *cali'*—walking; *prabhu*—Śrī Caitanya Mahāprabhu; *bhuvaneśvara āilā*—reached the place known as Bhuvaneśvara.

TRANSLATION

After taking prasāda, Śrī Caitanya Mahāprabhu remained there for the night. Early in the morning, He began walking and finally reached Bhuvaneśvara.

TEXT 100

'কটকে' আসিয়া কৈল 'গোপাল' দরশন ।
স্বপ্নেশ্বর-বিপ্র কৈল প্রভুর নিমন্ত্রণ ॥ ১০০ ॥

'kaṭake' āsiyā kaila 'gopāla' daraśana
svapneśvara-vipra kaila prabhura nimantraṇa

SYNONYMS

kaṭake—to the city of Kaṭaka; *āsiyā*—coming; *kaila*—did; *gopāla daraśana*—seeing Lord Gopāla; *svapneśvara-vipra*—the *brāhmaṇa* named Svapneśvara; *kaila*—did; *prabhura*—of Śrī Caitanya Mahāprabhu; *nimantraṇa*—invitation.

TRANSLATION

After reaching the city of Kaṭaka, He saw the temple of Gopāla, and a brāhmaṇa there named Svapneśvara invited the Lord to eat.

TEXT 101

রামানন্দ-রায় সব-গণে নিমন্ত্রিল ।
বাহির উদ্যানে আসি' প্রভু বাসা কৈল ॥ ১০১ ॥

rāmānanda-rāya saba-gaṇe nimantrila
bāhira udyāne āsi' prabhu vāsā kaila

SYNONYMS

rāmānanda-rāya—Rāmānanda Rāya; *saba-gaṇe*—all the followers of Śrī Caitanya Mahāprabhu; *nimantrila*—invited; *bāhira udyāne*—in an outside garden; *āsi'*—coming; *prabhu*—Śrī Caitanya Mahāprabhu; *vāsā kaila*—made His resting place.

TRANSLATION

Rāmānanda Rāya invited all the others for their meals, and Śrī Caitanya Mahāprabhu made His resting place in a garden outside the temple.

TEXT 102

ভিক্ষা করি' বকুল-তলে করিলা বিশ্রাম।
প্রতাপরুদ্র-ঠাঞি রায় করিল পয়ান॥ ১০২॥

bhikṣā kari' bakula-tale karilā viśrāma
pratāparudra-ṭhāñi rāya karila payāna

SYNONYMS

bhikṣā kari'—after taking lunch; *bakula-tale*—underneath a *bakula* flower tree; *karilā viśrāma*—took rest; *pratāparudra-ṭhāñi*—to the presence of Mahārāja Pratāparudra; *rāya*—Rāmānanda Rāya; *karila payāna*—departed.

TRANSLATION

While Śrī Caitanya Mahāprabhu was taking rest beneath a bakula tree, Rāmānanda Rāya immediately went to Mahārāja Pratāparudra.

TEXT 103

শুনি' আনন্দিত রাজা অতিশীঘ্র আইলা।
প্রভু দেখি' দণ্ডবৎ ভূমেতে পড়িলা॥ ১০৩॥

śuni' ānandita rājā ati-śīghra āilā
prabhu dekhi' daṇḍavat bhūmete paḍilā

SYNONYMS

śuni'—hearing; *ānandita*—very pleased; *rājā*—the King; *ati-śīghra*—hastily; *āilā*—came; *prabhu dekhi'*—seeing Lord Śrī Caitanya Mahāprabhu; *daṇḍavat*—obeisances offered falling flat; *bhūmete*—on the ground; *paḍilā*—fell down.

TRANSLATION

The King was very happy to hear the news, and he hastily went there. Upon seeing the Lord, he fell flat to offer Him obeisances.

TEXT 104

পুনঃ উঠে, পুনঃ পড়ে প্রণয়-বিহ্বল ।
স্তুতি করে, পুলকাঙ্গ, পড়ে অশ্রুজল ॥ ১০৪ ॥

punaḥ uṭhe, punaḥ paḍe praṇaya-vihvala
stuti kare, pulakāṅga, paḍe aśru-jala

SYNONYMS

punaḥ—again; *uṭhe*—he arose; *punaḥ*—again; *paḍe*—he fell down; *praṇaya-vihvala*—overwhelmed with love; *stuti kare*—offers prayers; *pulaka-aṅga*—the entire body quivering in joy; *paḍe*—fell down; *aśru-jala*—tears.

TRANSLATION

Being overwhelmed with love, the King again and again got up and fell down. When he offered prayers, his whole body shivered, and tears fell from his eyes.

TEXT 105

তাঁর ভক্তি দেখি' প্রভুর তুষ্ট হৈল মন ।
উঠি' মহাপ্রভু তাঁরে কৈলা আলিঙ্গন ॥ ১০৫ ॥

tāṅra bhakti dekhi' prabhura tuṣṭa haila mana
uṭhi' mahāprabhu tāṅre kailā āliṅgana

SYNONYMS

tāṅra bhakti—his devotion; *dekhi'*—seeing; *prabhura*—of Śrī Caitanya Mahāprabhu; *tuṣṭa*—pleased; *haila*—was; *mana*—mind; *uṭhi'*—standing up; *mahāprabhu*—Śrī Caitanya Mahāprabhu; *tāṅre*—him; *kailā āliṅgana*—embraced.

TRANSLATION

Śrī Caitanya Mahāprabhu was very pleased to see the King's devotion, and He therefore stood up and embraced him.

TEXT 106

পুনঃ স্তুতি করি' রাজা করয়ে প্রণাম ।
প্রভু-কৃপা-অশ্রুতে তাঁর দেহ হৈল স্নান ॥ ১০৬ ॥

punaḥ stuti kari' rājā karaye praṇāma
prabhu-kṛpā-aśrute tāṅra deha haila snāna

SYNONYMS

punaḥ—again; *stuti kari'*—offering prayers; *rājā*—the King; *karaye praṇāma*—offered obeisances; *prabhu kṛpā*—of the mercy of the Lord; *aśrute*—by the tears; *tāṅra*—of the Lord; *deha*—the body; *haila*—became; *snāna*—bathed.

TRANSLATION

When the Lord embraced the King, the King again and again offered prayers and obeisances. In this way, the Lord's mercy brought tears from the King, and the Lord's body was bathed with these tears.

TEXT 107

সুস্থ করি, রামানন্দ রাজারে বসাইলা ।
কায়মনোবাক্যে প্রভু তাঁরে কৃপা কৈলা ॥ ১০৭ ॥

sustha kari, rāmānanda rājāre vasāilā
kāya-mano-vākye prabhu tāṅre kṛpā kailā

SYNONYMS

sustha kari—comforting him; *rāmānanda*—Rāya Rāmānanda; *rājāre vasāilā*—made the King sit down; *kāya-mano-vākye*—with body, mind and words; *prabhu*—Śrī Caitanya Mahāprabhu; *tāṅre*—unto the King; *kṛpā kailā*—showed His mercy.

TRANSLATION

Finally Rāmānanda Rāya pacified the King and made him sit down. The Lord also bestowed mercy upon him through His body, mind and words.

TEXT 108

ঐছে তাঁহারে কৃপা কৈল গৌররায় ।
"প্রতাপরুদ্র-সংত্রাতা" নাম হৈল যায় ॥ ১০৮ ॥

aiche tāṅhāre kṛpā kaila gaurarāya
"pratāparudra-santrātā" nāma haila yāya

SYNONYMS

aiche—such; *tāṅhāre*—unto the King; *kṛpā*—mercy; *kaila*—showed; *gaurarāya*—Śrī Caitanya Mahāprabhu; *pratāparudra-santrātā*—the deliverer of Mahārāja Pratāparudra; *nāma*—the name; *haila*—became; *yāya*—by which.

TRANSLATION

Śrī Caitanya Mahāprabhu showed such mercy to the King that from that day on the Lord became known as Pratāparudra-santrātā, the deliverer of Mahārāja Pratāparudra.

TEXT 109

রাজ-পাত্রগণ কৈল প্রভুর বন্দন ।
রাজারে বিদায় দিলা শচীর নন্দন ॥ ১০৯ ॥

rāja-pātra-gaṇa kaila prabhura vandana
rājāre vidāya dilā śacīra nandana

SYNONYMS

rāja-pātra-gaṇa—the officers of the King; *kaila*—did; *prabhura vandana*—glorifying the Lord; *rājāre*—unto the King; *vidāya dilā*—bade farewell; *śacīra nandana*—the son of mother Śacī.

TRANSLATION

All the governmental officers also paid their respects to the Lord, and finally the King and his men were bade farewell by the son of mother Śacī.

TEXT 110

বাহিরে আসি' রাজা আজ্ঞা-পত্র লেখাইল ।
নিজ-রাজ্যে যত 'বিষয়ী', তাহারে পাঠাইল ॥ ১১০ ॥

bāhire āsi' rājā ājñā-patra lekhāila
nija-rājye yata 'viṣayī', tāhāre pāṭhāila

SYNONYMS

bāhire āsi'—coming outside; *rājā*—the King; *ājñā-patra*—letters of command; *lekhāila*—had written; *nija-rājye*—in his own kingdom; *yata*—all; *viṣayī*—government servants; *tāhāre*—unto them; *pāṭhāila*—sent.

TRANSLATION

The King then went outside and had orders written down and sent to the government servants within his kingdom.

TEXT 111

'গ্রামে-গ্রামে' নূতন আবাস করিবা ।
পাঁচ-সাত নব্যগৃহে সামগ্র্যে ভরিবা ॥ ১১১ ॥

'grāme-grāme' nūtana āvāsa karibā
pāṅca-sāta navya-gṛhe sāmagrye bharibā

SYNONYMS

grāme-grāme—in every village; *nūtana*—new; *āvāsa*—residential places; *karibā*—you should construct; *pāṅca-sāta*—five to seven; *navya-gṛhe*—in new houses; *sāmagrye*—with food; *bharibā*—you should fill.

TRANSLATION

His orders read: "In every village you should construct new residences, and in five or seven new houses, you should store all kinds of food.

TEXT 112

আপনি প্রভুকে লঞা তাহাঁ উত্তরিবা ।
রাত্রি-দিবা বেত্রহস্তে সেবায় রহিবা ॥ ১১২ ॥

āpani prabhuke lañā tāhāṅ uttaribā
rātri-dibā vetra-haste sevāya rahibā

SYNONYMS

āpani—personally, yourself; *prabhuke*—Śrī Caitanya Mahāprabhu; *lañā*—taking; *tāhāṅ uttaribā*—you should go there; *rātri-dibā*—night and day; *vetra-haste*—with a cane in the hands; *sevāya rahibā*—should remain engaged in His service.

TRANSLATION

"You should personally take the Lord to these newly constructed houses. Day and night you should engage in His service with a stick in your hands."

TEXT 113

দুই মহাপাত্র,—'হরিচন্দন', 'মর্দরাজ' ।
তাঁরে আজ্ঞা দিল রাজা —'করিহ সর্ব কায ॥ ১১৩ ॥

dui mahā-pātra,——'haricandana', 'mardarāja'
tāṅre ājñā dila rājā——'kariha sarva kāya

SYNONYMS

dui mahā-pātra—two respectable officers; *haricandana*—Haricandana; *mardarāja*—Mardarāja; *tāṅre*—to them; *ājñā dila*—gave orders; *rājā*—the King; *kariha*—do; *sarva kāya*—everything needed.

TRANSLATION

The King ordered two respectable officers named Haricandana and Mardarāja to do whatever was necessary to carry out these orders.

TEXTS 114-115

এক নব্য-নৌকা আনি' রাখহ নদী-তীরে ।
যাহাঁ স্নান করি' প্রভু যা'ন নদী-পারে ॥ ১১৪ ॥
তাহাঁ স্তম্ভ রোপণ কর 'মহাতীর্থ' করি' ।
নিত্য স্নান করিব তাহাঁ, তাহাঁ যেন মরি ॥ ১১৫ ॥

eka navya-naukā āni' rākhaha nadī-tīre
yāhāṅ snāna kari' prabhu yā'na nadī-pāre

tāhāṅ stambha ropaṇa kara 'mahā-tīrtha' kari'
nitya snāna kariba tāhāṅ, tāhāṅ yena mari

SYNONYMS

eka—one; *navya*—new; *naukā*—boat; *āni'*—bringing; *rākhaha*—keep; *nadī-tīre*—on the bank of the river; *yāhāṅ*—where; *snāna kari'*—taking bath; *prabhu*—Śrī Caitanya Mahāprabhu; *yā'na*—goes; *nadī-pāre*—on the other bank of the river; *tāhāṅ*—there; *stambha*—a memorial column; *ropaṇa kara*—establish; *mahā-tīrtha kari'*—making that place a great place of pilgrimage; *nitya*—daily; *snāna kariba*—I shall bathe; *tāhāṅ*—there; *tāhāṅ*—there; *yena mari*—let me die.

TRANSLATION

The King also ordered them to maintain a new boat on the banks of the river, and wherever Śrī Caitanya Mahāprabhu took His bath or crossed to the other side of the river, they should establish a memorial column and make that place a great place of pilgrimage. "Indeed," said the King, "I will take my bath there. And let me also die there."

TEXT 116

চতুর্দ্বারে করহ উত্তম নব্য বাস ।
রামানন্দ, যাহ তুমি মহাপ্রভু-পাশ ॥ ১১৬ ॥

caturdvāre karaha uttama navya vāsa
rāmānanda, yāha tumi mahāprabhu-pāśa

SYNONYMS

caturdvāre—at the place named Caturdvāra; *karaha*—make; *uttama*—very nice; *navya vāsa*—new residential quarters; *rāmānanda*—Rāmānanda Rāya; *yāha tumi*—you please go; *mahāprabhu-pāśa*—near Śrī Caitanya Mahāprabhu.

TRANSLATION

The King continued, "At Caturdvāra, please construct new residential quarters. Now, Rāmānanda, you can return to Śrī Caitanya Mahāprabhu."

TEXT 117

সন্ধ্যাতে চলিবে প্রভু,—নৃপতি শুনিল ।
হস্তী-উপর তাম্বুগৃহে স্ত্রীগণে চড়াইল ॥ ১১৭ ॥

sandhyāte calibe prabhu,——nṛpati śunila
hastī-upara tāmbu-gṛhe strī-gaṇe caḍāila

SYNONYMS

sandhyāte—in the evening; *calibe prabhu*—the Lord will start; *nṛpati śunila*—the King heard; *hastī-upara*—upon the backs of elephants; *tāmbu-gṛhe*—in tents; *strī-gaṇe*—all the ladies; *caḍāila*—made get up.

TRANSLATION

When the King heard that the Lord was leaving that evening, he immediately made arrangements for some elephants with small tents on their backs to be brought there. Then all the ladies of the palace got on the elephants.

TEXT 118

প্রভুর চলিবার পথে রহে সারি হঞা ।
সন্ধ্যাতে চলিলা প্রভু নিজগণ লঞা ॥ ১১৮ ॥

prabhura calibāra pathe rahe sāri hañā
sandhyāte calilā prabhu nija-gaṇa lañā

SYNONYMS

prabhura—of the Lord; *calibāra pathe*—on the route of walking; *rahe*—remained; *sāri hañā*—being in a line; *sandhyāte*—in the evening; *calilā prabhu*—the Lord departed; *nija-gaṇa lañā*—taking His own men.

TRANSLATION

All these ladies went to the road the Lord was taking and remained there in a line. That evening, the Lord departed with His devotees.

TEXT 119

'চিত্রোৎপলা-নদী' আসি' ঘাটে কৈল স্নান ।
মহিষীসকল দেখি' করয়ে প্রণাম ॥ ১১৯ ॥

'citrotpalā-nadī' āsi' ghāṭe kaila snāna
mahiṣī-sakala dekhi' karaye praṇāma

SYNONYMS

citrotpalā-nadī—to the river named Citrotpalā; *āsi'*—coming; *ghāṭe*—on the bank; *kaila snāna*—took a bath; *mahiṣī-sakala*—all the queens and ladies of the palace; *dekhi'*—seeing; *karaye praṇāma*—offered their obeisances.

TRANSLATION

When Śrī Caitanya Mahāprabhu went to the bank of the River Citrotpalā to take His bath, all the queens and ladies of the palace offered their obeisances to Him.

TEXT 120

প্রভুর দরশনে সবে হৈল প্রেমময় ।
'কৃষ্ণ' 'কৃষ্ণ' কহে, নেত্র অশ্রু বরিষয় ॥ ১২০ ॥

prabhura daraśane sabe haila premamaya
'kṛṣṇa' 'kṛṣṇa' kahe, netra aśru variṣaya

SYNONYMS

prabhura daraśane—by seeing the Lord; *sabe*—all of them; *haila*—became; *prema-maya*—overwhelmed with love; *kṛṣṇa kṛṣṇa kahe*—chanted the holy name of Kṛṣṇa; *netra*—the eyes; *aśru*—tears; *variṣaya*—poured.

TRANSLATION

Upon seeing the Lord, they all felt themselves overwhelmed with love of Godhead, and, tears pouring from their eyes, they began to chant the holy name, "Kṛṣṇa! Kṛṣṇa!"

TEXT 121

এমন কৃপালু নাহি শুনি ত্রিভুবনে ।
কৃষ্ণপ্রেমা হয় যাঁর দূর দরশনে ॥ ১২১ ॥

emana kṛpālu nāhi śuni tribhuvane
kṛṣṇa-premā haya yāṅra dūra daraśane

SYNONYMS

emana kṛpālu—such a merciful person; *nāhi*—not; *śuni*—we hear; *tri-bhuvane*—within the three worlds; *kṛṣṇa-premā haya*—one gets love of Kṛṣṇa; *yāṅra*—of whom; *dūra daraśane*—by seeing from a distance.

TRANSLATION

There is no one as merciful as Śrī Caitanya Mahāprabhu within all three worlds. Simply by seeing Him from a distance, one is overwhelmed with love of Godhead.

TEXT 122

নৌকাতে চড়িয়া প্রভু হৈল নদী পার ।
জ্যোৎস্নাবতী রাত্র্যে চলি' আইলা চতুর্দ্বার ॥১২২॥

naukāte caḍiyā prabhu haila nadī pāra
jyotsnāvatī rātrye cali' āilā caturdvāra

SYNONYMS

naukāte caḍiyā—getting on the boat; *prabhu*—Śrī Caitanya Mahāprabhu; *haila*—was; *nadī pāra*—across the river; *jyotsnāvatī*—lighted by the full moon; *rātrye*—in the night; *cali'*—walking; *āilā*—came; *caturdvāra*—to Caturdvāra.

TRANSLATION

The Lord then got into a new boat and crossed the river. Walking in the full moonlight, He finally reached the town known as Caturdvāra.

TEXT 123

রাত্র্যে তথা রহি' প্রাতে স্নানকৃত্য কৈল ।
হেনকালে জগন্নাথের মহাপ্রসাদ আইল ॥ ১২৩ ॥

rātrye tathā rahi' prāte snāna-kṛtya kaila
hena-kāle jagannāthera mahā-prasāda āila

SYNONYMS

rātrye—on that night; *tathā rahi'*—staying there; *prāte*—in the morning; *snāna-kṛtya kaila*—took His bath; *hena-kāle*—at that time; *jagannāthera*—of Lord Jagannātha; *mahā-prasāda āila*—remnants of food arrived.

TRANSLATION

The Lord spent the night there and in the morning took His bath. At that time, remnants of Lord Jagannātha's food arrived.

TEXT 124

রাজার আজ্ঞায় পড়িছা পাঠায় দিনে-দিনে ।
বহুত প্রসাদ পাঠায় দিয়া বহু-জনে ॥ ১২৪ ॥

rājāra ājñāya paḍichā pāṭhāya dine-dine
bahuta prasāda pāṭhāya diyā bahu-jane

SYNONYMS

rājāra ājñāya—by the order of the King; *paḍichā*—the superintendent of the temple; *pāṭhāya*—sent; *dine-dine*—day after day; *bahuta prasāda*—a large quantity of food; *pāṭhāya*—he sent; *diyā bahu-jane*—carried by many persons.

TRANSLATION

Following the King's orders, the superintendent of the temple sent large quantities of prasāda every day, and it was carried by many persons.

TEXT 125

স্বগণ-সহিতে প্রভু প্রসাদ অঙ্গীকরি' ।
উঠিয়া চলিলা প্রভু বলি' 'হরি' 'হরি' ॥ ১২৫ ॥

svagaṇa-sahite prabhu prasāda aṅgīkari'
uṭhiyā calilā prabhu bali' 'hari' 'hari'

SYNONYMS

sva-gaṇa-sahite—with His personal associates; *prabhu*—Śrī Caitanya Mahāprabhu; *prasāda*—the remnants of food; *aṅgīkari'*—accepting; *uṭhiyā*—standing up; *calilā*—started; *prabhu*—Śrī Caitanya Mahāprabhu; *bali'*—uttering; *hari hari*—Hari, Hari.

TRANSLATION

After accepting the prasāda, Śrī Caitanya Mahāprabhu stood up and started to go, chanting the holy names, "Hari! Hari!"

TEXT 126

রামানন্দ, মর্দরাজ, শ্রীহরিচন্দন ।
সঙ্গে সেবা করি' চলে এই তিন জন ॥ ১২৬ ॥

rāmānanda, mardarāja, śrī-haricandana
saṅge sevā kari' cale ei tina jana

SYNONYMS

rāmānanda—Rāmānanda; *mardarāja*—Mardarāja; *śrī-haricandana*—Śrī Haricandana; *saṅge*—in company; *sevā kari'*—rendering service; *cale*—went; *ei tina jana*—these three gentlemen.

TRANSLATION

Rāmānanda Rāya, Mardarāja and Śrī Haricandana always went with Śrī Caitanya Mahāprabhu and rendered various services.

TEXTS 127-129

প্রভু-সঙ্গে পুরী-গোসাঞি, স্বরূপ-দামোদর ।
জগদানন্দ, মুকুন্দ, গোবিন্দ, কাশীশ্বর ॥ ১২৭ ॥
হরিদাস-ঠাকুর, আর পণ্ডিত-বক্রেশ্বর ।
গোপীনাথাচার্য, আর পণ্ডিত-দামোদর ॥ ১২৮ ॥
রামাই, নন্দাই, আর বহু ভক্তগণ ।
প্রধান কহিলুঁ, সবার কে করে গণন ॥ ১২৯ ॥

prabhu-saṅge purī-gosāñi, svarūpa-dāmodara
jagadānanda, mukunda, govinda, kāśīśvara

haridāsa-ṭhākura, āra paṇḍita-vakreśvara
gopīnāthācārya, āra paṇḍita-dāmodara

rāmāi, nandāi, āra bahu bhakta-gaṇa
pradhāna kahiluṅ, sabāra ke kare gaṇana

SYNONYMS

prabhu-saṅge—with Śrī Caitanya Mahāprabhu; *purī-gosāñi*—Paramānanda Purī; *svarūpa-dāmodara*—Svarūpa Dāmodara; *jagadānanda*—Jagadānanda; *mukunda*—Mukunda; *govinda*—Govinda; *kāśīśvara*—Kāśīśvara; *haridāsa-ṭhākura*—Haridāsa Ṭhākura; *āra*—and; *paṇḍita-vakreśvara*—Paṇḍita Vakreśvara; *gopīnātha-ācārya*—Gopīnātha Ācārya; *āra*—and; *paṇḍita-dāmodara*—Paṇḍita Dāmodara; *rāmāi*—Rāmāi; *nandāi*—Nandāi; *āra*—and; *bahu bhakta-gaṇa*—many devotees; *pradhāna*—the chief; *kahiluṅ*—I have mentioned; *sabāra*—of all of them; *ke*—who; *kare gaṇana*—can make an account.

TRANSLATION

Paramānanda Purī Gosvāmī, Svarūpa Dāmodara, Jagadānanda, Mukunda, Govinda, Kāśīśvara, Haridāsa Ṭhākura, Vakreśvara Paṇḍita, Gopīnātha Ācārya, Dāmodara Paṇḍita, Rāmāi, Nandāi and many other devotees accompanied the Lord. I have mentioned only the chief devotees. No one can describe the total number.

TEXT 130

গদাধর-পণ্ডিত যবে সঙ্গেতে চলিলা ।
'ক্ষেত্র-সন্ন্যাস না ছাড়িহ'—প্রভু নিষেধিলা ॥ ১৩০ ॥

gadādhara-paṇḍita yabe saṅgete calilā
'kṣetra-sannyāsa nā chāḍiha'—prabhu niṣedhilā

SYNONYMS

gadādhara-paṇḍita—Gadādhara Paṇḍita; *yabe*—when; *saṅgete*—with Śrī Caitanya Mahāprabhu; *calilā*—started to go; *kṣetra-sannyāsa*—the renounced order of life at a holy place of pilgrimage; *nā chāḍiha*—do not give up; *prabhu niṣedhilā*—Lord Śrī Caitanya Mahāprabhu forbade.

TRANSLATION

When Gadādhara Paṇḍita started to go with the Lord, he was forbidden to come and was asked not to give up the vow of kṣetra-sannyāsa.

PURPORT

When one takes *kṣetra-sannyāsa,* he leaves his household life and goes to a place of pilgrimage devoted to Lord Viṣṇu. Such places include Puruṣottama (Jagannātha Purī), Navadvīpa-dhāma and Mathurā-dhāma. The *kṣetra-sannyāsī* lives in these places alone or with his family. Śrīla Bhaktivinoda Ṭhākura considers *kṣetra-sannyāsa* to be the preferable *vānaprastha* situation in this age of Kali. Sārvabhauma Bhaṭṭācārya lived in this way, and he has been called a *kṣetra-sannyāsī*—that is, a *sannyāsī* living in Jagannātha Purī.

TEXT 131

পণ্ডিত কহে,—"যাহাঁ তুমি, সেই নীলাচল ।
ক্ষেত্রসন্ন্যাস মোর যাউক রসাতল ॥" ১৩১ ॥

paṇḍita kahe,——"yāhāṅ tumi, sei nīlācala
kṣetra-sannyāsa mora yāuka rasātala"

SYNONYMS

paṇḍita kahe—Gadādhara Paṇḍita said; *yāhāṅ*—wherever; *tumi*—You are situated; *sei*—that; *nīlācala*—Jagannātha Purī; *kṣetra-sannyāsa*—vow to remain in a holy place of pilgrimage; *mora*—my; *yāuka*—let it go; *rasātala*—to hell.

TRANSLATION

When he was requested to return to Jagannātha Purī, Gadādhara Paṇḍita told the Lord, "Wherever You are staying is Jagannātha Purī. Let my so-called kṣetra-sannyāsa go to hell."

TEXT 132

প্রভু কহে,–"ইঁহা কর গোপীনাথ সেবন" ।
পণ্ডিত কহে,—"কোটি-সেবা ত্বৎপাদ-দর্শন" ॥ ১৩২॥

prabhu kahe,——"iṅhā kara gopīnātha sevana"
paṇḍita kahe,——"koṭi-sevā tvat-pāda-darśana"

SYNONYMS

prabhu kahe—Śrī Caitanya Mahāprabhu said; *iṅhā*—here; *kara*—just do; *gopīnātha sevana*—worship of Gopīnātha; *paṇḍita kahe*—the *paṇḍita* said; *koṭi-sevā*—millions of times the service; *tvat-pāda-darśana*—seeing Your lotus feet.

TRANSLATION

When Śrī Caitanya Mahāprabhu asked Gadādhara Paṇḍita to remain at Jagannātha Purī and engage in Gopīnātha's service, Gadādhara Paṇḍita replied, "One renders service to Gopīnātha a million times simply by seeing Your lotus feet."

TEXT 133

প্রভু কহে,—"সেবা ছাড়িবে, আমায় লাগে দোষ।
ইঁহা রহি' সেবা কর,—আমার সন্তোষ॥" ১৩৩॥

prabhu kahe,——"sevā chāḍibe, āmāya lāge doṣa
iṅhā rahi' sevā kara,——āmāra santoṣa"

SYNONYMS

prabhu kahe—Lord Śrī Caitanya Mahāprabhu said; *sevā chāḍibe*—you will give up the service; *āmāya*—to Me; *lāge*—will attach; *doṣa*—fault; *iṅhā rahi'*—staying here; *sevā kara*—just be engaged in service; *āmāra*—My; *santoṣa*—satisfaction.

TRANSLATION

Śrī Caitanya Mahāprabhu then said, "If you abandon His service, it will be My fault. It is better that you remain here and render service. That will be My satisfaction."

TEXT 134

পণ্ডিত কহে,—"সব দোষ আমার উপর।
তোমা-সঙ্গে না যাইব, যাইব একেশ্বর॥ ১৩৪॥

paṇḍita kahe,——"saba doṣa āmāra upara
tomā-saṅge nā yāiba, yāiba ekeśvara

SYNONYMS

paṇḍita kahe—the Paṇḍita said; *saba*—all; *doṣa*—fault; *āmāra upara*—upon me; *tomā-saṅge*—with You; *nā yāiba*—I shall not go; *yāiba*—I shall go; *ekeśvara*—alone.

TRANSLATION

The Paṇḍita replied, "Do not worry. All the faults will be on my head. I shall not accompany You but shall go alone.

TEXT 135

আই'কে দেখিতে যাইব, না যাইব তোমা লাগি'।
'প্রতিজ্ঞা'-'সেবা'-ত্যাগ-দোষ, তার আমি ভাগী॥"১৩৫

āi'ke dekhite yāiba, nā yāiba tomā lāgi'
'pratijñā'-'sevā'-tyāga-doṣa, tāra āmi bhāgī"

SYNONYMS

āi'ke—mother Śacīdevī; *dekhite*—to see; *yāiba*—I shall go; *nā yāiba*—I shall not go; *tomā lāgi'*—for Your sake; *pratijñā-sevā*—the vow and service to Gopīnātha; *tyāga-doṣa*—the fault of giving up; *tāra*—for that; *āmi bhāgī*—I am responsible.

TRANSLATION

"I shall go to see Śacīmātā, but I shall not go for Your sake. I shall be responsible for the abandoning of my vow and service to Gopīnātha."

TEXT 136

এত বলি' পণ্ডিত-গোসাঞি পৃথক্ চলিলা ।
কটক আসি' প্রভু তাঁরে সঙ্গে আনাইলা ॥ ১৩৬ ॥

eta bali' paṇḍita-gosāñi pṛthak calilā
kaṭaka āsi' prabhu tāṅre saṅge ānāilā

SYNONYMS

eta bali'—saying this; *paṇḍita-gosāñi*—Gadādhara Paṇḍita; *pṛthak calilā*—proceeded separately; *kaṭaka āsi'*—when He came to Kaṭaka; *prabhu*—Śrī Caitanya Mahāprabhu; *tāṅre*—him; *saṅge*—with Him; *ānāilā*—brought.

TRANSLATION

Thus Gadādhara Paṇḍita Gosvāmī traveled alone, but when they all arrived at Kaṭaka, Śrī Caitanya Mahāprabhu called him, and he went in the Lord's company.

TEXT 137

পণ্ডিতের গৌরাঙ্গ-প্রেম বুঝন না যায় ।
'প্রতিজ্ঞা', 'শ্রীকৃষ্ণ-সেবা' ছাড়িল তৃণপ্রায় ॥ ১৩৭ ॥

paṇḍitera gaurāṅga-prema bujhana nā yāya
'pratijñā', 'śrī-kṛṣṇa-sevā' chāḍila tṛṇa-prāya

SYNONYMS

paṇḍitera—of Gadādhara Paṇḍita; *gaurāṅga-prema*—the love for Śrī Caitanya Mahāprabhu; *bujhana*—understanding; *nā yāya*—is not possible; *pratijñā*—a vow; *śrī-kṛṣṇa-sevā*—the service of the Lord; *chāḍila*—gave up; *tṛṇa-prāya*—almost like straw.

TRANSLATION

No one can understand the loving intimacy between Gadādhara Paṇḍita and Śrī Caitanya Mahāprabhu. Gadādhara Paṇḍita gave up his vow and service to Gopīnātha just as one gives up a piece of straw.

PURPORT

Just to get Śrī Caitanya Mahāprabhu's association, Gadādhara Paṇḍita gave up his life's vow to engage in Gopīnātha's service. This kind of loving affection can be understood only by very confidential devotees. Ordinarily, no one can understand its purport.

TEXT 138

তাঁহার চরিত্রে প্রভু অন্তরে সন্তোষ ।
তাঁহার হাতে ধরি' কহে করি' প্রণয়-রোষ ॥ ১৩৮ ॥

tāṅhāra caritre prabhu antare santoṣa
tāṅhāra hāte dhari' kahe kari' praṇaya-roṣa

SYNONYMS

tāṅhāra caritre—in his behavior; *prabhu*—Śrī Caitanya Mahāprabhu; *antare*—within His heart; *santoṣa*—very satisfied; *tāṅhāra hāte dhari'*—catching his hand; *kahe*—says; *kari'*—exhibiting; *praṇaya-roṣa*—anger in love.

TRANSLATION

Gadādhara Paṇḍita's behavior was very pleasing to Śrī Caitanya Mahāprabhu's heart. Nevertheless, the Lord took his hand and spoke to him, displaying the anger of love.

TEXT 139

'প্রতিজ্ঞা', 'সেবা' ছাড়িবে,—এ তোমার 'উদ্দেশ' ।
সে সিদ্ধ হইল—ছাড়ি' আইলা দূর দেশ ॥ ১৩৯ ॥

'pratijñā', 'sevā' chāḍibe,——e tomāra 'uddeśa'
se siddha ha-ila——chāḍi' āilā dūra deśa

SYNONYMS

pratijñā—the vow; *sevā*—and service; *chāḍibe*—will give up; *e*—this; *tomāra*—your; *uddeśa*—purpose; *se*—that; *siddha*—complete; *ha-ila*—has become; *chāḍi'*—giving up; *āilā*—have come; *dūra deśa*—to a distant place.

TRANSLATION

"You have abandoned Gopīnātha's service and broken your vow to live in Purī. All that is now complete because you have come so far.

TEXT 140

আমার সঙ্গে রহিতে চাহ,—বাঞ্ছ নিজ-সুখ ।
তোমার দুই ধর্ম যায়,—আমার হয় 'দুঃখ' ॥ ১৪০ ॥

āmāra saṅge rahite cāha,——vāñcha nija-sukha
tomāra dui dharma yāya,——āmāra haya 'duḥkha'

SYNONYMS

āmāra saṅge—with Me; *rahite*—to remain; *cāha*—you want; *vāñcha*—you desire; *nija-sukha*—your own sense gratification; *tomāra*—your; *dui dharma*—two principles; *yāya*—go away; *āmāra*—of Me; *haya*—there is; *duḥkha*—unhappiness.

TRANSLATION

"Your wanting to go with Me is simply a desire for sense gratification. In this way, you are breaking two religious principles, and because of this I am very unhappy.

TEXT 141

মোর সুখ চাহ যদি, নীলাচলে চল ।
আমার শপথ, যদি আর কিছু বল ॥ ১৪১ ॥

mora sukha cāha yadi, nīlācale cala
āmāra śapatha, yadi āra kichu bala

SYNONYMS

mora—of Me; *sukha*—the satisfaction; *cāha*—you want; *yadi*—if; *nīlācale cala*—go back to Jagannātha Purī (Nīlācala); *āmāra śapatha*—My condemnation; *yadi*—if; *āra*—more; *kichu*—something; *bala*—you say.

TRANSLATION

"If you want My happiness, please return to Nīlācala. You will simply condemn Me if you say any more about this matter."

TEXT 142

এত বলি' মহাপ্রভু নৌকাতে চড়িলা।
মূর্চ্ছিত হঞা পণ্ডিত তথাই পড়িলা ॥ ১৪২ ॥

eta bali' mahāprabhu naukāte caḍilā
mūrcchita hañā paṇḍita tathāi paḍilā

SYNONYMS

eta bali'—saying this; *mahāprabhu*—Śrī Caitanya Mahāprabhu; *naukāte caḍilā*—got on a boat; *mūrcchita hañā*—fainting; *paṇḍita*—Gadādhara Paṇḍita Gosvāmī; *tathāi*—there; *paḍilā*—fell down.

TRANSLATION

Saying this, Śrī Caitanya Mahāprabhu got into a boat, and Gadādhara Paṇḍita immediately fell down in an unconscious state.

TEXT 143

পণ্ডিতে লঞা যাইতে সার্বভৌমে আজ্ঞা দিলা।
ভট্টাচার্য কহে,—"উঠ, ঐছে প্রভুর লীলা ॥ ১৪৩ ॥

paṇḍite lañā yāite sārvabhaume ājñā dilā
bhaṭṭācārya kahe,——"uṭha, aiche prabhura līlā

SYNONYMS

paṇḍite lañā—taking the Paṇḍita; *yāite*—to go; *sārvabhauma*—unto Sārvabhauma Bhaṭṭācārya; *ājñā dilā*—gave an order; *bhaṭṭācārya kahe*—Sārvabhauma Bhaṭṭācārya said; *uṭha*—please get up; *aiche*—such; *prabhura līlā*—the way of the Lord's pastimes.

TRANSLATION

Śrī Caitanya Mahāprabhu ordered Sārvabhauma Bhaṭṭācārya to take Gadādhara Paṇḍita with him. The Bhaṭṭācārya told Gadādhara Paṇḍita, "Get up! Such are the pastimes of Śrī Caitanya Mahāprabhu.

TEXT 144

তুমি জান, কৃষ্ণ নিজ-প্রতিজ্ঞা ছাড়িলা।
ভক্ত কৃপা-বশে ভীষ্মের প্রতিজ্ঞা রাখিলা ॥ ১৪৪ ॥

tumi jāna, kṛṣṇa nija-pratijñā chāḍilā
bhakta kṛpā-vaśe bhīṣmera pratijñā rākhilā

SYNONYMS

tumi jāna—you know; *kṛṣṇa*—Lord Kṛṣṇa; *nija-pratijñā*—His own promise; *chāḍilā*—gave up; *bhakta kṛpā-vaśe*—being obliged by the devotional service of a devotee; *bhīṣmera*—of Grandfather Bhīṣma; *pratijñā rākhilā*—kept the promise.

TRANSLATION

"You should know that Lord Kṛṣṇa Himself violated His own promise just to keep the promise of Grandfather Bhīṣma.

TEXT 145

স্বনিগমমপহায় মৎপ্রতিজ্ঞা-
মৃতমধিকর্তুমবপ্লুতো রথস্থঃ।
ধৃতরথচরণোঽভ্যয়াচ্চলদ্গু-
র্হরিরিব হন্তুমিভং গতোত্তরীয়ঃ ॥ ১৪৫ ॥

svanigamam apahāya mat-pratijñām
ṛtam adhikartum avapluto ratha-sthaḥ
dhṛta-ratha-caraṇo 'bhyayāc caladgur
harir iva hantum ibhaṁ gatottarīyaḥ

SYNONYMS

sva-nigamam—His own promise not to take a weapon and fight on behalf of the Pāṇḍavas; *apahāya*—giving up; *mat-pratijñām*—my promise; *ṛtam*—true; *adhikartum*—to make more; *avaplutaḥ*—having jumped down; *ratha-sthaḥ*—who was on the chariot (Lord Kṛṣṇa); *dhṛta*—who took up; *ratha-caraṇaḥ*—the wheel of the chariot; *abhyayāt*—ran forward; *calat-guḥ*—making the entire planet tremble; *hariḥ*—a lion; *iva*—like; *hantum*—to kill; *ibham*—an elephant; *gata-uttarīyaḥ*—losing the outer garment.

TRANSLATION

" 'Intending to make my promise true, Lord Kṛṣṇa broke His own promise not to take up a weapon at Kurukṣetra. With His outer garment falling off,

Lord Śrī Kṛṣṇa jumped from His chariot, picked up a wheel and came running at me to kill me. Indeed, He rushed at me like a lion going to kill an elephant, and He caused the whole earth to tremble.'

PURPORT

Lord Kṛṣṇa promised not to fight in the battle of Kurukṣetra or even take up a weapon. But when Bhīṣma wanted to keep his own promise to break the promise of the Lord, the Lord immediately got down from the chariot, and to make Bhīṣma's promise true He picked up a chariot wheel and rushed forward to kill him. This is a quotation from *Śrīmad-Bhāgavatam* (1.9.37).

TEXT 146

এইমত প্রভু তোমার বিচ্ছেদ সহিয়া ।
তোমার প্রতিজ্ঞা রক্ষা কৈল যত্ন করিয়া ॥" ১৪৬ ॥

ei-mata prabhu tomāra viccheda sahiyā
tomāra pratijñā rakṣā kaila yatna kariyā"

SYNONYMS

ei-mata—in this way; *prabhu*—Śrī Caitanya Mahāprabhu; *tomāra*—of you; *viccheda sahiyā*—tolerating the separation; *tomāra pratijñā*—your vow; *rakṣā kaila*—protected; *yatna kariyā*—with great endeavor.

TRANSLATION

"Similarly, tolerating your separation, Śrī Caitanya Mahāprabhu has protected your vow with great endeavor."

TEXT 147

এইমত কহি' তাঁরে প্রবোধ করিলা ।
দুইজনে শোকাকুল নীলাচলে আইলা ॥ ১৪৭ ॥

ei-mata kahi' tāṅre prabodha karilā
dui-jane śokākula nīlācale āilā

SYNONYMS

ei-mata—in this way; *kahi'*—speaking; *tāṅre*—him; *prabodha karilā*—awoke; *dui-jane*—the two persons; *śoka-ākula*—overwhelmed with grief; *nīlācale*—to Jagannātha Purī; *āilā*—went back.

TRANSLATION

In this way Sārvabhauma Bhaṭṭācārya revived Gadādhara Paṇḍita. Then both of them, very much grief-stricken, returned to Jagannātha Purī, Nīlācala.

TEXT 148

প্রভু লাগি' ধর্ম-কর্ম ছাড়ে ভক্তগণ ।
ভক্ত-ধর্ম-হানি প্রভুর না হয় সহন ॥ ১৪৮ ॥

prabhu lāgi' dharma-karma chāḍe bhakta-gaṇa
bhakta-dharma-hāni prabhura nā haya sahana

SYNONYMS

prabhu lāgi'—for the sake of Śrī Caitanya Mahāprabhu; *dharma-karma*—all prescribed duties; *chāḍe*—give up; *bhakta-gaṇa*—all the devotees; *bhakta-dharma*—of the duty of a devotee; *hāni*—the abandonment; *prabhura*—to Śrī Caitanya Mahāprabhu; *nā haya*—is not; *sahana*—tolerable.

TRANSLATION

All the devotees would abandon all kinds of duties for Śrī Caitanya Mahāprabhu's sake, yet the Lord did not like the devotees' giving up their promised duties.

TEXT 149

'প্রেমের বিবর্ত' ইহা শুনে যেই জন ।
অচিরে মিলিয়ে তাঁরে চৈতন্য-চরণ ॥ ১৪৯ ॥

'premera vivarta' ihā śune yei jana
acire miliye tāṅre caitanya-caraṇa

SYNONYMS

premera vivarta—the misgivings of loving affairs; *ihā*—this; *śune*—listens; *yei jana*—any person who; *acire*—very soon; *miliye*—meet; *tāṅre*—him; *caitanya-caraṇa*—the lotus feet of Śrī Caitanya Mahāprabhu.

TRANSLATION

All these are the misgivings of loving affairs. Whoever listens to these incidents gets Śrī Caitanya Mahāprabhu's shelter very soon.

TEXT 150

দুই রাজপাত্র যেই প্রভু-সঙ্গে যায়।
'যাজপুর' আসি' প্রভু তারে দিলেন বিদায়॥ ১৫০॥

dui rāja-pātra yei prabhu-saṅge yāya
'yājapura' āsi' prabhu tāre dilena vidāya

SYNONYMS

dui rāja-pātra—the two government officers; *yei*—who; *prabhu-saṅge*—with Śrī Caitanya Mahāprabhu; *yāya*—go; *yājapura āsi'*—when coming to Yājapura; *prabhu*—Śrī Caitanya Mahāprabhu; *tāre*—unto them; *dilena vidāya*—bade farewell.

TRANSLATION

When Śrī Caitanya Mahāprabhu and His party arrived at Yājapura, the Lord asked the two government officers who had come with Him to return.

PURPORT

The place called Yājapura is very well known in Orissa. It is a subdivision of the Kaṭaka district and is situated on the southern side of the Vaitaraṇī River. Formerly great sages performed sacrifices on the northern bank of the Vaitaraṇī River; consequently the place is known as Yājapura—"the place where sacrifices are performed." Some people say that this was one of the capital cities of King Yayāti and that from the name Yayāti-nagara the name Yājapura has come. As stated in *Mahābhārata* (*Vana-parva* Chapter 114):

ete kaliṅgāḥ kaunteya
yatra vaitaraṇī nadī
yatrāyajata dharmo 'pi
devān śaraṇam etya vai
atra vai ṛṣayo 'nye ca
purā kratubhir ījire

According to the *Mahābhārata*, great sages formerly performed sacrifices in this place. There are still many temples of demigods and incarnations there, and there is also a Deity of Śrī Varāhadeva. This Deity is especially important and is visited by many pilgrims. Those who worship the Supreme Lord's energy worship Vārāhī, Vaiṣṇavī and Indrāṇī, as well as many similar forms of Devī, the internal energy. There are many deities of Lord Śiva, and there are many places along the river known as Daśāśvamedha-ghāṭa. Sometimes Yājapura is also called Nābhi-gayā or Virajā-kṣetra.

TEXT 151

প্রভু বিদায় দিল, রায় যায় তাঁর সনে ।
কৃষ্ণকথা রামানন্দ-সনে রাত্রি-দিনে ॥ ১৫১ ॥

prabhu vidāya dila, rāya yāya tāṅra sane
kṛṣṇa-kathā rāmānanda-sane rātri-dine

SYNONYMS

prabhu vidāya dila—the Lord bade them farewell; *rāya*—Rāmānanda Rāya; *yāya*—goes; *tāṅra sane*—with Him; *kṛṣṇa-kathā*—discussion of topics of Lord Kṛṣṇa; *rāmānanda-sane*—with Rāmānanda; *rātri-dine*—day and night.

TRANSLATION

Śrī Caitanya Mahāprabhu bade farewell to the officers, and Rāya Rāmānanda continued on with the Lord. The Lord talked to Rāmānanda Rāya about Śrī Kṛṣṇa day and night.

TEXT 152

প্রতিগ্রামে রাজ-আজ্ঞায় রাজভৃত্যগণ ।
নব্য গৃহে নানা-দ্রব্যে করয়ে সেবন ॥ ১৫২ ॥

prati-grāme rāja-ājñāya rāja-bhṛtya-gaṇa
navya gṛhe nānā-dravye karaye sevana

SYNONYMS

prati-grāme—in each village; *rāja-ājñāya*—by the order of the King; *rāja-bhṛtya-gaṇa*—the government servants; *navya gṛhe*—in newly constructed houses; *nānā-dravye*—with all kinds of food grains; *karaye sevana*—rendered service.

TRANSLATION

In each and every village, in compliance with the King's order, government officers constructed new houses and filled each of them with stocks of grains. Thus they served the Lord.

TEXT 153

এইমত চলি' প্রভু 'রেমুণা' আইলা ।
তথা হৈতে রামানন্দ-রায়ে বিদায় দিলা ॥ ১৫৩ ॥

ei-mata cali' prabhu 'remuṇā' āilā
tathā haite rāmānanda-rāye vidāya dilā

SYNONYMS

ei-mata—in this way; *cali'*—walking; *prabhu*—Śrī Caitanya Mahāprabhu; *remuṇā āilā*—came to Remuṇā; *tathā haite*—from there; *rāmānanda-rāye*—unto Rāmānanda Rāya; *vidāya dilā*—bade farewell.

TRANSLATION

Śrī Caitanya Mahāprabhu finally arrived at Remuṇā, where He bade farewell to Śrī Rāmānanda Rāya.

PURPORT

It was stated in the First Chapter of *Madhya-līlā,* verse 149, that Rāmānanda Rāya was bade farewell from Bhadraka. Śrīla Bhaktisiddhānta Sarasvatī Ṭhākura states that in those days the place called Remuṇā also included Bhadraka.

TEXT 154

ভূমেতে পড়িলা রায় নাহিক চেতন ।
রায়ে কোলে করি' প্রভু করয়ে ক্রন্দন ॥ ১৫৪ ॥

bhūmete paḍilā rāya nāhika cetana
rāye kole kari' prabhu karaye krandana

SYNONYMS

bhūmete paḍilā—fell down on the ground; *rāya*—Rāmānanda Rāya; *nāhika cetana*—there was no consciousness; *rāye*—Rāmānanda Rāya; *kole kari'*—taking on the lap; *prabhu*—Śrī Caitanya Mahāprabhu; *karaye krandana*—began crying.

TRANSLATION

When Rāmānanda Rāya fell to the ground and lost consciousness, Śrī Caitanya Mahāprabhu took him upon His lap and began to cry.

TEXT 155

রায়ের বিদায়-ভাব না যায় সহন ।
কহিতে না পারি এই তাহার বর্ণন ॥ ১৫৫ ॥

rāyera vidāya-bhāva nā yāya sahana
kahite nā pāri ei tāhāra varṇana

SYNONYMS

rāyera vidāya-bhāva—feelings of separation from Rāmānanda Rāya; *nā yāya*—not possible; *sahana*—to tolerate; *kahite*—to speak; *nā pāri*—I am not able; *ei*—this; *tāhāra*—of that; *varṇana*—a description.

TRANSLATION

Rāmānanda Rāya's separation from Caitanya Mahāprabhu is very difficult to describe. It is almost intolerable, and therefore I cannot describe it further.

TEXT 156

তবে 'ওড্র দেশ-সীমা' প্রভু চলি' আইলা ।
তথা রাজ-অধিকারী প্রভুরে মিলিলা ॥ ১৫৬ ॥

tabe 'oḍhra-deśa-sīmā' prabhu cali' āilā
tathā rāja-adhikārī prabhure mililā

SYNONYMS

tabe—thereafter; *oḍhra-deśa-sīmā*—the boundary of Orissa; *prabhu*—Lord Śrī Caitanya Mahāprabhu; *cali'*—taveling; *āilā*—reached; *tathā*—there; *rāja-adhikārī*—a government officer; *prabhure*—Śrī Caitanya Mahāprabhu; *mililā*—met.

TRANSLATION

When Śrī Caitanya Mahāprabhu finally arrived at the border of the state of Orissa, a government officer came there to meet Him.

TEXT 157

দিন দুই-চারি তেঁহো করিল সেবন ।
আগে চলিবারে সেই কহে বিবরণ ॥ ১৫৭ ॥

dina dui-cāri teṅho karila sevana
āge calibāre sei kahe vivaraṇa

SYNONYMS

dina dui-cāri—two or four days; *teṅho*—he; *karila sevana*—served the Lord; *āge*—forward; *calibāre*—for going; *sei*—that officer; *kahe*—spoke; *vivaraṇa*—detailed information.

TRANSLATION

For two or four days, the government officer served the Lord. He also gave the Lord detailed information of what was ahead.

TEXT 158

মদ্যপ যবন-রাজার আগে অধিকার ।
তাঁর ভয়ে পথে কেহ নারে চলিবার ॥ ১৫৮ ॥

madyapa yavana-rājāra āge adhikāra
tāṅra bhaye pathe keha nāre calibāra

SYNONYMS

madyapa—drunkard; *yavana*—Mohammedan; *rājāra*—of a king; *āge*—ahead; *adhikāra*—the government; *tāṅra bhaye*—being afraid of such a king; *pathe*—on the road; *keha*—anyone; *nāre*—not able; *calibāra*—to travel.

TRANSLATION

He informed the Lord that the territory ahead was ruled by a Moslem governor, who was a drunkard. Out of fear for this king, no one could walk the road freely.

TEXT 159

পিছলদা পর্যন্ত সব তাঁর অধিকার ।
তাঁর ভয়ে নদী কেহ হৈতে নারে পার ॥ ১৫৯ ॥

pichaladā paryanta saba tāṅra adhikāra
tāṅra bhaye nadī keha haite nāre pāra

SYNONYMS

pichaladā—the place named Pichaladā; *paryanta*—up to; *saba*—everything; *tāṅra*—of him; *adhikāra*—under the authority; *tāṅra bhaye*—because of fear of him; *nadī*—the river; *keha*—anyone; *haite*—to cross; *nāre*—not able; *pāra*—to the other side.

TRANSLATION

The jurisdiction of the Mohammedan government extended up to Pichaladā. Due to fear of the Mohammedans, no one would cross the river.

PURPORT

During the old days, Pichaladā was part of Tamaluka and Bengal. Pichaladā is located about fourteen miles south of Tamaluka. The River Rūpa-nārāyaṇa is well known in Tamaluka, and Pichaladā was situated on the bank of the Rūpa-nārāyaṇa River.

TEXT 160

দিন কত রহ – সন্ধি করি' তাঁর সনে ।
তবে সুখে নৌকাতে করাইব গমনে ॥ ১৬০ ॥

dina kata raha——sandhi kari' tāṅra sane
tabe sukhe naukāte karāiba gamane

SYNONYMS

dina kata raha—stay here for a few days; *sandhi kari'*—making peaceful negotiations; *tāṅra sane*—with him; *tabe*—then; *sukhe*—in happiness; *naukāte*—on the boat; *karāiba gamane*—I will help You start.

TRANSLATION

Mahārāja Pratāparudra's government officer further informed Śrī Caitanya Mahāprabhu that He should stay at the Orissa border for some days so that a peaceful agreement could be negotiated with the Mohammedan governor. In that way, the Lord would be able to cross the river peacefully in a boat.

TEXT 161

সেই কালে সে যবনের এক অনুচর ।
'উড়িয়া-কটকে' আইল করি' বেশান্তর ॥ ১৬১ ॥

sei kāle se yavanera eka anucara
'uḍiyā-kaṭake' āila kari' veśāntara

SYNONYMS

sei kāle—at that time; *se yavanera*—of the Mohammedan governor; *eka anucara*—one follower; *uḍiyā-kaṭake*—to the camp of Orissan soldiers; *āila*—came; *kari' veśa-antara*—changing the dress.

TRANSLATION

At that time, a follower of the Mohammedan governor arrived at the Orissa encampment dressed in disguise.

TEXTS 162-163

প্রভুর সেই অদভুত চরিত্র দেখিয়া ।
হিন্দু-চর কহে সেই যবন-পাশ গিয়া ॥ ১৬২ ॥
'এক সন্ন্যাসী আইল জগন্নাথ হইতে ।
অনেক সিদ্ধ-পুরুষ হয় তাঁহার সহিতে ॥ ১৬৩ ॥

prabhura sei adabhuta caritra dekhiyā
hindu-cara kahe sei yavana-pāśa giyā

'eka sannyāsī āila jagannātha ha-ite
aneka siddha-puruṣa haya tāṅhāra sahite

SYNONYMS

prabhura—of Śrī Caitanya Mahāprabhu; *sei*—that; *adabhuta caritra*—wonderful characteristics; *dekhiyā*—seeing; *hindu-cara*—the Hindu spy; *kahe*—says; *sei*—that; *yavana-pāśa giyā*—going to the Mohammedan king; *eka sannyāsī*—one mendicant; *āila*—has come; *jagannātha ha-ite*—from Jagannātha Purī; *aneka*—many; *siddha-puruṣa*—liberated persons; *haya*—are; *tāṅhāra sahite*—with Him.

TRANSLATION

The Mohammedan spy saw the wonderful characteristics of Śrī Caitanya Mahāprabhu, and when he returned to the Mohammedan governor, he told him, "A mendicant has come from Jagannātha Purī with many liberated persons.

TEXT 164

নিরন্তর করে সবে কৃষ্ণ-সংকীর্তন ।
সবে হাসে, নাচে, গায়, করয়ে ক্রন্দন ॥ ১৬৪ ॥

nirantara kare sabe kṛṣṇa-saṅkīrtana
sabe hāse, nāce, gāya, karaye krandana

SYNONYMS

nirantara—without stopping; *kare*—perform; *sabe*—all; *kṛṣṇa-saṅkīrtana*—chanting of the holy name of the Lord; *sabe*—all of them; *hāse*—laugh; *nāce*—dance; *gāya*—sing; *karaye krandana*—and cry.

TRANSLATION

"All these saintly people incessantly chant the Hare Kṛṣṇa mahā-mantra, and they all laugh, dance, chant and cry.

TEXT 165

লক্ষ লক্ষ লোক আইসে তাহা দেখিবারে ।
তাঁরে দেখি' পুনরপি যাইতে নারে ঘরে ॥ ১৬৫ ॥

lakṣa lakṣa loka āise tāhā dekhibāre
tāṅre dekhi' punarapi yāite nāre ghare

SYNONYMS

lakṣa lakṣa—millions upon millions; *loka*—people; *āise*—come; *tāhā*—that; *dekhibāre*—to see; *tāṅre dekhi'*—after seeing Him; *punarapi*—again; *yāite*—to go; *nāre*—are not able; *ghare*—home.

TRANSLATION

"Many millions upon millions of people come to see Him, and after they see Him, they cannot return home.

TEXT 166

সেই সব লোক হয় বাউলের প্রায় ।
'কৃষ্ণ' কহি' নাচে, কান্দে, গড়াগড়ি যায় ॥ ১৬৬ ॥

sei saba loka haya bāulera prāya
'kṛṣṇa' kahi' nāce, kānde, gaḍāgaḍi yāya

SYNONYMS

sei saba loka—all those persons; *haya*—are; *bāulera prāya*—almost like madmen; *kṛṣṇa kahi'*—chanting the holy name of Kṛṣṇa; *nāce*—they dance; *kānde*—they cry; *gaḍāgaḍi yāya*—they roll on the ground.

TRANSLATION

"All these people become like madmen. They simply dance and chant the holy name of Kṛṣṇa. Sometimes they even cry and roll on the ground.

TEXT 167

কহিবার কথা নহে—দেখিলে সে জানি ।
তাঁহার প্রভাবে তাঁরে 'ঈশ্বর' করি' মানি ॥' ১৬৭ ॥

kahibāra kathā nahe——dekhile se jāni
tāṅhāra prabhāve tāṅre 'īśvara' kari' māni'

SYNONYMS

kahibāra kathā—describable topic; *nahe*—this is not; *dekhile*—if one sees; *se jāni*—he can understand; *tāṅhāra prabhāve*—by His influence; *tāṅre*—Him; *īśvara kari'*—as the Supreme Personality of Godhead; *māni*—I accept.

TRANSLATION

"Actually these things cannot even be described. One can understand them only by seeing. By His influence, I accept Him as the Supreme Personality of Godhead."

TEXT 168

এত কহি' সেই চর 'হরি' 'কৃষ্ণ' গায়।
হাসে, কান্দে, নাচে, গায় বাউলের প্রায়॥ ১৬৮ ॥

eta kahi' sei cara 'hari' 'kṛṣṇa' gāya
hāse, kānde, nāce, gāya bāulera prāya

SYNONYMS

eta kahi'—saying this; *sei cara*—that messenger; *hari*—Hari; *kṛṣṇa*—Kṛṣṇa; *gāya*—chants; *hāse*—laughs; *kānde*—cries; *nāce*—dances; *gāya*—sings; *bāulera prāya*—just like a madman.

TRANSLATION

After saying this, the messenger began to chant the holy names of Hari and Kṛṣṇa. He also began to laugh and cry, dance and sing exactly like a madman.

TEXT 169

এত শুনি' যবনের মন ফিরি' গেল।
আপন-'বিশ্বাস' উড়িয়া স্থানে পাঠাইল॥ ১৬৯ ॥

eta śuni' yavanera mana phiri' gela
āpana-'viśvāsa' uḍiyā sthāne pāṭhāila

SYNONYMS

eta śuni'—after hearing this; *yavanera*—of the Mohammedan governor; *mana*—the mind; *phiri' gela*—became changed; *āpana*—own; *viśvāsa*—secretary; *uḍiyā*—of the representative of the Orissan government; *sthāne*—to the place; *pāṭhāila*—sent.

TRANSLATION

Upon hearing this, the mind of the Mohammedan governor was changed. He then sent his own secretary to the representative of the Orissan government.

TEXT 170

'বিশ্বাস' আসিয়া প্রভুর চরণ বন্দিল।
'কৃষ্ণ' 'কৃষ্ণ' কহি' প্রেমে বিহ্বল হইল ॥ ১৭০ ॥

'viśvāsa' āsiyā prabhura caraṇa vandila
'kṛṣṇa' 'kṛṣṇa' kahi' preme vihvala ha-ila

SYNONYMS

viśvāsa—the secretary; *āsiyā*—coming; *prabhura*—of Lord Śrī Caitanya Mahāprabhu; *caraṇa*—the lotus feet; *vandila*—worshiped; *kṛṣṇa kṛṣṇa*—the holy name of the Lord, Kṛṣṇa, Kṛṣṇa; *kahi'*—uttering; *preme*—in ecstasy; *vihvala*—overwhelmed; *ha-ila*—became.

TRANSLATION

The Mohammedan secretary came to see Śrī Caitanya Mahāprabhu. When he offered his respects to the Lord's lotus feet and uttered the holy name of the Lord, "Kṛṣṇa, Kṛṣṇa," he also was overwhelmed with ecstatic love.

TEXT 171

ধৈর্য হঞা উড়িয়াকে কহে নমস্করি'।
'তোমা-স্থানে পাঠাইলা ম্লেচ্ছ অধিকারী ॥ ১৭১ ॥

dhairya hañā uḍiyāke kahe namaskari'
'tomā-sthāne pāṭhāilā mleccha adhikārī

SYNONYMS

dhairya hañā—becoming calm; *uḍiyāke*—to the representative of the Orissan government; *kahe*—says; *namaskari'*—offering respect; *tomā-sthāne*—to your place; *pāṭhāilā*—has sent; *mleccha*—the Mohammedan; *adhikārī*—governor.

TRANSLATION

After calming down, the Mohammedan secretary offered his respects and informed the representative of the Orissan government, "The Mohammedan governor has sent me here.

TEXT 172

তুমি যদি আজ্ঞা দেহ' এথাকে আসিয়া ।
যবন অধিকারী যায় প্রভুকে মিলিয়া ॥ ১৭২ ॥

tumi yadi ājñā deha' ethāke āsiyā
yavana adhikārī yāya prabhuke miliyā

SYNONYMS

tumi—you; *yadi*—if; *ājñā*—order; *deha'*—give; *ethāke*—here; *āsiyā*—coming; *yavana adhikārī*—the Mohammedan governor; *yāya*—may go; *prabhuke*—Lord Śrī Caitanya Mahāprabhu; *miliyā*—after meeting.

TRANSLATION

"If you agree, the Mohammedan governor will come here to meet Śrī Caitanya Mahāprabhu and then return.

TEXT 173

বহুত উৎকণ্ঠা তাঁর, কর্যাছে বিনয় ।
তোমা-সনে এই সন্ধি, নাহি যুদ্ধ-ভয় ॥' ১৭৩ ॥

bahuta utkaṇṭhā tāṅra, karyāche vinaya
tomā-sane ei sandhi, nāhi yuddha-bhaya'

SYNONYMS

bahuta—very much; *utkaṇṭhā*—anxiety; *tāṅra*—his; *karyāche*—has made; *vinaya*—submissive petition; *tomā-sane*—with you; *ei*—this; *sandhi*—a peace proposal; *nāhi*—there is not; *yuddha-bhaya*—fear of fighting.

TRANSLATION

"The Mohammedan governor is very eager, and he has submitted this petition with great respect. It is a proposal for peace. You need not fear that we will fight."

TEXT 174

শুনি' মহাপাত্র কহে হঞা বিস্ময়।
'মদ্যপ যবনের চিত্ত ঐছে কে করয়! ১৭৪ ॥

śuni' mahā-pātra kahe hañā vismaya
'madyapa yavanera citta aiche ke karaya!

SYNONYMS

śuni'—hearing; *mahā-pātra*—the representative of the Orissan government; *kahe*—says; *hañā vismaya*—becoming astonished; *madyapa*—drunkard; *yavanera*—of the Mohammedan; *citta*—the heart; *aiche*—in this way; *ke karaya*—who has made.

TRANSLATION

Upon hearing this proposal, the representative of the Orissan government, the mahā-pātra, was very astonished. He thought, "The Mohammedan governor is a drunkard. Who has changed his mind?

TEXT 175

আপনে মহাপ্রভু তাঁর মন ফিরাইল।
দর্শন-স্মরণে যাঁর জগৎ তারিল॥' ১৭৫ ॥

āpane mahāprabhu tāṅra mana phirāila
darśana-smaraṇe yāṅra jagat tārila'

SYNONYMS

āpane—personally; *mahāprabhu*—Śrī Caitanya Mahāprabhu; *tāṅra*—his; *mana*—mind; *phirāila*—changed; *darśana*—by a personal visit; *smaraṇe*—by remembrance; *yāṅra*—of whom; *jagat*—the whole world; *tārila*—He has delivered.

TRANSLATION

"It must be Śrī Caitanya Mahāprabhu Himself who has changed the Mohammedan's mind. Due to His presence and even due to His remembrance, the whole world is liberated."

PURPORT

From this we can understand that the Mohammedan governor was a drunkard (*madyapa*). Ordinarily, there was no chance that he would change, but Lord Śrī

Caitanya Mahāprabhu could turn anyone's mind to Kṛṣṇa consciousness. One can be delivered from material existence simply by remembering Śrī Caitanya Mahāprabhu's holy name or by visiting Him. This Kṛṣṇa consciousness movement is being spread throughout the world, but not even one *yavana* or *mleccha* addicted to drinking could have changed and accepted Kṛṣṇa consciousness without Śrī Caitanya Mahāprabhu's grace. People are often astonished to see many thousands of Westerners converted to Vaiṣṇavism. Generally Westerners are addicted to meat-eating, drinking, gambling and illicit sex; therefore their taking up Kṛṣṇa consciousness is astonishing. In India, especially, there is much astonishment at this. The answer, however, is given here: *darśana-smaraṇe yāṅra jagat tārila.* This change is made possible simply by the remembrance of Śrī Caitanya Mahāprabhu. The Western devotees are very sincerely chanting the holy names of Śrī Caitanya Mahāprabhu and His associates: *śrī-kṛṣṇa-caitanya prabhu nityānanda śrī-advaita gadādhara śrīvāsādi-gaura-bhakta-vṛnda.* By the mercy of Śrī Caitanya Mahāprabhu and His associates, people are being purified and their consciousness directed from *māyā* to Kṛṣṇa.

The word *viśvāsa* refers to a secretary. This title is generally found among the *kāyastha* caste in the Hindu community. In Bengal, the title *viśvāsa* is still used by the *kāyasthas.* The word *viśvāsa* means "faithful," and a *viśvāsī* is a person in whom one can place faith. Śrī Bhaktivinoda Ṭhākura states that during the Mohammedan reign in Bengal, there was a secretariat entitled *viśvāsa-khānā.* The office of *viśvāsa-khānā* was a secretariat office in which only the most reliable people were employed. They were elected from the *kāyastha* community, a community that is still very expert in managing business and government affairs. The secretariat, or *viśvāsa-khānā,* is generally a very reliable and faithful servant. Whenever some confidential service was needed, these officers were employed.

TEXT 176

এত বলি' বিশ্বাসেরে কহিল বচন ।
"ভাগ্য তাঁর—আসি' করুক প্রভু দরশন ॥ ১৭৬ ॥

eta bali' viśvāsere kahila vacana
"bhāgya tāṅra——āsi' karuka prabhu daraśana

SYNONYMS

eta bali'—saying this; *viśvāsere*—unto the secretary of the Mohammedan governor; *kahila vacana*—spoke the following words; *bhāgya*—great fortune; *tāṅra*—his; *āsi'*—coming; *karuka*—let him do; *prabhu daraśana*—visiting Śrī Caitanya Mahāprabhu.

TRANSLATION

After thinking this, the mahā-pātra immediately informed the Mohammedan secretary, "It is a great fortune for your governor. Let him come visit Śrī Caitanya Mahāprabhu.

TEXT 177

প্রতীত করিয়ে—যদি নিরস্ত্র হঞা।
আসিবেক পাঁচ-সাত ভৃত্য সঙ্গে লঞা ?" ১৭৭ ॥

pratīta kariye——yadi nirastra hañā
āsibeka pāñca-sāta bhṛtya saṅge lañā?"

SYNONYMS

pratīta—understood; *kariye*—I make; *yadi*—if; *nirastra hañā*—being without weapons; *āsibeka*—he will come; *pāñca-sāta*—five to seven; *bhṛtya*—servants; *saṅge*—in company; *lañā*—taking.

TRANSLATION

"However, let me make it understood that he should come here without weapons. He may bring with him five or seven servants."

TEXT 178

'বিশ্বাস' যাঞা তাঁহারে সকল কহিল।
হিন্দুবেশ ধরি' সেই যবন আইল ॥ ১৭৮ ॥

'viśvāsa' yāñā tāṅhāre sakala kahila
hindu-veśa dhari' sei yavana āila

SYNONYMS

viśvāsa—the secretary; *yāñā*—returning; *tāṅhāre*—unto the Mohammedan governor; *sakala kahila*—told everything; *hindu-veśa dhari'*—accepting the dress of a Hindu; *sei yavana*—that Mohammedan governor; *āila*—came.

TRANSLATION

The secretary returned to the Mohammedan governor and informed him of this news. Dressing himself like a Hindu, the Mohammedan governor then came to see Śrī Caitanya Mahāprabhu.

TEXT 179

দূর হৈতে প্রভু দেখি' ভূমেতে পড়িয়া।
দণ্ডবৎ করে অশ্রু-পুলকিত হঞা॥ ১৭৯॥

dūra haite prabhu dekhi' bhūmete paḍiyā
daṇḍavat kare aśru-pulakita hañā

SYNONYMS

dūra haite—from a distance; *prabhu*—Śrī Caitanya Mahāprabhu; *dekhi'*—seeing; *bhūmete paḍiyā*—falling down on the ground; *daṇḍavat kare*—offered obeisances; *aśru*—tears; *pulakita*—jubilant; *hañā*—becoming.

TRANSLATION

Upon seeing Śrī Caitanya Mahāprabhu from a distant place, the Mohammedan governor fell to the ground and offered obeisances. Tears came to his eyes, and he was jubilant with ecstatic emotions.

TEXT 180

মহাপাত্র আনিল তাঁরে করিয়া সম্মান।
যোড়হাতে প্রভু-আগে লয় কৃষ্ণনাম॥ ১৮০॥

mahā-pātra ānila tāṅre kariyā sammāna
yoḍa-hāte prabhu-āge laya kṛṣṇa-nāma

SYNONYMS

mahā-pātra—the Orrisan representative; *ānila*—brought; *tāṅre*—him; *kariyā sammāna*—showing great respect; *yoḍa-hāte*—with folded hands; *prabhu-āge*—before Śrī Caitanya Mahāprabhu; *laya kṛṣṇa-nāma*—chanted the holy name of Kṛṣṇa.

TRANSLATION

Arriving in that way, the Mohammedan governor was respectfully brought before Śrī Caitanya Mahāprabhu by the mahā-pātra. The governor then stood before the Lord with folded hands, and he chanted the holy name of Kṛṣṇa.

TEXT 181

"অধম যবনকুলে কেন জন্ম হৈল।
বিধি মোরে হিন্দুকুলে কেন না জন্মাইল॥ ১৮১॥

"adhama yavana-kule kena janma haila
vidhi more hindu-kule kena nā janmāila

SYNONYMS

adhama—low; *yavana-kule*—in the family of a Mohammedan; *kena*—why; *janma haila*—there was birth; *vidhi*—providence; *more*—me; *hindu-kule*—in the family of a Hindu; *kena*—why; *nā*—not; *janmāila*—caused to be born.

TRANSLATION

The governor then submissively asked, "Why was I born in a Mohammedan family? This is considered a low birth. Why didn't supreme Providence grant me a birth in a Hindu family?

TEXT 182

'হিন্দু' হৈলে পাইতাম তোমার চরণ-সন্নিধান।
ব্যর্থ মোর এই দেহ, যাউক পরাণ॥" ১৮২॥

'hindu' haile pāitāma tomāra caraṇa-sannidhāna
vyartha mora ei deha, yāuka parāṇa"

SYNONYMS

hindu haile—if I was born in a Hindu family; *pāitāma*—I would have gotten; *tomāra*—of You; *caraṇa*—of the lotus feet; *sannidhāna*—proximity; *vyartha*—useless; *mora*—my; *ei*—this; *deha*—body; *yāuka parāṇa*—let me die immediately.

TRANSLATION

"If I had taken birth in a Hindu family, it would have been easy for me to remain near Your lotus feet. Since my body is now useless, let me die immediately."

TEXT 183

এত শুনি' মহাপাত্র আবিষ্ট হঞা।
প্রভুকে করেন স্তুতি চরণে ধরিয়া॥ ১৮৩॥

eta śuni' mahā-pātra āviṣṭa hañā
prabhuke karena stuti caraṇe dhariyā

SYNONYMS

eta śuni'—hearing this; *mahā-pātra*—the representative of the Orissan government; *āviṣṭa hañā*—being overwhelmed; *prabhuke*—unto Śrī Caitanya Mahāprabhu; *karena*—makes; *stuti*—prayers; *caraṇe dhariyā*—catching His feet.

TRANSLATION

Upon hearing the governor's submissive statement, the mahā-pātra was overwhelmed with joy. He clasped the lotus feet of Śrī Caitanya Mahāprabhu and began to offer the following prayers.

TEXT 184

'চণ্ডাল—পবিত্র যাঁর শ্রীনাম-শ্রবণে ।
হেন-তোমার এই জীব পাইল দরশনে ॥ ১৮৪ ॥

'caṇḍāla——pavitra yāṅra śrī-nāma-śravaṇe
hena-tomāra ei jīva pāila daraśane

SYNONYMS

caṇḍāla—the dog-eater, the lowest of mankind; *pavitra*—purified; *yāṅra*—of whom; *śrī-nāma-śravaṇe*—by hearing the holy name; *hena-tomāra*—of such a one as You; *ei jīva*—this conditioned living entity; *pāila*—has gotten; *daraśane*—the personal visit.

TRANSLATION

"Simply by hearing Your holy name, a caṇḍāla, lowest of men, can be purified. Now this conditioned soul has received Your personal interview.

TEXT 185

ইঁহার যে এই গতি, ইথে কি বিস্ময় ?
তোমার দর্শন-প্রভাব এইমত হয় ॥' ১৮৫ ॥

iṅhāra ye ei gati, ithe ki vismaya?
tomāra darśana-prabhāva ei-mata haya'

SYNONYMS

iṅhāra—of this Mohammedan governor; *ye*—which; *ei*—this; *gati*—result; *ithe*—in this; *ki*—what; *vismaya*—the wonder; *tomāra*—of You; *darśana-prabhāva*—influence of seeing; *ei-mata haya*—is like this.

TRANSLATION

"It is no wonder that this Mohammedan governor has attained such results. Simply by seeing You, all this is possible.

TEXT 186

যন্নামধেয়শ্রবণানুকীর্তনাদ্
যৎপ্রহ্বণাদ্ যৎস্মরণাদপি ক্বচিৎ ।
শ্বাদোঽপি সদ্যঃ সবনায় কল্পতে
কুতঃ পুনস্তে ভগবন্নু দর্শনাৎ ॥ ১৮৬ ॥

yan-nāmadheya-śravaṇānukīrtanād
yat-prahvaṇād yat-smaraṇād api kvacit
śvādo 'pi sadyaḥ savanāya kalpate
kutaḥ punas te bhagavan nu darśanāt

SYNONYMS

yat—of whom; *nāmadheya*—of the name; *śravaṇa*—from hearing; *anukīrtanāt*—and thereafter from chanting; *yat*—to whom; *prahvaṇāt*—from offering respects; *yat*—of whom; *smaraṇāt*—from simply remembering; *api*—also; *kvacit*—sometimes; *śvādaḥ*—a dog-eater; *api*—even; *sadyaḥ*—immediately; *savanāya*—for performing Vedic sacrifices; *kalpate*—becomes eligible; *kutaḥ*—what to speak; *punaḥ*—again; *te*—of You; *bhagavan*—O Supreme Personality of Godhead; *nu*—certainly; *darśanāt*—from seeing.

TRANSLATION

" 'To say nothing of the spiritual advancement of persons who see the Supreme Person face to face, even a person born in a family of dog-eaters becomes immediately eligible to perform Vedic sacrifices if he once utters the holy name of the Supreme Personality of Godhead, or chants about Him, hears about His pastimes, offers Him obeisances or even remembers Him.' "

PURPORT

This is a quotation from *Śrīmad-Bhāgavatam* (3.33.6). According to this verse, it doesn't matter what position a person holds. One may be the lowest of the low—a *caṇḍāla,* or dog-eater—but if he takes to chanting and hearing the holy name of the Lord, he is immediately eligible to perform Vedic sacrifices. This is especially true in this age of Kali.

harer nāma harer nāma
harer nāmaiva kevalam
kalau nāsty eva nāsty eva
nāsty eva gatir anyathā
(*Bṛhan-nāradīya Purāṇa,* 38.126)

A person born in a *brāhmaṇa* family cannot perform Vedic sacrifices until he is properly purified and has attained his sacred thread. However, according to this verse, it is understood that even a lowborn person can immediately perform sacrifices if he sincerely chants and hears the holy name of the Lord. Sometimes envious people ask how Europeans and Americans in this Kṛṣṇa consciousness movement can become *brāhmaṇas* and perform sacrifices. They do not know that the Europeans and Americans have already been purified by chanting the holy name of the Lord—Hare Kṛṣṇa, Hare Kṛṣṇa, Kṛṣṇa Kṛṣṇa, Hare Hare/ Hare Rāma, Hare Rāma, Rāma Rāma, Hare Hare. This is the proof. *Śvādo 'pi sadyaḥ savanāya kalpate.* One may be born in a family of dog-eaters, but he can perform sacrifices simply by chanting the *mahā-mantra.*

Those who find fault in the Western Vaiṣṇavas should consider this statement from *Śrīmad-Bhāgavatam* and the commentary on this verse by Śrīla Jīva Gosvāmī. In this regard, Śrīla Jīva Gosvāmī has stated that to become a *brāhmaṇa,* one has to wait for purification and undergo the sacred thread ceremony, but a chanter of the holy name does not have to wait for the sacred thread ceremony. We do not allow devotees to perform sacrifices until they are properly initiated in the sacred thread ceremony. Yet according to this verse, an offenseless chanter of the holy name is already fit to perform a fire ceremony, even though he is not doubly initiated by the sacred thread ceremony. This is the verdict given by Lord Kapiladeva in His instructions to His mother, Devahūti. It was Lord Kapiladeva who instructed Devahūti in pure Sāṅkhya philosophy.

TEXT 187

তবে মহাপ্রভু তাঁরে কৃপা-দৃষ্টি করি'।
আশ্বাসিয়া কহে,– তুমি কহ 'কৃষ্ণ' 'হরি' ॥ ১৮৭ ॥

tabe mahāprabhu tāṅre kṛpā-dṛṣṭi kari'
āśvāsiyā kahe,——tumi kaha 'kṛṣṇa' 'hari'

SYNONYMS

tabe—thereafter; *mahāprabhu*—Śrī Caitanya Mahāprabhu; *tāṅre*—unto him; *kṛpā-dṛṣṭi kari'*—glancing with mercy; *āśvāsiyā*—giving assurance; *kahe*—says; *tumi*—you; *kaha*—utter; *kṛṣṇa*—the holy name Kṛṣṇa; *hari*—the holy name Hari.

TRANSLATION

Śrī Caitanya Mahāprabhu then glanced with mercy at the Mohammedan governor. Giving him assurance, He asked him to chant the holy names Kṛṣṇa and Hari.

PURPORT

It is Śrī Caitanya Mahāprabhu's mercy that He advises everyone—even *caṇḍālas, mlecchas* and *yavanas*—to chant the holy name of the Lord. In other words, one who has taken to chanting the holy names Kṛṣṇa and Hari has already received Śrī Caitanya Mahāprabhu's mercy. The Lord's request to chant the holy name of Kṛṣṇa is now extended to everyone in the world through this Kṛṣṇa consciousness movement. Whoever follows Śrī Caitanya Mahāprabhu's instructions will certainly be purified, and one who sincerely chants the holy name offenselessly is already more than a *brāhmaṇa.* Unfortunately there are many fools and rascals in India who do not allow Western Vaiṣṇavas to enter certain temples. Such rascals do not clearly understand the *Vedas.* As stated previously: *yan-nāmadheya-śravaṇānukīrtanād.*

TEXT 188

সেই কহে,—'মোরে যদি কৈলা অঙ্গীকার ।
এক আজ্ঞা দেহ,—সেবা করি যে তোমার ॥ ১৮৮ ॥

sei kahe,—'more yadi kailā aṅgīkāra
eka ājñā deha,—sevā kari ye tomāra

SYNONYMS

sei kahe—the Mohammedan governor said; *more*—me; *yadi*—if; *kailā aṅgīkāra*—You have accepted; *eka ājñā*—one order; *deha*—give; *sevā*—service; *kari*—I may render; *ye*—so that; *tomāra*—Your.

TRANSLATION

The Mohammedan governor then said, "Since You have so kindly accepted me, please give me some order so that I can render You some service."

PURPORT

If one is purified by following Śrī Caitanya Mahāprabhu's orders—that is, by chanting the holy name of Kṛṣṇa—one must certainly be eager to render service to the Lord. This is the test. When one engages enthusiastically in the Lord's service, it is to be understood that he is reaping the results of chanting the names of Kṛṣṇa and Hari.

TEXT 189

গো-ব্রাহ্মণ-বৈষ্ণবে হিংসা কর্য়াছি অপার।
সেই পাপ হইতে মোর হউক নিস্তার ॥ ১৮৯ ॥

go-brāhmaṇa-vaiṣṇave hiṁsā karyāchi apāra
sei pāpa ha-ite mora ha-uka nistāra

SYNONYMS

go-brāhmaṇa-vaiṣṇave—to the cows, *brāhmaṇas* and Vaiṣṇavas; *hiṁsā*—violence and envy; *karyāchi*—I have done; *apāra*—unlimitedly; *sei pāpa ha-ite*—from those sinful activities; *mora*—my; *ha-uka*—let there be; *nistāra*—liberation.

TRANSLATION

The Mohammedan governor then prayed for liberation from the unlimited sinful activities he had previously incurred by being envious of brāhmaṇas and Vaiṣṇavas and killing cows.

PURPORT

By chanting the holy names Kṛṣṇa and Hari, one is certainly liberated from sinful activities, such as killing cows or insulting *brāhmaṇas* and Vaiṣṇavas. It is most sinful to kill cows and insult *brāhmaṇas* and Vaiṣṇavas. The *karma* incurred by such activity is very great, but one can immediately nullify all this *karma* by surrendering to Lord Kṛṣṇa and chanting His holy name. After being released from one's sinful reactions (*karma*), one becomes eager to serve the Lord. This is the test. Since the Mohammedan governor was immediately purified in the presence of Śrī Caitanya Mahāprabhu, he could utter the names of Kṛṣṇa and Hari. Consequently he was anxious to render some service, and the Lord, anxious to fulfill his desires, immediately had the devotee Mukunda Datta inform the governor that there was some service to render.

TEXT 190

তবে মুকুন্দ দত্ত কহে,—'শুন, মহাশয়।
গঙ্গাতীর যাইতে মহাপ্রভুর মন হয় ॥ ১৯০ ॥

tabe mukunda datta kahe,——'śuna, mahāśaya
gaṅgā-tīra yāite mahāprabhura mana haya

SYNONYMS

tabe—thereafter; *mukunda datta kahe*—Mukunda Datta, a devotee of *Śrī Caitanya Mahāprabhu* said: *śuna mahāśaya*—my dear sir, kindly hear me; *gaṅgā-*

tīra yāite—to go to the bank of the Ganges; *mahāprabhura*—of Śrī Caitanya Mahāprabhu; *mana*—the mind or desire; *haya*—is.

TRANSLATION

Mukunda Datta then told the Mohammedan governor, "My dear sir, please hear. Śrī Caitanya Mahāprabhu wishes to go to the bank of the Ganges.

TEXT 191

তাহাঁ যাইতে কর তুমি সহায়-প্রকার ।
এই বড় আজ্ঞা, এই বড় উপকার ॥' ১৯১ ॥

tāhāṅ yāite kara tumi sahāya-prakāra
ei baḍa ājñā, ei baḍa upakāra'

SYNONYMS

tāhāṅ yāite—to go there; *kara*—do; *tumi*—you; *sahāya-prakāra*—all kinds of assistance; *ei baḍa ājñā*—this is a great order; *ei baḍa upakāra*—this is a great favor.

TRANSLATION

"Please give Him all assistance so that He can go there. This is your first great order, and if you can comply, you will render a great service."

TEXT 192

তবে সেই মহাপ্রভুর চরণ বন্দিয়া ।
সবার চরণ বন্দি' চলে হৃষ্ট হঞা ॥ ১৯২ ॥

tabe sei mahāprabhura caraṇa vandiyā
sabāra caraṇa vandi' cale hṛṣṭa hañā

SYNONYMS

tabe—thereafter; *sei*—the governor; *mahāprabhura*—of Śrī Caitanya Mahāprabhu; *caraṇa vandiyā*—after worshiping the lotus feet; *sabāra caraṇa vandi'*—offering respect to the feet of all the other devotees; *cale*—departed; *hṛṣṭa hañā*—being very pleased.

TRANSLATION

After this, the Mohammedan governor offered prayers to the lotus feet of Śrī Caitanya Mahāprabhu as well as to the lotus feet of all His devotees. After that, the governor departed. Indeed, he was very pleased.

TEXT 193

মহাপাত্র তাঁর সনে কৈল কোলাকুলি।
অনেক সামগ্রী দিয়া করিল মিতালি ॥ ১৯৩ ॥

mahā-pātra tāṅra sane kaila kolākuli
aneka sāmagrī diyā karila mitāli

SYNONYMS

mahā-pātra—the Orissan representative; *tāṅra sane*—with him; *kaila*—performed; *kolākuli*—embracing; *aneka*—various; *sāmagrī*—materials; *diyā*—giving as gift; *karila mitāli*—established friendship.

TRANSLATION

Before the governor left, the mahā-pātra embraced him and offered him many material gifts. He thus established a friendship with him.

TEXT 194

প্রাতঃকালে সেই বহু নৌকা সাজাঞা।
প্রভুকে আনিতে দিল বিশ্বাস পাঠাঞা ॥ ১৯৪ ॥

prātaḥ-kāle sei bahu naukā sājāñā
prabhuke ānite dila viśvāsa pāṭhāñā

SYNONYMS

prātaḥ-kāle—in the morning; *sei*—the governor; *bahu*—many; *naukā*—boats; *sājāñā*—decorating; *prabhuke*—Śrī Caitanya Mahāprabhu; *ānite*—to bring; *dila*—gave; *viśvāsa*—the secretary; *pāṭhāñā*—sending.

TRANSLATION

The next morning the governor sent his secretary with many nicely decorated boats to bring Śrī Caitanya Mahāprabhu to the other side of the river.

TEXT 195

মহাপাত্র চলি' আইলা মহাপ্রভুর সনে।
ম্লেচ্ছ আসি' কৈল প্রভুর চরণ বন্দনে ॥ ১৯৫ ॥

mahā-pātra cali' āilā mahāprabhura sane
mleccha āsi' kaila prabhura caraṇa vandane

SYNONYMS

mahā-pātra—the Orissan government representative; *cali'*—moving; *āilā*—went; *mahāprabhura sane*—with Śrī Caitanya Mahāprabhu; *mleccha*—the governor of the other side; *āsi'*—coming; *kaila*—performed; *prabhura caraṇa vandane*—worshiping the lotus feet of the Lord.

TRANSLATION

The mahā-pātra crossed the river with Śrī Caitanya Mahāprabhu, and when they reached the other shore, the Mohammedan governor personally received the Lord and worshiped His lotus feet.

TEXT 196

এক নবীন নৌকা, তার মধ্যে ঘর ।
স্বগণে চড়াইলা প্রভু তাহার উপর ॥ ১৯৬ ॥

eka navīna naukā, tāra madhye ghara
svagaṇe caḍāilā prabhu tāhāra upara

SYNONYMS

eka—one; *navīna*—new; *naukā*—boat; *tāra*—of which; *madhye*—in the middle; *ghara*—a room; *sva-gaṇe*—with His associates; *caḍāilā*—put on board; *prabhu*—Śrī Caitanya Mahāprabhu; *tāhāra upara*—on it.

TRANSLATION

One of the boats had been newly constructed, and it had a room in the middle. It was on this boat that they put Śrī Caitanya Mahāprabhu and His associates.

TEXT 197

মহাপাত্রে মহাপ্রভু করিলা বিদায় ।
কান্দিতে কান্দিতে সেই তীরে রহি' চায় ॥ ১৯৭ ॥

mahā-pātre mahāprabhu karilā vidāya
kāndite kāndite sei tīre rahi' cāya

SYNONYMS

mahā-pātre—unto the *mahā-pātra; mahāprabhu*—Śrī Caitanya Mahāprabhu; *karilā vidāya*—bade farewell; *kāndite kāndite*—crying and crying; *sei*—that *mahā-pātra; tīre*—on the bank; *rahi' cāya*—stood and watched.

TRANSLATION

Finally Śrī Caitanya Mahāprabhu bade farewell to the mahā-pātra. Standing on the river bank and looking at the boat, the mahā-pātra began to cry.

TEXT 198

জলদস্যুভয়ে সেই যবন চলিল ।
দশ নৌকা ভরি' বহু সৈন্য সঙ্গে নিল ॥ ১৯৮ ॥

jala-dasyu-bhaye sei yavana calila
daśa naukā bhari' bahu sainya saṅge nila

SYNONYMS

jala-dasyu-bhaye—because of fearing pirates; *sei*—that; *yavana*—Mohammedan governor; *calila*—went along; *daśa naukā bhari'*—filling ten boats; *bahu*—many; *sainya*—soldiers; *saṅge*—with him; *nila*—took.

TRANSLATION

The Mohammedan governor then personally accompanied Śrī Caitanya Mahāprabhu. Because of pirates, the governor took ten boats, which were full with many soldiers.

TEXT 199

'মন্ত্রেশ্বর'-দুষ্টনদে পার করাইল ।
'পিছল্‌দা' পর্যন্ত সেই যবন আইল ॥ ১৯৯ ॥

'mantreśvara'-duṣṭa-nade pāra karāila
'pichaldā' paryanta sei yavana āila

SYNONYMS

mantreśvara—named Mantreśvara; *duṣṭa-nade*—at a dangerous spot in the river; *pāra karāila*—arranged to cross; *pichaldā paryanta*—up to the place named Pichaldā; *sei*—that; *yavana*—Mohammedan governor; *āila*—accompanied Śrī Caitanya Mahāprabhu.

TRANSLATION

The Mohammedan governor accompanied Śrī Caitanya Mahāprabhu past Mantreśvara. This place was very dangerous due to pirates. He took the Lord to a place named Pichaldā, which was near Mantreśvara.

PURPORT

The very wide mouth of the Ganges near present-day Diamond Harbor was called Mantreśvara. Through the Ganges, the boat entered the Rūpa-nārāyaṇa River and reached the village of Pichaldā. Pichaldā and Mantreśvara are located very close together. After passing Mantreśvara, the Mohammedan governor accompanied the Lord as far as Pichaldā.

TEXT 200

তাঁরে বিদায় দিল প্রভু সেই গ্রাম হৈতে।
সে-কালে তাঁর প্রেম-চেষ্টা না পারি বর্ণিতে ॥ ২০০ ॥

tāṅre vidāya dila prabhu sei grāma haite
se-kāle tāṅra prema-ceṣṭā nā pāri varṇite

SYNONYMS

tāṅre—unto the governor; *vidāya dila*—bade farewell; *prabhu*—Śrī Caitanya Mahāprabhu; *sei grāma haite*—from the village known as Pichaldā; *se-kāle*—in those days; *tāṅra*—his; *prema-ceṣṭā*—activities in ecstatic love; *nā pāri*—I am not able; *varṇite*—to describe.

TRANSLATION

Finally Śrī Caitanya Mahāprabhu bade the governor farewell. The intense ecstatic love exhibited by the governor cannot be described.

PURPORT

Śrī Caitanya Mahāprabhu bade farewell to the Mohammedan governor at Pichaldā. Kṛṣṇadāsa Kavirāja Gosvāmī herein states that the governor experienced symptoms of ecstatic love due to being separated from Śrī Caitanya Mahāprabhu. These symptoms, he admits, cannot be described.

TEXT 201

অলৌকিক লীলা করে শ্রীকৃষ্ণচৈতন্য।
যেই ইহা শুনে তাঁর জন্ম, দেহ ধন্য ॥ ২০১ ॥

alaukika līlā kare śrī-kṛṣṇa-caitanya
yei ihā śune tāṅra janma, deha dhanya

SYNONYMS

alaukika—uncommon; *līlā*—pastimes; *kare*—performs; *śrī-kṛṣṇa-caitanya*—Śrī Caitanya Mahāprabhu; *yei*—anyone who; *ihā*—this; *śune*—hears; *tāṅra*—his; *janma*—birth; *deha*—body; *dhanya*—glorified.

TRANSLATION

Lord Śrī Caitanya Mahāprabhu's pastimes are all uncommon. Whoever listens to His activities becomes glorious, and his life becomes perfect.

TEXT 202

সেই নৌকা চড়ি' প্রভু আইলা 'পানিহাটি'।
মাবিকেরে পরাইল নিজ-কৃপা-সাটী ॥ ২০২ ॥

sei naukā caḍi' prabhu āilā 'pānihāṭi'
nāvikere parāila nija-kṛpā-sāṭī

SYNONYMS

sei naukā caḍi'—boarding the same boat; *prabhu*—Śrī Caitanya Mahāprabhu; *āilā*—reached; *pānihāṭi*—the place named Pānihāṭi; *nāvikere*—the captain of the boat; *parāila*—He put on; *nija-kṛpā-sāṭī*—His own used cloth as special mercy.

TRANSLATION

The Lord finally reached Pānihāṭi, and, as an act of mercy, He gave the captain of the boat one of His personal garments.

TEXT 203

'প্রভু আইলা' বলি' লোকে হৈল কোলাহল।
মনুষ্য ভরিল সব, কিবা জল, স্থল ॥ ২০৩ ॥

'prabhu āilā' bali' loke haila kolāhala
manuṣya bharila saba, kibā jala, sthala

SYNONYMS

prabhu āilā—the Lord has arrived; *bali'*—saying; *loke*—among the residents; *haila*—there was; *kolāhala*—great broadcasting; *manuṣya*—all kinds of men; *bharila*—filled; *saba*—all; *kibā jala*—either on the water; *sthala*—or on land.

TRANSLATION

The place called Pānihāṭi was located on the bank of the Ganges. After hearing that Śrī Caitanya Mahāprabhu had arrived, all kinds of men assembled both on land and on the water.

PURPORT

The village of Pānihāṭi is situated on the banks of the Ganges near Khaḍadaha.

TEXT 204

রাঘব-পণ্ডিত আসি' প্রভু লঞা গেলা ।
পথে যাইতে লোকভিড়ে কষ্টে-সৃষ্টে আইলা ॥২০৪॥

rāghava-paṇḍita āsi' prabhu lañā gelā
pathe yāite loka-bhiḍe kaṣṭe-sṛṣṭye āilā

SYNONYMS

rāghava-paṇḍita—Rāghava Paṇḍita; *āsi'*—coming; *prabhu*—Śrī Caitanya Mahāprabhu; *lañā*—taking; *gelā*—went to his place; *pathe yāite*—passing on the road; *loka-bhiḍe*—in the crowd of men; *kaṣṭe-sṛṣṭye*—with great difficulty; *āilā*—reached.

TRANSLATION

At length Śrī Caitanya Mahāprabhu was taken away by Rāghava Paṇḍita. There was a great crowd assembled along the way, and the Lord reached Rāghava Paṇḍita's residence with great difficulty.

TEXT 205

একদিন প্রভু তথা করিয়া নিবাস ।
প্রাতে কুমারহট্টে আইলা,—যাহাঁ শ্রীনিবাস ॥ ২০৫ ॥

eka-dina prabhu tathā kariyā nivāsa
prāte kumārahaṭṭe āilā,——yāhāṅ śrīnivāsa

SYNONYMS

eka-dina—one day; *prabhu*—Śrī Caitanya Mahāprabhu; *tathā*—there; *kariyā nivāsa*—residing; *prāte*—in the morning; *kumārahaṭṭe*—the town named Kumārahaṭṭa; *āilā*—reached; *yāhāṅ*—where; *śrīnivāsa*—the home of Śrīnivāsa Ṭhākura.

TRANSLATION

The Lord stayed at Rāghava Paṇḍita's place for only one day. The next morning, He went to Kumārahaṭṭa, where Śrīvāsa Ṭhākura lived.

PURPORT

The present name of Kumārahaṭṭa is Hālisahara. After Śrī Caitanya Mahāprabhu accepted *sannyāsa,* Śrīvāsa Ṭhākura—due to separation from Śrī Caitanya Mahāprabhu—left Navadvīpa and went to Hālisahara to live.

From Kumārahaṭṭa, Śrī Caitanya Mahāprabhu went to Kāñcanapallī (known as Kāṅcaḍāpāḍā), where Śivānanda Sena lived. After staying two days at Śivānanda's house, the Lord went to the house of Vāsudeva Datta. From there He went to the western side of Navadvīpa to the village called Vidyānagara. From Vidyānagara He went to Kuliyā-grāma and stayed at Mādhava dāsa's house. He stayed there one week and excused the offenses of Devānanda and others. Due to Kavirāja Gosvāmī's mentioning the name of Śāntipurācārya, some people think that Kuliyā is a village near Kāṅcaḍāpāḍā. Due to this mistaken idea, they invented another place known as New Kuliyāra Pāṭa. Actually such a place does not exist. Leaving the house of Vāsudeva Datta, Śrī Caitanya Mahāprabhu went to the house of Advaita Ācārya. From there He went to the western side of Navadvīpa to Vidyānagara and stayed at the house of Vidyā-vācaspati. These accounts are given in the *Caitanya-bhāgavata, Caitanya-maṅgala, Caitanya-candrodaya-nāṭaka* and *Caitanya-carita-kāvya.* Śrīla Kavirāja Gosvāmī has not vividly described this entire tour; therefore, on the basis of *Caitanya-caritāmṛta,* some unscrupulous people have invented a place called Kuliyāra Pāṭa near Kāṅcaḍāpāḍā.

TEXT 206

তাহাঁ হৈতে আগে গেলা শিবানন্দ-ঘর ।
বাসুদেব-গৃহে পাছে আইলা ঈশ্বর ॥ ২০৬ ॥

tāhāṅ haite āge gelā śivānanda-ghara
vāsudeva-gṛhe pāche āilā īśvara

SYNONYMS

tāhāṅ haite—from there; *āge*—ahead; *gelā*—Lord Śrī Caitanya Mahāprabhu proceeded; *śivānanda-ghara*—to the house of Śivānanda Sena; *vāsudeva-gṛhe*—to the house of Vāsudeva Datta; *pāche*—after this; *āilā*—came; *īśvara*—the Lord.

TRANSLATION

From the house of Śrīvāsa Ṭhākura, the Lord went to the house of Śivānanda Sena and then to the house of Vāsudeva Datta.

TEXT 207

'বাচস্পতি-গৃহে' প্রভু যেমতে রহিলা।
লোক-ভিড় ভয়ে যৈছে 'কুলিয়া' আইলা ॥ ২০৭ ॥

'vācaspati-gṛhe' prabhu yemate rahilā
loka-bhiḍa bhaye yaiche 'kuliyā' āilā

SYNONYMS

vācaspati-gṛhe—at the house of Vidyā-vācaspati; *prabhu*—the Lord; *yemate*—as; *rahilā*—stayed there for some time; *loka-bhiḍa bhaye*—due to fear of crowds of people; *yaiche*—just as; *kuliyā āilā*—He came to Kuliyā, the present city of Navadvīpa.

TRANSLATION

The Lord remained some time at the house of Vidyā-vācaspati, but then, because it was too crowded, He went to Kuliyā.

PURPORT

The house of Vidyā-vācaspati was located at Vidyānagara, which was near Koladvīpa, or Kuliyā. It was here that Devānanda Paṇḍita was residing. This information is found in *Caitanya-bhāgavata* (*Madhya-līlā,* Chapter Twenty-one). In *Caitanya-candrodaya-nāṭaka,* the following statement is given about Kuliyā. *Tataḥ kumārahaṭṭe śrīvāsa-paṇḍita-vāṭyām abhyāyayau:* "From there the Lord went to the house of Śrīvāsa Paṇḍita in Kumārahaṭṭa." *Tato 'dvaita-vāṭīm abhyetya haridāsenābhivanditas tathaiva taraṇī-vartmanā navadvīpasya pāre kuliyā-nāma-grāme mādhava-dāsa-vāṭyām uttīrṇavān. evaṁ sapta-dināni tatra sthitvā punas taṭa-vartmanā eva calitavān:* "From the house of Śrīvāsa Ācārya, the Lord went to the house of Advaita Ācārya, where He was offered obeisances by Haridāsa Ṭhākura. The Lord then took a boat to the other side of Navadvīpa to a place called Kuliyā, where He stayed seven days at the house of Mādhava dāsa. He then proceeded along the banks of the Ganges."

In the *Śrī Caitanya-carita-mahā-kāvya,* it is stated, *anyedyuḥ sa śrī-navadvīpa-bhūmeḥ pāre gaṅgaṁ paścime kvāpi deśe, śrīmān sarva-prāṇināṁ tat-tad-aṅgair netrānandaṁ samyag āgatya tene:* "The Lord went to the eastern side of the Ganges at Navadvīpa, and everyone was pleased to see the Lord coming."

In the *Caitanya-bhāgavata* (*Antya-khaṇḍa,* Chapter Three), it is stated, *sarva-pāriṣada-saṅge śrī-gaurasundara/ ācambite āsi' uttarilā tāṅra ghara:* "The Lord suddenly came to Vidyānagara with a full party and stayed there in the house of Vidyā-vācaspati," *Navadvīpādi sarva-dike haila dhvani:* "Thus throughout Navadvīpa, the Lord's arrival was made known." *Vācaspati-ghare āilā nyāsi-*

cūḍāmaṇi: "Thus the chief of all the *sannyāsīs,* Śrī Caitanya Mahāprabhu, arrived at the house of Vidyā-vācaspati." As further stated:

ananta arbuda loka bali' 'hari' 'hari'
calilena dekhibāre gaurāṅga śrī-hari

patha nāhi pāya keho lokera gahale
vanaḍāla bhāṅgi' loka daśa-dike cale

lokera gahale yata araṇya āchila
kṣaṇeke sakala divya pathamaya haila

kṣaṇeke āila saba loka kheyā-ghāṭe
kheyārī karite pāra paḍila saṅkaṭe

satvare āsilā vācaspati mahāśaya
karilena aneka naukāra samuccaya

naukāra apekṣā āra keho nāhi kare
nānā mate pāra haya ye yemate pāre

hena-mate gaṅgā pāra ha-i' sarva-jana
sabhei dharena vācaspatira caraṇa

lukāñā gelā prabhu kuliyā-nagara
kuliyāya āilena vaikuṇṭha-īśvara

sarva-loka 'hari' bali' vācaspati-saṅge
sei-kṣaṇe sabhe calilena mahā-raṅge

kuliyā-nagare āilena nyāsi-maṇi
sei-kṣaṇe sarva-dike haila mahā-dhvani

sabe gaṅgā madhye nadīyāya-kuliyāya
śuni' mātra sarva-loke mahānande dhāya

vācaspatira grāme (vidyānagare) chila yateka gahala

tāra koṭi koṭi-guṇe pūrila sakala

lakṣa lakṣa naukā vā āila kothā haite
nā jāni kateka pāra haya kata-mate

lakṣa lakṣa loka bhāse jāhnavīra jale
sabhe pāra hayena parama kutūhale

gaṅgāya hañā pāra āpanā-āpani
kolākoli kari' sabhe kare hari-dhvani

kṣaṇeke kuliyā-grāma——nagara prāntara
paripūrṇa haila sthala, nāhi avasara

kṣaṇeke āilā mahāśaya vācaspati
teṅho nāhi pāyena prabhura kothā sthiti

kuliyāya prakāśe yateka pāpī chila
uttama, madhyama, nīca,——sabe pāra haila

kuliyā-grāmete āsi' śrī-kṛṣṇa-caitanya
hena nāhi, yāre prabhu nā karilā dhanya

"When Śrī Caitanya Mahāprabhu stayed at Vidyā-vācaspati's house, many hundreds and thousands of people went to see Him and chant the holy name of Hari. It was so crowded that people could not even find a place to walk; therefore they made room by clearing out the jungles near the village. Many roads were automatically excavated, and many people also came by boat to see the Lord. So many came that it was difficult for the boatmen to get them across the river. When Vidyā-vācaspati suddenly arrived, he made arrangements for many boats to receive these people, but the people would not wait for the boats. Somehow or other they crossed the river and hurried toward the house of Vidyā-vācaspati. Due to this great crowd, Śrī Caitanya Mahāprabhu secretly went to Kuliyā-nagara. After the Lord left Vidyānagara, however, all the people heard news of His leaving. They then accompanied Vācaspati to Kuliyā-nagara. Since the news of the Lord's arrival was immediately broadcast, large crowds arrived and greeted Śrī Caitanya Mahāprabhu with great jubilation. Indeed, when the crowd went to see Śrī Caitanya Mahāprabhu, it increased ten thousand times in number. No one could say how many people crossed the river to see Him, but many hundreds of thousands made a great tumult when crossing the River Ganges. After crossing the river, everyone began to embrace one another because they heard the good news of Śrī Caitanya Mahāprabhu's arrival. Thus all the inhabitants of Kuliyā, the sinful, intermediate, and spiritually advanced, were delivered and glorified by Śrī Caitanya Mahāprabhu."

As stated in *Caitanya-bhāgavata* (*Antya-khaṇḍa,* Chapter Six):

khānāyoḍā, baḍagāchi, āra dogāchiyā
gaṅgāra opāra kabhu yāyena 'kuliyā'

As stated in *Caitanya-maṅgala:*

gaṅgā-snāna kari prabhu rāḍha-deśa diyā
krame krame uttarilā nagara 'kuliyā'

māyera vacane punaḥ gelā navadvīpa
vārakoṇā-ghāṭa, nija vāḍīra samīpa

In the commentary of Premadāsa it is said:

nadīyāra mājhakhāne, sakala lokete
jāne, 'kuliyā-pāhāḍapura' nāme sthāna.

Śrī Narahari Cakravartī, or Ghanaśyāma dāsa, has written in his *Bhakti-ratnākara:*

kuliyā pāhāḍapura dekha śrīnivāsa
pūrve 'koladvīpa'-parvatākhya——e pracāra

In a book named *Navadvīpa-parikrama,* also written by Ghanaśyāma dāsa, it is stated: *kuliyā-pāhāḍapura grāma pūrve koladvīpa-parvatākhyānanda nāma.* Therefore one can conclude that the present-day city of Navadvīpa and the places known as Bāhirdvīpa, Kolera Gañja, Kola-āmāda, Kolera Daha, Gadakhāli, etc. were known as Kuliyā, but the so-called Kuliyāra Pāṭa is not the original Kuliyā.

TEXT 208

মাধবদাস-গৃহে তথা শচীর নন্দন ।
লক্ষ-কোটি লোক তথা পাইল দরশন ॥ ২০৮ ॥

mādhava-dāsa-gṛhe tathā śacīra nandana
lakṣa-koṭi loka tathā pāila daraśana

SYNONYMS

mādhava-dāsa-gṛhe—at the house of Mādhava dāsa; *tathā*—there; *śacīra nandana*—the son of mother Śacī; *lakṣa-koṭi loka*—many hundreds and thousands of people; *tathā*—there; *pāila daraśana*—got His audience.

TRANSLATION

When the Lord stayed at the house of Mādhava dāsa, many hundreds and thousands of people came to see Him.

PURPORT

Mādhava dāsa is identified as follows. In the family of Śrīkara Caṭṭopādhyāya, Yudhiṣṭhira Caṭṭopādhyāya took his birth. Formerly, he and his family members lived in Bilvagrāma and Pāṭūli. From there he went to Kuliyā Pāhāḍapura, formerly known as Pāḍapura. The eldest son of Yudhiṣṭira Caṭṭopādhyāya is known as Mādhava dāsa, the second son was called Haridāsa, and the youngest son was called Kṛṣṇasampatti Caṭṭopādhyāya. The three brothers' nicknames were Chakaḍi, Tinakaḍi and Dukaḍi. The grandson of Mādhava dāsa was named Vaṁśīvadana, and his grandson Rāmacandra and their descendants are still living at Vāghnāpāḍā, or Vaiñcī.

TEXT 209

সাত দিন রহি' তথা লোক নিস্তারিলা ।
সব অপরাধিগণে প্রকারে তারিলা ॥ ২০৯ ॥

sāta dina rahi' tathā loka nistārilā
saba aparādhi-gaṇe prakāre tārilā

SYNONYMS

sāta dina—seven days; *rahi'*—staying; *tathā*—there; *loka*—the people; *nistārilā*—He liberated; *saba*—all; *aparādhi-gaṇe*—the offenders; *prakāre*—in some fashion; *tārilā*—delivered.

TRANSLATION

The Lord stayed there for seven days and delivered all kinds of offenders and sinners.

TEXT 210

'শান্তিপুরাচার্য'-গৃহে ঐছে আইলা ।
শচী-মাতা মিলি' তাঁর দুঃখ খণ্ডাইলা ॥ ২১০ ॥

'śāntipurācārya'-gṛhe aiche āilā
śacī-mātā mili' tāṅra duḥkha khaṇḍāilā

SYNONYMS

śāntipura-ācārya—of Advaita Ācārya; *gṛhe*—to the house; *aiche*—similarly; *āilā*—went; *śacī-mātā*—mother Śacī; *mili'*—meeting; *tāṅra*—her; *duḥkha*—unhappiness; *khaṇḍāilā*—pacified.

TRANSLATION

After leaving Kuliyā, Śrī Caitanya Mahāprabhu visited the house of Advaita Ācārya at Śāntipura. It was there that the Lord's mother, Śacīmātā, met Him and was thus relieved of her great unhappiness.

TEXT 211

তবে 'রামকেলি'-গ্রামে প্রভু যৈছে গেলা ।
'নাটশালা' হৈতে প্রভু পুনঃ ফিরি' আইলা ॥ ২১১ ॥

tabe 'rāmakeli'-grāme prabhu yaiche gelā
'nāṭaśālā' haite prabhu punaḥ phiri' āilā

SYNONYMS

tabe—thereafter; *rāmakeli-grāme*—in the village known as Rāmakeli; *prabhu*—Lord Śrī Caitanya Mahāprabhu; *yaiche*—similarly; *gelā*—went; *nāṭaśālā*—the place known as Kānāi Nāṭaśālā; *haite*—from; *prabhu*—Śrī Caitanya Mahāprabhu; *punaḥ*—again; *phiri' āilā*—returned.

TRANSLATION

The Lord then visited the village known as Rāmakeli and the place known as Kānāi Nāṭaśālā. From there He returned to Śāntipura.

TEXT 212

শান্তিপুরে পুনঃ কৈল দশ-দিন বাস ।
বিস্তারি' বর্ণিয়াছেন বৃন্দাবন-দাস ॥ ২১২ ॥

śāntipure punaḥ kaila daśa-dina vāsa
vistāri' varṇiyāchena vṛndāvana-dāsa

SYNONYMS

śāntipure—at Śāntipura; *punaḥ*—again; *kaila*—made; *daśa-dina*—for ten days; *vāsa*—residence; *vistāri'*—elaborating; *varṇiyāchena*—has described; *vṛndāvana-dāsa*—Vṛndāvana dāsa Ṭhākura.

TRANSLATION

Śrī Caitanya Mahāprabhu stayed in Śāntipura for ten days. This has all been described very elaborately by Vṛndāvana dāsa Ṭhākura.

TEXT 213

অতএব ইহাঁ তার না কৈলুঁ বিস্তার ।
পুনরুক্তি হয়, গ্রন্থ বাড়য়ে অপার ॥ ২১৩ ॥

ataeva ihāṅ tāra nā kailuṅ vistāra
punarukti haya, grantha bāḍaye apāra

SYNONYMS

ataeva—therefore; *ihāṅ*—here; *tāra*—of that incident; *nā kailuṅ*—I did not give; *vistāra*—elaboration; *punarukti*—repetition; *haya*—it is; *grantha*—the book; *bāḍaye*—increases; *apāra*—unlimitedly.

TRANSLATION

I will not narrate these incidents because they have already been described by Vṛndāvana dāsa Ṭhākura. There is no need to repeat the same information, for such repetition would unlimitedly increase the size of this book.

TEXTS 214-215

তার মধ্যে মিলিলা যৈছে রূপ-সনাতন ।
নৃসিংহানন্দ কৈল যৈছে পথের সাজন ॥ ২১৪ ॥
সূত্রমধ্যে সেই লীলা আমি ত' বর্ণিলুঁ ।
অতএব পুনঃ তাহা ইহাঁ না লিখিলুঁ ॥ ২১৫ ॥

tāra madhye mililā yaiche rūpa-sanātana
nṛsiṁhānanda kaila yaiche pathera sājana

sūtra-madhye sei līlā āmi ta' varṇiluṅ
ataeva punaḥ tāhā ihāṅ nā likhiluṅ

SYNONYMS

tāra madhye—within that; *mililā*—He met; *yaiche*—how; *rūpa-sanātana*—the two brothers Rūpa and Sanātana; *nṛsiṁhānanda*—Nṛsiṁhānanda; *kaila*—did; *yaiche*—how; *pathera sājana*—decoration of the road; *sūtra-madhye*—in the synopsis; *sei līlā*—those pastimes; *āmi*—I; *ta'*—indeed; *varṇiluṅ*—have described; *ataeva*—therefore; *punaḥ*—again; *tāhā*—that; *ihāṅ*—here; *nā likhiluṅ*—I have not written.

TRANSLATION

Those narrations tell how Śrī Caitanya Mahāprabhu met the brothers Rūpa and Sanātana and how Nṛsiṁhānanda decorated the road. I have already de-

scribed these in an earlier synopsis of this book; therefore I will not repeat the narrations here.

PURPORT

This information is given in *Ādi-līlā* (Chapter Ten, verse 35) and *Madhya-līlā* (Chapter One, verses 155-162 and 175-226).

TEXT 216

পুনরপি প্রভু যদি 'শান্তিপুর' আইলা ।
রঘুনাথ-দাস আসি' প্রভুরে মিলিলা ॥ ২১৬ ॥

punarapi prabhu yadi 'śāntipura' āilā
raghunātha-dāsa āsi' prabhure mililā

SYNONYMS

punarapi—again; *prabhu*—Śrī Caitanya Mahāprabhu; *yadi*—when; *śāntipura āilā*—came to Śāntipura; *raghunātha-dāsa*—Raghunātha dāsa; *āsi'*—coming; *prabhure mililā*—met Śrī Caitanya Mahāprabhu.

TRANSLATION

When Śrī Caitanya Mahāprabhu returned to Śāntipura, Raghunātha dāsa came to meet Him.

TEXT 217

'হিরণ্য,' 'গোবর্ধন',—দুই সহোদর ।
সপ্তগ্রামে বারলক্ষ মুদ্রার ঈশ্বর ॥ ২১৭ ॥

'hiraṇya', 'govardhana',——dui sahodara
saptagrāme bāra-lakṣa mudrāra īśvara

SYNONYMS

hiraṇya—Hiraṇya; *govardhana*—Govardhana; *dui sahodara*—two brothers; *saptagrāme*—in the village named Saptagrāma; *bāra-lakṣa*—1,200,000; *mudrāra*—of coins; *īśvara*—the masters.

TRANSLATION

Two brothers named Hiraṇya and Govardhana, who were residents of Saptagrāma, had an income of 1,200,000 rupees.

PURPORT

Hiraṇya and Govardhana were inhabitants of Saptagrāma in the district of Hugalī. Actually they were inhabitants not of Saptagrāma, but a nearby village named Kṛṣṇapura. They took their birth in a big *kāyastha* family, and although their family title has not been ascertained, it is known that they came from an aristocratic family. The elder brother's name was Hiraṇya Majumadāra, and the younger brother's name was Govardhana Majumadāra. Śrī Raghunātha dāsa was the son of Govardhana Majumadāra. Their family priest was Balarāma Ācārya, who was a favorite of Haridāsa Ṭhākura's, and the family's spiritual master was Yadunandana Ācārya, a favorite of Vāsudeva Datta's.

The village of Saptagrāma is located on the eastern railway from Calcutta to Burdwan, and presently the railway station is called Triśabighā. In those days there was a large river there known as the Sarasvatī, and present-day Triśabighā is a great port. In 1592, the Pāṭhānas invaded, and due to a flooding of the Sarasvatī River in the year 1632, this great port was partially destroyed. It is said that in the Seventeenth and Eighteenth Centuries, Portuguese businessmen used to come aboard their ships. In those days, Saptagrāma, situated on the southern side of Bengal, was very rich and popular. The merchants, who were the principal residents, were called Saptagrāma *suvarṇa-vaṇik*. There were very many rich people there, and Hiraṇya Majumadāra and Govardhana Majumadāra belonged to the *kāyastha* community. They also were very rich, so much so that it is mentioned in this verse that their annual income as landlords amounted to 1,200,000 rupees. In this connection, one may refer to *Ādi-līlā* (Chapter Eleven, verse 41), which describes Uddhāraṇa Datta, who also belonged to the Saptagrāmī *suvarṇa-vaṇik* community.

TEXT 218

মহৈশ্বর্যযুক্ত দুঁহে—বদান্য, ব্রহ্মণ্য ।
সদাচারী, সৎকুলীন, ধার্মিকাগ্রগণ্য ॥ ২১৮ ॥

mahaiśvarya-yukta duṅhe——vadānya, brahmaṇya
sadācārī, satkulīna, dhārmikāgra-gaṇya

SYNONYMS

mahā-aiśvarya-yukta—very opulent in riches; *duṅhe*—both the brothers; *vadānya*—very magnanimous; *brahmaṇya*—devoted to brahminical culture; *sat-ācārī*—well-behaved; *sat-kulīna*—aristocratic; *dhārmika-agra-gaṇya*—on the top of the list of religious persons.

TRANSLATION

Both Hiraṇya Majumadāra and Govardhana Majumadāra were very opulent and magnanimous. They were well-behaved and devoted to brahminical

culture. They belonged to an aristocratic family, and among religionists they were predominant.

TEXT 219

নদীয়া-বাসী ব্রাহ্মণের উপজীব্য-প্রায় ।
অর্থ, ভূমি, গ্রাম দিয়া করেন সহায় ॥ ২১৯ ॥

nadīyā-vāsī, brāhmaṇera upajīvya-prāya
artha, bhūmi, grāma diyā karena sahāya

SYNONYMS

nadīyā-vāsī—inhabitants of Nadia; *brāhmaṇera*—of all *brāhmaṇas; upajīvya-prāya*—almost the entire source of income; *artha*—money; *bhūmi*—land; *grāma*—villages; *diyā*—giving as charity; *karena sahāya*—give help.

TRANSLATION

Practically all the brāhmaṇas residing in Nadia were dependent on the charity of Hiraṇya and Govardhana, who gave them money, land and villages.

PURPORT

Although Navadvīpa was very opulent and populous during Śrī Caitanya Mahāprabhu's time, practically all the *brāhmaṇas* depended on the charity of Hiraṇya and Govardhana. Because the brothers highly respected the *brāhmaṇas,* they very liberally gave them money.

TEXT 220

নীলাম্বর চক্রবর্ত্তী – আরাধ্য দুঁহার ।
চক্রবর্ত্তী করে দুঁহায় 'ভ্রাতৃ'-ব্যবহার ॥ ২২০ ॥

nīlāmbara cakravartī——ārādhya duṅhāra
cakravartī kare duṅhāya 'bhrātṛ'-vyavahāra

SYNONYMS

nīlāmbara cakravartī—the grandfather of Śrī Caitanya Mahāprabhu; *ārādhya duṅhāra*—very worshipable for these two; *cakravartī*—Nīlāmbara Cakravartī; *kare*—does; *duṅhāya*—to the two of them; *bhrātṛ-vyavahāra*—treating as brothers.

TRANSLATION

Nīlāmbara Cakravartī, the grandfather of Śrī Caitanya Mahāprabhu, was much worshiped by the two brothers, but Nīlāmbara Cakravartī used to treat them as his own brothers.

TEXT 221

মিশ্র-পুরন্দরের পূর্বে করয়াছেন সেবনে ।
অতএব প্রভু ভাল জানে দুইজনে ॥ ২২১ ॥

miśra-purandarera pūrve karyāchena sevane
ataeva prabhu bhāla jāne dui-jane

SYNONYMS

miśra-purandarera—to Purandara Miśra, the father of Śrī Caitanya Mahāprabhu; *pūrve*—previously; *karyāchena sevane*—had rendered service; *ataeva*—therefore; *prabhu*—Śrī Caitanya Mahāprabhu; *bhāla*—very well; *jāne*—knew; *dui-jane*—the two brothers.

TRANSLATION

Formerly, these two brothers rendered much service to Miśra Purandara, the father of Śrī Caitanya Mahāprabhu. Because of this, the Lord knew them very well.

TEXT 222

সেই গোবর্ধনের পুত্র –রঘুনাথ দাস ।
বাল্যকাল হৈতে তেঁহো বিষয়ে উদাস ॥ ২২২ ॥

sei govardhanera putra——raghunātha dāsa
bālya-kāla haite teṅho viṣaye udāsa

SYNONYMS

sei—that; *govardhanera putra*—son of Govardhana Majumadāra; *raghunātha dāsa*—Raghunātha dāsa; *bālya-kāla haite*—from his very childhood; *teṅho*—he; *viṣaye udāsa*—indifferent to material happiness.

TRANSLATION

Raghunātha dāsa was the son of Govardhana Majumadāra. From childhood, he was uninterested in material enjoyment.

TEXT 223

সন্ন্যাস করি' প্রভু যবে শান্তিপুর আইলা ।
তবে আসি' রঘুনাথ প্রভুরে মিলিলা ॥ ২২৩ ॥

sannyāsa kari' prabhu yabe śāntipura āilā
tabe āsi' raghunātha prabhure mililā

SYNONYMS

sannyāsa kari'—after accepting the *sannyāsa* order; *prabhu*—the Lord; *yabe*—when; *śāntipura āilā*—went to Śāntipura; *tabe*—at that time; *āsi'*—coming; *raghunātha*—Raghunātha dāsa; *prabhure*—Śrī Caitanya Mahāprabhu; *mililā*—met.

TRANSLATION

When Śrī Caitanya Mahāprabhu returned to Śāntipura after accepting the renounced order, Raghunātha dāsa met Him.

TEXT 224

প্রভুর চরণে পড়ে প্রেমাবিষ্ট হঞা ।
প্রভু পাদস্পর্শ কৈল করুণা করিয়া ॥ ২২৪ ॥

prabhura caraṇe paḍe premāviṣṭa hañā
prabhu pāda-sparśa kaila karuṇā kariyā

SYNONYMS

prabhura—of Śrī Caitanya Mahāprabhu; *caraṇe*—at the lotus feet; *paḍe*—fell down; *prema-āviṣṭa*—absorbed in ecstatic love; *hañā*—becoming; *prabhu*—Śrī Caitanya Mahāprabhu; *pāda-sparśa kaila*—touched with His feet; *karuṇā*—mercy; *kariyā*—showing.

TRANSLATION

When Raghunātha dāsa went to see Śrī Caitanya Mahāprabhu, he fell at the Lord's lotus feet in ecstatic love. Showing him mercy, the Lord touched him with His feet.

TEXT 225

তাঁর পিতা সদা করে আচার্য-সেবন ।
অতএব আচার্য তাঁরে হৈলা পরসন্ন ॥ ২২৫ ॥

tāṅra pitā sadā kare ācārya-sevana
ataeva ācārya tāṅre hailā parasanna

SYNONYMS

tāṅra pitā—his father; *sadā*—always; *kare*—performs; *ācārya-sevana*—worship of Advaita Ācārya; *ataeva ācārya*—therefore Advaita Ācārya; *tāṅre*—upon him; *hailā parasanna*—became pleased.

TRANSLATION

Raghunātha dāsa's father, Govardhana, always rendered much service to Advaita Ācārya. Consequently Advaita Ācārya was very pleased with the family.

TEXT 226

আচার্য-প্রসাদে পাইল প্রভুর উচ্ছিষ্ট-পাত ।
প্রভুর চরণ দেখে দিন পাঁচ-সাত ॥ ২২৬ ॥

ācārya-prasāde pāila prabhura ucchiṣṭa-pāta
prabhura caraṇa dekhe dina pāṅca-sāta

SYNONYMS

ācārya-prasāde—by the mercy of Advaita Ācārya; *pāila*—got; *prabhura*—of Lord Śrī Caitanya Mahāprabhu; *ucchiṣṭa-pāta*—remnants of food; *prabhura*—of Śrī Caitanya Mahāprabhu; *caraṇa*—lotus feet; *dekhe*—sees; *dina*—days; *pāṅca-sāta*—five to seven.

TRANSLATION

When Raghunātha dāsa was there, Advaita Ācārya favored him by giving him the food remnants left by the Lord. Raghunātha dāsa was thus engaged for five or seven days by rendering service to the Lord's lotus feet.

TEXT 227

প্রভু তাঁরে বিদায় দিয়া গেলা নীলাচল ।
তেঁহো ঘরে আসি' হৈলা প্রেমেতে পাগল ॥ ২২৭ ॥

prabhu tāṅre vidāya diyā gelā nīlācala
teṅho ghare āsi' hailā premete pāgala

SYNONYMS

prabhu—Śrī Caitanya Mahāprabhu; *tāṅre*—unto Raghunātha dāsa; *vidāya diyā*—bidding farewell; *gelā*—went back; *nīlācala*—to Jagannātha Purī; *teṅho*—he; *ghare āsi'*—returning home; *hailā*—became; *premete pāgala*—mad in ecstatic love.

TRANSLATION

After bidding farewell to Raghunātha dāsa, Śrī Caitanya Mahāprabhu returned to Jagannātha Purī. After returning home, Raghunātha dāsa became mad with ecstatic love.

TEXT 228

বার বার পলায় তেঁহো নীলাদ্রি যাইতে ।
পিতা তাঁরে বান্ধি' রাখে আনি' পথ হৈতে ॥ ২২৮ ॥

bāra bāra palāya teṅho nīlādri yāite
pitā tāṅre bāndhi' rākhe āni' patha haite

SYNONYMS

bāra bāra—again and again; *palāya*—leaves home; *teṅho*—he; *nīlādri yāite*—to go to Jagannātha Purī; *pitā*—his father; *tāṅre*—him; *bāndhi'*—binding; *rākhe*—keeps; *āni'*—bringing back; *patha haite*—from the road.

TRANSLATION

Raghunātha dāsa used to run away from home again and again to go to Jagannātha Purī, but his father kept binding him and bringing him back.

TEXT 229

পঞ্চ পাইক তাঁরে রাখে রাত্রি-দিনে ।
চারি সেবক, দুই ব্রাহ্মণ রহে তাঁর সনে ॥ ২২৯ ॥

pañca pāika tāṅre rākhe rātri-dine
cāri sevaka, dui brāhmaṇa rahe tāṅra sane

SYNONYMS

pañca—five; *pāika*—watchmen; *tāṅre*—him (Raghunātha dāsa); *rākhe*—keep; *rātri-dine*—day and night; *cāri sevaka*—four personal servants; *dui brāhmaṇa*—two *brāhmaṇas* to cook; *rahe*—remain; *tāṅra sane*—with him.

TRANSLATION

His father even had five watchmen guard him day and night. Four personal servants were employed to look after his comfort, and two brāhmaṇas were employed to cook for him.

TEXT 230

একাদশ জন তাঁরে রাখে নিরন্তর ।
নীলাচলে যাইতে না পায়, দুঃখিত অন্তর ॥ ২৩০ ॥

ekādaśa jana tāṅre rākhe nirantara
nīlācale yāite nā pāya, duḥkhita antara

SYNONYMS

ekādaśa—eleven; *jana*—persons; *tāṅre*—him; *rākhe*—keep; *nirantara*—day and night; *nīlācale*—to Jagannātha Purī; *yāite*—to go; *nā pāya*—was not able; *duḥkhita antara*—very unhappy within the mind.

TRANSLATION

In this way, eleven people were incessantly keeping Raghunātha dāsa under control. Thus he could not go to Jagannātha Purī, and because of this he was very unhappy.

TEXT 231

এবে যদি মহাপ্রভু 'শান্তিপুর' আইলা ।
শুনিয়া পিতারে রঘুনাথ নিবেদিলা ॥ ২৩১ ॥

ebe yadi mahāprabhu 'śāntipura' āilā
śuniyā pitāre raghunātha nivedilā

SYNONYMS

ebe—now; *yadi*—when; *mahāprabhu*—Śrī Caitanya Mahāprabhu; *śāntipura*—to Śāntipura; *āilā*—came; *śuniyā*—hearing; *pitāre*—unto his father; *raghunātha*—Raghunātha dāsa; *nivedilā*—submitted.

TRANSLATION

When Raghunātha dāsa learned that Śrī Caitanya Mahāprabhu had arrived at Śāntipura, he submitted a request to his father.

TEXT 232

"আজ্ঞা দেহ', যাঞা দেখি প্রভুর চরণ ।
অন্যথা, না রহে মোর শরীরে জীবন" ॥ ২৩২ ॥

"ājñā deha', yāñā dekhi prabhura caraṇa
anyathā, nā rahe mora śarīre jīvana"

SYNONYMS

ājñā deha'—kindly give me permission; *yāñā*—going; *dekhi*—I may see; *prabhura caraṇa*—the lotus feet of the Lord; *anyathā*—otherwise; *nā rahe*—will not remain; *mora*—my; *śarīre*—within the body; *jīvana*—life.

TRANSLATION

Raghunātha dāsa asked his father, "Please give me permission to go see the lotus feet of the Lord. If you do not, my life will not remain within this body."

TEXT 233

শুনি' তাঁর পিতা বহু লোক-দ্রব্য দিয়া ।
পাঠাইল বলি' 'শীঘ্র আসিহ ফিরিয়া' ॥ ২৩৩ ॥

śuni' tāṅra pitā bahu loka-dravya diyā
pāṭhāila bali' 'śīghra āsiha phiriyā'

SYNONYMS

śuni'—hearing; *tāṅra*—his; *pitā*—father; *bahu*—many; *loka-dravya*—servants and materials; *diyā*—giving; *pāṭhāila*—sent; *bali'*—saying; *śīghra*—very soon; *āsiha*—come; *phiriyā*—returning.

TRANSLATION

Hearing this request, Raghunātha dāsa's father agreed. Giving him many servants and materials, the father sent him to see Śrī Caitanya Mahāprabhu, requesting him to return soon.

TEXT 234

সাত দিন শান্তিপুরে প্রভু-সঙ্গে রহে ।
রাত্রি-দিবসে এই মনঃকথা কহে ॥ ২৩৪ ॥

sāta dina śāntipure prabhu-saṅge rahe
rātri-divase ei manaḥ-kathā kahe

SYNONYMS

sāta dina—for seven days; *śāntipure*—at Śāntipura; *prabhu-saṅge*—in the association of Śrī Caitanya Mahāprabhu; *rahe*—stayed; *rātri-divase*—both day and night; *ei*—these; *manaḥ-kathā*—words in his mind; *kahe*—says.

TRANSLATION

For seven days Raghunātha dāsa associated with Śrī Caitanya Mahāprabhu in Śāntipura. During those days and nights, he had the following thoughts.

TEXT 235

'রক্ষকের হাতে মুঞি কেমনে ছুটিব !
কেমনে প্রভুর সঙ্গে নীলাচলে যাব ?' ২৩৫ ॥

'rakṣakera hāte muñi kemane chuṭiba!
kemane prabhura saṅge nīlācale yāba?'

SYNONYMS

rakṣakera hāte—from the clutches of the watchmen; *muñi*—I; *kemane*—how; *chuṭiba*—shall get release; *kemane*—how; *prabhura saṅge*—with Śrī Caitanya Mahāprabhu; *nīlācale*—to Jagannātha Purī; *yāba*—I shall go.

TRANSLATION

Raghunātha dāsa thought, "How shall I be able to get free from the hands of the watchmen? How shall I be able to go with Śrī Caitanya Mahāprabhu to Nīlācala?"

TEXT 236

সর্বজ্ঞ গৌরাঙ্গপ্রভু জানি' তাঁর মন ।
শিক্ষা-রূপে কহে তাঁরে আশ্বাস-বচন ॥ ২৩৬ ॥

sarvajña gaurāṅga-prabhu jāni' tāṅra mana
śikṣā-rūpe kahe tāṅre āśvāsa-vacana

SYNONYMS

sarva-jña—omniscient; *gaurāṅga-prabhu*—Śrī Caitanya Mahāprabhu; *jāni'*—knowing; *tāṅra*—his; *mana*—mind; *śikṣā-rūpe*—as an instruction; *kahe*—says; *tāṅre*—unto Raghunātha dāsa; *āśvāsa-vacana*—words of assurance.

TRANSLATION

Since Śrī Caitanya Mahāprabhu was omniscient, He could understand Raghunātha dāsa's mind. The Lord therefore instructed him with the following reassuring words.

TEXT 237

"স্থির হঞা ঘরে যাও, না হও বাতুল ।
ক্রমে ক্রমে পায় লোক ভবসিন্ধুকূল ॥ ২৩৭ ॥

"sthira hañā ghare yāo, nā hao vātula
krame krame pāya loka bhava-sindhu-kūla

SYNONYMS

sthira hañā—being patient; *ghare yāo*—go back home; *nā*—do not; *hao*—become; *vātula*—crazy; *krame krame*—gradually; *pāya*—gets; *loka*—a person; *bhava-sindhu-kūla*—the far shore of the ocean of material existence.

TRANSLATION

"Be patient and return home. Don't be a crazy fellow. By and by you will be able to cross the ocean of material existence.

PURPORT

As stated in *Śrīmad-Bhāgavatam* (10.14.58):

samāśritā ye pada-pallava-plavaṁ
mahat-padaṁ puṇya-yaśo-murāreḥ
bhavāmbudhir vatsa-padaṁ paraṁ padaṁ
padaṁ padaṁ yad vipadāṁ na teṣām

This material world is just like a big ocean. It begins with Brahmaloka and extends to Pātālaloka, and there are many planets, or islands, in this ocean. Not knowing about devotional service, the living entity wanders about this ocean, just as a man tries to swim to reach the shore. Our struggle for existence is similar to this. Everyone is trying to get out of the ocean of material existence. One cannot immediately reach the coast, but if one endeavors, he can cross the ocean by Śrī Caitanya Mahāprabhu's mercy. One may be very eager to cross this ocean, but he cannot attain success by acting like a madman. He must swim over the ocean very patiently and intelligently under the instructions of Śrī Caitanya Mahāprabhu or His representative. Then, one day, he will reach the shore and return home, back to Godhead.

TEXT 238

মর্কট-বৈরাগ্য না কর লোক দেখাঞা ।
যথাযোগ্য বিষয় ভুঞ্জ' অনাসক্ত হঞা ॥ ২৩৮ ॥

markaṭa-vairāgya nā kara loka dekhāñā
yathā-yogya viṣaya bhuñja' anāsakta hañā

SYNONYMS

markaṭa-vairāgya—monkey renunciation; *nā kara*—do not do; *loka*—to the people; *dekhāñā*—showing off; *yathā-yogya*—as it is befitting; *viṣaya*—material things; *bhuñja'*—enjoy; *anāsakta*—without attachment; *hañā*—being.

TRANSLATION

"You should not make yourself a showbottle devotee and become a false renunciant. For the time being, enjoy the material world in a befitting way and do not become attached to it."

PURPORT

The word *markaṭa-vairāgya,* indicating false renunciation, is very important in this verse. Śrīla Bhaktisiddhānta Sarasvatī Ṭhākura, in commenting on this word, points out that monkeys make an external show of renunciation by not accepting clothing and by living naked in the forest. In this way they consider themselves renunciants, but actually they are very busy enjoying sense gratification with dozens of female monkeys. Such renunciation is called *markaṭa-vairāgye*—the renunciation of a monkey. One cannot be really renounced until one actually becomes disgusted with material activity and sees it as a stumbling block to spiritual advancement. Renunciation should not be *phalgu,* temporary, but should exist throughout one's life. Temporary renunciation, or monkey renunciation, is like the renunciation one feels at a cremation ground. When a man takes a dead body to the crematorium, he sometimes thinks, "This is the final end of the body. Why am I working so hard day and night?" Such sentiments naturally arise in the mind of any man who goes to a crematorial *ghāṭa.* However, as soon as he returns from the cremation grounds, he again engages in material activity for sense enjoyment. This is called *śmaśāna-vairāgya,* or *markaṭa-vairāgya.*

In order to render service to the Lord, one may accept necessary things. If one lives in this way, he may actually become renounced. In the *Bhakti-rasāmṛta-sindhu* (1.2.108), it is said:

yāvatā syāt sva-nirvāhaḥ
svīkuryāt tāvad arthavit
ādhikye nyūnatāyāṁ ca
cyavate paramārthataḥ

"The bare necessities of life must be accepted, but one should not superfluously increase his necessities. Nor should they be unnecessarily decreased. One should simply accept what is necessary to help one advance spiritually."

In his *Durgama-saṅgamanī,* Śrī Jīva Gosvāmī comments that the word *sva-nirvāhaḥ* actually means *sva-sva-bhakti-nirvāhaḥ*. The experienced devotee will accept only those material things that will help him render service to the Lord. In *Bhakti-rasāmṛta-sindhu* (1.2.256), *markaṭa-vairāgya,* or *phalgu-vairāgya,* is explained as follows:

prāpañcikatayā buddhyā
hari-sambandhi-vastunaḥ
mumukṣubhiḥ parityāgo
vairāgyaṁ phalgu kathyate

"Whatever is favorable for the rendering of service to the Lord should be accepted and should not be rejected as a material thing." *Yukta-vairāgya,* or befitting renunciation, is thus explained:

anāsaktasya viṣayān
yathārham upayuñjataḥ
nirbandhaḥ kṛṣṇa-sambandhe
yuktaṁ vairāgyam ucyate

"Things should be accepted for the Lord's service and not for one's personal sense gratification. If one accepts something without attachment and accepts it because it is related to Kṛṣṇa, one's renunciation is called *yukta-vairāgya.*" Since Kṛṣṇa is the Absolute Truth, whatever is accepted for His service is also the Absolute Truth.

The word *markaṭa-vairāgya* is used by Śrī Caitanya Mahāprabhu to indicate so-called Vaiṣṇavas who dress themselves in loincloths trying to imitate Śrīla Rūpa Gosvāmī. Such people carry a beadbag and chant, but at heart they are always thinking about getting women and money. Unknown to others, these *markaṭa-vairāgīs* maintain women but externally present themselves as renunciants. Śrī Caitanya Mahāprabhu was very much opposed to these *markaṭa-vairāgīs,* or pseudo-Vaiṣṇavas.

TEXT 239

অন্তরে নিষ্ঠা কর, বাহ্যে লোকব্যবহার ।
অচিরাৎ কৃষ্ণ তোমায় করিবে উদ্ধার ॥" ২৩৯ ॥

antare niṣṭhā kara, bāhye loka-vyavahāra
acirāt kṛṣṇa tomāya karibe uddhāra

SYNONYMS

antare—within the heart; *niṣṭhā kara*—keep strong faith; *bāhye*—externally; *loka-vyavahāra*—behavior like ordinary men; *acirāt*—very soon; *kṛṣṇa*—Lord Kṛṣṇa; *tomāya*—unto you; *karibe*—will do; *uddhāra*—liberation.

TRANSLATION

Śrī Caitanya Mahāprabhu continued: "Within your heart, you should keep yourself very faithful, but externally you may behave like an ordinary man. Thus Kṛṣṇa will soon be very pleased and deliver you from the clutches of māyā.

TEXT 240

বৃন্দাবন দেখি' যবে আসিব নীলাচলে ।
তবে তুমি আমা-পাশ আসিহ কোন ছলে ॥ ২৪০ ॥

vṛndāvana dekhi' yabe āsiba nīlācale
tabe tumi āmā-pāśa āsiha kona chale

SYNONYMS

vṛndāvana dekhi'—after visiting Vṛndāvana; *yabe*—when; *āsiba*—I shall come back; *nīlācale*—to Jagannātha Purī; *tabe*—at that time; *tumi*—you; *āmā-pāśa*—to Me; *āsiha*—please come; *kona chale*—by some pretext.

TRANSLATION

"You may see me at Nīlācala, Jagannātha Purī, when I return after visiting Vṛndāvana. By that time you can think of some trick to escape.

TEXT 241

সে ছল সেকালে কৃষ্ণ স্ফুরাবে তোমারে ।
কৃষ্ণকৃপা যাঁরে, তারে কে রাখিতে পারে ॥" ২৪১ ॥

se chala se-kāle kṛṣṇa sphurābe tomāre
kṛṣṇa-kṛpā yāṅre, tāre ke rākhite pāre"

SYNONYMS

se chala—that trick; *se-kāle*—at that time; *kṛṣṇa*—Lord Kṛṣṇa; *sphurābe*—will show; *tomāre*—unto you; *kṛṣṇa-kṛpā*—the mercy of Kṛṣṇa; *yāṅre*—upon whom; *tāre*—him; *ke*—who; *rākhite*—to keep; *pāre*—is able.

TRANSLATION

"What kind of means you will have to use at that time will be revealed by Kṛṣṇa. If one has Kṛṣṇa's mercy, no one can check him."

PURPORT

Although Śrīla Raghunātha dāsa was very anxious to join Śrī Caitanya Mahāprabhu, the Lord advised him to wait for the mercy of Lord Kṛṣṇa. He recommended that Raghunātha dāsa keep his Kṛṣṇa consciousness firmly fixed in his heart while externally behaving like an ordinary man. This is a trick for everyone advanced in Kṛṣṇa consciousness. One can live in society like an ordinary human being, but at the same time one's own business should be to satisfy Kṛṣṇa and spread His glories. A Kṛṣṇa conscious person should not be absorbed in material things, for his only business is the devotional service of the Lord. If one is engaged in this way, Kṛṣṇa will certainly bestow His mercy. As Śrī Caitanya Mahāprabhu advised Raghunātha dāsa: *yathā-yogya viṣaya bhuñja' anāsakta hañā*. The same is repeated: *antare niṣṭhā kara, bāhye loka-vyavahāra*. This means that one must have no other desire within his heart than to serve Kṛṣṇa. On the basis of such a conviction, one can cultivate Kṛṣṇa consciousness. This is confirmed in *Bhakti-rasāmṛta-sindhu* (1.2.200):

laukikī vaidikī vāpi
yā kriyā kriyate mune
hari-sevānukūlaiva
sā kāryā bhaktim icchatā

A devotee may act as an ordinary human being or as a strict follower of Vedic injunctions. In either case, everything he does is favorable for the advancement of devotional service because he is in Kṛṣṇa consciousness.

TEXT 242

এত কহি' মহাপ্রভু তাঁরে বিদায় দিল ।
ঘরে আসি' মহাপ্রভুর শিক্ষা আচরিল ॥ ২৪২ ॥

eta kahi' mahāprabhu tāṅre vidāya dila
ghare āsi' mahāprabhura śikṣā ācarila

SYNONYMS

eta kahi'—saying this; *mahāprabhu*—Śrī Caitanya Mahāprabhu; *tāṅre*—unto Raghunātha dāsa; *vidāya dila*—bade farewell; *ghare āsi'*—returning home; *mahāprabhura*—of Śrī Caitanya Mahāprabhu; *śikṣā*—the instruction; *ācarila*—practiced.

TRANSLATION

In this way, Śrī Caitanya Mahāprabhu bade farewell to Raghunātha dāsa, who returned home and did exactly what the Lord told him.

TEXT 243

বাহ্য বৈরাগ্য, বাতুলতা সকল ছাড়িয়া ।
যথাযোগ্য কার্য করে অনাসক্ত হঞা ॥ ২৪৩ ॥

bāhya vairāgya, vātulatā sakala chāḍiyā
yathā-yogya kārya kare anāsakta hañā

SYNONYMS

bāhya vairāgya—external renunciation; *vātulatā*—craziness; *sakala*—all; *chāḍiyā*—giving up; *yathā-yogya*—as it is befitting; *kārya*—duties; *kare*—performs; *anāsakta hañā*—being without attachment.

TRANSLATION

After returning home, Raghunātha dāsa gave up all craziness and external pseudo renunciation and engaged in his household duties without attachment.

TEXT 244

দেখি' তাঁর পিতা-মাতা বড় সুখ পাইল ।
তাঁহার আবরণ কিছু শিথিল হইল ॥ ২৪৪ ॥

dekhi' tāṅra pitā-mātā baḍa sukha pāila
tāṅhāra āvaraṇa kichu śithila ha-ila

SYNONYMS

dekhi'—seeing; *tāṅra*—his; *pitā-mātā*—father and mother; *baḍa*—very much; *sukha*—happiness; *pāila*—got; *tāṅhāra āvaraṇa*—strong vigilance upon him; *kichu*—something; *śithila ha-ila*—became slackened.

TRANSLATION

When Raghunātha dāsa's father and mother saw that their son was acting like a householder, they became very happy. Because of this, they slackened their guard.

PURPORT

When Raghunātha dāsa's father and mother saw that their son was no longer acting like a crazy fellow and was responsibly attending to his duties, they became very happy. The eleven people—five watchmen, four personal servants and two *brāhmaṇas*—who were guarding him became less strict in their vigilance. When Raghunātha dāsa actually took up his household affairs, his parents reduced the number of guards.

TEXTS 245-246

ইহাঁ প্রভু একত্র করি' সব ভক্তগণ ।
অদ্বৈত-নিত্যানন্দাদি যত ভক্তজন ॥ ২৪৫ ॥
সবা আলিঙ্গন করি' কহেন গোসাঞি ।
সবে আজ্ঞা দেহ'—আমি নীলাচলে যাই ॥ ২৪৬ ॥

ihāṅ prabhu ekatra kari' saba bhakta-gaṇa
advaita-nityānandādi yata bhakta-jana

sabā āliṅgana kari' kahena gosāñi
sabe ājñā deha'——āmi nīlācale yāi

SYNONYMS

ihāṅ—here (at Śāntipura); *prabhu*—Śrī Caitanya Mahāprabhu; *ekatra kari'*—assembling in one place; *saba bhakta-gaṇa*—all the devotees; *advaita-nityānanda-ādi*—headed by Advaita Ācārya and Nityānanda Prabhu; *yata bhakta-jana*—all the devotees; *sabā āliṅgana kari'*—embracing every one of them; *kahena gosāñi*—Śrī Caitanya Mahāprabhu said; *sabe*—all of you; *ājñā deha'*—just give Me permission; *āmi*—I; *nīlācale*—to Nīlācala, Jagannātha Purī; *yāi*—may go.

TRANSLATION

Meanwhile, at Śāntipura, Śrī Caitanya Mahāprabhu assembled all His devotees—headed by Advaita Ācārya and Nityānanda Prabhu—embraced them all and asked their permission to return to Jagannātha Purī.

TEXT 247

সবার সহিত ইহাঁ আমার হইল মিলন ।
এ বর্ষ 'নীলাদ্রি' কেহ না করিহ গমন ॥ ২৪৭ ॥

sabāra sahita ihāṅ āmāra ha-ila milana
e varṣa 'nīlādri' keha nā kariha gamana

SYNONYMS

sabāra sahita—with everyone; *ihāṅ*—here; *āmāra*—of Me; *ha-ila*—there was; *milana*—meeting; *e varṣa*—this year; *nīlādri*—to Jagannātha Purī; *keha*—any of you; *nā*—not; *kariha gamana*—go.

TRANSLATION

Because He had met them all at Śāntipura, Śrī Caitanya Mahāprabhu requested all the devotees not to go to Jagannātha Purī that year.

TEXT 248

তাহাঁ হৈতে অবশ্য আমি 'বৃন্দাবন' যাব ।
সবে আজ্ঞা দেহ', তবে নির্বিঘ্নে আসিব ॥ ২৪৮ ॥

tāhāṅ haite avaśya āmi 'vṛndāvana' yāba
sabe ājñā deha', tabe nirvighne āsiba

SYNONYMS

tāhāṅ haite—from there; *avaśya*—certainly; *āmi*—I; *vṛndāvana yāba*—shall go to Vṛndāvana; *sabe*—all of you; *ājñā deha'*—give Me permission; *tabe*—then; *nirvighne*—without disturbance; *āsiba*—I shall come back.

TRANSLATION

Śrī Caitanya Mahāprabhu said, "I shall certainly go to Vṛndāvana from Jagannātha Purī. If all of you give Me permission, I shall return here again without difficulty."

TEXT 249

মাতার চরণে ধরি' বহু বিনয় করিল ।
বৃন্দাবন যাইতে তাঁর আজ্ঞা লইল ॥ ২৪৯ ॥

mātāra caraṇe dhari' bahu vinaya karila
vṛndāvana yāite tāṅra ājñā la-ila

SYNONYMS

mātāra—of Śacīmātā; *caraṇe*—the feet; *dhari'*—catching; *bahu vinaya karila*—submitted most humbly; *vṛndāvana yāite*—to go to Vṛndāvana; *tāṅra*—her; *ājñā*—permission; *la-ila*—took.

TRANSLATION

Clasping the feet of His mother, Śrī Caitanya Mahāprabhu very humbly requested her permission. Thus she gave Him leave to go to Vṛndāvana.

TEXT 250

তবে নবদ্বীপে তাঁরে দিল পাঠাঞা।
নীলাদ্রি চলিলা সঙ্গে ভক্তগণ লঞা ॥ ২৫০ ॥

tabe navadvīpe tāṅre dila pāṭhāñā
nīlādri calilā saṅge bhakta-gaṇa lañā

SYNONYMS

tabe—thereafter; *navadvīpe*—to Navadvīpa; *tāṅre*—her; *dila pāṭhāñā*—sent back; *nīlādri*—to Jagannātha Purī; *calilā*—departed; *saṅge*—with Him; *bhakta-gaṇa lañā*—taking all the devotees.

TRANSLATION

Śrīmatī Śacīdevī was sent back to Navadvīpa, and the Lord and His devotees started for Jagannātha Purī, Nīlādri.

TEXT 251

সেই সব লোক পথে করেন সেবন।
সুখে নীলাচল আইলা শচীর নন্দন ॥ ২৫১ ॥

sei saba loka pathe karena sevana
sukhe nīlācala āilā śacīra nandana

SYNONYMS

sei saba loka—all those persons; *pathe*—on the road; *karena sevana*—rendered all service; *sukhe*—in great happiness; *nīlācala*—to Jagannātha Purī; *āilā*—came back; *śacīra nandana*—the son of mother Śacī.

TRANSLATION

The devotees who accompanied Śrī Caitanya Mahāprabhu rendered all kinds of service on the way to Nīlācala, Jagannātha Purī. Thus in great happiness the Lord returned.

TEXT 252

প্রভু আসি' জগন্নাথ দরশন কৈল।
'মহাপ্রভু আইলা'—গ্রামে কোলাহল হৈল ॥ ২৫২ ॥

prabhu āsi' jagannātha daraśana kaila
'mahāprabhu āilā'——grāme kolāhala haila

SYNONYMS

prabhu—Śrī Caitanya Mahāprabhu; *āsi'*—returning; *jagannātha*—to Lord Jagannātha; *daraśana*—visit; *kaila*—made; *mahāprabhu āilā*—Śrī Caitanya Mahāprabhu has come back; *grāme*—in the town; *kolāhala haila*—there was great agitation.

TRANSLATION

When Śrī Caitanya Mahāprabhu arrived in Jagannātha Purī, He visited the temple of the Lord. News then spread all over the city that He had returned.

TEXT 253

আনন্দিত ভক্তগণ আসিয়া মিলিলা ।
প্রেম-আলিঙ্গন প্রভু সবারে করিলা ॥ ২৫৩ ॥

ānandita bhakta-gaṇa āsiyā mililā
prema-āliṅgana prabhu sabāre karilā

SYNONYMS

ānandita—very pleased; *bhakta-gaṇa*—all the devotees; *āsiyā*—came; *mililā*—met; *prema-āliṅgana*—embracing in love; *prabhu*—the Lord; *sabāre*—to all devotees; *karilā*—offered.

TRANSLATION

All the devotees then came and met the Lord with great happiness. The Lord also embraced each of them in great ecstatic love.

TEXT 254

কাশীমিশ্র, রামানন্দ, প্রদ্যুম্ন, সার্বভৌম ।
বাণীনাথ, শিখি-আদি যত ভক্তগণ ॥ ২৫৪ ॥

kāśī-miśra, rāmānanda, pradyumna, sārvabhauma
vāṇīnātha, śikhi-ādi yata bhakta-gaṇa

SYNONYMS

kāśī-miśra—Kāśī Miśra; *rāmānanda*—Rāmānanda; *pradyumna*—Pradyumna; *sārvabhauma*—Sārvabhauma; *vāṇīnātha*—Vāṇīnātha; *śikhi-ādi*—Śikhi Māhiti and others; *yata bhakta-gaṇa*—all the devotees.

TRANSLATION

Kāśī Miśra, Rāmānanda Rāya, Pradyumna, Sārvabhauma Bhaṭṭācārya, Vāṇīnātha Rāya, Śikhi Māhiti and all the other devotees met Śrī Caitanya Mahāprabhu.

TEXT 255

গদাধর-পণ্ডিত আসি' প্রভুরে মিলিলা ।
সবার অগ্রেতে প্রভু কহিতে লাগিলা ॥ ২৫৫ ॥

gadādhara-paṇḍita āsi' prabhure mililā
sabāra agrete prabhu kahite lāgilā

SYNONYMS

gadādhara-paṇḍita—Gadādhara Paṇḍita; *āsi'*—coming; *prabhure mililā*—met the Lord; *sabāra agrete*—in front of all the devotees; *prabhu*—the Lord; *kahite lāgilā*—began to say.

TRANSLATION

Gadādhara Paṇḍita also came and met the Lord. Then, before all the devotees, Śrī Caitanya Mahāprabhu began to speak as follows.

TEXT 256

'বৃন্দাবন যাব আমি গৌড়দেশ দিয়া ।
নিজ-মাতার, গঙ্গার চরণ দেখিয়া ॥ ২৫৬ ॥

'vṛndāvana yāba āmi gauḍa-deśa diyā
nija-mātāra, gaṅgāra caraṇa dekhiyā

SYNONYMS

vṛndāvana yāba—shall go to Vṛndāvana; *āmi*—I; *gauḍa-deśa diyā*—through Bengal; *nija-mātāra*—of My own mother; *gaṅgāra*—of the River Ganges; *caraṇa*—the feet; *dekhiyā*—seeing.

TRANSLATION

"It was My decision to go to Vṛndāvana through Bengal in order to see My mother and the River Ganges.

TEXT 257

এত মতে করি' কৈলুঁ গৌড়েরে গমন ।
সহস্রেক সঙ্গে হৈল নিজ-ভক্তগণ ॥ ২৫৭ ॥

eta mate kari' kailuṅ gauḍere gamana
sahasreka saṅge haila nija-bhakta-gaṇa

SYNONYMS

eta—such; *mate*—decision; *kari'*—making; *kailuṅ*—I did; *gauḍere*—to Bengal; *gamana*—going; *sahasreka*—thousands of men; *saṅge*—with Me; *haila*—there were; *nija-bhakta-gaṇa*—My own devotees.

TRANSLATION

"Thus I went to Bengal, but thousands of devotees began to follow Me.

TEXT 258

লক্ষ লক্ষ লোক আইসে কৌতুক দেখিতে।
লোকের সংঘট্টে পথ না পারি চলিতে ॥ ২৫৮ ॥

lakṣa lakṣa loka āise kauṭuka dekhite
lokera saṅghaṭṭe patha nā pāri calite

SYNONYMS

lakṣa lakṣa loka—many thousands of people; *āise*—came; *kauṭuka*—out of curiosity; *dekhite*—to see; *lokera saṅghaṭṭe*—by the assembly of so many men; *patha*—the road; *nā pāri*—I was not able; *calite*—to pass through.

TRANSLATION

"Many hundreds and thousands of people came to see Me out of curiosity, and due to such a large crowd I could not travel very freely on the road.

TEXT 259

যথা রহি, তথা ঘর-প্রাচীর হয় চূর্ণ।
যথা নেত্র পড়ে তথা লোক দেখি পূর্ণ ॥ ২৫৯ ॥

yathā rahi, tathā ghara-prācīra haya cūrṇa
yathā netra paḍe tathā loka dekhi pūrṇa

SYNONYMS

yathā rahi—wherever I stayed; *tathā*—there; *ghara-prācīra*—the building and the boundary walls; *haya*—became; *cūrṇa*—broken; *yathā*—wherever; *netra*—the eyes; *paḍe*—fell; *tathā*—there; *loka*—people; *dekhi*—I see; *pūrṇa*—filled.

TRANSLATION

"Indeed, the crowd was so large that the house and the boundary walls of the house where I stayed were destroyed, and wherever I looked I could see only large crowds.

TEXT 260

কষ্টে-সৃষ্ট্যে করি' গেলাঙ রামকেলি-গ্রাম ।
আমার ঠাঞি আইলা 'রূপ' 'সনাতন' নাম ॥ ২৬০ ॥

kaṣṭe-sṛṣṭye kari' gelāṅa rāmakeli-grāma
āmāra ṭhāñi āilā 'rūpa' 'sanātana' nāma

SYNONYMS

kaṣṭe-sṛṣṭye—with great difficulty; *kari'*—doing; *gelāṅa*—I went; *rāmakeli-grāma*—to the village of Rāmakeli; *āmāra ṭhāñi*—before me; *āilā*—came; *rūpa sanātana nāma*—the two brothers named Rūpa and Sanātana.

TRANSLATION

"With great difficulty I went to the town of Rāmakeli, where I met two brothers named Rūpa and Sanātana.

TEXT 261

দুই ভাই—ভক্তরাজ, কৃষ্ণকৃপা-পাত্র ।
ব্যবহারে—রাজমন্ত্রী হয় রাজপাত্র ॥ ২৬১ ॥

dui bhāi——bhakta-rāja, kṛṣṇa-kṛpā-pātra
vyavahāre——rāja-mantrī haya rāja-pātra

SYNONYMS

dui bhāi—two brothers; *bhakta-rāja*—kings of devotees; *kṛṣṇa-kṛpā-pātra*—suitable candidates for Kṛṣṇa's mercy; *vyavahāre*—in behavior; *rāja-mantrī*—ministers of the government; *haya*—are; *rāja-pātra*—government officers.

TRANSLATION

"These two brothers are great devotees and suitable recipients of Kṛṣṇa's mercy, but in their ordinary dealings they are government officials, ministers to the King.

TEXT 262

বিদ্যা-ভক্তি-বুদ্ধি-বলে পরম প্রবীণ ।
তবু আপনাকে মানে তৃণ হৈতে হীন ॥ ২৬২ ॥

vidyā-bhakti-buddhi-bale parama pravīṇa
tabu āpanāke māne tṛṇa haite hīna

SYNONYMS

vidyā—education; *bhakti*—devotion; *buddhi*—and intelligence; *bale*—in strength; *parama*—very; *pravīṇa*—experienced; *tabu*—still; *āpanāke*—themselves; *māne*—they think; *tṛṇa*—a straw; *haite*—than; *hīna*—lower.

TRANSLATION

"Śrīla Rūpa and Sanātana are very experienced in education, devotional service, intelligence and strength, yet they think themselves inferior to straw in the street.

TEXTS 263-264

তাঁর দৈন্য দেখি' শুনি' পাষাণ বিদরে ।
আমি তুষ্ট হঞা তবে কহিলুঁ দোঁহারে ॥ ২৬৩ ॥
"উত্তম হঞা হীন করি' মানহ আপনারে ।
অচিরে করিবে কৃষ্ণ তোমার উদ্ধারে ॥" ২৬৪ ॥

tāṅra dainya dekhi' śuni' pāṣāṇa bidare
āmi tuṣṭa hañā tabe kahiluṅ doṅhāre

"uttama hañā hīna kari' mānaha āpanāre
acire karibe kṛṣṇa tomāra uddhāre"

SYNONYMS

tāṅra dainya dekhi'—by seeing their humility; *śuni'*—or even hearing about it; *pāṣāṇa*—stone; *bidare*—becomes melted; *āmi*—I; *tuṣṭa hañā*—being very pleased; *tabe*—then; *kahiluṅ doṅhāre*—said to both of them; *uttama hañā*—being actually superior in every respect; *hīna*—inferior; *kari'*—proposing as; *mānaha*—you accept; *āpanāre*—yourselves; *acire*—very soon; *karibe*—will do; *kṛṣṇa*—Lord Kṛṣṇa; *tomāra*—of you; *uddhāre*—liberation.

TRANSLATION

"Indeed, the humility of these two brothers could even melt stone. Because I was very pleased with their behavior, I told them, 'Although you are both very exalted, you consider yourselves inferior, and because of this, Kṛṣṇa will very soon deliver you.'

PURPORT

Such are the qualifications of a pure devotee. Materially one may be very opulent, experienced, influential and educated, but if one still thinks himself lower than straw in the street, one attracts the attention of Śrī Caitanya Mahāprabhu or Lord Kṛṣṇa. Although Mahārāja Pratāparudra was a king, he took up a broom to cleanse the road for Lord Jagannātha's Ratha chariot. Because of this humble service, Śrī Caitanya Mahāprabhu was very pleased with the King, and for that reason the Lord embraced him. According to Śrī Caitanya Mahāprabhu's instructions, a devotee should never be puffed up by material power. He should know that material power is the result of one's past good activities (*karma*) and is consequently transient. At any moment all one's material opulence can be finished; therefore a devotee is never proud of such opulence. He is always humble and meek, considering himself lower than a piece of straw. Because of this, the devotees are eligible to return home, back to Godhead.

TEXTS 265-266

এত কহি' আমি যবে বিদায় তাঁরে দিল ।
গমনকালে সনাতন 'প্রহেলী' কহিল ॥ ২৬৫ ॥
যাঁর সঙ্গে হয় এই লোক লক্ষ কোটি ।
বৃন্দাবন যাইবার এই নহে পরিপাটী ॥ ২৬৬ ॥

eta kahi' āmi yabe vidāya tāṅre dila
gamana-kāle sanātana 'prahelī' kahila

yāṅra saṅge haya ei loka lakṣa koṭi
vṛndāvana yāibāra ei nahe paripāṭī

SYNONYMS

eta kahi'—saying this; *āmi*—I; *yabe*—when; *vidāya*—farewell; *tāṅre*—unto them; *dila*—gave; *gamana-kāle*—while going; *sanātana*—Sanātana; *prahelī*—enigma; *kahila*—said; *yāṅra saṅge*—with whom; *haya*—is; *ei*—this; *loka*—crowd of people; *lakṣa koṭi*—hundreds of thousands; *vṛndāvana*—to Vṛndāvana-dhāma; *yāibāra*—for going; *ei*—this; *nahe*—not; *paripāṭī*—the method.

TRANSLATION

"After speaking to them in this way, I bade them farewell. As I was leaving, Sanātana told Me, 'It is not appropriate for one to be followed by a crowd of thousands when one goes to Vṛndāvana.'

TEXT 267

তবু আমি শুনিলুঁ মাত্র, না কৈলুঁ অবধান ।
প্রাতে চলি' আইলাঙ 'কানাইর নাটশালা'-গ্রাম ॥২৬৭॥

tabu āmi śuniluṅ mātra, nā kailuṅ avadhāna
prāte cali' āilāṅa 'kānāira nāṭaśālā'-grāma

SYNONYMS

tabu—still; *āmi*—I; *śuniluṅ*—heard; *mātra*—only; *nā*—not; *kailuṅ*—paid; *avadhāna*—any attention; *prāte*—in the morning; *cali' āilāṅa*—I walked; *kānāira nāṭaśālā*—to Kānāi Nāṭaśālā; *grāma*—the place.

TRANSLATION

"Although I heard this, I did not pay it any attention. In the morning, however, I went to the place named Kānāi Nāṭaśālā.

TEXT 268

রাত্রিকালে মনে আমি বিচার করিল ।
সনাতন মোরে কিবা 'প্রহেলী' কহিল ॥ ২৬৮ ॥

rātri-kāle mane āmi vicāra karila
sanātana more kibā 'prahelī' kahila

SYNONYMS

rātri-kāle—at night; *mane*—in the mind; *āmi*—I; *vicāra karila*—considered; *sanātana*—Sanātana; *more*—unto Me; *kibā*—what; *prahelī*—enigma; *kahila*—spoke.

TRANSLATION

"At night, however, I considered what Sanātana had told Me.

TEXT 269

ভালত' কহিল,—মোর এত লোক সঙ্গে ।
লোক দেখি' কহিবে মোরে—'এই এক ঢঙ্গে' ॥২৬৯॥

bhālata' kahila,——mora eta loka saṅge
loka dekhi' kahibe more——'ei eka ḍhaṅge'

SYNONYMS

bhālata' kahila—he has spoken very well; *mora*—of Me; *eta*—so much; *loka*—crowd; *saṅge*—in the company; *loka*—the people; *dekhi'*—seeing; *kahibe more*—will speak about Me; *ei*—this; *eka*—one; *ḍhaṅge*—imposter.

TRANSLATION

"I decided that Sanātana had spoken very well. I was certainly being followed by a large crowd, and when people would see so many men, they would surely rebuke Me, saying, 'Here is another imposter.'

TEXT 270

'দুর্লভ' "দুর্গম' সেই 'নির্জন' বৃন্দাবন ।
একাকী যাইব, কিবা সঙ্গে একজন ॥ ২৭০ ॥

'durlabha' 'durgama' sei 'nirjana' vṛndāvana
ekākī yāiba, kibā saṅge eka-jana

SYNONYMS

durlabha—very rare; *durgama*—invincible; *sei*—that; *nirjana*—solitary; *vṛndāvana*—the land of Vṛndāvana; *ekākī*—alone; *yāiba*—I shall go; *kibā*—or; *saṅge*—with Me; *eka-jana*—only one person.

TRANSLATION

"I then began to consider that Vṛndāvana is a very solitary place. It is invincible and very difficult to attain. I therefore decided to go there alone or, at the most, take only one person with Me.

TEXT 271

মাধবেন্দ্রপুরী তথা গেলা 'একেশ্বরে' ।
দুগ্ধদান-চ্ছলে কৃষ্ণ সাক্ষাৎ দিল তাঁরে ॥ ২৭১ ॥

mādhavendra-purī tathā gelā 'ekeśvare'
dugdha-dāna-cchale kṛṣṇa sākṣāt dila tāṅre

SYNONYMS

mādhavendra-purī—Mādhavendra Purī; *tathā*—there; *gelā*—went; *ekeśvare*—alone; *dugdha-dāna-chale*—on the plea of giving milk in charity; *kṛṣṇa*—Lord Kṛṣṇa; *sākṣāt*—direct audience; *dila*—gave; *tāṅre*—unto him.

TRANSLATION

"Mādhavendra Purī went to Vṛndāvana alone, and Kṛṣṇa, on the pretext of giving him milk, granted him an audience.

TEXT 272

বাদিয়ার বাজি পাতি' চলিলাঙ তথারে ।
বহু-সঙ্গে বৃন্দাবন গমন না করে ॥ ২৭২ ॥

bādiyāra bāji pāti' calilāṅa tathāre
bahu-saṅge vṛndāvana gamana nā kare

SYNONYMS

bādiyāra—of a gypsy; *bāji*—the magic; *pāti'*—demonstrating; *calilāṅa*—I went; *tathāre*—there; *bahu-saṅge*—with many men; *vṛndāvana*—to Vṛndāvana-dhāma; *gamana*—going; *nā kare*—no one does.

TRANSLATION

"I then understood that I was going to Vṛndāvana like a magician with his show, and this is certainly not good. No one should go to Vṛndāvana with so many men.

TEXT 273

একা যাইব, কিবা সঙ্গে ভৃত্য একজন ।
তবে সে শোভয় বৃন্দাবনের গমন ॥ ২৭৩ ॥

ekā yāiba, kibā saṅge bhṛtya eka-jana
tabe se śobhaya vṛndāvanera gamana

SYNONYMS

ekā yāiba—I shall go alone; *kibā*—or; *saṅge*—with Me; *bhṛtya*—servant; *eka-jana*—one; *tabe*—in that way; *se*—that; *śobhaya*—is beautiful; *vṛndāvanera gamana*—going to Vṛndāvana.

TRANSLATION

"I have therefore resolved to go alone or, at the utmost, with one servant. In this way, My journey to Vṛndāvana will be beautiful.

TEXT 274

বৃন্দাবন যাব কাহাঁ 'একাকী' হঞা !
সৈন্য সঙ্গে চলিয়াছি ঢাক বাজাঞা ! ২৭৪ ॥

vṛndāvana yāba kāhāṅ 'ekākī' hañā!
sainya saṅge caliyāchi ḍhāka bājāñā!

SYNONYMS

vṛndāvana yāba—I should go to Vṛndāvana; *kāhāṅ*—whereas; *ekākī hañā*—being alone; *sainya*—soldiers; *saṅge*—along with; *caliyāchi*—I am going; *ḍhāka bājāñā*—beating the drum.

TRANSLATION

"I thought, 'Instead of going to Vṛndāvana alone, I am going with soldiers and the beating of drums.'

TEXT 275

ধিক্, ধিক্ আপনাকে বলি' হইলাঙ অস্থির ।
নিবৃত্ত হঞা পুনঃ আইলাঙ গঙ্গাতীর ॥ ২৭৫ ॥

dhik, dhik āpanāke bali' ha-ilāṅa asthira
nivṛtta hañā punaḥ āilāṅa gaṅgā-tīra

SYNONYMS

dhik dhik—fie! fie!; *āpanāke*—on Myself; *bali'*—saying; *ha-ilāṅa*—I became; *asthira*—agitated; *nivṛtta hañā*—stopping such an action; *punaḥ*—again; *āilāṅa*—I came back; *gaṅgā-tīra*—to the bank of the Ganges.

TRANSLATION

"I therefore said, 'Fie upon Me!' and being very agitated, I returned to the banks of the Ganges.

TEXT 276

ভক্তগণে রাখিয়া আইনু নিজ নিজ স্থানে ।
আমা-সঙ্গে আইলা সবে পাঁচ-ছয় জনে ॥ ২৭৬ ॥

bhakta-gaṇe rākhiyā āinu nija nija sthāne
āmā-saṅge āilā sabe pāṅca-chaya jane

SYNONYMS

bhakta-gaṇe—the devotees; *rākhiyā*—keeping; *āinu*—I came; *nija nija sthāne*—in their respective places; *āmā-saṅge*—with Me; *āilā*—came; *sabe*—only; *pāṅca-chaya jane*—five or six men.

TRANSLATION

"I then left all the devotees there and brought only five or six persons with Me.

TEXT 277

নির্বিঘ্নে এবে কৈছে যাইব বৃন্দাবনে ।
সবে মেলি' যুক্তি দেহ' হঞা পরসন্নে ॥ ২৭৭ ॥

nirvighne ebe kaiche yāiba vṛndāvane
sabe meli' yukti deha' hañā parasanne

SYNONYMS

nirvighne—without obstacles; *ebe*—now; *kaiche*—how; *yāiba*—I shall go; *vṛndāvane*—to Vṛndāvana; *sabe meli'*—altogether; *yukti deha'*—give Me consultation; *hañā parasanne*—being very pleased with Me.

TRANSLATION

"Now I wish that you all will be pleased with Me and give Me good consultation. Tell Me how I shall be able to go to Vṛndāvana without impediments.

TEXT 278

গদাধরে ছাড়ি' গেনু, ইঁহো দুঃখ পাইল ।
সেই হেতু বৃন্দাবন যাইতে নারিল ॥ ২৭৮ ॥

gadādhare chāḍi' genu, iṅho duḥkha pāila
sei hetu vṛndāvana yāite nārila

SYNONYMS

gadādhare chāḍi'—leaving aside Gadādhara Paṇḍita; *genu*—I went; *iṅho*—Gadādhara Paṇḍita; *duḥkha pāila*—became unhappy; *sei hetu*—for that reason; *vṛndāvana*—to Vṛndāvana-dhāma; *yāite nārila*—I was unable to go.

TRANSLATION

"I left Gadādhara Paṇḍita here, and he became very unhappy. For this reason I could not go to Vṛndāvana."

TEXT 279

তবে গদাধর-পণ্ডিত প্রেমাবিষ্ট হঞা ।
প্রভু-পদ ধরি' কহে বিনয় করিয়া ॥ ২৭৯ ॥

tabe gadādhara-paṇḍita premāviṣṭa hañā
prabhu-pada dhari' kahe vinaya kariyā

SYNONYMS

tabe—thereupon; *gadādhara paṇḍita*—Gadādhara Paṇḍita; *prema-āviṣṭa hañā*—being absorbed in ecstatic love; *prabhu-pada dhari'*—catching hold of the lotus feet of the Lord; *kahe*—says; *vinaya kariyā*—with great humility.

TRANSLATION

Being encouraged by Śrī Caitanya Mahāprabhu's words, Gadādhara Paṇḍita became absorbed in ecstatic love. Immediately clasping the lotus feet of the Lord, he began to speak with great humility.

TEXT 280

তুমি যাহাঁ-যাহাঁ রহ, তাহাঁ 'বৃন্দাবন' ।
তাহাঁ যমুনা, গঙ্গা, সর্বতীর্থগণ ॥ ২৮০ ॥

tumi yāhāṅ-yāhāṅ raha, tāhāṅ 'vṛndāvana'
tāhāṅ yamunā, gaṅgā, sarva-tīrtha-gaṇa

SYNONYMS

tumi—You; *yāhāṅ-yāhāṅ*—wherever; *raha*—stay; *tāhāṅ vṛndāvana*—that place is Vṛndāvana; *tāhāṅ*—there; *yamunā*—the River Yamunā; *gaṅgā*—the River Gaṅgā; *sarva-tīrṭha-gaṇa*—all other holy places of pilgrimage.

TRANSLATION

Gadādhara Paṇḍita said, "Wherever You stay is Vṛndāvana, as well as the River Yamunā, the River Ganges and all other places of pilgrimage.

TEXT 281

তবু বৃন্দাবন যাহ' লোক শিখাইতে।
সেইত করিবে, তোমার যেই লয় চিত্তে ॥ ২৮১ ॥

tabu vṛndāvana yāha' loka śikhāite
seita karibe, tomāra yei laya citte

SYNONYMS

tabu—still; *vṛndāvana yāha'*—You go to Vṛndāvana; *loka śikhāite*—to teach the people in general; *seita*—that; *karibe*—You will do; *tomāra*—of You; *yei*—what; *laya*—takes; *citte*—in the mind.

TRANSLATION

"Although wherever You stay is Vṛndāvana, You still go to Vṛndāvana just to instruct people. Otherwise, You do whatever You think best."

PURPORT

It was not essential for Śrī Caitanya Mahāprabhu to go to Vṛndāvana, for wherever He stayed was immediately converted to Vṛndāvana. Indeed, there was also the River Ganges, the River Yamunā and all other places of pilgrimage. This was also expressed by Śrī Caitanya Mahāprabhu Himself when He danced in the Ratha-yātrā. At that time He said that His very mind was Vṛndāvana (*mora-mana——vṛndāvana*). Because His mind was Vṛndāvana, all the pastimes of Rādhā and Kṛṣṇa were taking place within Himself. Nonetheless, just to teach people, He visited *bhauma-vṛndāvana,* Vṛndāvana-dhāma in this material world. In this way the Lord instructed everyone to visit Vṛndāvana-dhāma, which is a very holy place. Materialists consider Vṛndāvana-dhāma an unclean city because there are many monkeys and dogs there, and along the bank of the Yamunā there is refuse. Some time ago, a materialistic man asked me, "Why are you living in Vṛndāvana? Why have you selected such a dirty place to live after retiring?" Such a person cannot understand that Vṛndāvana-dhāma is always a representation of the original Vṛndāvana-dhāma. Consequently Vṛndāvana-dhāma is as worshipable as Lord Kṛṣṇa. *Ārādhyo bhagavān vrajeśa-tanayas tad-dhāma vṛndāvanam:* according to Śrī Caitanya Mahāprabhu's philosophy, Lord Śrī Kṛṣṇa and His abode, Vṛndāvana, are equally worshipable. Sometimes materialistic people who have no spiritual understanding go to Vṛndāvana as tourists. One who goes to Vṛndāvana with such materialistic vision cannot derive any spiritual benefit. Such a person is not convinced that Kṛṣṇa and Vṛndāvana are identical. Since they are identical, Vṛndāvana is as worshipable as Lord Kṛṣṇa. Śrī Caitanya Mahāprabhu's vision (*mora-mana——vṛndāvana*) is different from the vision of an ordinary materialistic person. At the Ratha-yātrā festival, Śrī Caitanya Mahāprabhu, absorbed in the ecstasy of Śrīmatī Rādhārāṇī, dragged Lord Kṛṣṇa back to Vṛndāvana-dhāma. Śrī Caitanya Mahāprabhu spoke of this in the verses beginning *āhuś ca te* (*Madhya* 13.136).

In *Śrīmad-Bhāgavatam* (10.84.13) it is stated:

yasyātma-buddhiḥ kuṇape tridhātuke
svadhīḥ kalatrādiṣu bhauma ijya-dhīḥ
yat-tīrtha-buddhiḥ salile na karhicij
janeṣv abhijñeṣu sa eva gokharaḥ

"A human being who identifies this body made of three elements with his self, who considers the by-products of the body to be his kinsmen, who considers the land of birth as worshipable, and who goes to the place of pilgrimage simply to take a bath rather than meet men of transcendental knowledge there, is to be considered like an ass or a cow."

Śrī Caitanya Mahāprabhu personally renovated Vṛndāvana-dhāma and advised His chief disciples, Rūpa and Sanātana, to develop it and open it to attract the spiritual vision of the general populace. At present there are about five thousand temples in Vṛndāvana, and still our society, the International Society for Krishna Consciousness, is constructing a huge, magnificent temple for the worship of Lord Balarāma, Rādhā-Kṛṣṇa and Guru-Gaurāṅga. Since there is no prominent Kṛṣṇa-Balarāma temple in Vṛndāvana, we are attempting to construct one so that people will be attracted to Kṛṣṇa-Balarāma, or Nitāi-Gauracandra. *Vrajendra-nandana yei, śacī suta haila sei.* Narottama dāsa Ṭhākura says that Balarāma and the son of Mahārāja Nanda have advented Themselves as Gaura-Nitāi. To propagate this fundamental principle, we are establishing a Kṛṣṇa-Balarāma temple to broadcast to the world that worship of Gaura-Nitāi is the same as worship of Kṛṣṇa-Balarāma.

Although it is very difficult to enter into the Rādhā-Kṛṣṇa pastimes, most of the devotees of Vṛndāvana are attracted to the Rādhā-Kṛṣṇa *līlā.* However, since Nitāi-Gauracandra are direct incarnations of Balarāma and Kṛṣṇa, we can be directly in touch with Lord Balarāma and Lord Kṛṣṇa through Śrī Caitanya Mahāprabhu and Nityānanda Prabhu. Those who are highly elevated in Kṛṣṇa consciousness can enter into the pastimes of Rādhā-Kṛṣṇa through the mercy of Śrī Caitanya Mahāprabhu. It is said: *śrī-kṛṣṇa-caitanya rādhā-kṛṣṇa nahe anya.* Śrī Kṛṣṇa Caitanya Mahāprabhu is a combination of Rādhā and Kṛṣṇa.

Sometimes materialists, forgetting the pastimes of Rādhā-Kṛṣṇa and Kṛṣṇa-Balarāma, go to Vṛndāvana, accept the land's spiritual facilities and engage in material activity. This is against the teachings of Śrī Caitanya Mahāprabhu. The *prākṛta-sahajiyās* proclaim themselves *vraja-vāsī* or *dhāma-vāsī,* but they are mainly engaged in sense gratification. Thus they become more and more implicated in the materialistic way of life. Those who are pure devotees in Kṛṣṇa consciousness condemn their activities. The eternal *vraja-vāsīs* like Svarūpa Dāmodara did not even come to Vṛndāvana-dhāma. Śrī Puṇḍarīka Vidyānidhi, Śrī Haridāsa Ṭhākura, Śrīvāsa Paṇḍita, Śivānanda Sena, Śrī Rāmānanda Rāya, Śrī Śikhi Māhiti, Śrī Mādhavīdevī and Śrī Gadādhara Paṇḍita Gosvāmī never visited Vṛndāvana-dhāma. Śrīla Bhaktisiddhānta Sarasvatī Ṭhākura points out that we have no authorized documents stating that these exalted personalities visited Vṛndāvana. Nonetheless, we find many nondevotees, Māyāvādī *sannyāsīs, prākṛta-sahajiyās,* fruitive workers, mental speculators and many others with material motives going to Vṛndāvana to live. Many of these people go there to solve their economic problems by becoming beggars. Although anyone living in Vṛndāvana somehow or other is benefited, the real Vṛndāvana is appreciated only by a pure devotee. As stated in *Brahma-saṁhitā: premāñjana-cchurita-bhakti-vilocanena.* When one has purified eyes, he can see that Śrī Vṛndāvana and the original Goloka Vṛndāvana planet in the spiritual sky are identical.

Śrīla Narottama dāsa Ṭhākura, Śrīnivāsa Ācārya, Śrī Jagannātha dāsa Bābājī Mahārāja, Śrī Bhagavān dāsa Bābājī Mahārāja, Śrīla Gaurakiśora dāsa Bābājī Mahārāja and later Śrī Bhaktivinoda Ṭhākura of Calcutta always engaged in *nāma-bhajana* and certainly did not live anywhere but Vṛndāvana. Presently, the members of the Hare Kṛṣṇa movement throughout the world live in materially opulent cities, such as London, New York, Los Angeles, Paris, Moscow, Zurich and Stockholm. However, we are satisfied with following in the footsteps of Śrīla Bhaktivinoda Ṭhākura and other *ācāryas.* Because we live in the temples of Rādhā-Kṛṣṇa and continuously hold *hari-nāma-saṅkīrtana*—the chanting of Hare Kṛṣṇa—we consequently live in Vṛndāvana and nowhere else. We are also following in the footsteps of Śrī Caitanya Mahāprabhu by attempting to construct a temple in Vṛndāvana for our disciples throughout the world to visit.

TEXT 282

এই আগে আইলা, প্রভু, বর্ষার চারি মাস ।
এই চারি মাস কর নীলাচলে বাস ॥ ২৮২ ॥

ei āge āilā, prabhu, varṣāra cāri māsa
ei cāri māsa kara nīlācale vāsa

SYNONYMS

ei—just; *āge*—ahead; *āilā*—have come; *prabhu*—my Lord; *varṣāra cāri māsa*—the four months of the rainy season; *ei cāri māsa*—these four months; *kara*—just do; *nīlācale*—at Jagannātha Purī; *vāsa*—living.

TRANSLATION

Taking this opportunity, Gadādhara Paṇḍita said, "Just now the four months of the rainy season have begun. You should therefore spend the next four months in Jagannātha Purī.

TEXT 283

পাছে সেই আচরিবা, যেই তোমার মন ।
আপন-ইচ্ছায় চল, রহ,— কে করে বারণ ॥" ২৮৩ ॥

pāche sei ācaribā, yei tomāra mana
āpana-icchāya cala, raha,——ke kare vāraṇa"

SYNONYMS

pāche—thereafter; *sei*—that; *ācaribā*—You will do; *yei*—what; *tomāra mana*—You like; *āpana-icchāya*—by Your sweet will; *cala*—You always go; *raha*—You remain; *ke*—who; *kare vāraṇa*—can stop You.

TRANSLATION

"After remaining here for four months, You may be free to do as You like. Actually no one can stop You from going or remaining."

TEXT 284

শুনি' সব ভক্ত কহে প্রভুর চরণে ।
সবাকার ইচ্ছা পণ্ডিত কৈল নিবেদনে ॥ ২৮৪ ॥

śuni' saba bhakta kahe prabhura caraṇe
sabākāra icchā paṇḍita kaila nivedane

SYNONYMS

śuni'—hearing; *saba*—all; *bhakta*—devotees; *kahe*—said; *prabhura caraṇe*—unto the lotus feet of the Lord; *sabākāra icchā*—everyone's desire; *paṇḍita*—Gadādhara Paṇḍita; *kaila*—has made; *nivedane*—submission.

TRANSLATION

Upon hearing this statement, the devotees present at the lotus feet of Śrī Caitanya Mahāprabhu stated that Gadādhara Paṇḍita had properly presented their desire.

TEXT 285

সবার ইচ্ছায় প্রভু চারি মাস রহিলা ।
শুনিয়া প্রতাপরুদ্র আনন্দিত হৈলা ॥ ২৮৫ ॥

sabāra icchāya prabhu cāri māsa rahilā
śuniyā pratāparudra ānandita hailā

SYNONYMS

sabāra icchāya—because of everyone's desire; *prabhu*—Śrī Caitanya Mahāprabhu; *cāri māsa*—for four months; *rahilā*—remained; *śuniyā*—hearing; *pratāparudra*—King Pratāparudra; *ānandita hailā*—became very, very happy.

TRANSLATION

Being requested by all the devotees, Śrī Caitanya Mahāprabhu agreed to remain at Jagannātha Purī for four months. Hearing this, King Pratāparudra became very happy.

TEXT 286

সেই দিন গদাধর কৈল নিমন্ত্রণ ।
তাহাঁ ভিক্ষা কৈল প্রভু লঞা ভক্তগণ ॥ ২৮৬ ॥

sei dina gadādhara kaila nimantraṇa
tāhāṅ bhikṣā kaila prabhu lañā bhakta-gaṇa

SYNONYMS

sei dina—that day; *gadādhara*—Gadādhara Paṇḍita; *kaila nimantraṇa*—gave an invitation; *tāhāṅ*—at his place; *bhikṣā kaila*—took lunch; *prabhu*—Śrī Caitanya Mahāprabhu; *lañā*—with; *bhakta-gaṇa*—His devotees.

TRANSLATION

That day Gadādhara Paṇḍita extended an invitation to Śrī Caitanya Mahāprabhu, and the Lord took His lunch at his place with the other devotees.

TEXT 287

ভিক্ষাতে পণ্ডিতের স্নেহ, প্রভুর আস্বাদন ।
মনুষ্যের শক্ত্যে দুই না যায় বর্ণন ॥ ২৮৭ ॥

bhikṣāte paṇḍitera sneha, prabhura āsvādana
manuṣyera śaktye dui nā yāya varṇana

SYNONYMS

bhikṣāte—in feeding; *paṇḍitera*—of Gadādhara Paṇḍita; *sneha*—the affection; *prabhura*—of Śrī Caitanya Mahāprabhu; *āsvādana*—tasting; *manuṣyera*—of an ordinary human being; *śaktye*—in the power; *dui*—these two; *nā yāya*—not possible; *varṇana*—the description.

TRANSLATION

No ordinary human being can possibly describe Gadādhara Paṇḍita's affectionate presentation of food and Śrī Caitanya Mahāprabhu's tasting this food.

TEXT 288

এই মত গৌরলীলা— অনন্ত, অপার ।
সংক্ষেপে কহিয়ে, কহা না যায় বিস্তার ॥ ২৮৮ ॥

ei mata gaura-līlā——ananta, apāra
saṅkṣepe kahiye, kahā nā yāya vistāra

SYNONYMS

ei mata—in this way; *gaura-līlā*—pastimes of Lord Śrī Caitanya Mahāprabhu; *ananta*—unlimited; *apāra*—unfathomed; *saṅkṣepe*—in brief; *kahiye*—I describe; *kahā*—describing; *nā yāya vistāra*—no one can do elaborately and completely.

TRANSLATION

In this way, Śrī Caitanya Mahāprabhu performs His pastimes, which are unlimited and unfathomable. Somehow or other, these have briefly been described. It is not possible to describe them elaborately.

TEXT 289

সহস্র-বদনে কহে আপনে 'অনন্ত' ।
তবু এক লীলার তেঁহো নাহি পায় অন্ত ॥ ২৮৯ ॥

sahasra-vadane kahe āpane 'ananta'
tabu eka līlāra teṅho nāhi pāya anta

SYNONYMS

sahasra-vadane—in thousands of mouths; *kahe*—speaks; *āpane*—personally; *ananta*—Anantadeva; *tabu*—still; *eka līlāra*—of one pastime only; *teṅho*—He (Anantadeva); *nāhi*—not; *pāya*—gets; *anta*—the end.

TRANSLATION

Although Lord Anantadeva is always describing the pastimes of the Lord with His thousands of mouths, He cannot reach the end of even one of the Lord's pastimes.

TEXT 290

শ্রীরূপ-রঘুনাথ-পদে যার আশ ।
চৈতন্যচরিতামৃত কহে কৃষ্ণদাস ॥ ২৯০ ॥

śrī-rūpa-raghunātha pade yāra āśa
śrī-caitanya-caritāmṛta kahe kṛṣṇadāsa

SYNONYMS

śrī-rūpa—Śrīla Rūpa Gosvāmī; *raghunātha*—Śrīla Raghunātha dāsa Gosvāmī; *pade*—at the lotus feet; *yāra*—whose; *āśa*—expectation; *caitanya-caritāmṛta*—the book named *Caitanya-caritāmṛta; kahe*—describes; *kṛṣṇadāsa*—Śrīla Kṛṣṇadāsa Kavirāja Gosvāmī.

TRANSLATION

Praying at the lotus feet of Śrī Rūpa and Raghunātha, always desiring their mercy, I, Kṛṣṇadāsa, narrate Śrī Caitanya-caritāmṛta, following in their footsteps.

Thus end the Bhaktivedanta purports to the Śrī Caitanya-caritāmṛta, Madhya-līlā, *Sixteenth Chapter, describing Lord Caitanya's attempt to go to Vṛndāvana.*

References

The statements of *Śrī Caitanya-caritāmṛta* are all confirmed by standard Vedic authorities. The following authentic scriptures are quoted in this book on the pages listed. Numerals in bold type refer the reader to *Śrī Caitanya-caritāmṛta's* translations. Numerals in regular type are references to its purports.

Amṛta-pravāha-bhāṣya (Bhaktivinoda Ṭhākura), 159

Anubhāṣya (Bhaktisiddhānta Sarasvatī Ṭhākura), 21-22

Bhagavad-gītā, 21, 71, 88, 141, 144, 146

Bhakti-rasāmṛta-sindhu (Śrīla Rūpa Gosvāmī), 194, 278-279, 281

Bhakti-ratnākara (Narahari Cakravartī Ṭhākura), 263

Bhakti-sandarbha (Jīva Gosvāmī), 53, 54-57, 133, 195

Brahma-saṁhitā, **89,** 121, 300

Caitanya-bhāgavata (Vṛndāvana dāsa Ṭhākura), 184, 259-262

Caitanya-candrodaya-nāṭaka (Kavi-karṇapūra), 259-260

Caitanya-carita-mahā-kāvya (Kavi-karṇapūra), 259

Caitanya-maṅgala (Locana dāsa Ṭhākura), 259, 262-263

Durgama-saṅgamanī (Jīva Gosvāmī), 279

Dvārakā-māhātmya, 133

Garuḍa Purāṇa, 145

Hari-bhakti-vilāsa (Sanātana Gosvāmī), 54, 55, 56, 132-133

Mahābhārata, **139,** 231

Navadvīpa-parikrama, 263

Padma Purāṇa, 88-89

Glossary

A

Abhidheya—the stage of love of Godhead where one's relationship with God is expressed by one's activities.
Aprakaṭa-līlā—the unmanifested pastimes of the Lord.
Ārati—ceremony of Deity worship in which various pleasing articles are offered to the Lord.
Arcana—the devotional process of worshiping.
Ātma-nivedana—the devotional process of surrendering everything.

B

Bāla-gopāla—Deity of Kṛṣṇa as a cowherd boy.
Bhāgavata—A Vaiṣṇava.
Bhauma-ījya-dhīḥ—accepting something to be spiritual when it is actually material.
Bhoga—material enjoyment; or, articles of foodstuffs which have not been offered to the Deity.
Brahma-bandhu—an unqualified son of a *brāhmaṇa*.
Brāhmaṇa—the intelligent class of men.

C

Caṇḍāla—a dog-eater, the lowest of men.
Caraṇāmṛta—the Deities' bath water, mixed with yogurt and sugar.
Cāturmāsya—the four month rainy season when *sannyāsīs* do not travel.

D

Dāna—charity.
Dāsyam—the devotional process of serving.
Devī—the internal energy.
Dīkṣā—the process by which one can awaken his transcendental knowledge and vanquish all reactions caused by sinful activity.
Dola-yātrā—the swing festival of Rādhā and Kṛṣṇa.

G

Guṇas—the three modes of material nature.
Gauḍa-deśa—Bengal.
Gaura-Nitāi—Deity forms of Lord Caitanya and Lord Nityānanda.

H

Hari—the name of Kṛṣṇa which means "one who takes away all miseries."
Hlādinī—the pleasure potency of the Lord.

J

Janmāṣṭamī—the festival of Kṛṣṇa's birthday.
Jñānīs—mental speculators.

K

Kaḍāra—the ointment of Lord Jagannātha used by Lord Caitanya.
Kaniṣṭha-adhikārī—neophyte devotee.
Karma—fruitive work and its resultant reactions.
Karmīs—fruitive workers.
Kāśamdi—a kind of pickle.
Kārttika—the name of a Vedic month occuring around October-November of the Roman calendar in which the Dāmodara form of Lord Kṛṣṇa is worshiped.
Kāyastha caste—people of a Hindu community who are expert in managing business affairs and government affairs; very reliable and faithful servants.
Kīrtana—the devotional process of chanting.
Kṛṣṇa-bahirmukha—bereft of one's relationship with Kṛṣṇa.
Kṛṣṇa-bhakti—devotion to Kṛṣṇa.
Kṛṣṇa-dāsa—servant of Kṛṣṇa.
Kṣatriyas—the administrative and warrior class of men.
Kṣetra-sannyāsa—vow to leave household life and live in a place of pilgrimage devoted to Lord Viṣṇu.
Kṣīracorā—Gopīnātha Deity who stole condensed milk for Mādhavendra Purī.

M

Madhyama-adhikārī—the second-class devotee, usually a preacher.
Madhyama-bhāgavata—a devotee who has attained the intermediate stage between the neophyte and perfect devotee. Generally he becomes a preacher and is worshipable by neophytes and ordinary persons.
Mahā-bhāgavata—a first-class, unalloyed devotee.
Mahā-mantra—the great chanting for deliverance: Hare Kṛṣṇa, Hare Kṛṣṇa, Kṛṣṇa Kṛṣṇa, Hare Hare/ Hare Rāma, Hare Rāma, Rāma Rāma, Hare Hare.
Mahātmā—a great soul.
Mañjarīs—flowers of the *tulasī* plant.
Markaṭa-vairāgya—false renunciation; literally, the renunciation of a monkey.
Mantra—(*manaḥ*—mind, *tṝ*—to deliver) that which delivers the mind.
Māyā—illusion; the external energy of Kṛṣṇa.
Mlecchas—those who do not follow the regulative principles of the *Vedas*.

N

Nāmābhāsa—the stage above the offensive stage of chanting the name of God in which one gets a dim reflection of realization of the holy name.

Nanda-mahotsava—the festival of Nanda Mahārāja; Kṛṣṇa's birthday.
Nirantara—without cessation, continuously, constantly.
Nitya-siddha—an eternally liberated soul.

O

Oḍana-ṣaṣṭhī—ceremony at the beginning of winter when Lord Jagannātha gets a winter covering.

P

Pāda-sevana—the devotional process of serving the Lord's lotus feet.
Pañcarātra-vidhi—Deity worship.
Paramahaṁsa—topmost swanlike devotee.
Phalgu—temporary.
Prabhu—master.
Prajāpatis—progenitors of the human race.
Prakaṭa-līlā—the manifested pastimes of the Lord.
Prākṛta—on the material platform.
Prākṛta-sahajiyās—materialistic class of so-called Vaiṣṇavas who imagine themselves as confidential devotees.
Prasāda—(lit. mercy) remnants of foodstuffs, etc., offered to the Lord.
Puraścaryā—five preliminary devotional activities performed to qualify for intiation.

R

Rāsa-yātrā—festival of the *rāsa* dancing of Kṛṣṇa.

S

Sakhya—the devotional process of maintaining friendship.
Sākṣi-gopāla—the Deity of Kṛṣṇa who acted as a witness to the promise of an elder *brāhmaṇa* to a younger one.
Śālagrāma-śilā—a stone from the village of Śālagrāma which is worshiped as Nārāyaṇa.
Śāstras—revealed scriptures.
Smaraṇa—the devotional process of remembering.
Śravaṇa—the devotional process of hearing.
Śrī Kṛṣṇa-vijaya—a book of poems by Guṇarāja Khān, considered to be the first poetry book written in Bengal.
Śruti-gaṇa—the personified *Vedas.*
Sudarśana *cakra*—Kṛṣṇa's special weapon, a disc of light.
Śūdras—the servant class of men responsible for assisting the other three classes.

T

Ṭhākurāṇīs—the wives of devotees.

U

Uttama-adhikārī—first-class devotee who is expert in Vedic literature and has full faith in the Supreme Lord; he can deliver the whole world.

V

Vaiṣṇava—one who is a devotee of Viṣṇu, or Kṛṣṇa.
Vaiśyas—the mercantile and agricultural class of men.
Vandana—the devotional process of praying.
Vijayā-daśamī—the celebration of the conquest of Laṅkā by Lord Rāmacandra.
Virajā River—the river that divides the material world from the spiritual world.
Viṣṇu-tattva—having full status as Godhead.
Viśvāsa—(lit., faithful) a government secretary.

Y

Yavanas—meateaters.
Yukta-vairāgya—befitting renunciation.

Bengali Pronunciation Guide

BENGALI DIACRITICAL EQUIVALENTS AND PRONUNCIATION

Vowels

অ a আ ā ই i ঈ ī উ u ঊ ū ঋ ṛ

ৠ ṝ এ e ঐ ai ও o ঔ au

ং ṁ *(anusvāra)* ঁ ṅ *(candra-bindu)* ঃ ḥ *(visarga)*

Consonants

Gutterals:	ক ka	খ kha	গ ga	ঘ gha	ঙ ṅa
Palatals:	চ ca	ছ cha	জ ja	ঝ jha	ঞ ña
Cerebrals:	ট ṭa	ঠ ṭha	ড ḍa	ঢ ḍha	ণ ṇa
Dentals:	ত ta	থ tha	দ da	ধ dha	ন na
Labials:	প pa	ফ pha	ব ba	ভ bha	ম ma
Semivowels:	য ya	র ra	ল la	ব va	
Sibilants:	শ śa	ষ ṣa	স sa	হ ha	

Vowel Symbols

The vowels are written as follows after a consonant:

া ā ি i ী ī ু u ূ ū ৃ ṛ ৄ ṝ ে e ৈ ai ো o ৌ au

For example: কা kā কি ki কী kī কু ku কূ kū কৃ kṛ

কৄ kṝ কে ke কৈ kai কো ko কৌ kau

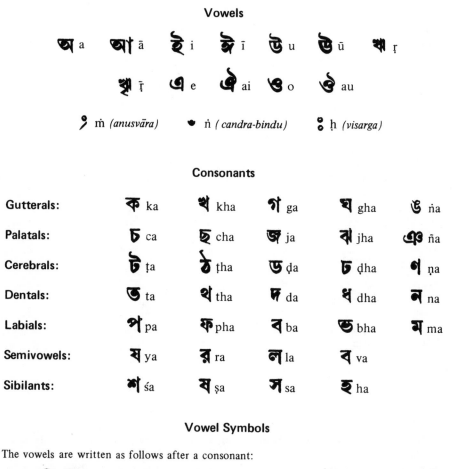

The letter *a* is implied after a consonant with no vowel symbol.

The symbol *virāma* (্) indicates that there is no final vowel. ক্ k

The letters above should be pronounced as follows:

a –like the *o* in h*o*t; sometimes like the *o* in go; final *a* is usually silent.
ā –like the *a* in f*a*r.
i, ī –like the *ee* in m*ee*t.
u, ū –like the *u* in r*u*le.
ṛ –like the *ri* in *ri*m.
ṝ –like the *ree* in *ree*d.
e –like the *ai* in p*ai*n; rarely like *e* in b*e*t.
ai –like the *oi* in b*oi*l.
o –like the *o* in g*o*.
au –like the *ow* in *ow*l.
ṁ –*(anusvāra)* like the *ng* in so*ng*.
ḥ –*(visarga)* a final *h* sound like in Ah.
ṅ – *(candra-bindu)* a nasal *n* sound like in the French word *bon*.
k –like the *k* in *k*ite.
kh –like the *kh* in Ec*kh*art.
g –like the *g* in *g*ot.
gh –like the *gh* in bi*g-h*ouse.
ṅ –like the *n* in ba*n*k.
c –like the *ch* in *ch*alk.
ch –like the *chh* in mu*ch-h*aste.
j –like the *j* in *j*oy.
jh –like the *geh* in colle*ge-h*all.
ñ –like the *n* in bu*n*ch.
ṭ –like the *t* in *t*alk.
ṭh –like the *th* in ho*t-h*ouse.
ḍ –like the *d* in *d*awn.
ḍh –like the *dh* in goo*d-h*ouse.
ṇ –like the *n* in g*n*aw.
t–as in *t*alk but with the tongue against the the teeth.
th–as in ho*t-h*ouse but with the tongue against the teeth.
d–as in *d*awn but with the tongue against the teeth.
dh–as in goo*d-h*ouse but with the tongue against the teeth.
n–as in *n*or but with the tongue against the teeth.
p –like the *p* in *p*ine.
ph –like the *ph* in *ph*ilosopher.
b –like the *b* in *b*ird.
bh –like the *bh* in ru*b-h*ard.
m –like the *m* in *m*other.
y –like the *j* in *j*aw. য
y –like the *y* in *y*ear. য়
r –like the *r* in *r*un.
l –like the *l* in *l*aw.
v –like the *b* in *b*ird or like the *w* in d*w*arf.
ś, ṣ –like the *sh* in *sh*op.
s –like the *s* in *s*un.
h–like the *h* in *h*ome.

This is a general guide to Bengali pronunciation. The Bengali transliterations in this book accurately show the original Bengali spelling of the text. One should note, however, that in Bengali, as in English, spelling is not always a true indication of how a word is pronounced. Tape recordings of His Divine Grace A. C. Bhaktivedanta Swami Prabhupāda chanting the original Bengali verses are available from the International Society for Krishna Consciousness, 3764 Watseka Ave., Los Angeles, California 90034.

Index of Bengali and Sanskrit Verses

This index constitutes a complete alphabetical listing of the first and third line of each four-line verse and both lines of each two-line verse in *Śrī Caitanya-caritāmṛta.* In the first column the transliteration is given, and in the second and third columns respectively the chapter-verse references and page number for each verse are to be found.

A

C

D

L

M

T

General Index

Numerals in bold type indicate references to *Śrī Caitanya-caritāmṛta's* verses. Numerals in regular type are references to its purports.

A

Abhinanda
as uncle of Kṛṣṇa, 123
Absolute Truth
three phases of, 144-145
See also: Kṛṣṇa, Supreme Lord
Ācāryaratna
See: Candraśekhara
Activities
determine position in disciplic succession, 189
for initiation not required for deliverance, **54**
of Vaiṣṇavas not easily understood, 64
pure devotee above fruitive, 194
Acyutānanda
as son of Sītādevī, **168**
Advaita Ācārya
Caitanya visited house of, **264**
communicates secretly with Caitanya, **186**
dances at Remuṇā, **171**
house of at Śāntipura, 174
instructed to spread *kṛṣṇa-bhakti,* **20**
invites Caitanya to lunch, **183-184**
served by Govardhana, **272**
travels to Jagannātha Purī, **165, 168**
worshiped by Caitanya, **6-7**
worshiped Caitanya, **5-6**
Age of Kali
See: Kali-yuga
Āmāra ājñāya guru hañā
quoted, 20
Āmāra 'duṣkara' karma
quoted, 189
Amogha
as son-in-law of Sārvabhauma, **125**
became devotee of Caitanya, **146-149, 154,** 156
criticizes Caitanya, **126**
Amṛta-pravāha-bhāṣya
Sixteenth Chapter summarized in, 159
Ānanda-cinmaya-rasa-pratibhāvitābhis
verses quoted, 121
Anantadeva
can't reach end of one of Lord's pastimes, **304**
Anāsaktasya viṣayān yathārham
verses quoted, 279
Anubhāṣya
quoted on Nityānanda as *viṣṇu-tattva,* 21-22
quoted on *prākṛta-sahajiyās'* beliefs, 21-22
Anyābhilāṣitā-śūnyaṁ
quoted, 194
Ārādhanānāṁ sarveṣāṁ
quoted, 189
Ārādhyo bhagavān vrajeśa-tanayas
quoted, 298
Arcāyām eva haraye
quoted, 51
Arcye viṣṇair śilā-dhīr guruṣu
quoted, 145
Arjuna
takes credit for victorious battle, 189-190
Association
of ordinary persons, 194
with faithful neophyte, 51
Ataeva kṛṣṇera 'nāma'
quoted, 58
Ataḥ śrī-kṛṣṇa-nāmādi
quoted, 58
Ātatāyinamāyāntam api vedānta
verses quoted, 136
Āṭhāranālā
Advaita Ācārya and Nityānanda receive garlands at, **176-177**
Atheists
regard Deity as material, 194-195

Ecstatic symptoms
of Pratāparudra Mahārāja's queens, **217**
Energies
Caitanya's unconceivable, **191**
Envy
demon loses everything by, 140-141
ete kaliṅgāḥ kaunteya
verses quoted, 231
Etiquette
for devotees, 119

F

Faith
devotees categorized according to, 52, 195
in chanting, 51
Fear
modes of nature keep conditioned souls in, 95
Fire
ceremony can be performed by offenseless chanter, 249
Food
Caitanya collects remnants of Lord Jagannātha's, **207**
from Balagaṇḍi taken by Caitanya, **182**
offered by wives of Caitanya, **170**
prepared for Caitanya by Sārvabhauma, **107-113**
See also: Prasāda

G

Gadādhara Paṇḍita
broke vow of *kṣetra-sannyāsa,* **221-226**
forbidden to accompany Caitanya, **221-226**
given place to live at Yameśvara, **97**
initiated by Puṇḍarīka Vidyānidhi, **200**
intimacy of Caitanya and, **225**
met Caitanya at Purī, **287**
never went to Vṛndāvana, 300
Ganges
as shelter of Caitanya, **205**
as Supreme Lord in form of water, **71**
Ganges
Caitanya is carried across, **252-257**
Vidyā-vācaspati ordered to worship, **71**
wherever Caitanya stays is, **297-298**
Garuḍa Purāṇa
quoted on exalted position of devotee, 145
Garuḍa-stambha
Caitanya stands near to see Jagannātha, 4
Gauḍa-deśa
Nityānanda as only qualified preacher from, **188**
Gaurāṅgera saṅgi-gaṇe
quoted, 85
Gaura-Nitāi
as incarnation for preaching, 189
as Kṛṣṇa-Balarāma, 299
Gaurāṅga-sundara
See: Caitanya Mahāprabhu
Gopāla
Deity installed by Mādhavendra Purī, **173**
Gopīnātha
at Remuṇā, **171**
Deity known as Kṣīracorā, 174
stole milk for Mādhavendra Purī, **174**
Govardhana Majumadāra
good qualities of, **268-269**
Raghunātha dāsa as son of, 268, **270**
served Advaita Ācārya, **272**
Govinda
See: Kṛṣṇa
Govinda
brings garlands to Āṭhāranālā, **176**
remained with Lord at Purī, **97**
travels to Jagannātha Purī, **166**
Guṇarāja Khān
as author of *Śrī Kṛṣṇa-vijaya,* **46**
life history of, 47
Guṇḍicā temple
cleansed at time of Ratha-yātrā, **180**
Śivānanda Sena instructed to go to, **45**
Guror labdhasya mantrasya
verses quoted, 55
Guru
Caitanya ordered everyone to become a, 20

L

M

N

R

S

T

U

The Author

His Divine Grace A. C. Bhaktivedanta Swami Prabhupāda appeared in this world in 1896 in Calcutta, India. He first met his spiritual master, Śrīla Bhaktisiddhānta Sarasvatī Gosvāmī, in Calcutta in 1922. Bhaktisiddhānta Sarasvatī, a prominent devotional scholar and the founder of sixty-four Gauḍīya Maṭhas (Vedic Institutes), liked this educated young man and convinced him to dedicate his life to teaching Vedic knowledge. Śrīla Prabhupāda became his student, and eleven years later (1933) at Allahabad he became his formally initiated disciple.

At their first meeting, in 1922, Śrīla Bhaktisiddhānta Sarasvatī Ṭhākura requested Śrīla Prabhupāda to broadcast Vedic knowledge through the English language. In the years that followed, Śrīla Prabhupāda wrote a commentary on the *Bhagavad-gītā,* assisted the Gauḍīya Maṭha in its work and, in 1944, without assistance, started an English fortnightly magazine, edited it, typed the manuscripts and checked the galley proofs. He even distributed the individual copies freely and struggled to maintain the publication. Once begun, the magazine never stopped; it is now being continued by his disciples in the West.

Recognizing Śrīla Prabhupāda's philosophical learning and devotion, the Gauḍīya Vaiṣṇava Society honored him in 1947 with the title "Bhaktivedanta." In 1950, at the age of fifty-four, Śrīla Prabhupāda retired from married life, and four years later he adopted the *vānaprastha* (retired) order to devote more time to his studies and writing. Śrīla Prabhupāda traveled to the holy city of Vṛndāvana, where he lived in very humble circumstances in the historic medieval temple of Rādhā-Dāmodara. There he engaged for several years in deep study and writing. He accepted the renounced order of life (*sannyāsa*) in 1959. At Rādhā-Dāmodara, Śrīla Prabhupāda began work on his life's masterpiece: a multivolume translation and commentary on the eighteen thousand verse *Śrīmad-Bhāgavatam* (*Bhāgavata Purāṇa*). He also wrote *Easy Journey to Other Planets.*

After publishing three volumes of *Bhāgavatam,* Śrīla Prabhupāda came to the United States, in 1965, to fulfill the mission of his spiritual master. Since that time, His Divine Grace has written over forty volumes of authoritative translations, commentaries and summary studies of the philosophical and religious classics of India.

In 1965, when he first arrived by freighter in New York City, Śrīla Prabhupāda was practically penniless. It was after almost a year of great difficulty that he established the International Society for Krishna Consciousness in July of 1966. Under his careful guidance, the Society has grown within a decade to a worldwide confederation of almost one hundred *āśramas,* schools, temples, institutes and farm communities.

In 1968, Śrīla Prabhupāda created New Vṛndāvana, an experimental Vedic community in the hills of West Virginia. Inspired by the success of New Vṛndāvana, now a thriving farm community of more than one thousand acres, his students have since founded several similar communities in the United States and abroad.

In 1972, His Divine Grace introduced the Vedic system of primary and secondary education in the West by founding the *Gurukula* school in Dallas, Texas. The school began with 3 children in 1972, and by the beginning of 1975 the enrollment had grown to 150.

Śrīla Prabhupāda has also inspired the construction of a large international center at Śrīdhāma Māyāpur in West Bengal, India, which is also the site for a planned Institute of Vedic Studies. A similar project is the magnificent Kṛṣṇa-Balarāma Temple and International Guest House in Vṛndāvana, India. These are centers where Westerners can live to gain firsthand experience of Vedic culture.

Śrīla Prabhupāda's most significant contribution, however, is his books. Highly respected by the academic community for their authoritativeness, depth and clarity, they are used as standard textbooks in numerous college courses. His writings have been translated into eleven languages. The Bhaktivedanta Book Trust, established in 1972 exclusively to publish the works of His Divine Grace, has thus become the world's largest publisher of books in the field of Indian religion and philosophy. Its latest project is the publishing of Śrīla Prabhupāda's most recent work: a seventeen-volume translation and commentary—completed by Śrīla Prabhupāda in only eighteen months—on the Bengali religious classic *Śrī Caitanya-caritāmṛta.*

In the past ten years, in spite of his advanced age, Śrīla Prabhupāda has circled the globe twelve times on lecture tours that have taken him to six continents. In spite of such a vigorous schedule, Śrīla Prabhupāda continues to write prolifically. His writings constitute a veritable library of Vedic philosophy, religion, literature and culture.